Borders of the Early Modern *Ius Commune*

The culture of the *ius commune* has been a unifying element of European and Western legal civilization. As shown by several recent studies, the influence of *ius commune* extended much farther than its traditional core area. This volume discusses the expansion and changes of *ius commune* in three significant corners of Europe, which in the classical narrative either totally or partially were left out of the picture: England, Scandinavia, and Venice. The study goes beyond the traditional question of the influence of *ius commune* in comparing the different constellations of normativity and legal pluralism in these regions. It investigates how not only *ius commune* but also other forms of normativity – such as customary law, written norms, and legal practice – were used and applied, and how they circulated. The approach helps create new narratives as to how the relationship between centers and peripheries in Europe evolved in the early modern period. These new narratives are built from bottom to top; thus, they are based on concrete source information, and they focus on the learned legal systems and their connection to the local legal sources. The collection further looks into the circulation of professors and doctors, students, and legal texts, starting from the idea that a theoretical understanding of the forms of normativity can emerge only through concrete, multidisciplinary research recognizing the tensions between global legal unification and differentiation. The book will be essential reading for researchers and academics in Legal History, Law and Religion, Comparative Legal Studies, and Early Modern History.

Dolores Freda is Professor of Legal History in the University "Federico II" of Naples, Italy.

Mario Piccinini has been Professor of Legal History at the University of Padua and is currently Senior Scholar at the same institution.

Heikki Pihlajamäki is Professor of Comparative Legal History and currently Academy Professor in the University of Helsinki

Chiara Maria Valsecchi is Professor of Legal History in the University of Padua.

Routledge Studies in Comparative Legal History

This series covers the general area of comparative legal history, including contributions focusing on both 'internal' legal history, i.e., doctrinal and disciplinary developments in the law, and 'external' legal history, i.e., legal ideas and institutions in wider contexts. Considering the various legal traditions worldwide, the series also welcomes works dealing with other laws and customs from around the globe. Temporal or geographical in approach, the series will consider both legal and similar law-like normative traditions. Works encompassing views from different schools of thought and contributions from comparative and transnational historiography, including interdisciplinary approaches, are encouraged. With a focus on higher level research in the form of monographs and edited collections, proposals for supplementary reading and textbooks are also welcomed.

Titles in this series:

English Law, the Legal Profession, and Colonialism
Histories, Parallels, and Influences
Edited by Cerian Griffiths and Łukasz Jan Korporowicz

Borders of the Early Modern *Ius Commune*
England, Venice, and Scandinavia
Edited by Dolores Freda, Mario Piccinini, Heikki Pihlajamäki, and Chiara Maria Valsecchi

For more information about this series, please visit:
https://www.routledge.com/Routledge-Studies-in-Comparative-Legal-History/book-series/COMPLEGHIST

Borders of the Early Modern *Ius Commune*

England, Venice, and Scandinavia

Edited by Dolores Freda, Mario Piccinini, Heikki Pihlajamäki, and Chiara Maria Valsecchi

Routledge
Taylor & Francis Group
LONDON AND NEW YORK

First published 2025
by Routledge
4 Park Square, Milton Park, Abingdon, Oxon OX14 4RN

and by Routledge
605 Third Avenue, New York, NY 10158

Routledge is an imprint of the Taylor & Francis Group, an informa business

British Library Cataloguing-in-Publication Data
A catalogue record for this book is available from the British Library

ISBN: 978-1-032-53584-5 (hbk)
ISBN: 978-1-032-54470-0 (pbk)
ISBN: 978-1-003-42506-9 (ebk)

DOI: 10.4324/9781003425069

Typeset in Galliard
by Deanta Global Publishing Services, Chennai, India

Contents

Contributors

Per Andersen is Professor of Legal History at the University of Southern Denmark. He has published several works on the development of the legal culture of medieval Denmark, especially legal procedure, and the continuous development of this during the early modern period.

Sir John Baker is Emeritus Downing Professor of the Laws of England at Cambridge University. He has written numerous books and articles on English legal history.

Dolores Freda is Professor of Legal History at the University "Federico II" of Naples, Italy. She has published several works in comparative legal history, with particular reference to the English common law in the early modern period and the history of emigration in the twentieth century.

Donato Gallo has been Researcher and Assistant Professor of Medieval History at the University of Padova. From 2010 to 2023, he also taught History of Universities. He studied the development of the *Studium* of Padua from the fourteenth to the early sixteenth centuries and published university records.

Silvia Gasparini is tenured Researcher of Legal History at the University of Padua. She teaches a course on Venetian Legal History and has published works on the Venetian legal system and legal culture in the medieval and modern ages.

Stefania Gialdroni is Professor of Medieval and Modern Legal History at the University of Padua. Her main research interests concern the history of commercial law and the relationship between law and language, as well as law and visual arts.

R.H. (Dick) Helmholz is a legal historian whose contributions to that subject have focused on the importance of the canon law and the European *ius commune* in England. This has led him to undertake research in the manuscript records of the English ecclesiastical courts as they existed prior to 1640. He has brought to light their relevance to the development of English common law in areas as diverse as defamation, marriage and divorce, contracts, and criminal law. Lately he has also studied the place which the law of nature occupied in cases brought before courts throughout medieval and early modern Europe.

David Ibbetson is Regius Professor of Civil Law Emeritus at the University of Cambridge. He has published widely on topics in legal history and is the author of *A Historical Introduction to the Law of Obligations*, attempting to put the modern English law of obligations into its historical context.

Sören Koch is Full Professor for Legal Science, Legal History, and Comparative Law at the University of Bergen in Norway. He has published works on the interplay between legal cultures and how to compare them based on legal historical understanding. He has recently focused on the pluralistic governance structures and dimensions of the Hanseatic League.

Mia Korpiola is Professor of Legal History at the University of Turku. Her broad research interests range from the history of legal literacy and the first Finnish women lawyers to the history of family and inheritance law.

Claudia Passarella is tenure-track Assistant Professor in Legal History at the Department of Private Law and Critique of Law in the University of Padua. Venetian law history represents one of her main fields of research. On this subject, she has published a book and several other works. In particular, she investigates the administration of criminal and civil justice in modern Venice (from the fifteenth to the eighteenth centuries).

Mario Piccinini has been Professor of Legal History at the Department of History, Geography and the Ancient World in the University of Padua and is currently Senior Scholar at the same Department. He works on the relations between political and legal thought and between legal and social normativity. He has written, among others, a book on Henry Sumner Maine and several essays on John of Salisbury, John Fortescue, Hobbes, F.W. Maitland, Harold Laski, Ernst Troeltsch, and Karl Marx.

Heikki Pihlajamäki is Professor of Comparative Legal History and is currently Academy Professor at the University of Helsinki. His research interests include history of commercial, criminal, and procedural law; colonial legal history; and history of the legal profession. Most of his works include comparative dimensions.

Chiara Valsecchi is Professor of Medieval and Modern Legal History at the University of Padua. One of her main fields of research is the history of family law in medieval, modern, and contemporary ages. She also studies the role of lawyers in the building of the modern state in different contexts (university, trial, *consilia*).

Alfredo Viggiano is Professor of Early Modern Political History at the University of Padua. His research concerns the analysis of judicial disputes, the study of political and legal cultures, and the strategies of legitimation of powers in the territories of the maritime and land states of the Venetian Republic (from the fifteenth to the eighteenth centuries). On this subject he has published several books and essays.

Introduction

1 Borders of *ius commune*

Ius commune at the Borders

Dolores Freda, Mario Piccinini, Heikki Pihlajamäki, and Chiara Maria Valsecchi

The European common law, *ius commune*, consisted of two main components, Roman law and the canon law of the Catholic Church, which both went through a period of vigorous scientification in the twelfth century. During the twelfth century, Justinian law books (which in the sixteenth century were to be called *Corpus iuris civilis*) became the object of intensive studies at the University of Bologna. Roughly at the same time, the authoritative legal texts of the church were collected into *Concordantia discordantium canonum* or *Decretum Gratiani*. *Corpus iuris* and Gratian's Decrete formed not only the basis of legal studies in medieval legal faculties but also the foundation of what came to be conceived as the common law of Europe.

Tracing the foundations of academic interest in *ius commune* as a concept, however, takes us to the early nineteenth century and the birth of legal history as an academic subject. Modern historiography of medieval Roman law started with Friedrich Carl von Savigny and his masterful, six-volume *Geschichte des römischen Rechts im Mittelalter* (1815–31). Savigny's concerns were not only intellectual but also practical. In the spirit of romanticism and nationalism, Savigny wished to contribute to a unified German private law on its medieval roots of Roman law. He presented a concrete roadmap to this end in his other great work, *System des heutigen römischen Rechts* (1840–49). Savigny's emphasis on Roman law as the healthiest part of the German legal heritage did not, however, appeal to all German legal scholars. In 1843, Georg Beseler published a book called *Volksrecht und Juristenrecht*, the main contention of which was that the reception of Roman law ("lawyers' law") had been a mistake, depriving the German people of its true, Germanic law. The split of Savigny's Historical School into Romanists and Germanists was finally sealed through the division of *Zeitschrift der Savigny-Stiftung* into Romanist and Germanist parts in 1880.

The division of legal history into Romanist and German camps was reproduced in many countries, although the separation was also criticized from at least the 1880s onwards. Among Romanists, the idea of following the fate of ancient Roman law after the fall of Rome until modern times remained the dominant concept for a long time.

DOI: 10.4324/9781003425069-2

Modern scholarship on medieval (and early modern) canon law began considerably later than studies on Roman or Germanic law. In 1905, Ulrich Stutz, a German professor of ecclesiastical law, addressed an academic audience at the University of Bonn. Instead of just pure dogmatics, Stutz called for a true legal history of the Christian churches. Just as French and German legal history had grown into independent disciplines during the nineteenth century, so should the history of canon law. Stephan Kuttner has called Stutz's contribution "a new departure." In the early years of the twentieth century, scholarly interest and specialization in the history of canon law was indeed rapidly taking shape, which shows in the fact that the canon law section of Savigny's *Zeitschrift* was established in 1911. Although not the first scholar to embark on the studies of medieval canon law, Kuttner himself was then certainly the first who, with his seminal works in the 1930s, brought the history of medieval canon law to the attention of a wider academic public.[1]

By the 1930s, all ingredients for serious discussions of *ius commune* were thus in place. Italian scholars came first. After debates on the theme in the 1930s, Francesco Calasso soon emerged as the most influential figure. Fruit of many years of work, his groundbreaking *Introduzione al diritto comune* appeared in 1951. According to him, medieval legal scholars were not to be treated as belonging to "external legal history," or something separated from practical legal life of their time. Instead, legal scholarship needed to be seen as in constant interaction with local legal orders, feudal law, and other legal courses.

Calasso divided the history of *ius commune* into three phases. The period of "absolute *ius commune*" extended from the twelfth to the thirteenth century. This is when, according to Calasso, *ius commune* reigned supreme over all other legal sources, such as statutory law, customary law, and feudal law. The second stage of *ius commune*, that of "subsidiary *ius commune*", covered the fourteenth and fifteenth centuries. The local laws (*iura propria*) had then priority over *ius commune*, which was applied only if the local laws did not provide an answer to the legal problem. The final phase of *ius commune*, that of "particular *ius commune*", began in the sixteenth century and lasted until the demise of *ius commune* in the nineteenth century. During this period, the early modern age, the reception and application of the *ius commune* depended on the local rulers. The third stage of *ius commune* coincided, not coincidentally, with the dissolution of European religious unity and the rise of national states, and, as legal scholarship is concerned, with the emergence of legal humanism. All these contextual reasons contributed to the diminishing significance of *ius commune*.[2] On the other hand, one might claim that the mixing of *ius*

1 Manlio Bellomo, *The Common Legal Past of Europe, 1000–1800* (Washington, DC: Catholic University of America Press, 1995).

2 Francesco Calasso, *Introduzione al diritto comune* (Milano: Giuffré, 1951).

commune with *iura propria* and its division into various regional common laws in Europe kept *ius commune* alive through the early modern period.[3]

Although much of Calasso's narrative, affected by the pandectist theory prevailing at the beginning of the twentieth century, has been received and handed down by most of the European legal scholarship, it has met with considerable criticism. In particular, the idea of a "system" of law (made by Roman and canon law) intended as unitary, exclusive, and universal has been recently questioned by, among others, Paolo Grossi, who highlighted that the recourse to legal categories typical of contemporary legal systems prevent us from catching the genuine (and pluralistic) nature of the *ius commune*.[4] At the same time, Calasso's description of the three phases of the *ius commune* has been challenged and much rescaled by subsequent historiography.[5]

It took decades until looking at medieval and early modern legal history in the traditional way became, if still not the only way of looking at medieval legal history, at least one of the most widespread scholarly orientations. In the 1950s, war-ridden Germany was again resuming its place as one of the leading nations in legal history research. This had important consequences for *ius commune* research. In 1959, the German legal historian Erich Genzmer proposed to the Max Planck Society that an institute for comparative legal history be established. Genzmer's proposal met with some support but also widespread criticism. Many general historians supported the idea, while several legal historians did not. Among the most influential critics were Fritz Pringsheim, Max Kaser, and Hans Thieme. The Max Planck Society nevertheless continued

3 Patrick Glenn has emphasized the existence of various regional common laws in the early modern period, such as the German *gemeines Recht*, the Dutch Roman–Dutch law, the Spanish *derecho común*, the French *droit comun*, and the English common law: Patrick Glenn, *On Common Laws* (Oxford: Oxford University Press, 2006). Few historians of medieval canon law now would believe that the *ius commune* of the glossators was based on Roman law only and that canon law would have remained the law of the Catholic Church only. See Caravale, *Alle origini del diritto europeo* (1985), for a compact description of the criticism against Calasso's work. Caravale has shown how *ius commune* as a scholarly concept was not a medieval invention but rather a product of early modern legal scholarship. Furthermore, the expression *utrumque ius*, "both laws," referred not to a unity of Roman and canon law but only to a double doctorate in law (*doctor in utroque iure*).

4 Paolo Grossi, *L'ordine giuridico medievale* (Roma–Bari: Laterza, 1995), 227–229. Already G. Astuti, *Recezione teorica e applicazione praticadel diritto romano nell'età del rinascimento giuridico*, in *Atti del Colloquio "Le droit romain et sa reception en Europe", Università di Varsavia, 8--10 ottobre 1973* (Varsavia, 1978), 2–58 (now in Id., *Tradizione romanistica e civiltà giuridica europea*, ed. by G. Diurni, vol. I (Napoli, 1984), 237–262), had affirmed that lawyers were not aware of the existence of a hierarchical relationship between *ius commune* and *iura propria*, resorting only to the norms of the *Corpus Iuris*, which, in their opinion, better met the needs of practice.

5 In particular, Gino Gorla, *La formazione del diritto moderno in Europa*, vol. I (Firenze: Olscki), 447–532; Id. *Diritto comparato e diritto comune europeo* (Milano: Giuffrè 1981), 651–703, highlighted the traditional legicentric approach thanks to the reappraisal of the role of the Great Tribunals in the development of law in the modern age.

with the plans and asked numerous leading scholars for their statement on whether an institute should be established and, if so, how it should be organized. Genzmer's idea had been to divide the institute into three departments, corresponding to the traditional division into Romanists, Germanists, and Canonists. Wolfgang Kunkel – a Romanist himself – was against this and suggested that, because all three groups often already worked together, the institute be organized according to projects. This solution eventually won the day. The proposed name of the future institute was no pushover either. Paul Mikat, not only a legal historian but also the Minister of Culture for the state of North Rhine–Westphalia at the time, thought that it would be better to call the legal history driven at the institute "European" instead of "comparative" so as not to provoke unnecessary competition with the existing comparative law institutes at the German universities. This view prevailed, and the Max Planck Institute for European Legal History was finally inaugurated in Frankfurt in 1964. In the political atmosphere of a unifying Europe of the early 1960s, "European" legal history no doubt also touched a chord.[6]

European *ius commune* became an important part of the life's work of Helmut Coing, the first director of the Institute. Besides editing the influential *Handbuch der Quellen und Literatur der neueren europäischen Privatrechtsgeschichte*, he published a book on European private law of the early modern period.[7] The Institute's journal, founded in 1967, also came to be called *Ius Commune*.

Most of the leading historians of *ius commune* no longer see medieval or early modern scholars as representatives of "learned law", isolated from its social context, but as legal actors involved in the complex network of legal and social relations. Most legal historians would expand the interest of the early *ius commune* researchers in private law to other branches of the law as well, such as criminal, procedural, and public law.

No consistent history of European *ius commune* has been written. Despite the current *ius commune* research, national legal histories have still dominated until this day in many countries, obscuring the effects of *ius commune* and often concealing connections of national legal histories to each other and to the common European past. France, England, and Spain are the main examples of nationalistic legal history tradition which have left little space for looking at legal history from a European, and even global, perspective.[8]

6 Jan Thiessen, "Das Max-Planck-Institut für europäische Rechtsgeschichte", in *Rechtswissenschaft in der Max-Planck-Gesellschaft, 1948–2002*, ed. by Thomas Duve, Jasper Kunstreich, Stefan Vogenauer (Göttingen: Max-Planck-Gesellschaft, 2023), 141–196, 141–150.

7 *Handbuch der Quellen und Literatur der neueren europäischen Privatrechtsgeschichte, Bd. 1–3*, ed. by Helmut Coing (München: Beck, 1973–1988); and Helmut Coing, *Europäisches Privatrecht: Älteres Gemeines Recht (1500 bis 1800). Bd. 1.* (München: Beck, 1985).

8 Alain Wijffels, "Le *ius commune* européen: 'hareng rouge' de l'approche comparative des traditions juridiques anglaise et française". *Clio@Themis* 5 (2012), https://journals.openedition

The influence of *ius commune* also extended much farther than its traditional core area of southern and western continental Europe – and this is the theme of this book. The chapters in this volume discuss the expansion and changes of *ius commune* in three significant corners of Europe, which in the classical narrative were either totally or partially left out of the picture: England, Scandinavia, and Venice. Our project is interested not only in the traditional question of the space of *ius commune*. In addition, the authors of this volume ask how not only *ius commune* but also other forms of normativity – such as customary law, written norms, and legal practice – were used and applied, and how they circulated. We will investigate the circulation of professors and doctors, students, and legal texts, starting from the idea that a theoretical understanding of the forms of normativity can emerge only through concrete, multidisciplinary research recognizing the tensions between legal unification and differentiation. The approach will hopefully help to create new narratives as to how the relationship between centres and peripheries in Europe evolved in the early modern period. These new narratives will be built from bottom to top; thus, they will be based on concrete source information, focusing on the learned legal systems and their connection to the local legal sources.

****

Part I of the volume has four chapters, approaching the *ius commune* in Venice from different points of view. These include the contributions of Silvia Gasparini, Claudia Passarella, Donato Gallo, and Alfredo Viggiano. In her chapter, Silvia Gasparini explains how, starting from the age of the *Comune* (ca. 1143–1297) and throughout the early modern age, Venetians controlled their advocates through law. Deeply mistrustful towards any form of autonomous guilds, Venetians aimed at keeping the two categories of private practitioners, *advocati extraordinarii* and *sollecitadori*, under control. In addition, the Venetian concept of justice as balance among private and public interests created the institution of elected, public advocates (*advocati ordinarii*). They provided counsel for either party in a judicial controversy, as well as those accused of crimes.

Claudia Passarella approaches the theme of *ius commune* through *De Usu et Authoritate Juris Civilis Romanorum* (1653) of the seventeenth-century English legal comparatist Arthur Duck. He noted that the Venetians lived according to their own customs and laws, without adopting the *ius civile Romanorum*, or Roman civil law. Duck remarked, however, that in modern Venice those same Roman laws were nevertheless recognized and even to some extent followed. Passarella investigates the issue through judicial practice in both criminal and civil matters. She shows how the authority of *ius commune*

.org/cliothemis/1733. On global legal history, see Thomas Duve, "What Is Global Legal History?", *Comparative Legal History*, 8:2 (2020), 73–115.

in criminal matters was often obvious, whereas in civil cases *ius commune* was applied only to the extent that it reflected natural justice and equity.

Donato Gallo writes on *peregrinationes iuridicae*, "legal wanderings," which involved young men from northern parts of Europe studying at Italian universities. Among them were, for instance, Englishmen and Swedes. Some obtained academic degrees, but for others, the Grand Tour was a means of accumulating social capital. Gallo shows how the University of Padua, which the Venetian youth also frequented to acquire knowledge of Roman and canon law, attracted students from other borders of the *ius commune* as well.

Alfredo Viggiano analyzes the relationship between Venetian law and the Ius Commune. The dominant interpretation in the historiography devoted to this relationship has emphasized the stark difference, the irreconcilability, between the two legal traditions. This essay seeks to question the basis of this narrative. Viggiano analyzes some modes of reception in the Republic of Venice of operational practices, interpretive typologies, and intellectual patterns typical of the *ius commune* in the period between the mid-fourteenth and the mid-sixteenth centuries. He pays particular attention to the conflicts and entanglements between the law elaborated in the capital and the plurality of rights existing in the provinces of the mainland (*stado da terra*) and the maritime state (*stado da mar*). In order to understand the real consistency of legal pluralism in the Republic of Venice, Viggiano considers the incidence of specific forms of conflict, the practices of some important institutions, and the profiles of some social actors.

Part II includes five contributions, which all explore the same issues from the perspective of the English legal world. Here we have chapters by Dolores Freda, Sir John Baker, Richard Helmholz, David Ibbetson, and Stefania Gialdroni. From their specific angles, all these chapters question the differences, often described as fundamental, between early modern continental and common law.

Dolores Freda's article also challenges the historiographic cliché, which goes back to F.W. Maitland and has been repeated by the European legal tradition ever since, of the dichotomy between common law and *ius commune*. Such an interpretation, taking the "Englishry" of English law for granted, contributed to constructing its past as insular with respect to Continental law. The chapter focuses on connections and commonalities between common law and *ius commune*, highlighting the existence of a common European legal tradition since the Middle Ages.

Similarly, Sir John Baker shows how modern England was not completely isolated from the canon law or the *ius gentium*. The courts which operated under those laws were the realm of a separate legal profession called the "civilians." Canon law and the *ius gentium* were, however, also sometimes applicable in the ordinary royal courts in Westminster Hall. In such cases the judges would discuss "their law" and apply it, without being themselves formally educated in it. In this chapter, Baker considers how the judges informed themselves, paying special attention to the role of the civilian and common law professions.

David Ibbetson's contribution is based on Thomas Smith's inaugural lecture given for the professorship of Civil Law in Cambridge in 1542 and is analyzed to understand the way the study of Roman law was seen in mid-sixteenth-century England. In his lecture Smith, embracing *mos italicus*, outlined his perception of the value (and advantages) of the study of Roman law in the context of the new humanism. Although the teaching of Roman law did not obtain a central position in Cambridge, in 1540 King Henry VIII established the chair, while the language of Roman law was the language of European diplomacy at the time. Ibbeston highlights that, although Smith's ambitions to revive the study of Roman law in England were not successful, he helped to bring some civilian learning into the English common law.

Richard Helmholz also approaches the subject of non-isolation of common law by looking at the two separate kinds of lawyers who existed in England: common lawyers, who practiced in the royal courts, and civil lawyers, active in courts of the church. Although, traditionally, historians have seen fundamental differences between these two branches of the legal profession, Helmholz shows, through a close examination of legal sources and practices, how several connections brought them together. He analyzes four such connections: shared religious and political allegiances, common roles in several English courts, close parallels in legal areas of substantive interest, and common procedural institutions.

Stefania Gialdroni's chapter analyzes Gerard Malynes's discussion of a body of customary laws uniformly and universally applied across medieval and early modern Europe (*lex mercatoria*) in his *Consuetudo, vel, Lex Mercatoria*: *or, the Ancient Law-Merchant (1622)*. The way Malynes discusses the role of the "learned doctors" and of the High Court of Admiralty is Gialdroni's point of interest. Both commercial law and England's common law being "at the border" of the *ius commune*, Malynes's treatise offers a rare insight on several "borderlands."

The four chapters in Part III (by Sören Koch, Per Andersen, Heikki Pihlajamäki, and Mia Korpiola) shift the reader's attention to northern Europe. Sören Koch, like Gialdroni, approaches the theme of borderlands from the point of view of commercial law. Koch asks how and to what extent the merchant court at the Hanse Kontor in Bergen court actively used *ius commune* in its jurisdiction. A case study from the early eighteenth century sheds light on the rather limited influence of learned law in that court. Even though a direct impact or active application of learned law is rare, the chapter nevertheless shows an indirect influence *of ius commune* and learned law in the Bergen merchant court.

The contribution of Per Andersen highlights the distinctive features of Danish legal history in comparison to many other parts of Europe. No legal education existed in Denmark before 1736, which explains why Danish legal actors were not particularly influenced by learned law after the *ius commune* - inspired legal changes in the High Middle Ages. For instance, this was the case in procedural law, as courts remained doubtful of parties being represented by others than themselves until 1638, when the profession of advocates emerged. Andersen offers an important insight into how law worked in practice at the border of early modern *ius commune.*

Heikki Pihlajamäki's chapter shows how the history of Swedish procedural law shares important characteristics with Danish law. From the Middle Ages onwards, the Swedish legal procedure – like the Danish – acquired features of *ius commune.* This occurred when the canon law of the church influenced the Swedish provincial laws, as they were put into written form in the thirteenth and fourteenth centuries. Under the increasing influence of learned lawyers in the sixteenth and seventeenth centuries, the impact of learned law on legal procedure continued and deepened. High courts, established from the beginning of the seventeenth century onwards, were instrumental here because many of their judges were trained in law. That the legal profession remained otherwise practically nonexistent for a long time set limits to learned influences on Swedish legal procedure. Elements of learned law were combined with traditional Swedish law, thus constructing a particular form of legal procedure specific for Sweden. Using concrete case examples, Mia Korpiola in her chapter shows how *ius commune* doctrines of criminal law and torture entered Sweden through Germany. She shows how the *Constitutio Criminalis Carolina* of 1532 and imperial police ordinances influenced Swedish norms, legal concepts, and practice. Although judicial torture was never formally accepted as part of Swedish criminal procedure, attempts at legalizing torture were made in the sixteenth and seventeenth centuries, and criminal suspects were sometimes – although rarely – also tortured.

The volume ends in an epilogue by Mario Piccinini and Chiara Maria Valsecchi. Focusing on Arthur Duck's *De Usu et Authoritate Juris Civilis Romani*, their essay cuts across many of the themes introduced previously in the volume. Written at the height of the Civil War, Duck's text analyses contemporaneous Roman law from the perspective of an English civilian operating in a country where the common law is not that of the other Christian dominions. This difference triggers Duck's cutting-edge research and, by multiplying the boundaries and relationships between inside and outside, provides a cognitive resource that allows us to question the nature of the late *ius commune* as a whole. The essay examines Duck's text by choosing two moments whose sources it reconstructs almost exhaustively. With reference to the beginning of Book I, it addresses Duck's conceptual and doctrinal toolkit (the divergence between *arma* and *leges*, the theological–political background linked to the apocalyptic question, and the relationship between rationality and authorization). Furthermore, for Chapter IV of Book II, Duck analyses how these tools are at work in the investigation of the legal conditions of the Italian states.

Although much research exists on the history of *ius commune*, this volume points to future investigations, for the subject has by no means been exhausted. A lot remains to be done, and the definitive history of *ius commune* remains far from written. Such a history would include not only the

European areas included in this book, but it would also ask how much space *ius commune* acquired outside Europe, and how it changed when interacting with local normativities in Africa, America, and Asia. We suspect that such an investigation would further contribute to dismantling the traditional way of looking at southern and western Europe as centers and the rest of the world as periphery.

The editors express their gratitude to Dr Luca Crisma and Dr Giulio Abbate for the valuable help they provided at the editing stage of this volume. All remaining errors are the sole responsibility of the editors.

This book has been published under the frame of the Mobility and Humanities project of the University of Padova's Department of Historical and Geographical Sciences and the Ancient World (DiSSGeA). The Mobility and Humanities project is funded as a Project of Excellence (2018–2022) by the Italian Ministry of Education, University, and Research (MIUR). The editors wish to thank the funding entities.

Part I

Ius Commune and Venice

2 Lawyers in Venice

A Curious Business

Silvia Gasparini

During the long life of the Venetian Republic the role played by legal counsel, and lawyers in general, was very different from that on the Italian mainland and in the rest of Europe. To understand the significance of this difference, we must look at it within the context of the equally important pecularities of the Venetian institutional and legal system.

It is well known that the Venetian Republic, just like any institution with *iurisdictio* in the medieval and modern periods, did not separate the powers of government, performing all three functions: legislation – the introduction of new rules of law; administration – their application outside judicial litigation; and jurisdiction – their application within the context of judicial conflicts. Only after the French Revolution did the long fight begin to separate powers into different and independent organs.[1]

Due to a lack of documents, little can be said about the early period of the Venetian *Ducatus*, when the territory was governed by a diarchy between the doge and the people in the form of direct democracy. All matters were discussed and decided by and within the assembly; judicial deliberations, such as those of a legislative and administrative nature, were proposed by the doge and approved by a majority vote.[2] Any interpretation and application of legal rules was thus a matter for the entire people: there was no need or place for lawyers.

The rules of law at the time were mainly customary, apart from a scattering of legislation introduced to manage occasional specific problems. Either the assembly swore to the doge that they would abide by the new rules they had just voted for, and accept the stated penalties, or the doge swore to the assembly that he would enforce them and pursue any violators. One instance is the deliberation taken in July 971, in which the people swore they would

1 Pietro Costa, *Iurisdictio: Semantica del potere politico nella pubblicistica medievale: 1100–1433* (Milano: Giuffrè, 1969, 2002); Mario A. Cattaneo, *Separazione dei poteri e certezza del diritto nella rivoluzione francese* (Sassari: Università di Sassari, 1988).

2 Giorgio Zordan, *L'ordinamento giuridico veneziano*, rev. ed. (Padova: Imprimitur, 2005), 20–22, 31–36.

DOI: 10.4324/9781003425069-4

not trade in military merchandise with the Saracens, under penalty of a heavy fine or death if unpaid.[3]

It would be a mistake to take the customs of the *Ducatus* as purely Roman. The unprecedented situation in which the refugees from the mainland found themselves after the Byzantines left them to their own devices in 741–742, together with the pressing need to maintain good relations with the neighbouring Langobards, and then with the Franks, as well as with trading partners along the coast of the eastern Mediterranean, introduced layer upon layer of foreign influences and created new national customs, which weakened the hold of the Theodosian institutes inherited from antiquity.[4] As for Justinian's compilation, it was never used in the *Ducatus*. Although it was referenced in the Pavia school's Langobardist analysis and was sporadically mentioned in early medieval documents in Italy, it was of no interest in the *Ducatus*.[5]

This oxymoronic "permeable isolation" created something entirely new, which owed less and less to Roman institutes as time went by. The Venetian *fraterne*, or *compagnie*, were managed by individual members, without the need to consult the others. This was very different from the way in which the Roman *societas* operated, because while the former aimed at regulating economic cooperation in financial investments abroad and, thus, required immediate responses to market conditions, the latter was largely concerned with exploiting agricultural land. The Venetian last wills lacked the constituent element of *institutio heredis* required by Roman law, and, while immediate powers (and responsibility) did not fall to the heir at the death of the testator, the Venetian legal institute of *commissarìa* required a *commissario* to actively manage the patrimony. In fact, most Venetian patrimonies were made up of invested currencies and precious but perishable merchandise, neither of which would survive unharmed a standstill in business.[6]

Things began to change when the direct democracy of the *Ducatus* evolved into the representative democracy of the *Commune*. It soon became necessary to relieve the elective councils of individual cases, allowing them to focus instead on political and legislative matters. Collegial magistrates were then created to deal with administrative and judicial tasks, although, when necessary, they could also enact legislation within the limits set by the laws in their

3 Ibidem, 135–147.

4 Enrico Besta, *Il diritto e le leggi civili di Venezia fino al dogado di Enrico Dandolo* (Venezia: Visentini, 1900); Lujo Margetic', "Il diritto", in *Storia di Venezia*, 1, *Origini-Età ducale*, ed. by Lellia Cracco Ruggini, Massimiliano Pavan, Giorgio Cracco, Gherardo Ortalli (Roma: Istituto dell'Enciclopedia italiana, 1992), 677–692.

5 Benvenuto Pitzorno, and Id., "Il *Liber Romanae legis* della *Ratio de lege Romana*. Per la storia del c.d. *Codi* in Italia", and "Il *Liber romanae legis* degli *Judicia a probis iudicibus promulgata*. Nota seconda per la storia del c. d. *Codi* in Italia", *Rivista italiana per le scienze giuridiche*, 43 (1907), 4–12, 101–136.

6 Zordan, *L'ordinamento giuridico*, 139.

capitolari.[7] Most jurisdiction was entrusted to collegial courts of justice, with individual and original areas of intervention. As was usually the case in the division of labour among the institutions of the Venetian State, their areas of intervention were not given on the basis of a preordained template but according to the workload arising from certain recurring problems. For instance, the *Curia del Forestier* granted full judicial protection to foreigners involved in controversies with Venetians or with other foreigners, the *Curia del Procurator* made judgements on controversies arising from the action of *Procuratori di San Marco* as *commissari* in the matter of *hereditas iacens* and *bona vacantia*, and the *Curia dell'Esaminador* preemptively evaluated the regularity of documents that were or could be claimed as evidence in court.[8]

But the most interesting development was the creation in 1244 of the *Curia di Petizion*, which solved a delicate legal problem. According to their capitulars, the courts could deliberate on sentences only on the basis of an already enforced legal rule. In the context of a State engaged in the fast-paced development of its markets, which meant maintaining relations with the whole of Europe and the Mediterranean, cases lacking any established discipline were the order of the day: the powers of the existing courts did not extend to solving them, and the Minor Council, which was tasked with providing solutions to unregulated cases, was already overworked. The role of the *Curia di Petizion* was to take over these cases and solve them *per iustitiam, laudum et arbitrium*: whatever solution (*arbitrium*) was deliberated by the Court by a majority vote (*laudum*) would be enforced as the right solution to the case (*iustitiam*). The solution worked so well that the capitular of *Petizion* was soon added to the statutes, extending the prerogative to apply the Venetian *arbitrium* to all magistrates in their judicial activity.[9]

Here we come to the heart of the problem in relation to the position of lawyers in the Venetian Republic: at this point in time the Venetian legal system clearly revealed its remedial, rather than substantive, nature.

For Venetians there was no point in having an exhaustive set or system of preordained rules that would only force the complexities of individual interests into artificial categories. Real-life situations were well known to be variable, and, as a consequence, any fixed rules would soon become obsolete.

As long as no problems arose, it was enough to allow custom, that is, by definition, rules that were shared and agreed upon, to discipline legal affairs. It was when public order was disrupted, whether by private litigation or by crime, that the State intervened. Civil legislation set parameters through flexible legal

7 Giorgio Cracco, "L'età del Comune", in *Storia di Venezia*, 2, *L'età del Comune*, ed. by Giorgio Cracco, Gherardo Ortalli (Roma: Istituto dell'Enciclopedia italiana, 1995), 1–30.

8 Melchiorre Roberti, *Le magistrature giudiziarie veneziane e i loro capitolari fino al 1300*, 1 (Padova: Tipografia del Seminario, 1906); 2–3 (Venezia: Deputazione di storia patria per le Venezie, 1909–11).

9 Giovanni I. Cassandro, *La curia di Petizion e il diritto processuale di Venezia: Con appendice di documenti* (Venezia: Deputazione di storia patria per le Venezie, 1937).

institutes, whose application in established practice was made consistent by turning it into law in publicly available texts. The backbone of these legal institutes was expressed in the statutes, whose deliberation procedure required, as a final step, approval by the people through a majority vote. Additional rules came from the legislation of the Major Council and the Senate.[10] Criminal repression was also the reserve of public institutions from the early days of the *Commune*: only the State could pursue crimes. Both substantive and procedural legislation, which were binding for the judges themselves, were put in place to restate custom, minimize its application, grant due process to the accused, and ensure consistency in repression in order to guarantee maximum effectiveness. The fines due to the State were imposed separately from damages due to the aggrieved parties. These developments of the legal system were gradually giving legislation (whether ordinary or statutory) primacy as a legal source.[11]

However, despite the burgeoning legislation, the Venetian legal system remained firmly focused on remedial justice. Legislation, where existent and applicable, was, of course, the first type of legal rule to be applied, slowly relegating custom to second place. But those who consulted the series of available legal sources were the judges, when they were called upon to solve a case, not lay lawyers aiming to build a theoretical system. Again, whenever a legal rule was not forthcoming, it was the duty of the judges themselves to employ *iustitiam, laudum et arbitrium* to find a solution. It comes as no surprise that, already by the mid-thirteenth century, custom had largely lost its substantive meaning and had come to refer instead to the practice of the courts, as documented in the archives of the recently established Chancery.[12]

The task of the lawyer has always been the interpretation of existing rules of law in view of their application to specific cases. In Venice, the interpreters were the judges themselves, whose appointment, indeed whose measure of *iurisdictio*, legitimately included the legislative power implicit in the Venetian idea of *arbitrium*.

From its outset the Venetian government was a shared endeavour and would remain so even after the so-called *Serrata* of the Major Council and the shift from a democratic to an aristocratic republic. All holders of political rights could be elected to the various magistrates, and while they were in office they performed all three functions of government. This made the Venetian

10 "Gli statuti civili di Venezia anteriori al 1242 editi per la prima volta", ed. by Enrico Besta, Riccardo Predelli, in *Nuovo Archivio Veneto*, n.s., 1 (1901), 205–300; *Gli statuti veneziani di Jacopo Tiepolo del 1242 e le loro glosse*, ed. by Roberto Cessi (Venezia: Istituto veneto di scienze, lettere ed arti, 1938).

11 Lamberto Pansolli, *La gerarchia delle fonti di dirittto nella legislazione medievale veneziana* (Milano: Giuffrè, 1970); Silvia Gasparini, "Bertaldo e il suo *Lucidarium*: Nuove riflessioni su un vecchio tema storiografico", in *Studi Veneziani*, 63 (2011), 15–47.

12 Marco Pozza, "La Cancelleria", in *Storia di Venezia*, 2, *L'età del Comune*, 349–369.

arbitrium very different from the *arbitrium* of the great courts of the modern absolutist States.[13]

In both instances, the legal system was known to be incomplete. The central courts of the modern States formulated their solutions to unregulated cases in unmotivated sentences, which stretched (or bent) the existing rules, while in Venice the judges were expressly appointed with the power to adopt a new rule through their sentences as an application of their all-round *iurisdictio*.

The Venetian legal system was thus not complete, but it could be judicially completed on a case-by-case basis. This flexibility was ensured due to the fact that they were not bound to follow precedents: they were consulted, but whenever the Venetian judges of a court agreed that a different outcome would yield better results, they were not obliged to motivate their disagreement with past rulings, unlike the technique of distinguishing in English common law.[14]

As interpreters of a substantive legal system that was preordained and independent from jurisdiction, lawyers had no place in Venice because any interpretation was always authentic, as it was given by the legislator itself.

That which needed a technical interpretation were the other, foreign legal systems that began to interact with the Venetian one, and for these needs provisions were taken. The *Curia del Forestier* bypassed the need for detailed knowledge of foreign legal rules by making the words of the agreements between the parties the first source of a solution for cases involving foreigners, thus anticipating by centuries the autonomy of the will of the parties in Napoleon's civil code.[15] Proficiency in foreign legal systems was instead needed in diplomacy and in the government of the dominions, both overseas and, from the fifteenth century, on the Italian mainland.

Of course, the most important of the various instances of foreign legislation was the Roman *ius commune*, employed as a supplementary law in Italy as well as in much of Europe. Lawyers knowledgeable in Justinian's compilation and in the doctrine built upon it were hired to posts in the major offices of the upper Chancery, where *acta* (acts of government) were written and archived. Note, however, that this knowledge did not reach the parish priests, who accounted for most of the chancery executive clerks until the second half of the fifteenth century. The Venetian priests also performed the function of *notarii ad instrumenta* as well as that of *notarii ad acta*, and remained, in the words of Attilio Bartoli Langeli, "a wedge of early medieval notarial practice"

13 Massimo Meccarelli, Arbitrium: *Un aspetto sistematico degli ordinamenti giuridici in età di diritto comune* (Milano: Giuffrè, 1998).

14 Joseph A.C. Thomas, "The Art of Distinguishing", in *L'educazione giuridica*, 2, *Profili storici* (Perugia: Libreria Editrice Universitaria, 1979), 207–216.

15 Maria Fusaro, "Politics of Justice/Politics of Trade: Foreign Merchants and the Administration of Justice from the Records of Venice's Giudici del Forestier", *Mélanges de l'École française de Rome – Italie et Méditerranée modernes et contemporaines*, 126:1 (2014), 2–24.

in Italy in the Middle Ages.[16] The rectors sent to oversee the various localities of the dominions had *assessori* at their side, who, in addition to being experts in *ius commune*, were also knowledgeable about local institutions, statutes, and customs.[17] The Signorìa would appoint *Consultori in iure* to analyse the most complex points of *ius commune* and *ius canonicum* arising from internal or international affairs.[18]

Andrea Padovani suggested that there was actual application of Roman rules in Venice at that time.[19] However, there is very little evidence for this hypothesis in the surviving documents from actual legal practice in the world of business and in court.[20] His opinion was largely based on the elaboration of *Statutum Novum* under doge Jacopo Tiepolo in 1242, an updated restatement of the statutory legislation introduced in the former five decades. The introductory part of the text includes a few references to Justinian's compilation, but they are indirect and careless,[21] sounding more like rhetorical tropes than a reference to principles within which to set enforceable rules of law.[22] Despite Padovani's intervention, doubts about a Romanization of the Venetian legal system in the age of the *Commune* remained, even though *Statutum Novum* was soon subjected to the addition of two sets of glosses. Only one set (the so-called Odofredian glosses) shows some knowledge of Roman law teachings at the University of Bologna, while the other usefully comments on matters of practical procedure in the Venetian courts at that time. However, the Odofredian glosses expressly stop short of giving an interpretation of the Venetian rules whenever they discipline legal institutes unknown to Roman law. Moreover, all glosses were soon after deleted and further glosses were forbidden in a deliberation by the Major Council.[23] Nothing, especially not legal

16 Attilio Bartoli Langeli, "Documentazione e notariato", in *Storia di Venezia*, 1, *Origini-Età ducale*, 861.

17 *L'amministrazione della giustizia penale nella Repubblica di Venezia, secoli XVI–XVIII*, 2, *Retoriche, stereotipi, prassi*, ed. by Giovanni Chiodi, Claudio Povolo (Sommacampagna: Cierre, 2004).

18 Antonella Barzazi, "I Consultori *in iure*", in *Storia della cultura veneta*, 5, *Il Settecento*, 2 (Vicenza: Neri Pozza, 1986), 179–199.

19 Andrea Padovani, "La politica del diritto", in *Storia di Venezia*, 2, *L'età del Comune*, 303–329.

20 Many private deeds can be found in Section 3, *Archivi notarili*, published by Comitato per la pubblicazione delle fonti relative alla storia di Venezia, 1950-. See also Benvenuto Pitzorno, *Le consuetudini giudiziarie veneziane anteriori al 1229* (Venezia: Tipografia Emiliana, 1910), including *Iudicia a probis iudicibus promulgata*, 37-59; and Roberti, *Le magistrature giudiziarie*, esp. 2, 61–91, 103–119, and 3, 135–168, 171–196.

21 Justinian began his introduction to the *Digestum*, a compilation of *iura*, with the words "*Deo auctore*". They were copied by Tiepolo in his first Prologue to the *Statutum*, a compilation of *leges*.

22 *Statutum Novum* can be found in *Novissimum Statutorum ac Venetorum legum volumen duabus in partibus divisum* (Venezia: Pinelli, 1729), part 1, cc. 2–71, esp. *Prologus primus*, c. 2.

23 Enrico Besta, "Le glosse agli statuti civili veneziani di Jacopo Tiepolo", in *Rendiconti dell'Istituto lombardo di Scienze e lettere*, 72:3:1 (1938–39), 65-83; Roberto Cessi, "Odofredo e la 'glossa' agli statuti veneti di Jacopo Tiepolo", in *Archivio veneto*, s. 5, 84 (1968), 29–44.

science, was to be tolerated as a limitation on the freedom of the Venetian government. Law experts were to be employed as consultants whenever necessary, but none of them (whether *ministeriali*, *assessori*, or *Consultori*) were ever given powers of decision or the right to vote.[24]

The Venetian State was truly independent and sovereign from the start. The Byzantine Empire did not demand or expect compliance with its legislation after 742, and clear boundaries with the Holy Roman Empire were set by *pax Nikephori* in 812–814 following those previously drawn up in the *terminatio Liutprandina* and *largitio Astolfina* of earlier centuries.[25] Thus, no limits were set to the areas of public interest the Venetian government chose to pursue, while the mainland's Comuni and later Signorìe were bound to remaining within the limits of their hard-won autonomy under the Western empire.[26]

As well as demonstrating the remedial nature of the system, the development of the Venetian form of *arbitrium* shows how judges, who declared the rules of law with their judicial *terminazioni*, consistently strived to apply legal solutions that were just, rather than merely correct. They did not reason in terms of an abstract and preordained set of rules that, combined with one another according to some equally abstract meta-rules of interpretation, would issue only one possible result. They instead considered all the interests in play in the controversy (those of the parties in civil litigation, those of the accused in criminal cases, and the interests of the State and the public) and worked out the best way to balance them, not only in the short term, but also, they hoped, in the medium and long terms.

It was not sufficient to state that one of the parties was in the right and the other in the wrong: black-and-white, Occam's razor solutions were likely to overlook the grey areas inherent in human relationships. Such solutions could take into account only who, in that moment, had the upper hand, but they did not consider the possibility of future cases that could later arise from the same knot of legal relationships or behaviours between the parties. An economy of resources in the exercise of jurisdiction was one of the public interests at play, as well as economies of time and money for the private parties going before the judges. For instance, the right of creditors was better protected

24 Silvia Gasparini, "I giuristi veneziani e il loro ruolo tra istituzioni e potere nell'età del diritto comune", in *Diritto comune, diritto commerciale, diritto veneziano: Colloquio tenuto al Centro tedesco di studi veneziani dal 20 al 21 ottobre 1984*, ed. by Karin Nehlsen-von Stryk, Dieter Nörr (Venezia: Centro tedesco di studi veneziani, 1985), 67–105.

25 Roberto Cessi, "La terminatio liutprandina per la definizione del territorio di Cittanova" and "Pacta Veneta", in Id., *Le origini del ducato veneziano* (Napoli: Morano, 1951), 149–153, 175–321; Giorgio Ravegnani, "Tra due imperi. L'affermazione politica nel XII secolo", in *Storia di Venezia*, 2, *L'età del Comune*, 33–79.

26 Gianluca Raccagni, "Il diritto pubblico, la pace di Costanza e i *libri iurium* dei Comuni lombardi", in *Gli inizi del diritto pubblico*, 2, *Da Federico I a Federico II: Atti del convegno tenuto a Trento, 20–22 settembre 2007*, ed. by Diego Quaglioni, Gerhard Dilcher (Bologna: Il Mulino; Berlin: Duncker & Humblot, 2008), 309–340.

when the debtors were given some way to make up for the delay or omission in performing their obligation, without destroying their future ability to keep contributing to the national economy.[27] In the same way, penalties for lesser crimes (unless in the case of relapsed culprits) were first given in the form of fines, and corporal punishments were executed only if the condemned person could not afford to pay (some managed through borrowing the money) because citizens were seen as more beneficial to the public good if they were alive (and repentant).[28]

The ordinary form of procedure in the courts (and in the Council of Forty as a court of appeal) was accusatory in civil as well as in criminal matters. The judges directed the trial as neutral referees, gathering the evidence and arguments produced by the parties, and, at the end of the confrontation, they would deliberate on the sentence.[29] Each party thus had complete control over how to present their case, although not everybody knew how to do so effectively. Whether daunted by the formality of the courts, lacking experience, or having only a limited knowledge of the language, many chose to be assisted by a relative or friend. This practice had both its advantages and its disadvantages. Those who could pay an orator would tend to fare better than those who defended themselves, and the presence of additional voices in the discussion could obscure the actual facts of the interests being confronted.

The Venetian legal system in the Middle Ages did not include professional attorneys or pleaders with a specific knowledge in matters of law. Instead, the Venetian State assumed, as one of its own aims, the task of assisting the parties in court, and it created the magistrate of four *Advocati parvi*.

They were elected by the Major Council and their *capitolare* mirrored that of the Court where they practised.[30] Their term of office lasted one year, and they had to be at least twenty years old. They were paid small, fixed fees by the parties, in addition to an equally modest retribution from the State. In cases of a conflict of interest, substitutes were drawn from a supplementary body of eight *Advocatores per omnes Curias*, or *Avvocati di San Marco*, who in the fifteenth century would supplant the *Advocatores* in the individual courts.[31]

27 Giovanni I. Cassandro, *Le rappresaglie e il fallimento a Venezia nei secoli XIII–XVI* (Torino: Lattes, 1938), 123–127, 173–192.

28 See *Promissio maleficiorum* by Orio Mastropiero in 1181, in *Gli atti originali della Cancelleria veneziana*, 1, *1090–1198*, ed. by Marco Pozza (Venezia: Il Cardo, 1994), 92–96.

29 Peter G. Stein, *Legal Institutions: The Development of Dispute Settlement* (London: Butterworth, 1984), 25–38.

30 Melchiorre Roberti, *Le magistrature giudiziarie veneziane e i loro capitolari fino al 1300*, 1 (Padova: Tipografia del Seminario, 1906), 246–252; 2 (Padova: Tipografia del Seminario, 1909) 93–99; 3 (Padova: Tipografia del Seminario, 1911), 131–132, 250–253. See also Giovanni I. Cassandro, *La Curia di Petizion e il diritto processuale di Venezia: Con appendice di documenti* (Venezia: Deputazione di storia patria per le Venezie, 1937), 106–110.

31 ASVe, *Maggior Consiglio, Deliberazioni*, reg. *Zaneta*, c. 52.

But not all litigation was discussed in the *Curiae*: a number of magistrates whose areas of intervention touched on trade were located near the market in Rialto, rather than in the Ducal Palace in San Marco. They also had jurisdiction, for which they also needed *advocati*. In 1463, two *Avvocati di Rialto* were created for cases judged by the *Consoli dei Mercanti* and the *Sopraconsoli*, who dealt with litigation arising from business transactions in the city market and from outstanding debts, and issued acts aimed at preventing bankruptcies. From 1474, both sets of *Advocatores* adopted the Venetian name of *Avvocati ordinari*.[32]

Criminal matters were also considered: on June 29, 1443, the magistrate of *Avvocato dei Prigioni* was created. The office had a term of two years, with its primary task being to act as a *defensor libertatis* for prison inmates, whether already condemned or awaiting judgement, in order for none of them to be unduly retained or kept in prison beyond the prescribed time limits. Their fees and retributions were the same as those for the *Avvocati ordinari*, although the poorer convicts were defended for free.[33]

These magistrate-attorneys were not lawyers in the sense of being experts in the law. Their task, with the help of the notaries from the magistrates' offices, was to check that the evidence in the hands of the party they had been called to assist was fit to be presented in court, that the procedural terms were respected, and that an exhaustive recapitulation of the facts in favour of the party was pronounced before the judges. The presence in court of these *Avvocati* ensured that all aspects of their legal situation were considered, together with the effects of the final decision. They were required to highlight the evidence in favour of their party, as well as their personal merits: there was no place for subtle interpretations of legal texts or written deeds. Both law and deeds, in fact, were usually detailed and exhaustive in their analysis of how to deal with the various possible eventualities of their application, with the specific and very practical intention of minimizing litigation.

Evidence that the *Avvocati ordinari* and *dei Prigioni* were expected to cover all of the demands of legal counsel by the parties in litigation or criminal cases could be seen in January 1348 in the case of Giacobello Contarini at the Council of Forty, in its role as court of appeal. A certain Michele Falier appeared in court, wishing to *arengare et advocare supra dictam questionem … credens secundum formam Consiliorum hoc facere posse* ("to plead and defend in reference to the case being judged ... believing that he was allowed to do so according to the rules of the Council"), but he was not given permission to

32 ASVe, *Compilazione leggi*, b. 64, c. 128 e cc. 140–141.

33 Vittorio Lazzarini, "L'avvocato dei carcerati poveri a Venezia", in Id., *Proprietà e feudi, offizi, garzoni, carcerati in antiche leggi veneziane: Saggi seguiti da una notizia biografica e dalla bibliografia dell'autore* (Roma: Edizioni di storia e letteratura, 1960), 89–113; Giovanni Scarabello, *Carcerati e carceri a Venezia nell'età moderna* (Roma: Istituto dell'Enciclopedia italiana, 1979), 17–18.

speak *eo quia non erat Advocator et etiam quia non erat attinens* ("because he was not an *Advocator*, nor a relative by blood or marriage").[34]

However, the goal of only having non-professional attorneys cooperate with non-professional judges in the pursuit of a "just justice" would ultimately not be met. The idea of an interaction between the legal counsel and the judges did not completely work in practice, so that the monopoly granted to magistrate-attorneys was vulnerable, with the private sector taking advantage of this vacuum. The office of *Avvocato ordinario* was often no more than a short apprenticeship for young politicians, who would soon go on to take various political positions in pursuit of their careers. *Li Advocati nostri facti per el Gran Conseio stanno molto poco sopra al Palazzo, et nel tempo stanno, sono nudi de pratica et quando hanno impreso alcuna cosa, et che facti sono sufficienti, finisseno al suo officio* ("Our Advocates elected by the Major Council practice for only a short time in the Courts; while they do, they are yet inexperienced, and as soon as they have begun to learn something, and be proficient, their time is already up").[35]

The constant demand from the public for qualified legal counsel in court was thus largely unanswered by the magistrate-attorneys. This resulted in competing offers by private individuals: given the *Avvocati ordinari*'s general lack of interest in getting properly engaged in their cases, self-employed counselors invaded the Palace, threatening to marginalize the magistrates and take pleading into their own hands. They were viewed at the time as an unruly mob, ready to use any means possible to support the interests of their clients. Attempts at silencing them began as early as August 18, 1296, when the Major Council forbade the practice of professional pleading and the presence of third parties in court.[36]

This conflict between the State's provisions and the ambitions of self-styled providers of legal services would last two and a half centuries, in which restrictive decrees were often undermined by a plethora of *per gratiam* exceptions. These were supposed to have covered only specific pending cases but were, in fact, regularly alleged by private pleaders to cover all of their clients' cases. The exceptions were so numerous that unlawful pleaders could easily make their way into court without being challenged. The situation was aggravated by the fact that, since the *Serrata* of the Major Council in 1297,[37] only members of the governing class could cover public offices. The presence of non-magistrates offering their services as professional, private pleaders was a threat to

34 ASVe, *Compilazione leggi*, b. 64, c. 83.

35 ASVe, *Compilazione leggi*, b. 64, c. 190.

36 ASVe, *Compilazione leggi*, b. 64, cc. 10 e 39.

37 Frederic C. Lane, "The Enlargement of the Great Council of Venice", *Studies in Venetian Social and Economic History*, ed. by Benjamin G. Kohl, Reinhold C. Mueller (London: Variorum Reprint, 1987), 236–274.

the connection between the judges and the magistrate-attorneys as members of the same class.

In this context, better qualifications were requested for the *Avvocati ordinari*, in an attempt to ensure that elected magistrates had had more extensive training and to entice them to repeat their term of office.[38] However, this was in vain: by the time the neologism *avvocati extraordinari* appeared in a deliberation by the Major Council, it was clear that the battle had been lost, and that, whatever their reputation, professional legal counsellors were there to stay. *Adeo crevit numerus cum improbis moribus Advocatorum extraordinariorum*..., lamented a decree of the Major Council on March 20, 1474: "So much have grown the number and the knavish ways of the *avvocati extraordinari*".[39]

Once the Venetian State was resigned to the invasion of the courts by private practitioners, for the first time they were given some sort of discipline. The Senate took the matter in hand as early as October 15, 1489, when anyone who intended to practise as a professional attorney, was required to present themselves to the Chancery within eight days and to be registered in order to be allowed into court.[40] No special requisites were needed at this time. The enlisted professionals would be limited to the same fees as the *Avvocati ordinari* but, clearly, without the added State remuneration due to the latter.

A total of sixty-four individuals asked for admission. Four of them (Marino Sagredo, Marco Malipiero, Antonio Trevisan, and Marco Donà) were members of the aristocracy who chose professional practice in the courts over a political career, although, of course, even if they did not offer themselves as political candidates, they had to at least take part in the sessions of the Major Council. Twenty of them were *cittadini originari* who had been born in Venice (or had been naturalized after a long period of residence) and who constituted the pool from which the Chancery's personnel was drawn, with the exception of the lowest positions which were also open to common people. Among the remaining forty professionals, some also gave their provenance from the Dominions: Brescia, Bergamo, Bologna, Ravenna, Feltre, Verona, Vicenza, Bolzano Vicentino, and Arbe in Dalmazia. Some were even illiterate.[41]

It was the first instance of a professional register for attorneys compiled and managed by the State. As such, it was radically different from the colleges of doctors of law or of other legal practitioners widely operating in the areas of *ius commune*. These were autonomous institutions, endowed with *iurisdictio* and self-governing within the limits of the common interests of their co-opted members. In the modern age, colleges like these, together with the guilds of arts and crafts, would ultimately contribute to undermining policies

38 ASVe, *Compilazione leggi*, b. 64, c. 166–190; ASVe, *Maggior Consiglio, Deliberazioni*, reg. *Deda*, c. 109.
39 ASVe, *Compilazione leggi*, b. 64, cc. 166, March 20, 1474.
40 ASVe, *Senato Terra, Deliberazioni*, reg. 10, 1486–1489, c. 210.
41 ASVe, *Compilazione leggi*, b. 63, c. 554.

of centralization and the primacy of the king's legislation. In Venice, the question never arose: no form of originary self-government of colleges and guilds ever existed. The Venetian *Scuole* (guilds of arts and crafts) had legal existence only inasmuch as they were acknowledged, disciplined, and overseen by the State.[42] The newly defined *avvocati extraordinari* had a notoriously low ranking in the list of crafts, arts, and professions as they were not trusted: all the more reason to prevent them from having any form of self-organization.

The next step was to make *the avvocati extraordinari* pay taxes: in the first thirty years or so of the sixteenth century there were a series of provisions set by decrees of the Senate.

The most interesting came on October 12, 1521, when the *avvocati extraordinari* were subjected to a system based on presumed income: a fixed sum of money was to be paid by the professional each time they spoke in court as a pleader. The tax now due from the *avvocati* raised money for essential works needed for the maintenance of the city waterways. During the late fifteenth and early sixteenth centuries, a "little ice age" lowered the average sea level, lessening the rinsing action of the tides in the lagoon of Venice and exposing the shallower areas to silting and swamping. The State set out a plan for periodic works entrusted to the offices of the *Provveditori di Comun* and the *Savi alle Acque* (later joined by the *Esecutori*) aimed at cleaning up and recalibrating the *rii*, the city's narrow waterways. The taxes drawn from the *avvocati extraordinari* would be set aside to finance these works. This continued until the end of the Republic.[43] In the two and a half centuries after this deliberation, however, the professionals' non-compliance would produce several different iterations of the decree.[44]

It was soon clear that the practitioners of the newly established profession needed to be subjected to some sort of selection criteria so as to prevent undesirable elements from infiltrating the registers. The process started as early as the late fifteenth century and ended in the early eighteenth century with the requirement for a doctorate of law at the *Studium Patavinum*.

The first step was taken in 1497, when the Senate ruled that all candidates to the profession of *avvocati extraordinari* should be *ballottati* (approved by majority vote) by a committee formed of two *Avogadori di Comun*, two *Auditori Vecchi*, two *Auditori Nuovi*, and six members of the Council of Forty, drawn by lot each time the committee was called on to vote. The members of the committee were carefully chosen: the *Auditori Vecchi* and

42 Patricia Fortini Brown, "Le 'Scuole'", in *Storia di Venezia*, 5, *Il Rinascimento: Società ed economia*, ed. by Alberto Tenenti, Ugo Tucci (Roma: Istituto dell'Enciclopedia italiana, 1996), 307–354.

43 ASVe, *Compilazione leggi*, b. 64, c. 262. On the maintenance of waterways, see Silvia Gasparini, "Simon Contarini Inquisitore alle Revisioni e Appuntadure e le Leggi Inquisitoriali del 24 luglio 1755", in *Atti dell'Istituto Veneto di Scienze, Lettere e Arti: Classe di scienze morali, lettere e arti*, 151 (1992–93), 34–41 and 109–114.

44 Some examples can be found in ASVe, *Compilazione leggi*, b. 64, cc. 208, 221, 226, 228.

Auditori Nuovi were appointed to perform an assessment of merit on requests for appeal before the Council of Forty, the *Vecchi* against sentences given in the metropolitan territory and the *Nuovi* in the dominions. The *Avogadori* had the same role in relation to criminal cases, and they were also entrusted with the general control of the legitimacy of the acts of the government. This ensured that the approved *avvocati extraordinari* would be fit to interact with the judges, especially during the appeal stage, and that the chance of any flaw in the final outcome of cases would be minimized.[45]

The next provision was taken in 1537 and had a much wider remit, as befitted the strong political personality of doge Andrea Gritti who sponsored the innovation. The new discipline was set within a global reform of legal counsel given in court, both by *Avvocati ordinari* and *extraordinari*, and it took the form of a so-called *correzione*, that is an addition, to the statutes of Venice. This gave the new rules permanent application as statutory laws: it was not just another isolated decree but an organic new system of admission, management, and control of the process of pleading in court.[46]

The *Correzion Gritti* raised the number of *Avvocati ordinari*, extended their term of office to three years, redefined the cases of incompatibility, and provided detailed rules for preventing and prosecuting absenteeism. The law was to be applied immediately: even in cases already pending in the Courts of San Marco and Rialto, as well as those on civil matters in the Council of Forty, the judges were tasked with ensuring that all parties had at least one *Avvocato ordinario* at their side, with the possibility of adding one or two more *avvocati* that were either *ordinari* or *extraordinari*. The parties were allowed to defend themselves with no legal counsel, but at this point very few took that risk. At least one *Avvocato ordinario* was obliged to attend the discussion of each case, to make a closing speech summing up the arguments, and to be present when the judge gave the sentence. In cases coming under the judicial areas of intervention of other offices, the parties were free to appoint either an *Avvocato ordinario* or, as more often happened, an *extraordinario*. Destitute parties were assisted for free by an *Avvocato ordinario* and two *extraordinari*, together with the *Avvocato dei Prigioni*, who assisted the poor in cases before the criminal section of the Forty.

Other rules were applicable to both *Avvocati ordinari* and *extraordinari*. It was forbidden for clients to *condurre alcun advocato a salario fermo* (to permanently employ them as subordinate workers). Furthermore, their professional appointment had to be given by deed so as to make it easier to detect any contravention of the above rule.

Fees had to be proportional to the value of the case, that is, to the sum demanded by the plaintiff (also by the aggrieved party in criminal cases) or due

45 ASVe, *Compilazione leggi*, b. 64, c. 211.

46 *Correzion Gritti* (a *rogatio per saturam*) is included in *Novissimum statutorum*, part 1, cc. 171–180.

as a fine to the State. The attorney of the losing party had a right to only half of the fee: perhaps a discreet form of economic pressure to stimulate competition between the *avvocati extraordinari* in order to ensure they maintained high levels of technical proficiency. It is also interesting to note that in order to keep civil cases as short as possible, from the age of the *Commune* sentences excluded specific performance in favour of an equivalent monetary compensation. The losing parties thus had to pay the amount stated in the decision, plus half the fees to their pleader, plus *caratti*, the small, fixed fee due to the *Avvocato ordinario* for cases discussed before the major judges.

However, the most relevant part of the *Correzion Gritti* was the institution of a completely new system of criteria for being enlisted as *avvocati extraordinari*. Members of the Chancery and the clergy were excluded from the profession, barring a few exceptional cases.[47] Moreover, the candidates had to be members of the Major Council, or originary citizens, or at least to have been legitimately born in Venice (to married non-citizen parents) in order to be admitted to the Courts of San Marco and Rialto. Natives of the Dominions were allowed to appear only before those judges who covered cases arising in the mainland localities under Venetian rule, provided that they had resided in Venice for at least fifteen years. It was a question not only of being able to assess the trustworthiness of the candidates, but also of ensuring that they had had enough exposure to the workings of the Venetian legal and judicial system, which was so different from those elsewhere. No requisite of residence was necessary to plead before the *Auditori Novi* and the *Avogadori di Comun*, who, as we have seen, selected the requests for appeal against the sentences given in the Dominions.[48]

The procedure to be admitted as *avvocati extraordinari* was also laid out in detail. The candidates had to present themselves to the *Avogadori di Comun*, who would receive and audit the validity of the documents detailing the necessary requisites. The files were then passed on to the *Sindici e Giudici extraordinari di San Marco e Rialto* (a subset of the Council of Forty, which relieved it of some less significant areas of intervention), whose members, in turn, put the names into a register and compiled a list that was printed and put up for public viewing in the courts.

Moreover, a *comandadore* (town crier) was to read the text of the law aloud once a year, on the first workday in October, outside the offices of the courts at San Marco and Rialto.[49]

47 Ibidem, part 1, c. 174 *verso*.

48 See Ceferino Caro Lopez, "Gli Auditori Nuovi e il dominio di Terraferma", in *Stato società e giustizia nella Repubblica veneta (sec. XV–XVIII)*, 1, ed. by Gaetano Cozzi (Roma: Jouvence 1980), 259–316; Gaetano Cozzi, "Note sopra l'Avogaria di Comun", in *Venezia e la Terraferma attraverso le relazioni dei rettori: Atti del convegno*, Trieste 23–24 ottobre 1980, ed. by Amelio Tagliaferri (Trieste: Giuffrè, 1981), 547–557.

49 Andrea Da Mosto, *L'Archivio di Stato di Venezia*, 1, *Archivi dell'Amministrazione centrale della Repubblica veneta e archivi notarili* (Roma: Biblioteca d'arte, 1937), 144, and "Archivio

Applying such an innovative and complex reform as *Correzion Gritti* cannot have been easy: in fact, on October 29, 1553, the Major Council created a specific office of magistrates for the task, the *Conservatori ed Esecutori alle leggi*.[50] They were entrusted with the procedure for admission, the keeping of the register, and the compilation of the public list, which was posted in all offices with judicial areas of intervention. Despite being a world metropolis, Venice was still a comparatively small city, where people of all social classes mixed freely and were widely acquainted with each other. Evidence of this can be seen in the fact that the lists were written in alphabetical order on the basis of the *avvocati extraordinari*'s Christian names rather than their surnames.[51]

The new magistrate of the *Conservatori* was also tasked with punishing violations to the *Correzione*: the most common violations were extortionate fees, attempts to delay the process, and inappropriate oratory.[52]

Any private person could make a signed complaint against an *avvocato extraordinario* without their name being made know to the accused; notaries and other clerks in the judicial offices could also denounce them; and the *Conservatori* also had the power to proceed by inquisition on their own initiative. Inquisitorial procedures had been introduced as a reaction to the serious crisis posed by the conspiracy of 1310 by Baiamonte Tiepolo, Marco Querini, and Badoero Badoer. They were originally enacted by the newly instituted Council of Ten and helped to prevent the Marino Falier conspiracy in 1354. They were never abrogated and could even be delegated case by case to other magistrates, as and when necessary.[53] The fines paid by the *avvocati extraordinari* who had been found guilty were divided in equal parts among the private accuser, in cases in which there was one; the clerks of the office where the violation had taken place; and the funds of the *Arsenale*, the State shipyard.[54]

In the second half of the sixteenth century a second form of legal profession, distinct from that of the *avvocati extraordinari*, came to the attention of the government. The Venetian name given to the practitioners was

di Stato di Venezia", in *Guida generale degli Archivi di Stato italiani*, 4, *S–Z* (Roma: Ministero dei Beni Culturali e Ambientali, 1994), 994–995.

50 Da Mosto, *L'archivio di Stato*, 1, 79; "Archivio di Stato di Venezia", 1994, 986–987.

51 ASVe, *Compilazione leggi*, b. 63, c. 635.

52 ASVe, *Compilazione leggi*, b. 64, cc. 194, 596, 644, 1013; ASVe, *Conservatori alle leggi*, bb. 391-398, *Querele contro avvocati 1610–1760*.

53 Paolo Preto, "Baiamonte Tiepolo: traditore della patria o eroe e martire della libertà?", in *Continuità e discontinuità nella storia politica, economica e religiosa: Studi in onore di Aldo Stella*, ed. by Paolo Pecorari, Giovanni Silvano (Vicenza: Neri Pozza, 1993), 217–264; Gaetano Cozzi, "Autodifesa o difesa? Imputati e avvocati davanti al Consiglio dei Dieci", in *La società veneta e il suo diritto: Saggi su questioni matrimoniali, giustizia penale, politica del diritto, sopravvivenza del diritto veneto nell'Ottocento* (Venezia: Marsilio, 2000), 149–230; Silvia Gasparini, "Il processo veneziano 'col rito': riflessioni su un problema storiografico", in *Studi Veneziani*, n.s. 60 (2011), 38–51. On inquisition in general, see Franco Cordero, *Criminalia: Nascita dei sistemi penali* (Roma–Bari: Laterza, 1985).

54 ASVe, *Maggior Consiglio, Deliberazioni*, reg. *Rocca*, c. 20.

sollecitadori or *intervenienti*, and their function was to ensure that procedural rules and terms were respected by the party they assisted.[55] In theory, it was not their place to deal with the question of law, which would be the task of the attorneys, but only with the proper presentation of evidence on behalf of the client. They thus "intervened" in the procedure for the client. Another task was to encourage the clerks of the judiciary offices to set the nearest possible date for the case's discussion or to solicit delays when the interests of the client demanded it – which is why they were also called *sollecitadori*. They were also sometimes employed by *avvocati extraordinari* as glorified secretaries in order to relieve them of the more routine drudgery of casework.

They were never mandatory, and many cases were judged without them being present. However, in some minor offices they were tolerated as pleaders on behalf of those parties who could not or would not employ an attorney but would also not attempt to defend themselves.

The profession was not unique to the Venetian metropolitan area. There were *intervenienti* at least in some of the dominions, not only on the mainland but also in Corfu in the modern age (Panajota Tzivara pers. comm, October 2021), and, under the name of *causidici*, in the Republic of Genoa.[56] No link however can be made with solicitors in the British common law system: any similarity came from convergent evolution.

It is clear that this category of low-level professionals often operated at the edge of legality. After dealing with the main problem of regulating the *avvocati extraordinari*, it was the turn of the *sollecitadori*. Their earliest mention is in a 1564 deliberation of the criminal section of the Council of Forty: too many unwary members of the public involved in criminal cases but ignorant of law were accosted by these disreputable people who ensured them they would give them the best and fastest outcome, for a fee of course. This deliberation was modelled on the earliest provisions on *avvocati extraordinari*: the *Sindici e Giudici extraordinari di San Marco e Rialto* had to register the names of those who wanted to practise as *sollecitadori*, provided they certified to having no criminal convictions.[57]

It seems that the State's legalization of this secondary profession, however reluctant it was, led to an excess of practitioners. In 1582, a *terminazione* by the Sindici confirmed by a decree of the Forty enforced a stricter selection of candidates and mandated periodic revisions of the criteria. The subjects of the Republic and its dominions who resided in Venice had to certify that they had a clean criminal record, and they had to provide a trustworthy witness

55 See a later overview of the profession by Leone Ongarini, *Instruzioni utili e necessarie al veneto interveniente o sia sollecitadore di Palazzo* (Venezia: Costantini, 1775), and Silvia Gasparini, *Tra fatto e diritto: Avvocati e causidici a Venezia nell'eta moderna* (Padova: Imprimitur, 2005).

56 Riccardo Ferrante, "Il 'governo delle cause': La professione di causidico nell'esperienza genovese (XV–XVIII secolo)", in *Rivista di Storia del Diritto Italiano*, 52 (1989), 181–299.

57 This deliberation is summarized in the premise to the later *terminazione* of 1582, which will be expanded on later in this chapter.

who declared under oath where the candidate lived and that they had never practised subordinate jobs, crafts, or trades. Those who did not live in Venice also had to prove they had a clean criminal record in their locality of origin. Foreigners could be admitted by providing proof of their territorial origin and of having been resident in Venice for at least ten years.[58]

This first stage of selection was followed by a cultural and technical examination conducted by the notary of the *Sindici*, by their *cogidor* (from *coadiuvo, -are*: a subordinate clerk), and by an *Avvocato fiscale*. The two *Avvocati fiscali* were State attorneys who were appointed to protect the economic interests of the State; one was noble, and the other was a citizen, and, of course, both had to be knowledgeable about Venetian laws.[59] The aspiring *sollecitadore* had to pass an exam on judicial practices in which they also had to translate legal texts from Latin, as well as writing one or more judicial acts in Venetian. What is more, once approved, the newly appointed *sollecitadori* had to present a *piezaria* (surety) to be renewed every three years, in case they damaged the interests of the clients or incurred fines.

Fees were subjected to an inflexible limit of two ducats per month from each client, whatever the number of cases treated on their behalf, and they were due only if services had, in fact, been performed.

In 1586, the regulation of *sollecitadori* was raised to a statutory level with the *Correzion Cicogna* (under doge Pasquale Cicogna): the discipline was restated with some modifications. The *Correzion Cicogna* mandated the Chiefs of the Forty's direct involvement in the examinations. They approved the candidates through the vote of a qualified majority. The *correzione* also excluded foreigners from the profession.[60]

The problems would not end there: unauthorized individuals practised under the name of enlisted *sollecitadori*, who signed the papers of the case in their stead. The planned revisions of the requisites of the registered professionals did not, in fact, happen regularly. At most, occasional inspections led to new provisions with only temporary effects.[61]

The *Correzion Contarini* (under doge Carlo Contarini) of 1655–56 also marginally revised the discipline, making it slightly stricter and mandating a radical revision of the current authorizations, but with no real change in legislation or in practice.[62]

Meanwhile, the problem of a better professional qualification for the *avvocati extraordinari* was becoming increasingly urgent. The *Conservatori* took

58 ASVe, *Sindico, capitolare*, cc. 206–209.

59 Marco Ferro, *Dizionario del diritto comune e veneto che contiene le leggi civili, canoniche e criminali, i principj del jus naturale, di politica, di commercio con saggi di Storia civile Romana e Venete* (Venezia: Fenzo, 1778–81) *ad vocem* Avvocati fiscali.

60 *Novissimum statutorum*, part 1, cc. 190 v.-191.

61 ASVe, *Sindico, Revisioni e approvazioni*, 1620–1655, b. 30; sec. 18th, bb. in alphabetical order.

62 *Novissimum statutorum*, part 1, cc. 225 v.-233 v.

advantage of their normative powers to implement a series of increasingly strict evaluations and, when necessary, their *terminazioni* and proposals were confirmed or enacted by decrees of the Senate.

A decree on February 26, 1600 m.v. (= 1601), stated that the requisites to be certified by the candidates were their legitimate birth or prolonged residence in Venice, good behaviour, never having done *esercizj vili [o] arti mecaniche* (subordinate jobs or any sort of craft or trade), and, for the first time, to have been found proficient in an examination before the *Conservatori*, during which the *Avvocati fiscali* would question them about judicial procedures and matters pertaining to the legal profession.[63] The exam syllabus was extended in 1626 to include knowledge of the statutes and a reasoned solution to a question of Venetian civil law.[64] However, too many passed the exam. In 1656, a list was compiled of twenty-five points in Latin about the Venetian legal system, which was renewed every three years and was publicly posted in the office of the *Conservatori*. Two of the points, drawn by lots for each candidate, were discussed during the examination. In addition, the candidates had to translate and explain a passage randomly chosen by the *Avvocati fiscali* from legal books.[65]

Much more so than in its earlier expansion overseas, the acquisition of extensive dominions in the Italian mainland inevitably led to closer contact and interaction with the legal systems based on *ius commune*. The Republic had chosen to maintain the existing institutions and legal systems, which were medieval in their origins, in the conquered areas, submitting them to the control of Venetian rectors elected in the capital. After the wars of the League of Cambrai, the recovered territories were subjected to wider reaching and stricter management by the rectors, whose powers were inserted in updated versions of the local statutes and were approved by decrees of the Senate. The rectors' powers were not exactly the same in the different mainland dominions, but, in general, they could decide certain reserved cases in the first instance, judge local cases on appeal, and could also be delegated to judge individual cases, applying the accusatory rite delegated by the Senate or the inquisitorial rite delegated by the Ten. This made it necessary for all non-magistrate legal operators, especially for the notaries in the judicial offices, and, of course, for the attorneys. to have some knowledge of the Roman legal system, as well as of the local statutes, although this was not required of the rectors themselves.

From the Middle Ages, works of a legal character had been exceedingly rare in Venice, apart from the peculiarly Venetian production of practical handbooks about procedure. These were mostly on criminal law and, occasionally, on civil law. During the late seventeenth and eighteenth centuries, a different type of work flourished that strove to compare the peculiarities of

63 ASVe, *Conservatori alle leggi*, capit. 1, c. 41 v.
64 Ibidem, c. 43.
65 Ibidem, c. 68, and ASVe, *Compilazione leggi*, b. 64, c. 564.

the Venetian system with Roman law applied elsewhere and to find common ground between them.[66]

The new ideas were in line with the tendency of the Venetian State to bring the still moderately autonomous local colleges of lawyers, which had existed in the dominions before Venetian rule, under more direct control. In pursuit of this aim, in a *terminazione* on May 6, 1668, the *Riformatori allo Studio di Padova* (who were appointed with the governance of the university) made it necessary to have a doctorate of law in the *Studium Patavinum* in order to plead before the judges in the dominions. This innovation, confirmed by the Senate on August 14 and proclaimed publicly by all rectors in the *Terraferma*, reduced the prerogatives of the legal colleges, meaning that co-opted membership was no longer sufficient to practise before the judges.[67]

This renewed attention to Roman law and its application was also reflected in the policy adopted by the *Conservatori* for the technical selection of *avvocati extraordinari* in the capital. On September 10, 1700, the *Conservatori* expressed their disappointment that the candidates limited their studies to learning by heart the answers to the published twenty-five questions. They thus declared that the candidates would be able to take the exam only if they had a doctorate in law from the University of Padua or a certificate proving they had taken its course for at least a year.[68] In the following two decades, this led to a major innovation in the Venetian judicial system. This clean break with the past was introduced not by a *terminazione* of the *Conservatori* but by a decree of the Senate. On January 13, 1723 m.v., having a doctorate in law from the *Studium* was a necessary requirement for practising as an *avvocato extraordinario*. In the same decree, a doctorate in medicine became mandatory for medical doctors.[69]

However, this opening up to Roman law must not be understood as a surrender. On the contrary, on September 4, 1751, the Conservatori amended the admission test, making it more difficult in relation to Venetian matters. It included discussing two points of Roman law, drawn by lot from a new list of twenty-five questions, but also answering two questions in Venetian about the practice of the courts, drawn by lots from the existing list, and solving two analytical problems given on the spot by the *Avvocato fiscale*.[70] The selection of the qualified lawyers proceeded in parallel with the reform of their instruction in the *Studium*, where Roman law and its doctrine was no longer the only subject taught: the curricula were updated to give space to the Venetian legal system, with the introduction of such matters as public law, feudal legislation,

66 This form of scientific literature is discussed in this volume by Claudia Passarella.

67 ASVe, *Compilazione leggi*, b. 64, c. 585.

68 ASVe, *Compilazione leggi*, b. 64, c. 628; ASVe, *Senato Terra, Deliberazioni*, reg. 51, c. 28 *verso*.

69 ASVe, *Senato Terra, filza* 1618; *Conservatori alle leggi*, capit. 1, c. 182; *Compilazione leggi*, b. 64, c. 726.

70 ASVe, *Conservatori alle leggi*, capit. 1, c. 178.

ecclesiastical laws, and natural law. Thus having the doctorate implied not only that a person had expertise in Roman *ius commune*, but also in Venetian legislation.[71]

One of the last reforms of the ageing Republic was a further reassessment of the legal professions. In 1772, a committee gathered by the Major Council, made up of the Chiefs of the Forty, the *Sindici*, and the *Conservatori*, was tasked with evaluating possible updates to the existing regime for both *avvocati extraordinari* and *sollecitadori*.[72] However, a few months of discussion brought nothing more than suggestions to change minor details. On April 30, 1781, on the other hand, the Major Council created a College of *sollecitadori* made up of one hundred members, selected in the first instance by the *Avogadori* and, afterwards, by a panel elected within the College. This was a major innovation, a step towards giving the *sollecitadori* very limited self-government under the supervision of the State. Sadly, there is very little evidence of what effect this reform had in the final sixteen years of the republic.[73]

There can be little doubt that the development of *avvocati extraordinari* contributed to the further decline of *Avvocati ordinari*. The fourteenth-century competition between the Council of Forty and the Senate around their areas of intervention had ended with the latter stripping the former of most of its legislative functions. The Forty thus became one of the earliest formal courts of appeal in continental Europe. This, in turn, led to the informal introduction of a distinction between careers that led to progression in the judiciary offices in the orbit of the Forty and the more brilliant and promising senatorial careers of a political and legislative character.

While the *Avvocati dei Prigioni* were active and effective until the end of the eighteenth century,[74] the office of *Avvocato ordinario* remained in the lower ranks of judicial careers. Sometimes it was seen as a first step towards being elected to the Forty, but more often it was merely a way for members of the Major Council from poorer families to have an income. In the late modern age, technical qualifications for magistrate-attorneys were never achieved. These attorneys were often limited to signing trial documents, leaving the pleading to the *avvocati extraordinari*.[75]

71 Giorgio Zordan, *Dall'Università dei Giuristi alla Facoltà di Giurisprudenza nello Studio patavino* (Padova: CEDAM, 2006), 24–27.

72 The proceedings are summarized in *Scrittura della Conferenza delli Capi della Quarantia Criminal e de' magistrati del Sindico e de' Conservatori alle leggi*, in ASVe, *Compilazione leggi*, b. 63.

73 Ernesto Garino, "Note sul problema dell'avvocatura in Lombardia e a Venezia nella seconda metà del XVIII secolo", in *Economia, istituzioni e cultura in Lombardia nell'età di Maria Teresa*, 2, *Cultura e società: Atti dei convegni per il 2° centenario di Maria Teresa d'Austria*, 2, *Cultura e società in Lombardia nell'età di Maria Teresa, Milano 6–9 novembre 1980*, ed. by Aldo De Maddalena, Ettore Rotelli, Gennaro Barbarisi (Bologna: Il Mulino, 1982), 1003–1006.

74 See for instance ASVe, *Compilazione leggi*, b. 64, c. 850.

75 Ferro, *Dizionario*, ad vocem Avvocati ordinari.

The ups and downs of the magistrate-attorneys are reflected in the election registers compiled by the *Segretario alle voci* in the Chancery.[76] The surviving documents begin with a register covering the years 1349–1353: the elected *Avvocati ordinari* appear to be young men of good prospects, eager to master the principles and rules of the legal system and to develop a political sense of Venetian justice which would remain fundamental in their future careers. When their term of office ended, they would often remain in court, being immediately elected as judges in one of the *Curiae*, and alternating between the office of judge and *Avvocato ordinario* according to the rhythm of the *contumacia* (the period within which magistrates could not be reelected to a previous office).[77] But in the early Modern Age the election registers already began to show signs of decline: prestigious families were still present, including Donà, Grimani, Barbaro, Querini, and Corner, but often they were the less ambitious members of those families, or they belonged to their minor branches, who usually moved on to the offices of judge in *Curia*, *Auditore*, *Avvocato fiscale*, or, at best, became members of the Forty.[78]

From the seventeenth century onwards, the registers of the *Avvocati ordinari* show an increase in *barnaboti*, members of destitute families of the aristocracy who rented cheap apartments in Dorsoduro, in the parish of St. Barnaba. Sometimes generation after generation made their livings as magistrate-attorneys, and so there was little turnover.[79]

Becoming a magistrate-attorney was a viable, if unambitious, choice. In the words of Vettore Sandi in the mid-eighteenth century: "there are some who, bent on their own pleasures and on doing whatever they wish, rather than on being of service to the public ... disappoint the aims of the government and only feign wanting to be a pleader so as to be unavailable for other duties ... and satisfied with the mere appearance of the title and the office, they care about everything except practising".[80]

ASVe = Archivio di Stato di Venezia
b., bb. = busta, buste (binder, binders)
c., cc. = carta, carte (front and back of a page)
capit. = capitolare (register of the deliberations defining the powers of a certain magistrate)
m.v. = more Veneto (the new year in Venice began on March 1; dates in the months of January and February were given more Veneto under the previous year)

76 Da Mosto, *L'Archivio di Stato*, 1, 221; "Archivio di Stato di Venezia", 905–906.
77 ASVe, *Maggior Consiglio, Deliberazioni*, reg. *Deda*, c. 16.
78 ASVe, *Segretario alle Voci*, serie *Maggior Consiglio*, regg. 4 e 7.
79 ASVe, *Segretario alle Voci*, serie *Maggior Consiglio*, reg. 27, cc. 66–68, 70, 111–112, 116–118.
80 Vettore Sandi, *Principj di storia civile della Repubblica di Venezia dalla sua fondazione sino all'anno di N.S. 1700*, 3.2, *Della parte terza che contiene i tempi dal 1500 al 1700, volume secondo dall'anno 1530 sino al 1700* (Venezia: Coleti, 1756), 618–619.

r. = recto (front of a page)
reg. = register
v. = verso (back of a page)

Note: I have used capitals for *Avvocati ordinari*, as well as for all names of magistrates, but not for *avvocati extraordinari* and *sollecitadori*, who had no powers of government.

3 "*Negari tamen non potest Venetos Ius Civile Romanorum colere et venerari*"

Venetian Law and *ius commune* between the Seventeenth and Eighteenth Centuries

Claudia Passarella

Introduction

This chapter takes its starting point from a famous passage in *De Usu et Authoritate Iuris Civilis Romanorum in Dominiis Principum Christianorum* by the English jurist Arthur Duck, in which he reflects on the relationship between Venice, the Roman Empire, and Roman laws in the medieval and early modern age.[1] Duck points out that the Venetians preserved their "primitive freedom" from the empire, not incorporating its laws into their legal system.[2] In fact, Roman law was not even included as a last resort to be drawn on as subsidiary legislation.[3] However, it was not completely foreign to the Venetian mainland, where it was taught and to a certain extent applied.[4]

1 As noted by Richard H. Helmholz a few years ago, *De Usu et Authoritate Iuris Civilis Romanorum in Dominiis Principum Christianorum* "was an impressive work of legal scholarship when it was published, and it remains impressive to this day". Richard H. Helmholz, "Arthur Duck (1580–1648)", *Ecclesiastical Law Journal*, 17: 2 (2015), 215–216.

2 See Book II, Chapter III in which he reflects on the authority and use of Roman law in *Dominiis Principum Italiae*. Paragraphs XVIII and XIX are devoted to Venice in particular and paragraph XVIII begins like this: "Veneti vero ex omnibus aliis Italiae Populis minime Romanas Leges admiserunt, et ut Libertatem suam primaevam contra omnem Imperatorum Romanorum vim et potestatem conservarunt, ita et Legibus semper suis usi sunt […]". Arthur Duck, *De Usu et Authoritate Iuris Civilis Romanourum in Dominiis Principum Christianorum* (Londini, apud Richardi Hodinksonne, 1653), 75r–76r.

3 The order of sources in the Venetian legal system is established in Jacopo Tiepolo's compilation of statutes (1242). In the text of the statute Venice''s "clear and absolute rejection" of *ius commune* as a source of law is very evident. Over the centuries, this rejection attracted the attention, first, of the most eminent medieval jurists – primarily Bartolo da Sassoferrato and Baldo degli Ubaldi – and, then, of Venetian doctrine, which, especially in the early modern age, emphasized the relationship between the rejection of the *ius commune* system and the concept of Venetian sovereignty. Giorgio Zordan, *L'ordinamento giuridico veneziano* (Padova: Imprimitur, 2005, 2ed.), 175–182.

4 "Negari tamen non potest Venetos Ius Civile Romanorum colere et venerari, immeritoque eos superbiae redarguunt aliqui, quod non dignentur Legibus Imperialibus parere, quia Iuris Civilis Professorum ut Assessorum in Iudiciis suis opera et Consilio utuntur […]". Duck, *De Usu et Authoritate Iuris Civilis Romanourum*, chapter III, par. XIX, 194.

DOI: 10.4324/9781003425069-5

Duck refers to various illustrious professors of law at the University of Padua – from Tiberio Deciani to Giacomo Menochio, and from Francesco Mantica to Marc'Antonio Pellegrini – who gave the law course its excellent reputation and whose teachings benefitted multiple generations of students. He also mentions the role of the *assessori* (judges) who administered justice in the mainland courts, although he does not go into further detail on this subject.

Duck thus gives us a sense of the complexity of a legal system that eschewed traditional categories, placing itself – not without some difficulty – between two different conceptions of law. This chapter aims to explore its intersections and reciprocal contaminations, focusing on legal and judicial practice in the Venetian mainland, which evolved slowly but continuously over the centuries.[5]

The intersections between Venetian legislation, Roman law, and the *ius commune* tradition can be found at both the level of doctrine and in the field of jurisprudence, where different practical methods were used in criminal matters and in the regulation of civil law. This chapter will consider a variety of key figures who worked as judges, chancellors, lawyers, and prosecutors, demonstrating a diversity of approaches and a multiplicity of voices. The research, which lends itself to various levels of investigation, has taken its lead from the fundamental points in Gaspare Morari's *Prattica de' Reggimenti in Terraferma* (Prattica of the territorial districts in the mainland), published in 1708.[6] Morari drew on his experience as an *assessor* serving the rectors who had been sent to administer the mainland cities and was thus able to lay out the basic coordinates of a system characterized by legislative and judicial pluralism.[7]

As shown by the historiography, Venetian patricians sent to the mainland regions to take up positions as rectors remained in office for limited periods – of approximately 16 months – during which they were called upon to perform a series of civil, military, and judicial functions.[8] They did this as a step

5 For a reflection on the relationship between Venice and the *ius commune* system between the Middle Ages and the modern age, see my article, Claudia Passarella, "Venezia e il diritto comune: Dall'orgoglio nazionalistico alla ricerca delle concordanze", *Archivio Giuridico*, 153 (2021), 155–200. In that article I proposed a diachronic reflection on the sources from Jacopo Tiepolo's *Statutum Novum* to the attempts at codification in the late eighteenth century. In this chapter, however, I intend to privilege a predominantly procedural approach by focusing on the judicial sphere and the works of a number of authors, who, in various ways, developed all or part of their professional experience in the Venetian mainland between the seventeenth and eighteenth centuries. This is thus a slightly different line of research, allowing the topic to be examined from a new perspective.

6 Gaspare Morari, *Prattica de' Reggimenti in Terraferma* (Padova: Giuseppe Corona, 1708).

7 For a reflection on the concept of pluralism within the Republic of Venice, see Elisabetta Fusar Poli, *Relativo e plurale. Dinamiche, processi e fonti di diritto in Terraferma veneta, secc. XVI–XVIII* (Torino: Giappichelli, 2020).

8 Since the 1970s, the historiography on the subject has been enriched by countless contributions. Since it is not possible here to give an account of all the studies published on the subject, I will limit myself to mentioning the fourteen volumes of the *Relazioni dei rettori veneti in ter-*

in a *cursus honorum* that they hoped would lead to prominent positions in the most important magistracies of Venice, in which Roman law had no place even as a last resort in the absence of other laws. Inclined more to pragmatism than to legal technicalities, the Venetian patricians sent to the mainland needed the help of a number of assistants – mainly chancellors and assessors – who were chosen very carefully, because, as Morari rightly noted, "the condemnation or the glory" of the rector's government very often depended on their work.[9]

The assessors had to have proven experience and be discerning, judicious, and resolute in their deliberations. The office could be taken up only by subjects of the Venetian state – as long as they came from a city other than that in which they were being called on to work – who had been awarded a doctorate from the University of Padua, where they had been taught by the most important jurists of the time.[10] The emphasis placed on the skills required of assessors embarking on their professional careers reveals an important juncture which is fundamental to our research, bringing to light an early form of interaction between the politics of law proper to Venice – applied by the rectors – and the legal tradition of *ius commune*, to which the assessors referred, although not necessarily explicitly. The courts on the mainland provided the physical space in which these two different legal systems interacted, with rectors and assessors as their respective exponents. There was a daily balancing act between the two systems, with the rules of their coexistence often remaining implicit in the various stages of a judgment. The judicial sphere thus became the main context for this dialogue, which could either be constructive or, on the contrary, reveal potentially divisive approaches.

Without entering procedural technicalities, Morari describes the tasks assigned to the assessors engaged in delivering justice.[11] With regard to the management of civil litigation, a key role was given to the assessor appointed as deputy of the *podestà* – a rector with civil and judicial functions. They heard the demands of all the parties, examined the arguments put forward by the lawyers, and considered the depositions made by the witnesses before making their decision on the dispute, with the important clarification that the decisions made by them in their role as deputy of the rector had the same value

---

raferma published by the Institute of Economic History at the University of Trieste between 1973 and 1979. These reports – which Venetian representatives had to present to the Senate at the end of their term in office – reveal the problems that the rectors were called upon to deal with in the various regions of the republic. Among the items on their agendas, the administration of justice undoubtedly played a prominent role.

9 Morari, *Prattica de' Reggimenti*, 10.

10 A study of this specific professional category was made by Claudio Povolo, *Il giudice assessore nella Terraferma veneta* (Pordenone: Tipografia Sartor, 1991). For a focus on the requirements for entering the profession in the first half of the eighteenth century, see Alfredo Viggiano, "Ascesa sociale e burocrazia di stato: La carriera di assessore nello stato di terraferma veneto", *Annali Veneti*, 2 (1985), 67–74.

11 Morari, *Prattica de' Reggimenti*, 14–28.

and force as the sentences given by the rector himself. In criminal matters, on the other hand, the central figure was the judge at the *maleficio* (who was in charge of criminal cases), who was the second most important of the assessors. Their competence in judgments *in criminalibus* covered all stages of the proceedings: they had to attend the *visum et repertum*, preside over the interrogation of the offender, have the witnesses examined, admit the suspect's defences, supervise the use of torture, oversee the whole trial from beginning to end, and present their opinion on the case immediately after hearing the deputy's opinion.

Morari's study therefore examines civil litigation and criminal justice separately, as they were governed by different rules, although with important similarities in the regulation of certain institutions and in the terminology used by legal practitioners.[12] Our analysis will also follow two distinct tracks, given that, as we shall see in the following pages, the interaction between Venetian law and the *ius commune* tradition followed slightly different logics in criminal and civil law. We will begin from a variety of sources that will allow us to rethink some long-established categories, raising questions that, in turn, open new opportunities for reflection.

Ius Commune and the Administration of Criminal Justice: From Lorenzo Priori to Bartolomeo Melchiori

The study of criminal justice in the Venetian Republic during the *ancien régime* lends itself to various levels of interpretation that consider its legislative aspects and doctrinal works, its case files, and the numerous letters and communication sent from the mainland to Venice and vice versa. Worthy of special mention are the *practicae criminales*, which became a very successful literary genre in the modern age and an indispensable reference for generations of jurists across the Italian Peninsula.[13] The *practicae* were widely circulated in the Republic, where, from the early seventeenth century onwards, several manuals were published in which the criminal process was described in its entirety, including both theoretical analyses and practical advice based on daily experience.[14]

12 For a reflection on the legal language used in legislative and procedural acts in eighteenth-century Venice, see Lorenzo Tomasin, *Il volgare e la legge: Storia linguistica del diritto veneziano, secoli XIII–XVIII* (Padova: Esedra, 2001), 235–290.

13 The *Pratiche criminali*, the *Istruzioni criminali*, and the *Ristretti* made up "the chosen scope" of seventeenth- and eighteenth-century jurists. See Michele Pifferi, "Criminalistica in antico regime", *Il contributo italiano alla storia del pensiero: Diritto* (Roma: Istituto dell'Enciclopedia Italiana Treccani, 2012), 141–148. In recent years, the genre of *praticae* has been of particular interest to researchers. See, in particular, Loredana Garlati, "Per una storia del processo penale: Le pratiche criminali", *Rivista di storia del diritto italiano*, 89 (2016), 71–109.

14 For an overview of Venetian criminal practices in the modern age, see Claudio Povolo, "Retoriche giudiziarie, dimensioni del penale e prassi processuale nella Repubblica di Ven-

The title of the first Venetian *practica criminalis* written in the vernacular clearly identifies its field of interest. The chancellor Lorenzo Priori's *Prattica criminale secondo il ritto delle leggi della Serenissima Repubblica di Venetia* (Criminal practice according to the legal procedure and laws in the Venetian Republic) was written at the end of the sixteenth century but was published posthumously in 1622, with numerous reissues up until the end of the eighteenth century.[15] It has two parts: the first is dedicated to the procedural dimension and the second to the examination of the main criminal offences, including, of course, various forms of homicide. In the first part Priori engages in a detailed examination of *ordo iudiciorum* in judgments carried out on the mainland, analyzing all stages of the trial from the presentation of the complaint to the considerations made by the judge before giving their sentence. Although many of its passages are stilted and difficult to read, the *Prattica* provides us with valuable information at a time when interactions between Venice and the mainland courts were somewhat limited.

These limited interactions did not mean, however, that Venice was uninterested in repressing criminal activity. On the contrary, from the second half of the sixteenth century onwards, the city had legislated heavily on criminal matters, encouraging targeted interventions and more extensive and complete reforms.[16] Priori's work is full of references to the laws issued by the Venetian authority in the various fields of law and procedure, clarifying that, in criminal proceedings, Venetian laws were the first to be applied: the judges could therefore have recourse to city statutes only in the absence of a sovereign law.

The abundance of legislative references is linked to the absence – or at least very low number – of explicit references to the tradition of *ius commune*, which, in the penal sector, was rooted in the analysis and application of the canonical inquisitorial process. Even on topics that were widely debated by jurists – such as rules of evidence, ways of interrogating an offender, and the use of torture – Priori generally avoided citing the great masters. However, we should not let this lack of citations fool us: as pointed out by Giovanni Chiodi, who has done extensive in-depth research on the *Prattica*, the doctrine of

ezia da Lorenzo Priori ai pratici settecenteschi", in *L'amministrazione della giustizia penale nella Repubblica di Venezia (secoli XVI–XVIII)*, II, *Retoriche, stereotipi, prassi*, ed. by Giovani Chiodi, Claudio Povolo (Sommacampagna: Cierre, 2004), 19–170.

15 Lorenzo Priori, *Prattica criminale secondo il ritto delle leggi della Serenissima Repubblica di Venetia* (Venezia: Girolamo Albrizzi, 1695). Unlike previous editions, the 1695 edition is improved by an alphabetical subject index. For information on the life of the Venetian chancellor, see Claudio Povolo, "Priori Lorenzo", in *Dizionario biografico dei giuristi italiani, sec. XII–XX* (Bologna: Il Mulino, 2013), vol. 2, 1628.

16 See, for example, the repression of banditry, which in the late sixteenth and early seventeenth centuries became a particular focus of the Venetian legislature. This topic was studied, among many others, by Claudio Povolo, "Nella spirale della violenza: Cronologia, intensità e diffusione del banditismo nella terraferma veneta (1550–1610)", in *Bande armate, banditi, banditismo e repressione di giustizia negli Stati europei di antico regime*, ed. by Gherardo Ortalli (Roma: Jouvence, 1986), 21–51.

ius commune was "widely and implicitly used" by Priori,[17] who made particular recourse to the opinions of Giulio Claro in his famous *Liber Quintus Sententiarum*. Chiodi argues that Priori's use of Claro's work demonstrates the "affinity of thought" between the Venetian chancellor and the Lombard senator and provides evidence of similarities in many areas.[18] This common basis, however, had to be adapted to the customs and practices of individual territories, which, in some cases, could diverge significantly, with solutions which were specific to a given geographical area.

Among the institutions typical of the Venetian Republic, we should mention the *bando ad inquirendum*, which was a particular type of ban used for serious crimes if no strong indications of guilt had emerged against the absent defendant. In such circumstances, the offender was banished for two years, during which they could decide to voluntarily turn themselves in to the justice system so that the trial could continue; otherwise, when the term was up, their ban would become permanent and would also be extended to the city of Venice and Dogado.[19] The *bando ad inquirendum* was emblematic of an institution particular to a specific geographical area that was part of a broader regulation characterized by common, or at least similar, rules in the different territories. Precisely by virtue of its specificity, this particular type of ban is mentioned in all the seventeenth and eighteenth centuries Venetian *practicae*, even though it would have been much less commonly used during the latter century.

In the following decades, Priori's example was followed by other jurists who wrote manuals characterized by a primarily practical approach. Indeed, the golden age of the Venetian *practicae* began in the 1630s, reaching its peak in the mid-eighteenth century and continuing until the final years of the republic.[20] Marc'Antonio Tirabosco's *Ristretto di pratica criminale*, published in 1636 and reprinted on numerous occasions due to its popularity among legal practitioners, must be understood in this context.[21]

17 Giovanni Chiodi, "Le relazioni pericolose: Lorenzo Priori, il senatore invisibile e gli eccelsi Consigli veneziani", in *L'amministrazione della giustizia penale nella Repubblica di Venezia (secoli XVI–XVIII)*, I, *Lorenzo Priori e la sua* Prattica criminale, ed. by Giovanni Chiodi, Claudio Povolo (Sommacampagna: Cierre, 2004), XXXII.

18 Ivi, XCIV.

19 Priori, *Prattica criminale*, 57. Further information on this particular category of "bando" can be found in the *Dizionario del diritto* compiled by the lawyer Marco Ferro: Marco Ferro, *Dizionario del diritto comune e veneto* (Venezia: Presso Andrea Santini e figlio, 1845, 2 ed.), I, 241–242.

20 The period of Venetian *practicae* came to an end in 1792 with the publication of the work of the lawyer Zeffirino Giovan Battista Grecchi with the title *Le formalità del processo criminale nel dominio veneto*. For more on this subject, see Gianni Buganza, "Tra scienza avvocatura e diritto: Zeffirino Giovan Battista Grecchi davanti alla corte pretoria di Padova (1789–1791)", *Studi veneziani*, 61 (2010), 237–379.

21 For this article, the following was consulted: Marc'Antonio Tirabosco, *Ristretto di prattica criminale che serve per la formation de' processi ad offesa* (Venezia: Domenico Lovisa, 1695).

Like Priori, Tirabosco also traced the various stages of a trial from the initiation of the proceedings to the pronouncing of the sentence, concluding with a succinct list of punishments. There are, however, clear differences in style between Priori's *Prattica* and Tirabosco's *Ristretto*: while the former is often stilted and difficult to read, the latter is written fluently and concisely, containing a high dose of pragmatism. The *Ristretto* does not have the plethora of legislative references we find in Priori's work but makes a series of clear distinctions between the procedures followed in Venice and those in the mainland courts. In Venice, for example, the offender was taken to the torture chamber before their defence, whereas in the mainland it was the other way around, i.e., first the defendant was given the opportunity to defend themselves and then, if deemed necessary, judicial torture was used.[22] At a time when interactions between Venice and the mainland were increasing – particularly through the use of delegations[23] – it became even more important to point out these procedural divergences, with a view to gradually increasing their interaction. However, this would never lead to a unitary system: Venice and the mainland remained two separate entities throughout the republic's life.

Just like Priori's *Prattica*, the *Ristretto* also lends itself to comparative analysis, bringing to light interconnections and reciprocal influences between Venetian practice and the *ius commune* system. And, once again, these connections are implicit, meaning that it is up to the researcher to identify and analyze them. Confirming the affinities between Venetian practice and the Lombard system, Loredana Garlati has linked Tirabosco's work with the *Ristretto della Prattica Criminale per lo Stato di Milano* drafted in the eighteenth century by an anonymous author. She studied the Milanese *Ristretto* in detail, discovering a connection between it and the text by Tirabosco, whose fame had evidently transcended narrow territorial boundaries.[24] She writes that the Milanese author faithfully reproduced Tirabosco's work on more than one occasion, demonstrating that it had been used as a reference model and proving the existence of a shared body of knowledge capable of forming a framework of common rules.

In this interweaving of invisible but substantial relations, institutions and customs emerged that were peculiar to each territory, as if their similarities reached a certain point and then gave way to the characteristic features of the respective legal systems, which would sometimes favour different solutions. The regulation of judicial torture is a clear example of this. In many respects, that proposed by Venetian jurists did not deviate from the dominant doctrine

22 Ivi, 107.

23 For a reflection on the emergence and development of delegations, see Giovanni Chiodi, "Il giardino dei sentieri che s'incontrano: Processo penale e forme di giustizia nella terraferma veneta (secoli XVI–XVIII)", in *Saggi in ricordo di Aristide Tanzi* (Milano: Giuffrè, 2009), 153–161.

24 Loredana Garlati, *Inseguendo la verità: Processo penale e giustizia nel Ristretto della prattica criminale per lo Stato di Milano* (Milano: Giuffrè, 1999), 7–8.

that, under certain conditions, legitimized the use of torture against defendants, accomplices, and even witnesses.[25] However, in the Venetian *practicae* – including in Tirabosco's *Ristretto* – we find some differences also from a linguistic point of view. Venetian jurists made a distinction that was not found in other geographical areas, that is, between torture with or without "*protesto*" (i.e., torture with or without a specific reason), and they made a further distinction depending on the stage of the trial when the torture was practiced.[26] This is a prime example of the attitude of Venetian legal practitioners who were familiar with the classifications drawn up by the most eminent jurists of *ius commune* – including Giulio Claro – but who had no problem adapting them to their own context.[27]

By the middle of the eighteenth century, the links that Priori and Tirabosco had decided not to make explicit started to become very clear. This shift can be seen in the 1740s with the publication of the first edition of the *Miscellanea di materie criminali volgari e latine composta secondo le leggi civili e venete*, written by one of the best-known jurists of the time, assessor Bartolomeo Melchiori.[28] The change of perspective is clear right from the work's preface, in which Melchiori addresses "the scholars of criminal law": he points out that the *Miscellanea* was built on two pillars, *ius civile* and Venetian law, "which admirably correspond to each other" and therefore have to be considered together in order to avoid undermining the study of the subject as a whole. This was the basis on which Melchiori built the *Miscellanea*, in which, in addition to the necessary references to Venetian laws, we find explicit references to the jurists of the *ius commune* tradition, in particular Egidio Bossi, Giulio Claro, Tiberio Deciani, Giacomo Menochio, Prospero Farinacci, and Benedikt Carpzov, alongside the names of the great jurists of the Roman era, from Ulpian to Marcian, from Paulus to Papinianus, whose teachings could

25 The use of torture in the medieval and modern ages has been widely researched. In recent decades the historiography has been enriched with numerous studies bringing to light the specific features of the practice. However, for a complete examination of the subject, it is necessary to refer to the now dated but indispensable study: Piero Fiorelli, *La tortura giudiziaria nel diritto comune* (Milano: Giuffrè, 1953–1954).

26 Tirabosco explained that torture without "protesto" was used against the defendant to "purge the proofs" against him and possibly arrive at an acquittal, whereas torture with "protesto" was used against the defendant in order to get the names of their accomplices and to discover the reasons that led them to commit the crime. Tirabosco, *Ristretto di prattica criminale*, 98–100.

27 For more detail on this issue, see Claudia Passarella, "La tortura giudiziaria nella Repubblica di Venezia nei secoli XVI-XVIII", *Historia et Ius*, 9 (2016), 1–29.

28 Bartolomeo Melchiori, *Miscellanea di materie criminali volgari e latine composta secondo le leggi civili e venete* (Venezia: Presso Gasparo Storti, 1776). For this chapter I consulted the second, augmented, and corrected edition of the text, which is divided into two volumes published in 1776. For more information on the life and works of Melchiori, see Loredana Garlati, "Melchiori Bartolomeo", in *Dizionario biografico dei giuristi italiani*, II, 1319–1320.

not be ignored given that "the civil laws of the Romans" expressed "the most certain measure of right and wrong".[29]

Melchiori appealed to Roman jurisprudence to answer a crucial question: whether the assessors should judge criminal cases "with the rigour of the law" or "with the temperance of equity". The very concept of equity necessitated a reference to the opinions and teachings formulated by Roman jurists who instructed "every learned man in the art of judging". As judge, Melchiori knew very well how important it was to give voice to mildness and clemency, carefully analyzing "the hidden feeling of those laws that seemed too harsh for the case", without, however, being afraid to impose severe punishments when necessary, because "it is one thing to use equity, another to betray discipline".[30]

Thus, unlike his predecessors, Melchiori openly and unhesitatingly cited Roman jurisprudence and the tradition of *ius commune*, acknowledging that both had functions that had long remained silent. At the same time, however, he paid a lot of attention to legislation in Venice – which, particularly in some areas, had intensified considerably[31] – and to a series of practices that characterized the administration of criminal justice in the territories of the Venetian mainland, with particular reference to the procedure adopted by the Council of Ten and the system of appeals.

From the seventeenth century onwards, the Council of Ten – established in 1310 and over time becoming the supreme criminal court of the city – had assumed a key role in the repression of criminal activity in the Venetian mainland through granting the rectors the possibility of using its own inquisitorial rules (called "il rito") both in the management of the trial and in the choice of punishment.[32] Recourse to delegated justice – which Priori had only briefly mentioned[33] – had significantly increased between the seventeenth and eighteenth centuries, to the point that Melchiori devoted an entire chapter of his *Miscellanea* to it, giving an account of the peculiarities of a procedure characterized by secrecy and rapid decision-making.

A similar reflection can be made in relation to the appeals system, which Priori and Tirabosco had ignored and which Melchiori instead dissected in all

29 Melchiori, *Miscellanea di materie criminali*, VI–VII.

30 Ivi, I, 34–44.

31 The regulation of firearms was a prime example of this: during the seventeenth century, Venice legislated widely on the matter, to such an extent that Melchiori felt the need to dedicate a specific dissertation to it, entitled *Trattato dell'Armi da Fuoco esposto secondo le Leggi Venete*. Ivi, I, 212–227.

32 Extensive studies have been made of the Council of Ten and its famous procedure. With particular reference to the seventeenth and eighteenth centuries, see Claudia Andreato, "Il rito inquisitorio del Consiglio dei Dieci nel XVI secolo," in *Processo e difesa penale in età moderna: Venezia e il suo stato territoriale*, ed. by Claudio Povolo (Bologna: il Mulino, 2007), 361–417; and Silvia Girardello, "La procedura inquisitoria in uno stato repubblicano: Il rito del Consiglio dei Dieci (sec. XVIII)", in *Processo e difesa penale*, 419–470.

33 Priori, *Prattica criminale*, 50.

its complexity. From the mid-seventeenth century, appeals had become a tool through which Venice centralized justice without renouncing the judicial pluralism that had always distinguished its politics. The court charged with examining the appeal was the *Quarantia Civil Vecchia*, which could either confirm the original decision taken by the mainland court or uphold the appeal and annul the sentence, possibly sending the case back to the local judge for a new trial.[34]

We thus find apparently opposing trends in the *Miscellanea* that are, in fact, not contradictory. On the one hand, Melchiori describes a scenario characterized by an increase in relations between the mainland and Venice and by the key role of the Venetian magistrates in the repression of crime, and, on the other hand, he structured his reasoning through a series of citations and references to the "civil laws of the Romans" and to the teachings of the most important jurists of the *ancien régime*, in search of correlations that could no longer be kept hidden.

As we shall see below, Melchiori's approach is in keeping with an attitude that was widespread in the second half of the eighteenth century: in most manuals published in the final decades of the republic there is an openness towards the system of *ius commune*, which had in fact always played a role in the training of legal practitioners in the Venetian mainland. Thus, a presence that had for decades remained latent was finally coming to light, initiating a period of dialogue and confrontation. In some cases, the comparison revealed what Melchiori called "admirable correspondences", while in other cases it exposed profound disagreements, which were stressed by some authors in order to reaffirm the specificity of Venice and its *stylus curiae*. One such author was Carlo Goldoni, a lawyer who, at a certain point in his career, decided to abandon the legal profession to devote himself body and soul to the theatre.

Ius Commune and the Administration of Civil Justice: Between Claims to Uniqueness and the Search for Similarities

In 1750, during the carnival period, the play *The Venetian Lawyer* by Carlo Goldoni was staged in the city for the first time. On the strength of his previous legal experience, Goldoni had decided to give the legal profession "that prominence that is rightly its due".[35] The comedy in three acts followed a legal

34 For more on the criminal appeals mechanism, see my article, Claudia Passarella, "Dalla Terraferma alla Dominante: Il sistema delle appellazioni all'ombra del leone di San Marco", in *History & Law Encounters. Lezioni per pensare da giurista*, II, ed. by Aldo Andrea Cassi, Elisabetta Fusar Poli, Federica Paletti (Torino: Giappichelli, 2022), 79–87.

35 Carlo Goldoni, "L'avvocato veneziano", in *Opere complete di Carlo Goldoni edite dal Municipio di Venezia nel II centenario dalla nascita* (Venezia: Istituto veneto di arti grafiche, 1908), vol. 3, 411. For information on the life of the celebrated Venetian playwright, see Lucia Strappini, "Goldoni Carlo" in *Dizionario Biografico degli Italiani*, 57 (2001), 581–592. For particular reference to Goldoni's professional experience in the legal field, see Mario A. Cattaneo,

dispute set in the city of Rovigo, on the Venetian mainland, between a woman named Rosaura and a young man named Florindo. The events depicted began in the 1720s when Anselmo Aretusi, married without children, had decided to adopt Rosaura, daughter of a Bolognese merchant named Pellegrino Balanzoni. By means of a legal contract Anselmo agreed to donate all his property to Rosaura. Two years later, Anselmo and his wife Ortensia had a son who they named Florindo. Before her death in 1744, Ortensia made a will in which she made it clear that all the assets of her dowry were to be given to Florindo. Anselmo died shortly afterwards without leaving any will. When her adoptive father died, Rosaura, defended by her uncle, Doctor Balanzoni – a Bolognese jurist who was expert in *ius commune* – decided to take legal action to ensure the fulfillment of the donation contract. Florindo, defended by a Venetian lawyer, Doctor Alberto Casaboni, opposed this by invoking the revocation of the donation due to the birth of children.

The aspect of interest in this dispute is not its subject matter, which was similar to many other cases that were debated daily in the courts, but rather in the contrast between the two lawyers. While Doctor Balanzoni was an expert in *ius commune*, Doctor Casaboni proudly belonged to the Venetian legal class.[36] The two professionals had very different styles: Balanzoni favoured a defensive line based on a "grand apparatus of doctrines" and a "great elegance in terminology", drawing up his *allegationes* in line with the *ius commune* tradition; while Casaboni opted for the Venetian style characterized by heated disputes in which the force of the argument was associated with incredibly passionate oratory. They were two completely antithetical strategies: the Bologna school in which "one writes and does not speak", and the Venetian method "which imitates the style of the ancient Roman orators".[37]

The difference between the Bolognese and the Venetian method, which Goldoni describes with the aim of making the former appear less effective than the latter, was not limited to the procedural strategy employed in court but concerned the very essence of the law in force in Bologna and Venice, respectively. Whereas Balanzoni made his arguments based on a long and inveterate tradition enriched over the centuries through the doctrine elaborated by numerous internationally renowned authors, Casaboni responded by citing

"Carlo Goldoni uomo di legge", *Quaderni per la storia dell'Università di Padova*, 30 (1997), 77–91. For a reflection on Venetian society at the time of Goldoni's plays, see Gaetano Cozzi, "Note su Carlo Goldoni, la società veneziana e il suo diritto", *Atti dell'Istituto veneto di scienze lettere e arti*, 137 (1978–79), 141–157. Finally, for a recent publication examining Carlo Goldoni's work through reflecting on the relationship between law and literature, see Christian Zendri, "Letteratura come diritto comune: Il caso di Carlo Goldoni", *Rivista internazionale di diritto comune*, 33 (2022), 233.

36 For an investigation on the legal counsel in the metropolitan courts of justice of the Venetian Republic, see Silvia Gasparini, "Conflitti e giustizia: Il patrocinio legale a Venezia", *Rivista di storia del diritto italiano*, 95 (2022), 179–233.

37 Goldoni, "L'avvocato veneziano", 419.

the Venetian statute that had been written with the law of nature as its only guide. Although he was familiar with Roman law and the system of *ius commune*, the Venetian lawyer chose to set them aside, having a statute at his disposal that, according to Goldoni, was "abundant, clear and instructive" and being able, in the absence of statutory rules, to appeal to previously judged cases, equity and the "weighing up of the circumstances", all elements that the Venetian playwright believed were infinitely more valuable than the sophisticated legal doctrines cited by the Bolognese jurist.[38]

The play deliberately accentuated the differences between the two models, with the declared intention of exalting the Venetian style "over what is called *ius commune*".[39] Being equally knowledgeable of the two systems due to his work experience as a lawyer first in Venice and then in Pisa, Goldoni made his preference clear, accentuating the characteristic traits of each system and the uniqueness of the Venetian style.

During the seventeenth and eighteenth centuries, other authors also emphasized the peculiarities of the Venetian system. In 1659, the Venetian author Alessandro Maria Vianoli published *L'oratore forense lodato & espresso* in which he extolled the eloquence of great men of the past, recommending that their example be followed.[40] In the Venetian tradition the oratorical skills of the Greeks and Romans were meant to provide inspiration to lawyers, who were expected to be fluent and eloquent, making speeches that were neither improvised nor impromptu, but the result of careful and methodical preparation.[41] Whereas in the tradition of *ius commune* a lawyer's skill was measured by the arguments and doctrinal citations in their *allegationes*, for the Venetians it was important to present the arguments in favour of their client "*a viva voce*", without resorting to scholarly writings as happened in "almost all other European nations".[42]

Few tangible traces remain of the vaunted oratorical skills of the Venetian court practitioners, most of which can be traced back to two collections of judicial cases published in the second half of the eighteenth century, thanks

38 Ivi, 484.

39 In the introductory note for the reader Goldoni immediately makes clear that he intends to "make a winner" of the Venetian style. Given these premises, it is obvious how the dispute would end: the case was won by Florindo, assisted by Casaboni, and the other party was made to pay the court costs. Discouraged by the outcome, Balanzoni decided not to appeal.

40 Alessandro Maria Vianoli, *L'oratore forense lodato & espresso* (Venezia: Gio. Pietro Pinelli, 1659).

41 The practical advice given by Constantino Pannà in his 1765 study, which is focused entirely on the art of argumentation, is crucial in this regard. In addition to providing technical pointers, the author provides concrete examples and points out mistakes to avoid when preparing speeches. Costantino Pannà, *Dell'artifizio della disputa veneziana* (Venezia: Presso Giambattista Pasquali, 1765).

42 Vettor Sandi, *Principi di storia civile della Repubblica di Venezia scritti da Vettor Sandi nobile veneto dall'anno di NS 1700 sino all'anno 1767* (Venezia: Presso Sebastiano Coletti, 1771), II, 282.

to which we can at least gain some insight into the ways in which cases were argued and discussed before Venetian judges.[43] Unfortunately, little else has survived. At best, a few documents can be found in family archives that have only recently been discovered and so are still undergoing study and analysis. An example of the latter is the documentation collected by the lawyer Francesco Maria Quarenghi, kept at the Biblioteca Civica Mai in Bergamo, which is an extremely heterogeneous collection that includes legal opinions and *allegationes*.[44] Those parts of it that have already been analyzed confirm the distance between the tradition of *ius commune* and the Venetian style, which is lacking in doctrinal citations and instead focuses on the concrete elements and circumstances of the case, favouring an extremely pragmatic approach.[45]

However, we must point out that the difference in method was not a symptom of a closure towards the system of *ius commune*, which the lawyers in the Venetian mainland were very knowledgeable about and which they constantly had to work with and confront. Eighteenth-century manuals tend to take a sober approach aimed at highlighting both the points of contact and the elements of diversity between the two legal cultures. This is the case with the works of legal practitioners such as Domenico Micheli, who, in 1733, published *L'ordine di procedere nei giudicj civili del foro di Verona*, and Antonio Lorenzoni, the author of three volumes of *Instituzioni del diritto civile privato per la provincia vicentina* published in the 1780s. Although he did not deal in detail with the thorny issue of the relationship between Venice, Roman laws, and the system of *ius commune*, Micheli demonstrated his mastery of concepts that originated from different legal systems, principally aiming to give laws "the order that naturally pertains to them".[46] Lorenzoni, on the other hand, addressed the issue in the first pages of his work by clarifying that, in the

43 Giuseppe Pavissi, *Storia delle cause civili agitate e diffinitivamente decise dagl'Eccellent. Consegli e Collegi della Serenissima Repubblica di Venezia* (Venezia: Presso Domenico Deregni, 1765); *Raccolta storica de' sovrani giudicj che seguono di tempo in tempo negli eccellentissimi Consegli e Collegj della Serenissima Repubblica di Venezia* (Venezia: Presso Giacomo Caroboli, 1775).

44 For a survey of the documents included in the collection, see https://www.bibliotecamai.org/wp-content/uploads/2017/11/Raccolta-Francesco-Maria-Quarenghi. (accessed 18 May 2023).

45 The first results of the current research on the wealth of documentation collected by the lawyer Francesco Maria Quarenghi were presented at a conference organized by the Department of Law at the University of Bergamo in December 2020: Francesco Maria Quarenghi (1741–1807) e le sue collezioni giuridiche fra età veneziana e periodo napoleonico. The conference proceedings were published in October 2023 under the title *Francesco Maria Quarenghi (1741–1807) e le sue collezioni fra erudizione e pratica del diritto*, ed. by Daniele Edigati (Torino: Giappichelli, 2023).

46 Domenico Micheli, *L'ordine di procedere nei giudicj civili del foro di Verona* (Verona: Per Dionigi Ramanzini, 1733). Domenico Micheli belonged to a family that was devoted to the study of law, as evidenced by the books in the library of his father, Carlo Maria Micheli. It included a number of legal texts from the tradition of *ius commune*, from Accursio's *Magna glossa* to the treaties on criminal law by Giulio Claro and Prospero Farinacci. For more on

resolution of a dispute, judges had to apply the statutory laws and, in their absence, Venetian laws, with the possibility – by no means given – of recourse to Roman or canonical laws that had been "accepted" by the system and thus had become proper to the state that had incorporated them.[47]

Although they were both important, Micheli's and Lorenzoni's manuals were situated within geographically limited horizons – the provinces of Verona and Vicenza, respectively – without any attempt at a general and in-depth reflection on the role assigned to Roman law as a source to be drawn upon in the resolution of a judicial dispute. This theme, touched on by many but rarely examined in all its complexity, was extensively analyzed by Antonio Bonsi, a jurist from Bergamo who, in 1788, published *Introduzione allo studio del diritto municipale privato della città di Bergamo, ossia considerazioni sulle leggi in generale* (An introduction to the study of private municipal law in the city of Bergamo, that is considerations on laws in general).[48]

From its very first pages, Bonsi made his position clear: although the private law in force in the Bergamo area was the result of a combination of rules deriving from the city statute and Venetian laws, there had to be recourse to the *ius commune*, thanks to which the system was "notably enriched and perfected". *Ius commune*, based on the Justinian Roman laws, was thus an indispensable reference for building a homogenous, coherent, and regular order. Bonsi obviously knew that the Venetians had never formally adopted Roman law as such, but he believed that in composing its own laws the city had had the foresight to take advantage of the wisdom of Roman law, transposing its "wisest" [49] principles and rules into its own practice. Venice had thus been able to profit from foreign knowledge, "making it its own", without renouncing the uniformity that was the distinctive feature of a nation proud of its freedom.

These general reflections also clearly indicated the order of the sources to be drawn from in the resolution of civil judgments. Recourse had to be made to Roman law in the absence of a statutory regulation, when not even Venetian laws were able to provide a rule applicable to the case in question. Thus, in these cases, legal practitioners could and should turn to Roman law

this, see Claudio Carcereri De Prati, *La biblioteca di Carlo Maria Micheli, causidico veronese del Seicento* (Padova: Imprimitur, 2006).

47 Antonio Lorenzoni, *Instituzioni del diritto civile privato per la provincia vicentina* (Vicenza: Nella stamperia Turra, 1785), 17–20. For information on the life and works of Lorenzoni, see Annamaria Monti, "Lorenzoni Antonio", in *Dizionario biografico dei giuristi italiani*, vol. 2, 1201–1202.

48 Antonio Bonsi, *Introduzione allo studio del dritto municipale privato della città di Bergamo, ossia considerazioni sulla legge in generale ed in particolare sulle fonti sistema ed uso del detto dritto* (Bergamo: Stamperia Locatelli), 1788.

49 Ivi, 152. Vettor Sandi also held that the Venetians had derived from Roman laws that which they believed to be "more equal, more natural and more suited to their own circumstances". Vettor Sandi, *Principi di storia civile della Repubblica di Venezia della sua fondazione sino all'anno di NS 1700 [...] Volume secondo dall'anno 1000 sino al 1300* (Venezia: Presso Sebastian Coletti, 1755), 851.

conceived as "an immense storehouse of universal rules ... equally appropriate for every society".[50] This had to be done *cum grano salis*, thus excluding all those laws that referred to customs or particular circumstances that had nothing to do with the legal system of the republic. Roman laws that did not have "the stamp of equity" were also to be excluded because, in the complete absence of a written rule, the judge had to be guided exclusively by the principles of reason and natural justice. Roman laws could therefore be used to the extent that they conformed to these principles. Bonsi specified that it was only on this condition that they deserved a place in the study of private municipal law in the city of Bergamo.[51]

In 1787, the year before the publication of Bonsi's work, Ubaldo Bregolini's work was published. Originally from Noale, in the province of Treviso, Bregolini was sent by his father to study law in Padua, where he obtained his doctoral degree at nineteen years old. He then moved to Treviso, where he embarked on an ecclesiastical career. Throughout his life, Bregolini devoted himself to teaching in various places, including at the Collegio Mariano in Bergamo.[52] His teaching career in the city of Bergamo lasted eleven years, from 1761 to 1772, when he was called upon to teach oratory and civil law in Venice, where he remained for thirty years. With his students in mind, whom he must have been very fond of, he drew up a study manual designed "for the instruction of the Venetian youth" to whom he thought it appropriate to provide the principles of civil jurisprudence according to Roman and Venetian laws.[53]

Published at the end of the 1780s, Bregolini's work is part of a literary genre of manuals that emphasized similarities between Roman and Venetian law and sought out points of correspondence between them.[54] The author infused his experience as a teacher – both in the mainland and in Venice – into the writing

50 Bonsi, *Introduzione allo studio del dritto*, 178.

51 Giuseppe Pavissi also discussed this subject more than twenty years earlier. He argued that Roman civil laws were welcomed into the Venetian legal system to the extent that they reflected the principles of reason, reason which itself had "the trusted escort" of the wisdom of nature. Pavissi, *Storia delle cause civili*, 14.

52 Nereo Vianello, "Bregolini Ubaldo", in *Dizionario Biografico degli Italiani*, 14 (1974), 116–118.

53 Ubaldo Bregolini, *Elementi di giurisprudenza civile secondo le leggi romane e venete* (Venezia: Nella stamperia di Carlo Palese, 1787), I, VI.

54 There are other noteworthy manuals in this vein, in particular the *Compendio della giurisprudenza civile romana e veneta* by Giuseppe Suzzi (1768) and Antonio Zuanelli's *Concordanza del diritto comune col veneto* (1772). Also the celebrated *Dizionario del diritto comune e veneto* by Marco Ferro, published between 1778 and 1781. Each in their own distinctive way, these authors all grappled with what Silvia Gasparini has called "the inevitable confrontation" between Venetian law and *ius commune*: Silvia Gasparini, "I giuristi veneziani e il loro ruolo tra istituzioni e potere nell'età di diritto comune", in *Diritto comune diritto commerciale diritto veneziano*, ed. by Karin Nehlsen von Stryck, Dieter Nörr (Venezia: Centro Tedesco di Studi Veneziani, 1985), 98–99.

of the manual, which was also successful beyond the state's borders. Thanks to his experience, Bregolini had the opportunity to reflect on the interaction between Venetian laws and the legal culture in the statutes of mainland cities. In all likelihood, Bregolini had come into contact with Bonsi during his teaching years in Bergamo, for Bonsi had also taught law at Collegio Mariano. What is certain is that both authors shared the same idea: they considered the principles of natural justice and equity to be that which ideally connected Roman jurisprudence and the Venetian statute.

Bregolini's work is divided into four volumes that are, in turn, sub-divided into dozens of titles that range from individual rights to succession law, and from contracts to obligations up to procedural matters. At several points, Bregolini engages in an explicit and detailed comparison between Roman and Venetian laws, inserting an appendix dedicated to the Venetian statute at the end of each chapter in order to "distinctly observe" the elements of dissimilarity between the former and the latter. However, the author was keen to emphasize how, alongside the unquestionable differences between the two systems in various spheres, including, for example, succession, there were aspects in which they were in "perfect agreement", dictated by common sense and the needs of society.[55]

But he also went further, importantly reflecting on the order in which sources were to be drawn on when making judgments. The judgments to which he was referring were those made in the Venetian magistrates' courts, which could include disputes that had initially been discussed and resolved in the mainland courts.[56] The first law to be applied was, of course, the provisions in the Venetian statute that all subjects had to observe and with which all judges had to comply. In the absence of a specific statutory provision, magistrates were to judge in accordance with customs "approved by the use of the people and authorized by the passage of time". When even customs were unable to provide an answer to the case in question, the magistrates were to refer to the provisions prescribed in similar cases with similar circumstances or analogous content. Where this was not possible, only one option remained, which was to settle the dispute "according to what they believe to be fair and equitable in their conscience".[57] The last resort in the Venetian legal system was therefore not Roman law, but *arbitrium*, understood as an instrument of dispute resolution based on equity and *iustitia*.[58]

55 Bregolini, *Elementi di giurisprudenza civile*, I, 28–29.

56 On the mechanism of appeals in civil judgments, see Claudia Passarella, *Interessi di parte e logiche del processo: La giustizia civile a Venezia in età moderna* (Torino: Giappichelli, 2018), 68–83, 133–143.

57 Bregolini, *Elementi di giurisprudenza civile*, I, 53.

58 In the Venetian legal system, *arbitrium* allowed judges to refer to non-formalistic criteria through which it was possible to get to the core of the relationship that had given rise to the dispute. For more on this, see Giovanni Cassandro, "Concetto caratteri e struttura dello stato veneziano", *Rivista di storia del diritto italiano*, 36 (1963), 43. On the role assigned

Bregolini delved into the intricacies of this concept, proposing his own personal and by no means obvious interpretation. The Venetian legal system asked judges to apply the principles of natural justice without specifying where they were to derive these principles from. According to Bregolini, they were to be drawn from Roman jurisprudence because it taught "in the most detailed manner the application of the principles of natural equity to possible cases". Its study, therefore, was absolutely essential.[59]

Bregolini's reflection goes beyond merely searching for points of agreement between Roman and Venetian laws, instead investigating the interaction between the two systems in practice, calling into play the concept of *arbitrium* that historiography has always considered a characteristic element of the Venetian legal system. Bregolini gives Roman jurisprudence a significant role precisely through the institution of *arbitrium*, overturning the established understanding. For him, *arbitrium*, which in the Venetian system of sources occupied the place traditionally reserved for Roman law, became the very way in which Roman law, to the extent that it reflected the principles of natural justice, entered the Venetian system. This change of perspective would have been impossible between the sixteenth and seventeenth centuries due to the dominant attitude in Venice at the time that attempted to exclude any reference to Roman law, seeing it as "foreign".[60]

Many eighteenth-century Venetian jurists wanted to distance themselves from this previous attitude, which had never reflected the complex relations characterizing the legal culture of the republic. Among them was Gaspare Morari, the Paduan assessor we mentioned at the beginning of this chapter. In the tenth chapter of his *Prattica*, Morari reflects on judgments in civil matters in the mainland courts and examines the possible recourse to Roman law, aware that such an opening could appear as a "great extravagance" in a republic that boasted of its "free, absolute and independent dominion".[61] For him, however, this hypothesis was not at all extravagant: the Roman laws were not to be considered foreign but "our Italian" laws, and consequently a Venetian judge could avail himself of them "as his own" in cases where Venetian laws were absent.[62] Morari thus wanted to give Roman law a direct

---

to *arbitrium* in the Venetian legal system, see Lamberto Pansolli, *La gerarchia delle fonti di diritto nella legislazione medievale veneziana* (Milano: Giuffrè, 1970), 113–192. On the concept of *arbitrium* in the tradition of *ius commune*, see Massimo Meccarelli, *Arbitrium: Un aspetto sistematico degli ordinamenti giuridici in età di diritto comune* (Milano: Giuffrè, 1998), 1–41.

59 Bregolini, *Elementi di giurisprudenza civile*, I, 53–54.

60 This was Giulio Dal Pozzo's thesis in the seventeenth century. The author denied that Roman laws had any margin of intervention within the Republic of Venice. Venice had given itself comprehensive and exhaustive legislation able to deal with any circumstances. Giulio Dal Pozzo, *Le instituzioni della prudenza civile fondate su le leggi romane e conformate alle leggi venete* (Venezia: Per Girolamo Albrizzi, 1697), 11–12.

61 Morari, *Prattica de' Reggimenti*, 175.

62 Ivi, 180–181.

sphere of intervention, whereas eighty years later Bregolini would give it space only to the extent that it expressed the principles of equity and justice.

Bregolini and the late eighteenth-century Venetian doctrine denied the binding force of Roman law as such, but recognized its value as an eminent doctrinal authority that could and should be a valid aid to various legal practitioners within the republic. At a time when the authority of Roman law was being called into question and, indeed, was in deep crisis, Venetian jurists recognized its importance, identifying relations and similarities that in the past had been hidden so as not to compromise the image of an autonomous and independent order that had been able to assert itself and prosper beyond the reach of Roman law and the tradition of *ius commune*.[63]

63 It is likely that this openness to dialogue and confrontation was motivated by the crisis faced by the Venetian legal system in the second half of the eighteenth century. Although the system of *ius commune* was itself in crisis at the time, in the eyes of Venetian jurists Roman laws and the doctrinal teachings of the most eminent jurists between the Middle Ages and the early modern age offered solid points of reference from which to draw inspiration and support in an attempt at normative renewal that was, however, destined to fail. Passarella, *Venezia e il diritto comune*, 183.

4 Students, Graduates, or "Tourists"

Scholars from across the Borders in Padua in the Sixteenth and Seventeenth Centuries

Donato Gallo

Venice and the *Studium* of Padua: Students and Teachers

On 21 November 1405, the Republic of Venice conquered the city of Padua, by which time Padua's *Studium* had been active for about 150 years. After an initial phase between 1222 and circa 1241, which was followed by a period of stagnation, it had been revived in the 1259–60 academic year. By the time Venice took over, Padua had become an attractive university town for *ultramontani* (transalpine students), who saw it as on a par with Bologna and an important stop on the *peregrinatio academica*.[1] Fundamental to this reputation were its prestigious professors in the main subjects. Venice followed a centuries-long principle: "students follow famous teachers".[2] Among those jurists who had taught in Padua were Iacopo dall'Arena, Riccardo Malombra, Ranieri Arsendi, Riccardo and Bartolomeo da Saliceto, Baldo (for three years: 1378–80) and his brother Angelo degli Ubaldi, and Francesco Zabarella. In the first 150 years of the Venetian period (1407–1550), the Venetian government employed Raffaele Fulgosio, Raffaele Raimondi, Giovanni Nicoletti da Imola, Paolo da Castro (who died in Padua in 1440), Antonio Roselli, Alessandro Tartagni, Bartolomeo Sozzini, Giason Del Maino, Filippo Decio, and Marco Mantova Benavides.

Arthur Duck was correct to claim that, although Roman law was not directly in force in the capital city, "the Athenaeum of Padua alone is sufficient to show the care Venice takes in preserving *ius civile*; offering lavish salaries they attract the most famous jurists in Italy to teach there; among many others, it included professors Tiberio Deciani, Giacomo Menochio, Cardinal Francesco Mantica

1 *Stranieri: Itinerari di vita studentesca tra XIII e XVIII secolo*, ed. by Maria Cristina La Rocca, Giulia Zornetta (Padova–Roma: PUP–Donzelli, 2023).

2 "Scolares sequuntur doctores famosos", cited in Donato Gallo, "Dal 1222 al 1509", in *L'Università di Padova nei secoli, 1222–1600: Documenti di storia dell'ateneo*, ed. by Piero Del Negro Piero, Francesco Piovan (Treviso: Antilia, 2017), 13–305, at 161.

DOI: 10.4324/9781003425069-6

and Marco Antonio Pellegrini, who brought great reputation and acclaim to *ius civile*".[3]

The 1509–10 war of the League of Cambrai waged by Emperor Maximilian I of Habsburg and his allies against the Republic of Venice made it more difficult for international students to attend in these years.[4] However, a few years later, the *Studium* regained its broad international appeal. The *Riformatori dello Studio di Padova* were founded temporarily in 1517 and definitively in 1528, and it were formed of three Venetian patricians who were members of the Senate (or *Consiglio dei Pregadi*) and were responsible for the management of the university and, in particular, the hiring of professors.[5]

Although, in theory, Venice respected the status quo, including the ancient organizational autonomy of the so-called Sacred Colleges of Doctors, in fact it often intervened for reasons of political expediency; it also guaranteed the preservation of student privileges, traditionally granted to scholastic corporations (*universitates*) but gradually restricted the ancient rights of students to choose and vote for professors, doing away with it completely in 1560. From the late sixteenth century onwards, the office of student *rector* was replaced by a *Syndicus* who acted as a prorector.

The sixteenth century was the epoch par excellence of the *Patavina Libertas*,[6] a cetual and corporate privilege that, together with the Venetian Republic's tolerant and pragmatic attitude, protected many Protestant students, particularly from Germany,[7] but also from France, England, Scotland, Hungary, and Poland.[8]

3 Arthur Duck, *De usu et authoritate Juris Ciuilis Romanorum in Dominiis Principum Christianorum, libri duo*, Londinii, Typis Richardi Hodgkinsonne, 1652, 76 (lib. II, cap. III, XIX) "Et Serenissimæ Respublicae Venetorum curam de conservando Jure Civili, unica Academia Patavina demonstrat, ad quam Clarissimos Italia Jurisconsultos magnis Stipendiis invitant pro docendo Jure Civili, in quâ præter alios plurimos Jus Civile nuper professi funt Tib. Decianus, Iacob, Menochius, Franc. Card. Mantica, & Anton. Peregrinus, qui tantum Lucis & Ornamenti Juri Civili attulerunt". See Claudia Passarella, "'*Negari tamen non potest Venetos ius civile Romanorum colere et venerari*': Venetian Law and *Ius Commune* between the Seventeenth and Eighteenth Centuries", in this volume.

4 Francesco Piovan, "Lo Studio di Padova e la guerra di Cambrai", *Quaderni per la storia dell'Università di Padova*, 43 (2010), 3–111.

5 François Dupuigrenet Desrousilles, "L'Università di Padova dal 1405 al Concilio di Trento", in *Storia della Cultura Veneta*, 3:2, *Dal primo Quattrocento al Concilio di Trento* (Vicenza: Neri Pozza, 1980), 607–646, here 627, 634–635.

6 *Libertas. Tra religione, politica e saperi*, ed. by Andrea Caracausi, Paola Molino, Dennj Solera (Padova–Roma: PUP-Donzelli, 2022).

7 Dennj Solera, Michaela Valente, "La *Patavina libertas* nell'età della Controriforma", in *Libertas. Tra religione, politica e saperi*, 167–184.

8 *Intellettuali e uomini di corte: Padova e lo spazio europeo fra Cinque e Seicento*, ed. by Ester Pietrobon (Padova–Roma: PUP-Donzelli, 2022).

Table 4.1 Matriculations of law students at Padua, 1591–1598

Ultramontani										*Citramontani*								*Total per year*						
Nations	Germana	Boema	Polona	Ungara	Provincialis	Burgunda	Anglica	Scota	Hyspana	Ultramarina	Romana	Sicula	MarchiaAnconitana	Lumbarda	Mediolana	Genuensis	Tusca	Veneta	Tarvisina	Foroiuliensis	Dalmata	Pedemontana	Patavina	
1591	51	5	6		12	5	4	4		2	1	1	5	31	3			8	14	5	1	3	1	**162**
1592	117	2	31	1	21	1	8		1	7	5	2	17	28	29	1	7	16	25	7		8	2	**341**
1593	135	5	9		17	4	9			1	8		11	27	10	1	3	8	30	4		1	2	**287**
1594	158		9	4	11	5	11	3		3	8		5	33	11	3	3	7	17	12		3	2	**311**
1595	125		3		13	2	10	2		2		1	9	15	16	3	5	4	19	2			9	**244**
1596	136	5	13	2	12	2	10	2		3	3	1	2	13	20	2	1	6	14	6		2	2	**257**
1597	110	4	8	1	3	2	14	3		8	3		11	26	6	2	8	17	23	6		2	1	**262**
1598	84	7	4		3	1	2	1		6	4	1	8	17	b	1	1	10	14	5				**181**
Per Per Natio	**916**	28	83	8	92	22	68	15	1		32	6	68	190	103	13	28	76	156	47	23		19	
1591-1598									*Ultra-montani*	**1265**												*Citra-mont-ani*	**780**	**2045**

From: Biagio Brugi, *Per la storia della scuola giuridica padovana* (Padova: Randi, 1889), 13

During the sixteenth century, at its height the *Studium* had around 1,000 students, sometimes reaching 1,100 according to official reports.[9] To begin with, about two-thirds were law students and one-third were philosophy and medicine students. Towards the middle of the century (1547) the number of physicians and philosophers surpassed that of the lawyers (300 jurists to 700 arts students), but it is not at all clear whether this was a trend or a one off.[10] Some registers of *general matriculations*, which recorded the different *nationes* of students, have been preserved only between 1591 and 1598. The total number of law students at that time showed that matriculations were significantly lower than they had been in the middle of the century.[11]

Problems Related to Graduation

In 1264, the *ius doctorandi* was assigned to the bishop of Padua, who was the chancellor of the *Studium* during the fourteenth century, assisted by the guild of city jurists, which functioned as a commission for granting degrees (a sort of faculty). As in Bologna, Perugia, Pavia, Siena, Ferrara, Florence, Pisa, and the other Italian *Studia* (except Naples and Rome), the so-called Sacred Colleges of Doctors in Padua (one of lawyers and one of philosophers and physicians) were made up of both real professors *(actu regentes)* and those in the city who had a doctorate but did not teach *(non regentes)*. There were many *doctores Paduani*, but only twelve were called "*numerari di collegio*", which meant that they were in the degree commission. In addition, from the 1540s until 1612, a number of palatine counts by imperial or papal investiture exercised their power to grant degrees, for instance, the Capodilista family in Padua.[12] As a palatine count, the famous jurist and teacher Marco Mantova Benavides (1489–1582) also granted several degrees.

While the Counter-Reformation restrictions imposed by Pope Pius IV's renowned papal bull *In sacrosancta* of 1564 obliged candidates for degrees and teaching posts to profess the Catholic faith, Venice maintained its tolerance towards the non-Catholic students who flocked to Padua. After a long preparatory phase, in 1616 Venice instituted the so-called *Collegio Veneto*, which, without demanding allegiance to Catholicism, granted degrees through the authority of the Venetian state ("auctoritate Veneta"), thus moving beyond the medieval idea of academic degrees requiring papal or imperial authority. It could give academic degrees to students who did not want to take an oath of Catholic faith (Protestant, Greek Orthodox, and Jewish students) and to "poor" students who could not afford the fees of the Sacred Colleges.

9 Emilia Veronese, "Dal 1509 al 1600" in *L'Università di Padova nei secoli, 1222–1600*, ed. by Piero Del Negro, Francesco Piovan, 341–526: 448.
10 Emilia Veronese, "Dal 1509 al 1600", 426.
11 See Table 1 in the Appendix.
12 Elda Martellozzo Forin, "Conti palatini e lauree conferite per privilegio: L'esempio padovano del sec. XV", *Annali di storia delle Università italiane*, 3 (1999), 79–119.

The Veneto College of Arts (philosophy and medicine) was the first to be founded.[13] Almost two decades later, in 1635, the Veneto College of Law was established,[14] consisting of an official professor who acted as president and eight professors of the main chairs of civil and canon law (two for each of the ordinary and extraordinary chairs of civil and canon law, because of the established system of "competition"). The examination methods were similar to those practised in the Sacred Colleges: the assignment of two civil law *puncta* from the Codex and the Digest,[15] and, in rare cases, also canon law (however the degree was said to be *in utroque iure*, "in both laws, civil and canon"); exposition; discussion with professors (*arguentes*) except in some specific cases; and the awarding and proclamation of the degree.

Although it had been championed by the *Natio Germanica*, the first students to graduate from the Veneto College of Law in 1637 were not of German origin but were three Englishmen and one Welshman (*Cambrobritannus*). The first person to obtain a degree in jurisprudence *auctoritate Veneta* was John Donne Jr (1604–67), a mature student who was the son of the well-known poet and dean of St. Paul's. However, only a few other Englishmen attained law degrees there in the following two decades.[16] This period partly covers what has rightly been referred to as the Anglo-Venetian moment, particularly evident in the first decades of the reign of King James I.[17]

From *peregrinatio academica* to the Grand Tour

Throughout the sixteenth and seventeenth centuries a large number of people arrived in Padua whom we could consider to be scholars, particularly because they participated in the student associations. Each *Natio* was a "container"

13 Lucia Rossetti, "I collegi per i dottorati 'auctoritate Veneta'", in *Viridarium flordum: Studi di storia veneta offerti dagli allievi a Paolo Sambin*, ed. by M.C. Billanovich, G. Cracco, A. Rigon (Padova: Antenore, 1984), 365–386; Piero Del Negro, "L'Università di Padova nei consulti di Paolo Sarpi", in *Ripensando Paolo Sarpi: Atti del Convegno internazionale di studi nel 450° anniversario della nascita di Paolo Sarpi*, ed. by Corrado Pin, (Venice: Ateneo Veneto, 2006), 417–437; Piero Del Negro, "Padova 1616: Una tappa verso l'università di Stato", in *La nascita delle università di Stato tra Medioevo ed età moderna*, ed. by Piero Del Negro (Bologna: Il Mulino, 2018), 15–32.

14 Francesca Zen Benetti, "Il Seicento", in *L'Università di Padova nei secoli, 1601–1805: Documenti di storia dell'ateneo*, ed. by Piero Del Negro, Francesco Piovan (Treviso: Antilia, 2002), 7–113: 64–65, 71.

15 *Puncta* were the sections of different widths into which the texts of Roman law and canon law were divided, since the mid-thirteenth century, for the purposes of teaching. Some *puncta* were also drawn by lot and assigned to the candidates before the degree examinations.

16 See Table 2 in the Appendix.

17 Michele Basso, Mario Piccinini, and Alfredo Viggiano, "The Anglo-Venetian Moment: Political and Legal Representations between the Republic of Venice and England in the Early Modern Age", in *Reimagining Mobilities across the Humanities*, vol. 1: *Theories, Methods and Ideas*, ed. by Lucio Biasiori, Francesco Mazzini, Chiara Rabbiosi (London: Routledge, 2023), 159–174.

of compatriots but not in the sense of the nation-state. Being enrolled meant enjoying scholastic privileges, the protection traditionally granted to the class of *scolares*, but it did not necessarily mean that person was actually a student. It is therefore not clear whether they came to study or to simply obtain an academic degree, in an era in which all preparation was aimed at the final examination and increasingly limited to *puncta*, explained by the so-called *puntisti*,[18] or whether they were tourists, travelling around Europe for education, culture, and leisure. The records from the late sixteenth century no longer clearly distinguish the "student" from the noble traveller, a distinction that became even less clear in the following century. Did people really go to Padua (or Bologna, Pavia, and Siena) to study in order to obtain an academic degree or did they just go as tourists? It was precisely at that time that the so-called art of travelling was born: Theodor Zwinger of Basel, a physician and man of letters, in his *Ars Apodemica* (first ed. 1577), lists Padua as one of the main places to travel for study, and he demonstrates a deep knowledge of the city (which he called *Athenae Italicae*) and its surroundings, as well as the complex structure of the *Studium*, where he graduated in medicine.[19]

A register relating to the *Natio Anglica et Scota* has been preserved, containing more than 2,000 signatures from 1618 to 1765.[20] The first pages list English and Scottish students of law and philosophy and medicine, as well as nobles and officials; then, over time, there are more and more names of English, Scottish, and Anglo-Irish gentlemen (and ladies) who passed through Padua on their tours of Italy, thanks to its proximity to Venice.[21] Thus, the *peregrinatio academica* became part of the Grand Tour and the *Kavaliersreise*.

Far more substantial are the registers of the matriculation of law students of the *Natio Germanica*, conserved from 1547 onwards.[22] Thousands of names appear in it: 6,045 from 1547 to 1605 (60 years), 5,860 from 1606 to 1729

18 In the seventeenth century there were private teachers (called *puntisti*) who explained the *puncta* to students in view of graduation, with a serious decline in the level of teaching and students' preparation. The Riformatori dello Studio intervened several times in the matter: see Sandro De Bernardin, "I Riformatori dello Studio: Indirizzi di politica culturale nell'Università di Padova", *Storia della cultura veneta, Il Seicento*, 4:1 (Vicenza: Neri Pozza, 1983), 61–91, at 80–81.

19 Paola Molino, "'E se un giorno tu volessi tornare in Italia, informamene immediatamente': L'influsso dell'esperienza padovana nell'organizzazione del sapere in età moderna", in *Stranieri*, ed. by Maria Cristina La Rocca, Giulia Zornetta, 183–197.

20 Horatio Brown, "Inglesi e Scozzesi all'università di Padova dall'anno 1618 sino al 1765", in *Monografie storiche sullo Studio di Padova: Contributo del R. Istituto Veneto di Scienze Lettere ed Arti alla celebrazione del VII centenario della Università* (Venezia: Grafiche Ferrari, 1922), 137–213.

21 Some travellers accompany their entries with notes of this sort: "All safe and sound arrived here from the Carnavale of Venice, Padua. Feb. 17th 1725" (Horatio Brown, "Inglesi e Scozzesi", 204).

22 *Matricula Nationis Germanicae Iuristarum in Gymnasio Patavino, I: 1547–1605; II: 1605–1801*, ed. by Elisabetta Dalla Francesca Hellman (Roma–Padova: Antenore: 2007–08) [hereafter cited: *MNGI* 1; *MNGI* 2].

Table 4.2 Englishmen and Welshmen who graduated *in utroque iure* at Padua from the Veneto College ol Law (1637–1657)

Abbreviations

Alumni = *Alumni Oxonienses 1500-1714* (ed. Joseph Foster; Oxford: OUP, 1891; online: https://www.british-history.ac.uk/alumni-oxon/1500-1714)
Andrich = Gian Luigi Andrich, *De Natione Anglica et Scota iuristarum Universitatis Patavinae ab a. MCCXXII ad a. MDCCXXXVII* (Padova: Gallina, 1892)
ASUP = Archivio Storico dell'Università di Padova, vols. 74–75
Brown = Horatio Brown, *Inglesi e Scozzesi all'università di Padova dall'anno 1618 sino al 1765*, cit.

nob. = nobilis
per. = perillustris
u.i. = utroque iure

1637
Ioannes Donne, Anglus perill. nob.
17.02.1637 (ASUP, 74, ff. 5r-v)
11.02.1637, presentatio et puncta (f. 3v): l. certi iuris 8 C. de test. mili. [C.6.21.8]; l. non dubitamus 20 ff. de condici. [D.35.1.20].
Alumni (John Donne jr, LL D, 1638 incorp. at Oxford).
Brown, n. 167 (1635).

Guilielmus Blake, Anglus, perill.
05.04.1637 (ASUP, 74, f. 7r)
04.04.1637, presentatio et puncta (f. 5v): l. collegium 8 C. de heredib. [C.6.24.8]; l. ex imperfecto 23 ff. de leg. 3. [D.32.23]
Alumni (William Blake, DCL, 1640 incorp. at Oxford).
Brown, n. 204 (30.3.1637).

Thomas Felectwood (sic), Anglus perill.
05.04.1637 (ASUP, 74, f. 7r)
05.04.1637, presentatio et puncta (ASUP, 74, f. 5v): l. proprias 13 C. de legat. [C.6.37.13]; l. non dubitamus ff. 20 de condit. [D.35.1.20]
Alumni (Thomas Fleetwod, "perhaps LL.D. Padua, and incorporated 10 July, 1639").
Andrich, 141 *Thomas Fleetzuvood* (3.4.1637).
Brown, n. 203 (30.3.1637).

Ioannes Nicolaus Vangonus (sic) Britannus
14.07.1637 (ASUP, 74, f. 8r)
11.07.1637 presentatio et puncta (ASUP, 74, f. 8r): l. si testament. C. de testa. [C.6.23.10]; l. obtinuit ff. de condi. et demo. [D.35.1.3]
Alumni (John Nicholas Vaughan; "B.C.L. Jesus Coll. 1628; LL.D. Padua, incorporated 5 July, 1638").
Brown, n. 228: *Johannes Nicholas Vaughan Cambrobritannus* (16.6.1637), from Wales.

(*Continued*)

Table 4.2 (Continued)

Abbreviations

1639

Guilelmus Blombleus nob. Anglus
20.04.1639 (ASUP, 74, f. 10r)
19.04.1639, presentatio et puncta (ASUP, 74, f. 9v): l. potes C. de ad. fisci. [C.2.8.2]; l. Femina ult. de tutelis [D.26.1.18].
Brown, n. 248; *William Bromley* (30.3.1639).

Thomas Gauuen (Gawen) nob. Anglus
20.04.1639 (ASUP, 74, f. 10r)
19.04.1639, presentatio et puncta (ASUP, 74, ff. 9v-10r): l. quod in uxorem C. de negot. gestis [C.2.18. 13]; l. extimate ff. soluto matrimonio [D.23.3.51].
Brown, n. 249: *Thomas Gawen* (30.3.1639) (n. 1612–1684).

1641

Galfredus Nightingale, Anglus
09.08.1641 (ASUP, 74, ff. 42r-v)
06.08.1641, presentatio (ASUP, 74, ff. 41v-42r); puncta (ASUP, 74, f. 42r): c. causam quam primo, de iuditiis [X.2.1.18]; l. certi iuris C. de test. militis [C.6.21.8].
Brown, n. 286: *Galfridus Nightingale Essexiensis* (1.5.1641).

Thomas Norton, Anglus
09.08.1641 (ASUP, 74, ff. 42r-43r)
06.08.1641, presentatio (ASUP, 74, ff. 41v-42r); puncta (ASUP, 74, f. 42r): c. iurgantium, c. de sent. et re iud. [X.2.27.2]; l. collegium C. de haeredibus instituendis [C.6.24.8].
Brown, n. 287 (1.5. 1641).

1651

Herbertus Ashby (sic) Anglus
15.9.1651 (ASUP, 74. f. 167r),
14.9.1651 (ASUP, 74, f. 167r): presentatio et puncta: 3 sane de foro competenti [X.2.3]; l. transactio 7 C. de transact. [C. 2.4.7].
Brown n. 463 *Herbertus Ashtley anglus Devoniensis* (30.8.1651).

1655

Henricus Wathinson (six) Anglus
15.01.1655 (ASUP, 75, ff. 27r-v)
12.01.1655, presentatio; 14.01 e puncta (ASUP, 75, f. 26v): c. de iure patro. [X.3.38]; l. omnibus ff. ad SC Trebell. [D.36.1.27].
Brown, n. 469 *Henricus Watkinson anglus Eboracensis* (18.12.1651).

1657

Georgius Croydon (Croyden) Anglus
20.03.1657 (ASUP, 75, ff. 32)
17.03.1657, presentatio; 19.03, puncta (ASUP, 75, f. 33r): l. dolum C. de dolo malo [C.2.20.6]: c. clericus 5 de vita et honest. clericorum [X.3.1.5].

(*Continued*)

Table 4.2 (Continued)

Abbreviations
Alumni (George Croyden, "of Temple Combe, Somerset, gent. Christ Church, matric. 1 Sept., 1634, aged 18; a student 1634 from Westminster School, B.A. 11 April, 1638, M.A. 8 July, 1641, and a canon 1666, and treasurer, created LL.D. Padua 20 March, 1656–57, and incorp. 4 Nov., 1662, under-master of Westminster School 1642–43, died 14 June, 1678")
Brown, n. 552. *John Croyden* (8.11.1656)

(ca. 120 years), and a few hundred in the years leading up to 1801. There is already a vast literature on German students (in the real sense) in Italian universities and in Padua in particular.[23] However, among those listed are also many people who were not real students, but who gave their names to the *Natio Germanica* either as a sign of honour or to obtain legal protection.

In fact, *Natio Germanica* does not mean "German", or even "of the Holy Roman Empire", but, as stated in the statutes of the *Natio Germanica Artistarum*, which was separated from *Natio Iuristarum* (the associations of "German" law students) in 1542, meant "those who use the Germanic language albeit in a corrupt form" (*qui utuntur lingua Gemanica licet corrupta*).[24] It thus includes not only Dutch and the Low Germanic dialects, but also the Nordic languages. Among the properly Germanic scholars (the area of the Holy Roman Empire), as stipulated by the statutes of the *Natio Germanica Iuristarum*,[25] there was a small minority of *Dani*, *Sueci*, *Livones*, that is, from the Baltic area, Denmark, Sweden, and Livonia.[26]

23 Biagio Brugi, "La nazione tedesca dei giuristi dello studio di Padova nel secolo XVII" in *Monografie storiche sullo Studio di Padova*, 95–106. This is an old and dated work, but still useful. Amongst the immense international literature on the theme, see Ariane Dröscher, "La mobilità degli studenti germanici tra i cinque maggiori Studi italiani tra il XVI e XVIII secolo: Primi risultati ed ipotesi di lavoro", *Annali di storia delle Università italiane*, 16 (2012), 275–295.

24 *Atti della Nazione germanica artista nello Studio di Padova*, ed. by A. Favaro (Venezia: Tipografia Emiliana, 1912), xxii.

25 *MNGI* 1, 2: "VIII. Ad matriculam hanc et commoda nationis Germanos nostros tam superiores quam inferiores, Danos praeterea, Suecos, Borussos, Livones, Boemos, Ungaros, Transylvanos, Moravos, Helvetios, Rhetos admittunto. IX. Illustres et generosi in hanc urbem etiam transitus gratia venientes a consiliario reliquisque officialibus oblata matricula excipiuntor" (transl. "VIII. Germans, from both upper and lower Germany, as well as Danes, Swedes, Prussians, Livonians, Bohemians, Hungarians, Transylvanians, Moravians, Swiss, Austrians will be admitted to the matriculation and to the advantages of the *Natio*. IX. The illustrious and noble personalities, who come to this city even just passing through, will be received in this register, which will be presented to them by the councilor and the other officials").

26 Here it is only possible to briefly mention other students from across the borders. In the registers of the matriculations of the *Natio Germanica* we find, between 1573 and 1603, various people from the eastern Baltic region, present-day Estonia, mainly from Riga (Livonia), and one person from Courland: see *MNGI* 1, 633, 644, 653; *MNGI* 2, 718, 743. Arvo Tering, *Eesti-liivi- ja kuramaalased Euroopa ülikoolides: 1561–1798* (Tartu: Kirjastus Eesti Aja-

Swedish Law Students (or Quasi-students) in Padua in the Sixteenth and Seventeenth Centuries

The registers of the *Natio Germanica Iuristarum*, which opens with a list of *inclyti* (the highest level aristocrats in the Empire's feudal hierarchy) includes various "travellers" passing through Padua at different times, and often several years apart, who described themselves in the *Natio* as *Sueci* or *Sveci*[27] (*Svezzesi* in old Italian, later *Svedesi*), thus from the Kingdom of Sweden.[28] Their journey was part of a tradition that became fundamental to the education of Swedish jurists.[29] From the research to date, however, no Swede appears to have obtained a legal degree from the Veneto College of Law at the *Studium* of Padua.[30]

The first documented case is a group of young nobles who arrived in Padua between January and February 1572 and enrolled in the *Natio Germanica*: Thure Bielke, Eric Sparr (21 years old), and his younger brother Johan (20 years old). Marginal annotations, which were evidently made many years later by someone who was well informed, record that the first two became royal councillors, treasurer and pro-chancellor, adding that they were sentenced to death in the year 1600 by Duke Charles, from 1604 King Charles IX Vasa when he ascended the throne of Sweden after defeating (in 1599) his nephew King Sigismund Vasa, a Catholic and also the King of Poland (as Sigismund III). The fourth, Axel Lovenkopf, according to later information noted next to his name, would later become governor of the Grand Duchy of Finland. Two more high-ranking Swedes passed through Padua in 1590.

However, almost half a century passed after the arrival of the first group before there was any trace of other Swedes in Padua, two of whom enrolled in

---

looarhiv, 2008), reports that there were, between 1571 and 1700, thirty-eight law students and seven arts students from Estonia-Livonia enrolled in the registers of matriculations of the two *Nationes Germanicae* of Padua. At a later time, we find on 4 September 1669, three *Norwegi* (Norvegians) *in itinere* (they were travellers): see *MNGI* 2, 4717. Johannes Smede; 4718. Jonas Smede; 4719. Nicolaus Stobaeus.

27 One student of canon law *Iohannes de Swecia* attends the graduation in medicine of a German from Regensburg in 1433; see *Acta graduum academicorum Gymnasii pataviniab anno 1406 ad annum 1450*, ed. by Caspar Zonta, Iospeph Brotto (Padova: Antenore, 1972), vol. 1, 298, but the context makes it doubtful that he was really a Swede. It probably means *de Swevia*, that is from Swabia (Schwaben, in Germany).

28 These names are given in chronological order in Table 3, with recerence to *MNGI*: we see the names of various noble families from the Kingdom of Sweden and other prominent people.

29 See Marianne Vasara-Aaltonen, *Learning Law and Travelling Europe: Study Journeys and the Developing Swedish Legal Profession, c. 1630–1800* (Leiden: Brill 2020).

30 For a comparison, four Danes graduated in the Veneto College of Law over little more than thirty years (1645–1677): Christianus Brunus, a nobleman, prorector et sindicus (1645: Archivio storico dell'Università di Padova, hereafter ASUP, vol. 74, f. 93r-v); Gasparus Bertholinus (1649: ASUP, vol. 74, ff. 141r-v); Petrus Resen (1653: ASUP, vol. 75, f. 10v); Christianus Sconegius (1660: ASUP, vol 75, ff. 46v–47r); Erasmus Bordinghius (1677: ASUP, 76, ff. 127r-v). About thirty Danes enrolled in the registers of *Natio Germanica* from 1547 to 1605 (*MNGI* 1, 633), they were 125 from 1605 to 1801 (*MNGI* 2, 718–719).

Table 4.3 Swedes at Padua in the registers of the *Natio Germanica* of law students (1572–1675)

1572
(*MNGI* 1.), 2196. Thuro a Bielke Gothus manu propria 3 nonas ianuarii anno 1572. *Consiliarius et thesaurarius regni Sueciae, capite postea a duce Carolo plexus.*
Thure Bielke: https://runeberg.org/sbh/bielketn.html
2197. Ericus a Sparr Swecus 22 februarii anno recuperatae salutis 1572. *Consiliarius et procancellarius regni Sueciae etc.*
Erik Larson Sparre 1550-1600: https://runeberg.org/sbh/b0489.html
2198. Iohannes a Sparr Suecus anno 1572, 22 februarii. *Hi tres Gothi sive Sueci a Carolo duce anno 1600 capite plexi.*
2199. Axellaus a Lovenkopf Suecus 22 februarii anno 1572. *Comes in Rassburg, baro in Grefnis et Kegelholrn, gubernator magni ducatus Finlandiae.*
Axel Lowenkopf: https://www.tandfonline.com/doi/full/10.1080/03468755.2023.2200805
1590
4131. 1590 Nicolaus Stake Gotthus 1 ianuarii.
https://runeberg.org/sbh/
4294. Svantho Bielke xvii novembris 1590. *Liber baro et magnus regni Sueciae cancellarius fuit. Obiit anno 1609.*
1620
(*MNGI*, 2.), 1662. Steno Bielke in Krakerum et Westanau liber baro eques auratus etc. Suecus 1 octobris anno 1620.
Sten Bielke: Vasara Altonen, p. 89
1663. Iohannes Hallenus Suecus 1 octobris 1620.
Johan Hallen (1588-1649): cf. Heiko Droste, *Im Dienst der Krone: Schwedische Diplomaten im 17. Jahrhundert* (Berlin: Lit Verlag, 2006), 395.
1628
2405. Thuro Bielke liber baro de Salestadt Suecus anno 1628 19 aprilis.
1650
3814. Gustav Adam Baner Suecus manu propria die 4 iulii anno 1650.

(*Continued*)

Table 4.3 (Continued)

1572
1651
3886. Henricus Hoghusen Svecus die 21 aprilis 1651
Author of *Dissertatio de verecundia seu ingenuo pudore* (Stockholmiae: 1642).
3914. Iohannes Sparre Svecus 5 augusti 1651.
3915. Jonas Boosl Svecus 5 augusti 1651.
1653
4057. Mauritius van Passe Svecus anno 1653 17 iunii.
4058. Henricus Ampelius Svecus 17 iunii 1653.
He was in journey: leaving Italy Padua, he went to Geneva in 1654: see *Le livre du recteur de l'Academie de Genève (1559–1878)*, sous la direction de Sven Stelling-Michaud (Genève: Droz, 1959), I, 207 n. 3674.
4060. Nicolaus Tungel Svecus 21 iulii 1653.
4076. Nicolaus Brahe comes de Wisingzborg Svecus l octobris 1653
4077. Petrus Sparre baro de Cronebergh Svecus l octobris 1653.
4079. Pontus Fredric de La Gardie comes de Leckoo et Arensbourc Suecus 17 octobris 1653.
Pontus Fredrik De la Gardie, 1630–1692: https://runeberg.org/sbh/delagpoo.html
1654
4131. Georgius Gyldhenstierna baro de Lundholm Svecus 31 iulii 1654.
4135. Abel Koch Westmannia Svecus die 29 augusti. 1654
1656
4215. Erland Camoenius Svecus 21 novembris 1656
Erland Caméen ,1631-1670: https://runeberg.org/biosvman/3/0180.html

(*Continued*)

Table 4.3 (Continued)

1572
1672 4813. Isaac Hedraeus Thomasson iuris utriusque licentiatus Svecus. anno 1672 die 17 novembris.
1675 4930. Carolus Gustavus Oxtenstierna comes de Morea Australi Svecus die 14 ianuarii anno 1675.

There are indicated: year; serial number in the *MNGI* edition (1.- 2.); the latin autograph signature (in Roman); any subsequent annotations (in italic); other references.

the *Natio Germanica* in 1620–22: Sven (Steno) Bielke, baron, and knight,[31] and Johan Hallenus. They immediately made an impression by becoming councillors of the *Natio*, and one later became *Prorector* and *Syndicus* of the university (then the highest office of the student body).[32] A few years later (1626) another, Ture Bielke, appears,[33] who was also a councillor to the *Natio Germanica*. His coat of arms can still be found among the thousands of shields in Palazzo Bo in Padua.[34]

The best-known case of an illustrious Swedish student (or quasi-student) falls in the middle of the seventeenth century, and it is that of Gustaf Adam Banér ("dulle Banér" "the foolish Banér", 1624–81), who arrived in Padua and first became councillor of the *Natio Germanica*, then prorector and *Syndicus* of the law students. He enrolled on 4 July 1650, and, within a few months, he became prorector and *Syndicus* (December 1650). At the end of his term in office, the *Natio Germanica* commissioned an engraving with a portrait of the young Gustaf Adam Banér, containing a long and adulatory Latin dedication to him.[35] Banér's presence in Padua, albeit brief, was honoured in the second half of the eighteenth century with a statue among the illustrious men in the so-called Isola Memmia in Prato della Valle, commissioned by Gustavus Adolphus III, king of Sweden, who had been to Venice on a private visit. He

31 Cf. Marianne Vasara-Aaltonen, *Learning Law and Travelling Europe*, cit. 89: "*Bielke* boys, Gustaf and Sten, serve as a good example. They had been born into a noble family in 1618 and 1624 ... *Ture* had travelled to England, Paris, and Padua".

32 *MNGI* 2, 322; *Acta Nationis Germanicae Iuristarum (1650–1709)*, ed. by Gilda Mantovani (Padova: Antenore, 1983), 7–8, 15, 23.

33 See Mariannae Vasara-Aaltonen, *Learning Law and Travelling Europe*, cit., 89: "*Bielke* boys, Gustaf and Sten, serve as a good example. They had been born into a noble family in 1618 and 1624 ... *Ture* had travelled to England, Paris, and Padua".

34 *Gli stemmi dello Studio di Padova*, ed. by Lucia Rossetti (Trieste: LINT, 1983), 160–161 (n. 691, 694); Lucia Rossetti and Elisabetta Dalla Francesca, *Stemmi di scolari dello Studio di Padova in manoscritti dell'Archivio antico* (Trieste: LINT, 1987).

35 Gilda Mantovani, *Acta Nationis Germanicae Iuristarum 1650–1709*, 8th ed., 7–8, 15, 20, 23, 29; and Lucia Rossetti, *Gli stemmi dello Studio*, 312 (n. 1529) The dedication says: "Hoc frontis honore placidoque fulgore luminum ac promissa caesarie avide populis spectabatur Gustavus Adamus Baner, quum a parentis fortissimi imperatoris trophaeis recens Patavini Gymnasii regimen capesseret et laureatis utrinque fascibus in complexu Musarum imperatoriae indolis flos, serpentibus inter victrices lauros hederis, in spem non unius triumphi assurgeret. Natio Germanica Martis ac Musarum alumna patri militari filio literariae gloriae reparatori felicissime memoriam posuit" ("With this crown on his head, in the calm radiance of his eyes and in his ample hair, Gustav Adam Banér was avidly admired by the people, since he had recently assumed the government of the University of Padua, after the victories of his father, a very brave commander; and he rose to the office in the hope of many triumphs, as the flower of a leader's nature, with bundles of laurel on both sides, with branches of ivy winding among the laurels of victory. The *Natio Germanica*, pupil of Mars and the Muses, placed this memory with the utmost favor to the son of a warrior father, restorer of literary glory").

also requested a statue of King Gustavus Adolphus II (1594–1632), who, according to a very dubious account, had been Galileo Galilei's student.[36]

The number of Swedes in the registers of matriculations increased between 1651 and 1654, with one also appearing in 1656, reaching about ten names in total over that period. However, in the following decades these journeys to Padua become very infrequent.[37] Thus ended the arrival of real or quasi-students who passed through Padua, even if sometimes very fleetingly, from the shores of the Baltic. But while the number of actual law students from across the borders was low, those who journeyed to Italy with a stop off in Padua were more numerous, as it added to one's "social capital", a clear mark of class distinction and a source of ostentation for members of the nobility.[38]

36 Lars Nystedt, "Due svedesi in Prato della Valle", *Padova e il suo territorio*, 69 (October 1997), 8–11.

37 Isaac Hedraeus Thomasson *iuris utriusque licentiatus* (1672, 17 novembre), who a few years earlier had written *De iure regio Svecorum dissertatio, qua imprimis ostenditur imperandi modum apud Suecos esse Monarchicum*, Jenae, 1669; Carolus Gustavus Oxtenstierna, *comes de Morea Australi Svecus* (1675, 14 January).

38 See Vasara-Aaltonen, *Learning Law and Travelling*, above all 89, 209, 340–343.

5 Venetian Law and *ius commune*

The Origins of a Controversy

Alfredo Viggiano

Conflicts and Hybridization

In a trial held at the Venetian court of the Criminal Council of Forty between 2 and 16 December 1529, the *avogadore of the commun* Marchionne Michiel indicted the Genoese merchant Andrea Grimaldi Corvara for the murder of his Venetian business partner, demanding he be put to death.[1] This story is recounted by the Venetian nobleman Marin Sanudo in his *Diari* (diaries), a monumental work full of accounts of everything that happened or was reported in Venice between 1496 and 1533.[2]

During the year he lived in Venice, the defendant had wasted 7,500 ducats – a considerable fortune earned from trading in Constantinople – "con zuogo e putane" (on gambling and prostitutes). Grimaldi Corvara was represented before the court by two leaders of the Venetian bar: Zuan Francesco Mocenigo and Francesco Filetti. Their defence was based on two pillars of common law founded in the major amendments it had undergone during the thirteenth and fourteenth centuries. First, according to them, the murder had not been carried out in cold blood, it was not premeditated (*pensato*); *and* the merchant was responding to the aggression of his partner, who had addressed him with defamatory words and struck him several times (*omicidio puro*).[3] For them, the semantic redefinition of the act was clear. But they also considered to be indisputable the second argument that they put to the court. Grimaldi Corvara had been taken from a sacred place ("tratto da luogo sacro") and so enjoyed ecclesiastical immunity. Mocenigo and Filetti had reviewed numerous classic passages in the Papal decretals and the letters of the Patriarch of

1 Marin Sanuto, *I Diarii*, vol. 1–58 (1496–1533), ed. by Rinaldo Fulin, Federico Stefani, Guglielmo Berchet, Marco Allegri (Venezia: A spese degli editori, 1879–1902). On Sanudo, see Gaetano Cozzi, *Marin Sanudo il Giovane: Dalla cronaca alla storia*, in Id., *Ambiente Veneziano, Ambiente veneto, saggi su politica, società, cultura nella Repubblica di Venezia in età moderna* (Venezia: Marsilio, 1997), 87–108.

2 Sanuto, *I Diarii*, vol. 52, coll. 294, 300, 317–318, 355–356, 359–360.

3 Per la distinzione fra *omicidio puro* e *omicidio pensato*, Claudio Povolo, *L'intrigo dell'onore: Poteri e istituzioni nella Repubblica di Venezia* (Sommacampagna: Cierre, 1998), 96.

DOI: 10.4324/9781003425069-7

Venice, which, if applied, would completely remove the secular court from the proceedings.[4]

The *avogadore* Marino Giustinian then took the floor, beginning with an imprecise evangelical quotation of Matthew, 21:13: "domus mea vocabitur, nunc est spelunca latronum" (mine was a house of prayer, now it is a den of thieves). The biblical references continue with a "proverb" by Solomon, which is not specified by Sanudo, and Chapter 19 of Deuteronomy. Although Sanudo does not expand on this, we can imagine Giustinian looked at Verses 3–5 of the Old Testament disciplinary decree, where the sovereign is ordered to create three areas within his territory to act as places to which the perpetrators of accidental and involuntary murders could retreat, so as to prevent the victims' family members taking revenge on them. Was he turning the judicial process into a theatre on which to stage a theological-political dispute? Was Giustinan advocating, about a century ahead of his time, an understanding of the relationship between law and politics in which the basis of the legitimacy of the sovereign's power is to be found in the pages of the Bible and, above all, the Old Testament[5]? The *avogadore* also skillfully responded to his antagonists by using their own repertoire, taking his cue from several passages of the *Decretum Gratiani* and the Comment on the Code of Justinian written by Bartolomeo da Saliceto (Bologna 1335?–1411), professor of civil law at the Universities of Bologna and Padua.[6] Through combining *ius civile* and "biblical law", the *avogadore* intended to demonstrate the legitimate foundations of the unlimited extension of the civil sovereign's power to guarantee the peace and life of his subjects; his sword must descend inexorably ("*severa justitia*") on the guilty.

It is worth taking a closer look at the institutional protagonists. The Criminal Council of Forty, together with its sister bodies, the Civil, Civil Nova, and Civil Nuovissima Councils of Forty, was one of the fundamental nuclei of the Venetian legal system.[7] The main function of these courts of justice, which became more clearly defined during the fifteenth century, consisted in hearing appeals on first instance sentences issued by Venetian magistrates

4 Carlotta Latini, *Il privilegio dell'immunità: Diritto d'asilo e giurisdizione nell'ordine giuridico dell'età moderna* (Milano: Giuffrè, 1998); for the case of the Republic of Venice, Alfredo Viggiano, "Fra violenza e protezione: l'ambigua natura dell'immunità: Il caso della Repubblica di Venezia nella prima età moderna", in *Exile, Asile, du droit aux pratiques*, ed. by Gilles Bertrand, Catherine Brice, Mario Infelise (Rome: Collection de l'École française de Rome, 2021), 49–76.

5 Lea Campos Boralevi, "Introduzione," in Petrus Cunæus, *De Repubilca Hebræorum* (Firenze: Centro Editoriale Toscano, 1996); *Politeia Biblica*, ed. by Lea Campos Boralevi, Diego Quaglioni (Firenze: Leo S. Olschki Editore, 2002). For the significant case of the United Provinces in the early modern age, see Simon Schama, *The Embarassment of Riches: An Interpretation of Dutch Culture in the Golden Age* (London: Harper & Collins), 1991.

6 Gianfranco Orlandelli, "*Voce 'Bartolomeo da Saliceto,'*" in *Dizionario biografico degli italiani*, vol. 6 (Roma: Istituto dell'Enciclopedia Italiana, 1964), 766–768.

7 Gaetano Cozzi, "Authority and the Law", in *Renaissance Venice*, ed. John R. Hale (London: Faber: 1973), 293–345.

and the rectors of the states *da terra* and *da mar* from Padua to Brescia, from Vicenza to Padua, from Koper to Zadar, and from Kotor to Corfu. In the Republic of Venice, the task of accepting lawsuits from a very wide territorial area with a diversity of languages, rights, and religious faiths was entrusted to incredibly large assemblies: the four courts of justice contained 160 Venetian nobles, and a complicated electoral system ensured that they could move from one to the other without breaks. This created a small class of "non-specialist" experts, whose expertise lay in their ability to float above the rough sea of the appeals system, adjudicating disputes according to criteria that we cannot always recognize.

Imagine the efforts lawyers went to translate into colloquial language the taxonomies on succession of the *ius civile* or the classifications of criminal types elaborated in the *Pratiche criminali* – the manuals for notaries, judges, and chancellors that spread throughout Europe from the fourteenth century onwards – for an audience that were not particularly interested in following inductive and deductive chains but were fascinated by dramatic twists and verbal fireworks. It seems that the elaboration of the ideal type of lawyer – who had a propensity for loquacity and a refined use of dialect – was conditioned not in their proclaimed defence of a peculiar *Venetian* understanding of law but in their position in a mobile network of social and institutional power relations that forced them to invent their own spaces of legitimation.[8]

The case we have discussed above serves as an introduction to the question of the relationship between *ius commune* and Venetian laws that I aim to address in this chapter. The date of the tragic affair of the Genoese merchant marks the end of this relationship; its origin can be found in the period in which the Venetian "*commune*" shifted its interests towards the mainland and the creation of the territorial state, beginning in the first decade of the fifteenth century. The "pure" forms of the Serenissima's system of government fit into Luca Mannori's schema of the constitutional family of the "jurisdictional state": a set of territories and rights, of forms of power and of class-based, corporative social organizations, each of which has a space in which they are free to "dire il diritto" (say the law) (*iurisdictio*). The sovereign receives and

8 Guseppe Trebbi, "Le professioni liberali", in *Storia di Venezia*, vol. 4, *Il Rinascimento*, ed. by Alberto Tenenti, Ugo Tucci (Roma: Istituto dell'Enciclopedia Italiana, 1996), 465–527.

Francesco Sansovino, *L'avvocato e il segretario*, ed. by Piero Calamandrei (Firenze: Le Monnier, 1942), 69; Elena Bonora, *Ricerche su Francesco Sansovino* (Venezia; Istituto veneto di Scienze Lettere ed Arti, 1994); Aldo Mazzacane, "Lo Stato e il Dominio nei giuristi veneti durante il secolo della Terraferma", in *Storia della cultura veneta*, 3/I, *Dal primo Quattrocento al Concilio di Trento*, ed. by Girolamo Arnaldo, Manlio Pastore Stocchi (Vicenza: Neri Pozza, 1980), 577–650; Ugo Petronio, "Civitas Venetiarum est edificata in mari," in *Studi veneti offerti a Gaetano Cozzi*, ed. by Gino Benzoni, Marino Berengo, Gherardo Ortalli, Giovanni Scarabello (Venezia: il Veltro, 1992), 171–185. Silvia Gasparini, "I giuristi veneziani e il loro ruolo tra istituzioni e potere nell'età del diritto comune", in *Diritto comune, diritto commerciale, diritto veneziano*, ed. by Karin Nehlsen von Stryk, Dieter Nörr (Venezia: Centro tedesco di studi veneziani, 1985), 80–81.

legitimates the various parts of the multiform complex of institutional subjects – as a supreme arbiter of justice they are able to recognize justice when one of these subjects, operating within the territory of which they are the legitimated guardian requests their intervention.[9] Thus, justice is not created by the sovereign, but it is given; it exists objectively in the order of the world, and the highest authority of the state helps to make it evident. According to this reading, the law is the common thread that holds together the pieces of the *composite state*, to use a well-known historiographical term.[10] To be more precise, the *legal pluralism* of the early modern states was guaranteed by the common law's capacity to foster the formation of a common idiom in which norm and exception could usually coexist – on the side of the subjects as privilege and obedience, on the side of the sovereign as mediation and authority.

The choice of the term "the long fifteenth century" is also significant.[11] I hold that within that period, various forms of communication were established between the capital and the provinces, between the Venetian nobility and the various different societies occupying the coastal and maininland states (stati *da terra* e *da mar*), and between different spheres of law and justice. At the end of a period of pronounced political and legal creativity and experimentation, these forms became more rigid, and they were integrated into the administrative routine. The development of those relations would not follow a preestablished path with the Italian Wars marking a significant watershed. In Venice the failed attempt – which was actually more tentative than has been claimed in the historiography – to introduce Roman law as the exclusive right of the state under Doge Andrea Gritti (1523–38) marks the end of a set of legal and political relations that I will now try to clarify.[12]

For Clifford Geertz, every law is a "local" law, in the sense that it is mixed with a set of idioms and (micro)rituals with explicit and implicit levels of rationality that are comprehensible and functional within a group of actors who are able to accurately decipher the meaning of the successive actions, but whose semantics may be enigmatic to an external observer who inserts

9 Luca Mannori, *Il sovrano tutore: Pluralismo istituzionale e accentramento istituzionale nel Principato dei Medici (secc. XVI–XVIII)* (Milano, Giuffrè, 1994); Antonio Hespanha, *La Gracia del Derecho: Economìa de la Cultura en la Edad Moderna* (Madrid: Centro de Estudios Constitucionales, 1983); Helmut Georg Koenisberger, "Monarchies and Parliaments in Europe – Dominium Regale or Dominium Politicum or Regale", *Theory and Society*, 5:2 (1978), 191–217.

10 John H. Elliott, "A Europe of Composite Monarchies", *Past & Present (The Cultural and Political Construction of Europe*, 137:1 (Nov 1992), 48–71; Marco Gentile, "Leviatano regionale o forma-stato composita: Sullo stato di idee vecchie e nuove", *Società e Storia*, 89 (2000), 561–573.

11 Isabella Lazzarini, *L'Italia degli Stati territoriali (sec. XIII–XV)* (Bologna: Il Mulino, 2007); E. Igor Mineo, "State, Order and Social Institutions, in Renaissance," in *The Italian Renaissance State*, ed. by Andrea Gamberini, Isabella Lazzarini Gamberini (Cambridge: Cambridge University Press, 2012), 332–344.

12 Cozzi, "Authority and the Law", 64–66.

what they see and hear into their own conceptual grids, thus misunderstanding them.[13] The unmistakable "local" colour of the Venetian legal system is characterized by the "hydraulic" function typical of the Councils of Forty: an enormous digestive system that metabolizes legal knowledge, rhetorical tactics, and procedural mechanisms, mixing together systems of expectations, ideas, and myths of justice.

Let us first note some "original features" of Venetian *law in action* that will serve as a guiding thread in our analysis. As well as the unusually high number of members of the Councils of Forty with respect to other European legal systems, we should add that the *Quarantiotti* – as they were called during the sixteenth century, reinforcing the idea of them as a micro-group – had a strong identity both within the circuit of the republican magistracies and in the eyes of external observers. Being part of the circuit of the supreme Venetian courts of appeal did not require a degree in law from the Padua law school; on the contrary, the members of the Councils of Forty themselves boasted of their ignorance. The obscurities of common law, the technicalities of feudal laws, and the incomprehensible deductions of canon law were completely foreign to their *Bildung*, and should remain so. This extraneousness to "Roman laws" (as the corpus of *ius comune* was called in Venice at the time) was reaffirmed by the rituals of the Councils of Forty. Debate was conducted in an *adversarial* manner, as it would be throughout the history of the Venetian state until its fall in 1797: lawyers' interventions often deviated from the system of evidence created in the construction phase of the trial dossier. This created a strange compromise between an "accusatory" (adversarial) and an inquisitorial procedure. Even the system of legal evidence appears contaminated by the inquest's mixing of the Venetian law with "civil law". Their coexistence can be seen in the ambivalent position of the *avogadore*: sometimes appearing as one of the accused party's lawyers, and other times as a representative of the republic's prosecution, similar to the role of an *attorney of law*. The *avogadore*'s role was often not so much of a judge engaged in an inquisition but of a particular kind of partisan lawyer. On attending a trial in the Council of Forty in the Venetian leg of his *Italianreise*, Johann Wolfgang von Goethe, who had not forgotten his legal training, described with amusement the survival of such an archaic way of doing justice.[14] We could hypothesize, following the indications of Mirjan Damaška's essay, "The Faces of Justice and State Authority. A comparative approach to the legal process", which evaluates the relations between constitutional structures and judicial organization, that the Venetian path to modernity saw the unstable and conflicting coexistence of an *active state*, in which the government dictated the agenda of judicial priorities through rigid

13 Clifford Geertz, *Local Knowledge: Further Essay in Interpretative Culture* (New York: Basic Books, 1985), 145.

14 Johann Wolfgang von Goethe, *Italian Journey* (Harmondsworth: Penguin Classics, 1970), 84–86.

hierarchical and bureaucratic control, and a *reactive state*, in which justice was, instead, understood as an instrument capable of fostering compromises and mediations between the various actors and agencies in the state's territory.[15]

The case that Grimaldi Corvara discussed above highlights the diffusion of a "learned" common law lexicon and legal culture in the mainland courts, and it offers us a lens through which to view the general question of the misfortunes, or fortunes, of *ius commune* in the Venetian Republic.

In Search of Origins

"Venice governs itself through its own statutes and laws, and not [through] those that govern in every other place, the Empire".[16] This sentence is taken from a celebratory operetta by Marin Sanudo. Hoping in vain to obtain the prestigious post of "public historiographer" of the republic, Sanudo carefully collected together official and private discussions: he recorded public orations and noted down every trace of city gossip; he transcribed judicial sentences and accounts of battles on land and sea, and, like a very precise seismograph, he recorded every ordinary and extraordinary event. The sheer size of the *Diarii* has made it a hugely significant source for the economic, military, religious, institutional, cultural, and literary history of the city, Italy, and Europe. His particular attention to judicial events also allows us to understand the central issue of this essay in all its forms: the relationship between local and civil law heritage in the Venetian Republic. The lines quoted at the beginning of this paragraph suggest a clear dichotomy between the Venetian Republic and other political systems, which he calls "places" (cities and territorial states). The Serenissima's own "statutes and laws" lent its political structures autonomous legitimacy, which ensured not only Venice's freedom and independence but was also an indispensable ingredient in the construction of its myth.[17] The performative nature of this myth was so effective and suggestive that it had a long-term influence on the historiographical discourse on the "Venetian constitution": first during the history of the republic until 1797 and then in the nineteenth and twentieth centuries.[18]

15 Mirjan Damaška, *The Faces of Justice and State Authority: A Comparative Approach to the Legal Process* (New Haven: Yale University Press, 1991).

16 Marin Sanuto, *De origine, situ et magistratibus urbis Venetae, ovvero la città di Venetia*, ed. by Angela Caracciolo Aricò (Venezia: Centro Cicogna, 2011), 98–99.

17 Franco Gaeta, "Alcune considerazioni sul mito di Venezia", *Biblioteque d'Humanisme et Renaissance*, 23:1 (1961), 58–75; Id., "Storiografia, coscienza nazionale e politica culturale nella Venezia del Rinascimento", in *Storia della cultura veneta: Dal primo Quattrocento al Concilio di Trento*, vol. 3:1, ed. by Girolamo Arnaldi, Manlio Pastore Stocchi (Vicenza; Neri Pozza, 1980), 1–90; Donald E. Queller, Francis R. Swietek, "The Myth of Venetian Patriciate", in *Two Studies on Venetian Government*, ed. by Donald E. Queller, Francis R. Swietek (Genève: Librairie Droz, 1997), 95–175.

18 James Grubb, "When Myths Lose Power: Four Decades of Venetian Historiography", *Journal of Modern History*, 58:1 (1984), 43–94.

The tension between the two legal fields – of the *ius commune* and of Venetian law – must be understood through considering two moments in the republic's historical-constitutional development, which, starting out distinct, then became strongly intertwined and ended up completely indistinguishable. The first of these two moments marked the origin and development of the *commune veneciarum* from the thirteenth century onwards.[19] The second, in the period between the mid-fourteenth century and the first two decades of the fifteenth century, was when Venice strengthened the network of its maritime colonies along the Dalmatian coast and towards the Peloponnese and the Greek islands, putting together, piece by piece, the jigsaw puzzle of its *Stado da Terra*.[20]

We can sum up the main elements of the historiographical discussion through posing a few questions.[21] What aspects of the new science of law, of the nascent *jus commune* coming from the great law schools of that time – Paris, Bologna, and Avignon, but also Oxford – reached Venice and influenced the practices of its courts of justice? How did fragments of the terminology and logical principles that were characteristic of *ius commune* become inserted into the rubric of the first great Venetian legal collection – such as the Statutes ordered by Doge Jacopo Tiepolo in 1244 and the subsequent Statute "reforms"? To what extent did a "Romanist patina" contaminate the norms (collected in the so-called *Capitolari*) specifying the spheres of jurisdiction of the Venetian courts of justice in matters of settling civil disputes between Venetian and foreign merchants, investigating reports of usury or of the counterfeiting of money, and assessing the validity of wills or the legitimacy of claims by parties to certain assets? If the main text of Venetian legislation, the Statute in its various editions and corrections, is a product of the common law culture, the assertion of a kind of autopoiesis of "local" law loses its foundation.

19 *Gli statuti veneziani di Jacopo Tiepolo del 1242 e le loro glosse*, ed. by Roberto Cessi, in *Memorie del Regio Istituto Veneto di Scienze, Lettere ed Arti*, 30:2 (1938), 78–95. For an introduction on the topic of Tiepolo's Statues, see Giorgio Cracco, "La cultura giuridico-politica nella Venezia della *Serrata*", in *Storia della cultura veneta*, vol. 2, *Il Trecento*, ed. by Girolamo Arnaldi (Vicenza: Neri Pozza, 1976), 238–271; Silvia Gasparini, "I giuristi veneziani e il loro ruolo tra istituzioni e potere nell'età di diritto comune", in *Diritto comune diritto commerciale, diritto veneziano*, ed. by Karin Nehlsen Von Stryck, Dieter Nörr (Venezia: Centro Tedesco di Studi Veneziani, 1985), 98–99. Giorgio Zordan, *L'ordinamento giuridico veneziano: Lezioni di storia del diritto veneziano, con una nota bibliografica* (Padova: Cleup, 1980); Enrico Besta, Riccardo Predelli, *Gli statuti civili di Venezia anteriori al 1242 editi per la prima volta* (Venezia: Federico Visentini, 1901), 5–117.

20 Gaetano Cozzi, Michael Knapton, *La repubblica di Venezia nell'età moderna: Dalla guerra di Chioggia al 1517* (Torino: UTET, 1986).

21 Mario Ascheri, *Medievo del potere: Le istituzioni laiche ed ecclesiastiche* (Bologna: Il Mulino, 2009); Paolo Grossi, *L'ordine giuridico medievale* (Roma–Bari: Laterza, 2006); *Jurists and Jurisprudence in Medieval Italy: Texts and Contexts*, ed. by Osvaldo Cavallar, Julius Kirshner (Toronto: University of Toronto Press, 2000).

The question of whether the legal system should recognize its filiation from "Imperial law" had already been raised during the Venetian Republic. Important research has shown that, by the beginning of the fifteenth century, "the question concerning the relationship between Venetian law, law, and custom had lost its force".[22] This hybridization had experienced its most extensive phase of expansion in the first two decades of the fourteenth century, and Riccardo Malombra was its most influential and refined interpreter. A Venetian citizen since 1312 and a lecturer in civil law at the Padua Studio from the beginning of the century until his death in 1344, Malombra provided the republic with numerous *consilia* (recommendations in which legal consideration supported the political motives of the clients[23]). For Malombra, Venetian liberty – threatened by Henry VII, the emperor, and John XII, the pope – could coexist with the authority of the emperor: the "*conservatio boni status rei publicae*" had to be guaranteed by carefully updating the ancient statutes with the "*scientia iuris*". This contamination continued without interruption until a law of the Senate (3 May 1401) sanctioned the total exclusion of the *doctores legum* from intervening in and contributing to the construction of the *law in action*. The magistracy of the *Avogaria di Comun*, to whose powers we shall return later, was tasked with removing all the *postilles* that had ended up in the statute books over time.[24] This memory of an intermixing between Venetian laws and the normative and ideological structures of the *ius commune* is not limited to the Late Middle Ages. We can find numerous traces of it when considering the creation of a kind of *institutional past*, of an inventing tradition, within and by the Venetian constitutional structure.[25]

The writer most aware of the existence of an underground and censored strand of the Venetian political and civic tradition was Marco Foscarini.[26] In his *Della letteratura veneziana* (1752), Foscarini reconstructs the origins and

22 Mazzacane. "Lo stato e il dominio nei giuristi veneti".

23 Mario Ascheri, *Tribunali, giuristi e istituzioni dal medioevo all'età moderna* (Bologna: Il Mulino, 1989).

24 Gaetano Cozzi, *Repubblica di Venezia e Stati italiani: Politica e giustizia dal secolo XVI al secolo XVIII* (Torino: Einaudi, 1962); Giovanni Casandro, *La Curia di Petizion e il diritto processuale veneziano* (Venezia: Regia Deputazione di Storia Patria, 1937); Claudia Passarella, "Venice and the *ius commune*: From Nationalistic Pride to the Search for Similarities", *Archivio Giuridico Italiano*, 153 (2021); Luigi Pansolli, *La gerarchia delle fonti di diritto nella legislazione medievale veneziana* (Milano: Giuffrè, 1970), 113–192; Massimo Meccarelli, *Arbitrium: Un aspetto sistematico degli ordinamenti giuridici in età di diritto comune* (Milano: Giuffrè, 1998).

25 Marco Bellabarba, "Introduzione: La memoria delle istituzioni", in *Identità territoriali e cultura politica nella prima età moderna/Territoriale Identität und politisches Kultur in der Frühen Neuzeit*, ed. by Marco Bellabarba and Reinhard Stauber (Bologna: Il Mulino; Berlin: Dunker & Humblot, 1998).

26 Piero Del Negro, "Marco Foscarini", in *Dizionario Biografico degli Italiani*, vol. 49 (1997), https://www.treccani.it/enciclopedia/marco-foscarini_(Dizionario-Biografico); Franco Venturi, *Settecento riformatore. Da Muratori a Beccaria* (Torino: Einaudi, 1969), 276–292; Id., *Utopia e riforma nell'Illuminismo* (Torino: Einaudi, 1970), 44–48; Erasmo Leso, "*Nota introduttiva a Marco Foscarini*", *Dal Muratori al Cesarotti*, vol. 5, *Politici ed economisti del*

structures of the "government of the Venetians" through an impressive study of chronicles and historiographical sources, letters, inscriptions, biographical and encomiastic collections, and legal dissertations. His work is also linked to the tradition of research that Arnaldo Momigliano defined as "antiquarian"[27] in his essay "Ancient History and the Antiquarian", and he certainly appears deaf to the demands for renewal coming from Enlightenment historiography. But this way of writing and style of analysis, its consequences (including sometimes interminable footnotes, forcing the reader to follow the author through the sometimes dead-end labyrinths of his arguments), and its close attention to an unclassified mass of documents, makes it a unique text for us. Reading between the lines of Book I of Foscarini's text, we can find the construction of principles of Venetian legal and institutional discourse and, at the same time, identify its ideological justification.[28]

According to Foscarini, it is undeniable that "Venetian law" existed from the end of the eleventh century onwards: the term appears for the first time in the text of the 1084 pact between Venice and the community of Loreo, but our commentator provides only a minimal reading of it: "a term meaning the union of laws and a certain comparison of them with each other, from which a coherent system of jurisprudence resulted". There is no doubt that Venice generated its "own laws"; but, as Foscarini suggests, what city?[29] However, this simple fact does not prevent us from questioning the claimed autonomy of 'Venetian law. Since the First Crusade, Venice had had contact with the world of the Greeks. The Eastern Latin Empire had preserved the legacy of classical Roman law and, above all, the principle of "natural equity", which the "fathers" of the Venetian homeland would directly transpose. This is the main way in which the compromise between the two legal systems was fostered. The *ius commune* did not come to Venice from the universities of Bologna, Paris, and Padua, where it was first discovered at the end of the twelfth century. Venetian nobles became acquainted with local statutes and *ordines iudiciarii* – the complicated rules of the procedural legal acts (*actiones*) and the system of legal evidence – when they were appointed rectors of the main cities of "Lombardia" (Foscarini's term for what is today northern Italy, including Tuscany).

---

primo Settecento, ed. by Raffaele Ajello, Marino Berengo, Alberto Caracciolo, Eric Cochrane, Erasmo Leso, Renzo Paci, Giuseppe Ricuperati (Milano-Napoli: Ricciardi, 1979), 167–202.

27 Arnaldo Momigliano, "Ancient History and the Antiquarian", *Journal of the Warburg and Courtauld Institutes*, 19 (1950), 147–168; *Momigliano and Antiquarianism: Foundations of the Modern Cultural Sciences*, ed. by Peter Miller (Toronto: University of Toronto Press, 2007), 385–399; Marco Caverzere, *Historical Culture and Political Reform in the Italian Enlightenment* (Oxford: Oxford University Press, 2020).

28 Marco Foscarini, *Della letteratura veneziana, libri otto* (Padova: Nella Stamperia del Seminario, 1752).

29 Ibidem, 7.

The attraction of the *ius commune* marks a *turning point* in the political and cultural history of the Serenissima: between Venice and the mainland there were no obstacles to communication but, instead, a fruitful exchange of experiences. There is a long list of Venetians between the beginning of the thirteenth and fifteenth centuries – and for this reason we will not go into all of them – who implemented a kind of civil cosmopolitanism (Foscarini's exclusion of any reference to war and conquest strikes me as significant here). This cosmopolitanism united the Italy of the medieval communes and fiefdoms with the East of Constantinople and the "kingdoms" of Candia (Heraklion, Crete) and Cyprus, the Peloponnese and Euboea and all of their original legislative bodies. Rectors of cities before Venice established its territorial state and, in that role, were protagonists of a gradual acculturation: Matteo Querini in Treviso; Stefano Badoer twice in Padua; Piero Tiepolo in Treviso and especially in Milan; Renier Zen in Piacenza; Nicolò Querini twice in Reggio; Maffeo Memmo on no less than four occasions in Padua; Andrea Zen, Filippo Belegno, and Giovanni Dandolo in Bologna, "three Venetians one after the other". Foscarini notes that five of them – Giovanni Soranzo, Pietro Ziani, Lorenzo Tiepolo, Jacopo Tiepolo, and Renier Zen – were given the ducal horn as soon as their term as Podestà was over. Giovanni Garzoni taught imperial law at the University of Vienna from 1394. When Venice annexed Padua to its "dominium" a large number of nobles enrolled in the law courses at the prestigious law school. The naturalness of this process of inclusion whereby the "Venetian laws" became segments, albeit among the most important, of a system of government of the "common good" was, however, hindered by an identitarian backlash in the form of a widespread vocation for particularism in the capital city. For Foscarini, the banning of Venetian nobles from professorships at Padua's law school was a sad day. Throughout the fifteenth century and then with the invention of printing, Venice remained the main center of publishing, even in legal subjects: "out of the Venetian printing presses came the Pandette, of which printed editions had not yet been seen"; followed by commentaries on the Corpus Juris and editions of *Consilia*. The epistolaries of the humanists, from Francesco Barbaro to Leonardo Contarini, tell of the further intermingling of literature and law in the name of Plato, Cicero, and Quintilian.

A close examination of the fresco painted by Marco Foscarini seems to suggest a reading of the complementarity of the relationship between the two spheres of law, the Venetian and the Roman-imperial. However, this relationship did not live up to its promise. In examining the wide range of literature on the original features of Venetian constitutional history, it becomes clear that the reading that has overwhelmingly prevailed emphasizes the extremely long and never resolved fracture between the capital and the *Terraferma*. Both are represented as monoliths, actors with fixed identities that are given once and for all, which remain unchanged in their increasingly frequent and necessary dialogues and confrontations throughout the republican age between the beginning of the fifteenth century and the end of the eighteenth century. It seems to me that the most knowledgeable and refined interpretations regarding the characteristics of the Venetian *legal system* also share this reading.

I use here the definition of *legal system* proposed by Lawrence Friedman, which takes into account not only the formal aspect of the law and the modalities of its production but also the legal "cultures" within a society. The power relations that are established within a given social environment, the need for order and motives for complaint, are understood in this reading as translated and mediated by the legal system.[30] This methodology is particularly useful for those wanting to study the early modern states, which are highly stratified and polycentric. However, having an awareness of the articulation of the different levels of political society has not been sufficient to stop even those readings which most closely study the contexts and dialogical forms of contamination and hybridization from proposing analyses in which abstract figures appear, if not Weberian *Idealtypen*. For example, the use of the category of "separateness" between the rulers and the ruled, in which normative production, the activities of the courts, and forms of legal acculturation are understood in their anthropological nature,[31] or the unresolved dialectic played out between two extremes, on the one hand, passive assimilation by the subjects and, on the other, the total impermeability between the Venetian and Veneto environments.[32]

If the role of those with institutional authority in the capital city and the territories was rigid, so too were the legal cultures that legitimized those subjects. On the one hand, the specificity of "Venetian law" is accentuated: it is the mark of the patriciate that governs the *stato da terra* and *the stato da mar* from the rooms of the ducal palace; on the other hand, there is a displacement of common law that guarantees the maintenance of the nobility's privileges in cities such as Verona, Padua, Brescia, Vicenza, and Udine and, within certain limits, justifies spaces of institutional and fiscal resistance that come from the capital city. According to this reading, the relations between rulers and ruled was dominated by a bipolar tension, and the conflicts and compositions that arose in the course of the modern age reinforced the isolation of both legal cultures. "The state structure of the Venetian aristocratic republic ensured that the relations of subjection between subjects and the *Dominante*

30 Lawrence M. Friedman, *The Legal System: A Social Science Perspective* (New York: Russell Sage Foundation, 1975).

31 Claudio Povolo, "Un sistema giuridico repubblicano: Venezia e il suo stato territoriale", in *Il diritto patrio: Tra diritto comune e codificazione (sec. XVI–XIX)*, ed. by Italo Birocchi and Antonello Mattone (Roma: Viella, 2006), 297–353; Id., "Dall'ordine della pace all'ordine pubblico", in *Processo e difesa penale in età moderna: Venezia e il suo stato territoriale*, ed. by Claudio Povolo (Bologna: Il Mulino, 2007), 15–107.

32 Cozzi, *Authority and the Law*, 293–345; Id., "Ambiente veneziano e ambiente veneto: Governanti e governati del Dominio di qua dal Mincio", in Id., *Ambiente veneziano, ambiente veneto: Saggi su società, cultura, giustizia nella Repubblica di Venezia in età moderna* (Venezia: Marsilio, 1997), 291–353.

were objectively determined by law".[33] This sentence is taken from an essay by Angelo Ventura, who, at the beginning of the 1960s, created the historiographic framework that interests us here. It is indicative of a general interpretation that underlies the foundation of the political discourse of the main treatise writers active from the mid-fifteenth century to the middle of the following century, from Paolo Morosini to Marc'Antonio Sabellico, from Lauro Quirini to Marin Sanudo.

A closer reading reveals it as an example of a confusion between the *etic* level – of the observer – and the *emic* level – of the actor – which, as Carlo Ginzburg warned, is a risk in any historical reconstruction.[34] Even more useful for reconstructing the relationship between *ius commune* and *ius veneto* is to try to grasp the interpretation of the concepts elaborated by Ventura. Rather than a huge number of magistracies, of instances of judgment and control, and of often conflicting deliberative bodies – a truly institutional labyrinth held together by functional interests – Ventura evidently believes that there is a "state structure" capable of articulating "relations of subjection" with Weberian vigour (these relations, which are anything but dialogical, guarantee the obedience of the subjects). Following Ventura's reasoning, the legitimacy of command and sovereignty is constituted in a kind of hermeneutic circularity: the objectivity of the law determines it and at the same time is determined by it. As we can see, Ventura does not recognize any space, except a subordinate and passive one, for the world of the "governed": their freedom is suffocated from birth by the "objectivity of the law" – in whose elaboration they do not participate and which they cannot influence.

Gaetano Cozzi takes a similar position to Angelo Ventura on the relations between politics and law and their indissoluble connection. Although their general frame of reference is similar, Cozzi's interpretation differs from Ventura's in terms of the field of analysis and the type of sources used to prove the working hypotheses. For Cozzi, who wrote his most important texts on the subject between the late 1960s and the 1980s, it is possible to trace the clear lines of what he defines as the "politics of law" through the centuries long historical experience of the republic. He attempts to highlight the legal and institutional role of the rectors, the Venetian nobles elected by the Maggior Consiglio to govern the major and minor cities of the mainland and maritime states. Cozzi describes how appointment was followed by the consignment of a "commission", which laid out the obligations and duties to which the representatives of the Serenissima had to adhere. According to Cozzi, the most important clauses on the investiture of the rectors concern the so-called hierarchy of sources (local statutes and common law, customs and Venetian law) to which the rectors had to swear an oath. Cozzi notes some differences

33 Angelo Ventura, *Nobiltà e popolo nella società veneta del Quattrocento e Cinquecento* (Bari–Roma: Laterza, 1964).

34 Carlo Ginzburg, *La lettera uccide* (Milano: Adelphi, 2021).

in priorities between the different commissions, which would produce a substantial dispute between Venice and its subjects, as well as a lot of work for the magistracy of the *Avogaria di comun*.[35]

Between Norms and Practices

Cozzi's refined analysis, which is limited to the reading of legislative and normative material, pays little attention to the daily practices of the rectors on the mainland. The key point of our reconstruction is that in the drafting of the rectors' commissions (*commissioni*) and in their responses to petitions from the mainland cities, the Venetian rulers continually affirmed their willingness to respect local prerogatives, already sanctioned by the so-called pacts of dedication (*pacta deditionis*) stipulated when the mainland was conquered.[36] However, there is no doubt that the republic's policy of law was capable of making interventions in the commissions that tended to deny, or suspend, the newly proclaimed openness. I was, in Cozzi's words: "A law based on *equitas*"[37]; the figure of "a pragmatic justice, founded on the *arbitrium* of the rector", emerged through cross-examination by numerous commissions.[38] Unlike for Ventura, for Cozzi law is not a form of action imposed on the subjects by the political will of the rulers; rather, it is an autonomous field that allows social actors to form their own identities and ideas of justice. Cozzi greatly reduced the complexity of the various forces at play and of the physiognomies of the protagonists of political and social life. According to this reading, the material and symbolic resources of law are understood as if they were the exclusive property of the nobles of the Serenissima.

For Cozzi, *equitas* and *arbitrium* represent the fundamental pillars of Veneto law by virtue of their ductility and practicality. These characteristics are opposed to the rigidity and abstraction that would prevail if common law was adopted. We have here highlighted a line of interpretation that contains original elements of considerable interest but at the same time makes evaluations that are worth questioning. The application of *arbitrium* and the recourse to *equitas* are certainly not peculiar to the policy of Venetian law, as Marco Foscarini had already realized: in Verona, in the first two decades of the fourteenth century, the members of Scaligeri chancellery recorded numerous

35 Alfredo Viggiano, *Governanti e governati: Legittimità del potere ed esercizio della sovranità nello stato veneziano della prima età moderna* (Treviso: Canova-Fondazione Benetton, 1993).
36 Antonio Menniti Ippolito, "Providebitur sicut melius videbitur: Milano e Venezia nel Bresciano nel primo Quattrocento", *Studi veneziani*, n.s 8 (1984), 37–76; Gherardo Ortalli, "Entrar nel Dominio: Le Dedizioni della città alla Repubblica Serenissima", in *Società, economia, istituzioni: Elementi per la conoscenza della repubblica di Venezia*, vol. 2, Gino Benzoni et alii, (Sommacampagna: Cierre, 2002), 63–73.
37 Cozzi, *Repubblica di Venezia*, 256.
38 Ibid., 259.

concessions to the governors of minor centres to apply *arbitrium*.[39] In other fifteenth-century Italian states, this principle was applied in various instances.[40] And so where does the Venetian peculiarity lie?

It has been noted that the strength of the common law idiom lies in its ability to adapt to the most diverse contexts. Hence, the inexhaustible hermeneutics exercised on them by jurists. *Arbitrium* and *equitas* in their various forms always refer to the question of *discretion*, a space of hermeneutic liberty, in the concrete exercise of justice. They are universal principles at the apex of the legal culture of the *ius commune*, which apply both in the field of civil justice and in that of punitive justice.[41] The flexibility with which these general concepts adapt to particular contexts is particularly striking, and their ability to lend legitimacy to those who apply them has guaranteed their success. They define the field of application of the law and the need to suspend its validity in order to "do justice"; they can also negatively characterize acts of the sovereign, who thus can be signalled as a "tyrant" who has betrayed the pact that unites him to his *populus* in order to defend the "bonum commune".[42]

The question of the original features of Venetian legal policy should therefore be posed comparatively. To what extent do the supporting structures of a republican constitutional system – modelled on a plurality of levels of judgment, on the equality of its various components, and on the respect of cetual and representative forms in the subject territories – establish peculiar political

39 Gian Maria Varanini, "Suppliche ai signori trecenteschi italiani fra *cancelleria* e corte: L'esempio *scaligero*", in *Suppliche e "gravamina". Politica, amministrazione e giustizia, secc. XIV–XVIII*, ed. by Andreas Würgler, Cecilia Nubola (Bologna: Il Mulino, 2002), 65–106. For a more general perspective, see Massimo Meccarelli, *Arbitrium: Un aspetto sistematico negli ordinamenti giuridici in età di diritto comune* (Milano: Giuffrè, 1998).

40 Andrea Zorzi, "Negoziazione penale, legittimazione giuridica e poteri urbani nell'Italia comunale", in *Criminalità e giustizia in Germania e in Italia: Pratiche giudiziarie e linguaggi giuridici tra tardo medioevo ed età moderna*, ed. by Marco Bellabarba, Gehrard Schwerhoff, Andrea Zorzi (Bologna: Il Mulino, 2001); Nadia Covini, *La "balanza drita", Pratiche di governo, leggi e ordinamenti nel ducato sforzesco* (Milano: Franco Angeli, 2007); Massimo Vallerani, "L'arbitrio negli statuti cittadini del Trecento: Note comparative", in *Tecniche di potere nel tardo medioevo: Regimi comunali e signorie in Italia*, ed. by Massimo Vallerani (Roma: Viella, 2011), 117–147.

41 Antonio Padoa Schioppa, "Equità nel diritto medievale e moderno: Spunti di dottrina", *Rivista di storia del diritto italiano*, 87 (2014), 5–44.

42 Diego Quaglioni, "'Quant tyranie sormonte, la justise est perdue': Alle origini del paradigma giuridico del tiranno", in *Tiranni e tirannide nel Trecento italiano*, ed. by Andrea Zorzi (Roma: Viella, 2013), 37–57; Angela De Benedicits, "Identità comunitarie e diritto di resistere", in *Identità collettive tra Medioevo ed età moderna: Atti del convegno internazionale (Bologna 28–30 settembre 2000)*, ed. by Paolo Prodi, Wolfgang Reinhard (Clueb: Bologna, 2002), 265–294; Otto Gerhard Oexle, "Die Kultur der Rebellion Schwureinung und Verschwörung im früh- und hochmittelalterlichen Okzident", in *Ordnung und Aufruhr im Mittelalter. Historische und juristische Studien zur Rebellion*, ed. by Marie Therese Fögen (Frankfurt am Main: Klostermann, 1995), 119–137; Peter Lantscher, *The Logic of Political Conflict in Medieval Cities: Italy and the Southern Low Countries, 1370–1440* (Oxford: Oxford University Press, 2015).

and judicial options? Which segments of the politics of law should we isolate in order to understand the similarities and differences between our territorial sample and Burgundy or Castile, Bavaria or Languedoc, Aragonese Naples or Tudor England? I have chosen here to point out the different modalities used for studying the system of appeals and to trace an initial identikit of the "'provincial" actors who played a leading role in the characterization of the Venetian legal system in order to propose a terrain for dialogue that is obviously open to other research avenues and hypotheses.

The research by Cozzi and by Ventura paid a lot of attention to the role of the rectors, the Venetian nobles sent to govern the main cities of the states *da terra* and *da mar*. What were the effects of the fact that they belonged to the sovereign body – and were not, as in the common European experience, officers appointed by the sovereign and completely subject to him? What consequences did this have on the relationship between the capital and the peripheries? We should not forget that Venice, taking the opposite position to Florence, decided that the policy of law in its *Dominium* hinged on respect for local statutes in which the rules of common law were embedded. The rectors had to comply with this obligation.[43] The *Avogaria di comun* was mandated to receive appeals on acts and sentences of Venetian representatives who did not observe this mandate. The investigations by the Venetian state on the effects of this system revealed practices that differed little from those in other Italian and foreign states and societies: the inability of rectors to resist clientelistic ties, cases of corruption, and a lack of respect for their subjects.[44]

The Venetian rectors of the early modern age who oscillated between excesses of severity and passivity did not resemble their more learned fellow citizens who ruled the cities of northern Italy in the thirteenth and fourteenth centuries and who were evoked by Marco Foscarini in his *Della letteratura veneziana*. To more clearly grasp the function of *ius commune* in the Venetian state, it is useful to turn to other states and societies. The most important and paradoxically the least studied are the mainland jurists, professors of the Padua law school, lawyers, and *assessori* (the technicians who were part of the court of rectors), who, through the drafting of reports, petitions, *consilia*, manuals of law, and sentences constituted the nerve nucleus of the system of mediation between Venice and the subject cities.

Venetian historiography (dazzled by the myth of "Venetian law") has neglected to study the formation and role of technicians and legal experts in

43 Gian Maria Varanini, "Gli statuti e l'evoluzione politico-istituzionale nella terraferma veneta quattrocentesca", in *La libertà di decidere: Realtà e parvenze di autonomia nella normativa locale del medioevo*, ed. by Rolando Dondarini (Cento: Deputazione provinciale di Storia Patria, 1995), 321–358.

44 Michael Knapton, "La condanna penale di Alvise Querini, ex *rettore* di *Rovereto* (1477): Solo un'altra smentita del mito di Venezia", *Atti Accademia roveretana degli Agiati*, 28:6 (1987), 303–332; Alfredo *Viggiano*, "Aspetti politici e giurisdizionali dell'attività dei *rettori* veneziani nello stato 'da terra' del Quattrocento", *Società e storia*, 17:65 (1994), 477–490.

the construction and maintenance of the institutions of the territorial states. To understand the importance of these figures, research should be conducted on the function of the colleges of judges and lawyers[45]; on the activity of the civil courts of the mainland cities; on the biographies, careers, and *networks* of legal experts; and on the contents of the '*consilia*'.

The study of appeals can act as an observatory, almost a seismograph, for understanding the tensions and accommodations between Venice and the powers of its territories and for understanding the attractiveness or otherwise of the capital's courts to its subjects. How much did the Serenissima's courts of appeal drive the inhabitants of Brescia, Zara, and Corfu, or – and this is even more important – rural communities to set off on the arduous, uncertain, and costly search for justice in the distant world of the capital? How much did this tension create new power relations, producing new opportunities for legitimization? How much did the Venetian attention to receiving appeals, which constituted the archaic patina of its myth of *dolce Justitia* (mild Justice), prevent more radical conflicts from arising in the world of the governed?

The fundamental role of the *avogaria di comun* emerged in the tangle of formal and informal relations from the early fifteenth century onwards, when Venice already occupied a substantial part of the Po Valley as far as Brescia and Bergamo and protected its territories by controlling rivers and mountain areas from Trentino to Friuli, and when it also controlled the strip of seaports that ran from Koper to the Ionian Islands, to which it added the republic's oldest colonial possession, the island of Crete. The *avogadori di comun* had a variety of attributes that are summed up by the definition repeated in all the treaties on the magistracies of the republic between the fifteenth and sixteenth centuries: they were "*observadori de la leze*" (observers and guardians of the law). This concise formulation conceals a very high power of jurisdictions. The *avogadori* appeared as promoters of the public prosecution in criminal trials held in Venice; they received appeals on verdicts in criminal matters pronounced by magistrates from the capital and the provinces of the Venetian state; they had the power to invalidate the decisions of sovereign councils – the Maggior Consiglio and the Senate, not the Council of Ten – that either conflicted with the Venetian Law or did not respect the principle of equity (*equitas*), the fundamental virtue of the Venetian political system.[46]

The freedom of the *avogadori* operated on different levels that seem to contradict each other: as receivers of the appeals of the "Dominii" they were

45 Lucien Faggion, *Les seigneurs du droit dans la République de Venise: Collège des Juges et société à Vicence à l'époque moderne (1530–1730 env.)* (Genève: Édition Slaktine, 2000).

46 For the development of Avogaria jurisdiction during the early modern age, Cristina Setti, "L'Avogaria di comun come magistratura media d'appello", *Il diritto della Regione: Il nuovo cittadino*, 1 (2009), 143–171; Ead., "La terza parte a Venezia: L'Avogaria di comun tra politica e prassi quotidiana (secoli XVI–XVIII)", *Acta Histriae*, 22 (2011), 128–140; Viggiano, *Governanti e governati*, 120–155, Id., "Interpretazione della legge e mediazione politica: Note sull'Avogaria di comun", in *Studi veneti offerti a Gaetano Cozzi*, 281–286.

obliged to protect local privileges (by virtue of the pacts stipulated between Venice and the subject centres when they were conquered[47]), but as guardians of the republican spirit and holders of discretionary powers they possessed a range of intervention that no other Venetian magistracy was allowed. We should add that both as public prosecutors and as receivers of appeals the *avogadori* could use their own discretion to present themselves to the magistrate that seemed to them to be best suited to solving the case in question (either the Maggior Consiglio and the Senate, the Serenissima Signoria, or the Council of Forty).

Thus, in some cases, they could appear as intransigent custodians of a higher order and, in other cases, as fastidious examiners of minor and sometimes trivial matters. Called upon to continually mediate between local legal systems and Venetian law, to disentangle the use of informal and consuetudinary procedures from the literal application of the written norm, to reconcile an attachment to archaic conventions with flexible adaptation to contingency and actuality, to oscillate between the political moods and emotions of the "piazza" and the labyrinths of the "palazzo", the *avogadori* were the chameleons of the Venetian constitution. The originality of their position in the interplay of the republic's institutions was both their strength and their weakness. The fragmentation of their duties may have served the noblemen elected to the office but risked blurring the profile of the institution.

We can propose the hypothesis that it was also for these reasons, in the hundred years between the mid-fifteenth and mid-sixteenth centuries, and with the aim of unequivocally and succinctly legitimizing the role of the *Avogaria*, numerous Venetian and non-Venetian political writers (including an anonymous French author from the late fifteenth century and the Florentine Donato Giannotti, who left after the restoration of Alessandro de Medici in 1530[48]) made comparisons between the magistracy and the tribunes of the plebs in republican Rome.[49]

The study of the so-called *intromissioni* (the acts with which the *avogadori* recognized the legitimacy of lawsuits and introduced them to the courts of justice) completely upends the question of the validity, use, and manipulation of the norms of the *ius commune*. The acts of the Avogaria during the fifteenth

47 Gaetano Cozzi, "Note sopra l'Avogaria di Comun", in *Atti del convegno "Venezia e la Terraferma attraverso le relazioni dei rettori" (Trieste, 23–24 ottobre 1980)*, ed. by Amelio Tagliaferri (Milano: Giuffrè, 1981), 547–557.

48 *Descripcion ou Traicté du gouvernement et regime de la cité et Seigneurie de Venise. Venezia vista dalla Francia ai primi del Cinquecento*, ed. by Philippe Braunstein, Reinhold Mueller (Venezia: Istituto Veneto di Scienze Lettere ed Arti, 2015); Felix Gilbert, "The Venetian Constitution in Florentine Political Thought", in *Florentine Studies: Politics and Society in Renaissance Florence*, ed. by Nicolai Rubinstein (London: Faber & Faber, 1968), 463–500.

49 On the genealogy and fortune of this paradigm in the early modern age, Massimo Galtarossa, "L'idea del Tribunato nella storia della Repubblica di Venezia", *Studi Veneziani*, 58 (2009), 405–419.

century demonstrate that it was an inexhaustible resource of knowledge, taxonomies, and opportunities for those who wished to assert their rights.

The *intromissioni* made by the Avogaria following appeals by subjects from the mainland grew from an annual average of twenty-three for the period 1430–40 to an average of eighty-five for the period 1480–90.[50] Through this filter, it is possible to identify the influence or otherwise of the use of the common law as a mechanism for regulating conflicts before the authorities. To this end, we could examine appeals of sentences by the rectors of Verona, Udine, and Padua punishing noblemen involved in acts of vengeance.[51] The procedural case in these instances tended not to recognize, indeed to dismiss, the spiral of ritual acts of violence that characterized the progress of the feud: somehow the procedures delegitimized the idiom of *vendetta* – the forms of *homicide* envisaged in the judicial manuals did not include vengeful practices as an extenuating circumstance, even though the statutes of a city such as Verona recognized the legitimacy of a murder committed by someone from a lineage offended and dishonoured by a rival belonging to another clan[52] – and thus promoted the formalization of the peace in the hands of the notaries.

Exemplary in this regard is a case from 1488.[53] The *avogadore* Nicolò Muazzo presented the case of Antonio da Rota of Bergamo to the Criminal Council of Forty. Muazzo challenged the legitimacy of an informative *littera* sent by the city's rector to the Serenissima Signoria in which it was stated that the murder committed by da Rota should be considered "*proditorio*" (treasonous). Rather, according to Muazzo, the papers collected following the appeal showed that there was a "capital hatred" between the defendant and the victim, Matteo de Bognatis. The rector would therefore have to carry out his investigation with this relationship in mind. The role played by clans and relatives did not feature in the case we have just heard and in many other similar cases in which "*antique inimicitie*" (ancient hatreds) were recognized as the origin of serious acts of bloodshed. For official justice, only single individuals were responsible. The writing down of lawsuits and testimonies, the translation of gestures into the formalized vocabulary of the *ius commune*, the journey of the case from the places in which it arose to Venice, created a spatial and temporal interval in which the social and anthropological atmosphere in which the "deed" was done appeared rarefied and therefore diminished in importance. A sort of "veil of ignorance", à la Rawls, was placed on the

50 Viggiano, *Governanti e governati*, 88–89.

51 Archivio di Stato di Venezia, Avogaria di comun, reg. 3647–3648.

52 Gian Maria Varanini, "Gli statuti delle città della Terraferma veneta nel Quattrocento", in *Statuti città territori in Italia e Germania tra medioevo ed età moderna*, ed. by Giorgio Chittolini, Dietmar Willoweit (Bologna: Il Mulino, 1991), 247–317; Id., "*La Terraferma veneta del Quattrocento e le tendenze recenti della storiografia*", in *1509–2009: L'ombra di Agnadello, Venezia e la terraferma: Atti del Convegno Internazionale di studi, Venezia 14–15–16 maggio 2009*, ed. by Giuseppe Del Torre, Alfredo Viggiano (Venezia: Ateneo Veneto, 2011).

53 Viggiano, *Governanti e governati*, 82.

whirlwind of passions, allowing the judicial machine to proceed. This example enables us to reaffirm Venice's belonging to the great family of common law: the core of judicial action is located in the inquisitorial process, another product of the law's revolution in the Middle Ages.[54]

Similar considerations to those just made on the intermingling of subjective demands and claims for cetual representation, institutional interventions, and legal idioms may also help to contextualize other aspects of the republic's system of government. These include the system of dispute settlement, which common law had greatly refined, and which differed from that adopted in Venice. The city's mercantile origins had made a mark on the arbitration procedures, giving the so-called *more veneto* arbitration process greater speed and informality.[55] The subjects of the mainland and maritime states could also access such jurisdiction, which meant mixing heteronomous legal traditions with sometimes unpredictable effects. Let us look at a case introduced by Avogadori Luca Tron and Dolfin Venier in Counsel of Quarantia on 21 April 1447. The Paduan citizen Rogato Rogati, belonging to one of the city's most eminent families, sent a complaint to Venice through his lawyers. For a long time there had been a civil conflict between him and one of his fellow citizens, Daniele Dottori, over the possession of some real estate. On 16 September 1446, the ducal councillors – six Venetian nobles entrusted with the task of hearing complaints and requests from their subjects and granting *gratie* if they considered such complaints well founded – intervened in favour of Dottori's request, deciding that the two contenders would have to produce evidence and writs in Padua before their "ordinary judge", the city's civil court. The lawyers defending the interests of the Rogati lineage were opposed to this request. The *avogadori* accepted the latter's version.

When retracing the phases of the dispute, the Venetian magistrates highlighted a passage in the argument – picking it out from many others – that, in their opinion, signalled the real will of both parties. The basis of the *avogadoris*' argument was that this consensual act had the force of law because of its chronological priority: Rogati and Dottori had, in fact, agreed together to entrust their destinies to Pietro Michiel, a Venetian nobleman. The relocation

54 Massimo Vallerani, *La giustizia pubblica medievale* (Bologna: Il Mulino, 2005).

55 On *arbitrato more veneto*, see Marco Bellabarba, *Le pratiche del diritto civile: Gli avvocati, le "Correzioni", i "conservatori delle leggi"*, in *Storia di Venezia*, vol. 6, *Dal Rinascimento al Barocco*, ed. by G. Cozzi, Paolo Prodi (Roma: Istituto dell'Enciclopedia Italiana, 1994), 795–824; Cozzi, *Repubblica di Venezia e stati italiani*, 222–224; On the topic of Venetian civil justice, see Claudia Passarella, *Interesse di parte e logiche del processo: La giustizia civile a Venezia in età moderna* (Giappichelli: Torino, 2018); Maria Fusaro, "Politics of Justice/ Politics of Trade: Foreign Merchants and the Administration of Justice from the Records of Venice's Giudici del Forestier", *Mélanges de l'École française de Rome – Italie et Méditerranée modernes et contemporaines* [online], 126:1 (21 July 2014), consulted online 9 March 2024, https://doi.org/10.4000/mefrim.1665 ; James E. Shaw, *The Justice of Venice: Authorities and Liberties in the Urban Economy, 1550–1700* (Oxford: Oxford University Press, 2006).

of the ongoing proceedings from Padua to Venice was thus founded on the unequivocal will of the subjects involved in the conflict; thus, there was a substantial motive to resort to a Venetian arbitrator to resolve the case. The recording of the affair in the archival registers is essential to the solution of the case, even though no details were recorded in the transcription by the court clerks that is particularly useful for reconstructing a more coherent and precise picture of the story. The arbitrator ruled in favour of a three-year extension (*prorogatio*) of the compromise. The *avogadori* played their hands well at this point: resorting to the "written memory" of the institution they represented, they proved that this extension had already been contested by some of their predecessors as contrary to customary practice; and this interpretation had been accepted (*laudata)* by the judges of the Council of Forty. This put the final seal on the case and consequently annulled the intervention of the Consiglieri.

A Provincial Elite: Expertise and Legitimacy

Among the various magistracies of the capital, I believe that the linchpin of the Venetian legal system – which impressed its procedural and political character on the entire fabric of public relations – was the Avogaria-Quarantia binomial (and not the "*tremendo tribunale*", the "terrifying court" of the Council of Ten or the State Inquisitors, as held by the narrative tradition that stretches back undisturbed to the Age of Enlightenment and Napoleon). If I am right, then we must look for an analogous institution in the mainland that mediated between and encouraged the hybridization of different legal cultures. The governors of the major cities of the Venetian mainland had a staff of legal experts to assist them in the tasks of civil and criminal justice: the *assessori*. This was not original to the republican state: already in the communal age the rectors of Tuscany and Lombardy were assisted by *doctores*.[56] An examination of the regulations concerning the *assessori*, along with some biographical sources, allows us to advance a few hypotheses on the Venetian version of the role. Giovanni Bonifacio, who occupied the position a number of times in the final years of the sixteenth century, dedicated a brief work to illustrating the appointment procedures and main duties of the *assessori*. The law stipulated that the rectors elected to govern the principal cities of the mainland state should appoint their own staff. Boniface specifies that the *assessori* had to be "*dottori di leggi*", but also had to be both Venetian subjects and graduates from the Padua law school. Following the principle adopted for the podestà of medieval cities, the *assessori* could not be natives of the cities "where they

56 Claudio Povolo, "Introduzione", in L'*Assessore, Discorso del Sig. Giovanni Bonifacio in Rovigo MDCXXVII*, ed. by Claudio Povolo (Rovigo: Tipografia Sartor, 1991); Alfredo Viggiano, "Ascesa sociale e burocrazia di Stato: La carriera di *assessore* nello Stato di Terraferma veneto", in *Annali Veneti: Società, Cultura, Istituzioni*, vol. 1, *Comunità del passato* (1985), 34–45.

judged". At the end of the sixteenth century, there were thirty-one *assessori*. Their numbers were proportionate to the importance of each city: four were elected in Padua and Verona; three in Brescia, Bergamo, and Vicenza; two in Udine, Treviso, Rovigo, and Crema; and only one in Belluno, Feltre, Cividale del Friuli, Salò, Palma, and Conegliano.

Thus, a group of civil servants began to form. Whereas in the capital city the Avogaria and the Quarantie constituted the point of verification, confrontation, and mediation between *jus civile* and Veneto law, in the major centres of the territorial state these tasks were entrusted to the group of experts whose features we will now attempt to outline. We should note that their careers did not depend on their election by one of the great magistrates of the republic, either the Maggior Consiglio or the Senate. The decision to place this mandate in the hands of the patricians appointed as rectors suggests some working hypotheses. Being a rector was not a profession: Venetian nobles took up the role once or twice in their lifetimes. How could they have sufficient knowledge of individuals and local realities to be able to carefully choose their collaborators or recommend names to another member of the patriciate about to enter the government of Padua or Verona? The scanty information available can provide only a partial response to this question. The situation in the fifteenth century appears more fluid than that described by Bonifacio. On 26 April 1458, a certain Simone de Chizolis, a "distinguished and loyal" Paduan (he and his family had contributed to uncovering Jacopo Scrovegni's conspiracy), made a plea to the Council of Ten, the most important penal court of the Serenissima, which was becoming very powerful at that time. Simone requested that three of his sons, "*doctores preclarissimi, intelligentes et doctos*" (highly cultured and very illustrious doctors), all be allowed to serve the state as *assessori* in Padua as well, making an exception to the legislation.[57] The Heads agreed: they could choose Padua, Vicenza, or Treviso. Thus, the choice of technicians appears to be based on clientelistic and paternalistic criteria, which are not without contradictions. The Heads therefore accepted nominations, but those who had obtained their favour were left with the far from easy task of seeking a patron.

The uncertainty of the procedures for admission to the office did not prevent the formation of a group of *assessori* who continuously occupied the roles in the mainland cities. This was the case for Girolamo Ferramosca from Vicenza: he held the role in 1486, 1488, 1489, 1494, and 1498 in Padua; 1491 in Crema; 1495 in Brescia; and 1500 in Treviso. The name of the Paduan Count Alvarotti also appears uninterrupted for fifteen years: 1488 and 1498 in Brescia; 1493 and 1500 in Bergamo; and 1495, 1497, and 1502 in Vicenza. They also included Giovanni della Scoffa from Vicenza; the Paduans Salione Buzzacarini, Antonio da Bassano, and Giovanni Antonio Pasini; and the Veronese Bartolomeo de Tomei and Girolamo Bravo. It should be noted,

57 Viggiano, *Governanti e governati*, 191.

however, that the role of *assessore* could not yet be said to be a "*profession*".[58] Many of those appointed through the rectors' oaths belonged to the colleges of local jurists or aspired to a position in the Studio. Others alternated their service to Venice with service to their local fatherland.

The extremely broad composition of the patriciate – the number of members of the Maggior Consiglio fluctuated between 2,000 and 2,500 from the mid-fifteenth century to the 1630s – made it very complicated when appointing state bureaucrats to form channels of communication or to donate the gifts and counter-gifts that characterized seigniorial or monarchical clientelistic systems. The difficulty of finding a functional match between demand (the nobles elected to the government of mainland cities) and supply (the aspiring lawyers to become *assessori*) was thus driven by a structural problem that was to be remedied only between the late seventeenth and early eighteenth centuries through the introduction of an exam for candidates.[59] A number of legislative measures were enacted during the fifteenth century in an attempt to improve the situation, but, if anything, they created further complications.

The republican ideology of public service postulates a sort of zero degree in the relations between the members of the political elite: favours and emotional inclinations were not allowed to influence choices. This was reiterated by a myriad of measures that, already during the fifteenth century, sought to restrict the rectors' networks of relationships: they could not receive gifts from their subjects, allow themselves to be represented in celebratory portraits, or mix their blood with their subjects by marriage or by assuming the role of godfather or witness in baptisms or marriages.[60]

Contact between the Venetian patricians and the legal experts was permitted only within public places: the Studio in Padua and the "Scuola" in Rialto. The spread of civil humanism – at times in opposition with cultural and legal practices – favoured the formation of new bonds through the exchange of, and commentary on, classical texts: the epistolaries of Francesco Barbaro and Ludovico Foscarini reveal the ways in which the study of ancient letters and the daily labours of state government could intersect. Both prominent humanists, they attended the Studio of Padua, and Foscarini was also a doctor in *utroque*

58 Michael Knapton, "Tribunali veneziani e proteste padovane nel secondo Quattrocento", *Studi veneti*, 168–169.

59 Alfredo Viggiano, "La repubblica degli esperti: Storie di Assessori nel Settecento veneziano", in *Tagiapiera, depentor, pennacchir, sonador: Il bergamasco a Venezia 1428–1797*, ed. by Maria Mencaroni Zoppetti (Bergamo: Atti dell'Ateneo di Bergamo, 2003), 189–208.

60 Marco Bellabarba, *Rettori veneti e città di Terraferma nel primo Seicento: immagini e parole*, in, *Rituali civici e continuità istituzionale nella città italiane in età moderna*, ed. by Gian Maria Varanini (Roma: Viella, 2023, 31–47; Claudio Povolo, "Il protettore amorevole (Magnifica Patria della Riviera del Garda 1570–1630)", in *Sul lago di Garda tra passato e futuro: Storia, lingua, letteratura*, vol. 1, ed. by Ateneo di Salò (Salò: Liberdizioni Salò, 2019), 87–124.

iure.[61] Their *cursus honorum* were studded with high-profile assignments: they were sent as ambassadors to pontiffs and emperors. Their names repeatedly appear in the lists of those elected to the highest magistracies (Avogadori di comun, Capi del Consiglio dei Dieci, Savi del Consiglio, Procuratori di San Marco). Similarly, and this is what is most interesting for our present purposes, they were repeatedly appointed as rectors in Treviso and Padua, Verona and Vicenza, and Brescia and Udine.[62]

True "bosses" of Venetian politics, Francesco Barbaro and Ludovico Foscarini weaved a broad network of friendships (a term that began to take on the weighty meaning of an indissoluble and exclusive bond typical of the classical age) with well-known men of letters, such as Lorenzo Valla or Guarino Veronese.[63] But, at the same time, when they governed the unstable provinces of the state *da terra*, they also frequented a wide range of individuals, who, thanks to the passepartout of the ancient language that lent them an air of distinction, pleaded with them to obtain an ecclesiastical benefit, an *officium* that would allow them to maintain their family. Among these individuals who were part of a kind of court of protégés revolving around the rector were numerous graduates either in both legal systems or only in *ius civile*, who facilitated continuous dialogue between the capital and their homelands. Among them, we find the names not only of several *assessori*, but also of individuals who, while providing important legal services in the network of relations between Venice and the mainland, remained in a liminal zone. Prominent among them is Erasmo de Erasmi from Udine.[64] He was a very active lawyer between the 1430s and 1450s in a wide range of disputes between feudal communities

61 Clémence Revest, "Naissance du cicéronianisme et émergence de l'humanisme comme culture dominante: Réflexions pour une étude de la rhétorique humaniste comme pratique sociale", *Mélanges de l'École française de Rome – Moyen Âge*, 125 (2013), 219–257.

62 Monique O'Connell, "Venetian Empire in Oratory and Print in the Later Fifteenth Century", in *Cultures of Empire: Rethinking Venetian Rule, 1400–1700: Essays in Honour of Benjamin Arbel*, ed. by Georg Christ, Franz-Julius Morche (Brill: Leiden, 2020), 41–62; Luka Špoljarić, "Power and Subversion in the Ducal Palace: Dalmatian Patrician Humanists and Congratulatory Orations to Newly Elected Doges", in *Neo Latin Contexts in Croatia and Tyrol: Challenges, Prospects, Case Studies*, ed. by Neven Jovanovic, Johanna Luggin, Luka Špoliarić (Wien: Böhlau Verlag, 2018), 81–106. An overview of the topic of representative institutions in the Republic of Venice, Giovanni Florio, *Micropolitica della rappresentanza: Dinamiche del potere a Venezia in età moderna* (Roma: Carocci, 2023).

63 On Francesco Barbaro, Percy Gothein, *Francesco Barbaro: Früh-Humanismus und Staats-Kunst in Venedig* (Berlino: Verlag die Runde, 1932); On Foscarini: Leonard Horsch, *Politisches Handlungswissen im Venedig des Quattrocento: Briefsammlung des Ludovico Foscarini*, vols. 1–2 (Berlin: De Gruyter, 2024); and Margaret L. King, *Venetian Humanism in an Age of Patrician Dominance* (Princeton: Princeton University Press, 1986); Vittore Branca, *La sapienza civile: Studi sull'Umanesimo a Venezia* (Firenze: Olschki, 1998).

64 Giuseppe Trebbi, "Umanesimo, erudizione e diritto nella disputa sull'antichità di Udine e Cividale (secoli XV–XVII)", in *Le subordinazioni delle città comunali a poteri maggiori in Italia dagli inizi del secolo XIV alla fine dell'Ancien Régime*, ed. by Miriam Davide (Trieste: Cerm, 2014), 187–262.

and noble jurists in Friuli and a leader of the bar in Udine. In his city he attended a *Schola Iuris*, of which very little evidence survives, but which we know provided sufficient acculturation for all those who wished to venture into the wilderness of the legal professions.[65] Thus – and the Friulian case is by no means exceptional – a group of *iurisperiti* emerged who did not necessarily graduate in the Studio of Padua but who provided essential services, such as composing pleas, organizing lawsuits, arbitrating hereditary disputes, and serving as "*vicario*" or "*cancelliere*" in the stately courts of justice (both secular and ecclesiastical) that had spread over the Friulian territory since the Middle Ages.[66]

Local chronicles, administrative papers, and family memoirs reflect the climate of lively hostility between the nobles and the peasants of well-structured micro-regions. For a handful of men in search of fortune, the "*banco del diritto*" (the law bench), which was the term used at the time, acted as a training ground for examining the relationship between customary feudal laws and Roman-canon law. The *paci* (a written act of pacification) recorded in the notaries' papers or the inquisition trials conducted in the curia of the Venetian rector (the Luogotenente) concern disputes around collective usage (the *commons*), relating to rights to hunt, graze, and fish. In cases of this kind we repeatedly find Erasmo de Erasmi and a handful of other lawyers (the *advocati* or *procuratori*) whose names recur frequently in the lawsuits in the second half of the fifteenth century.

The urgency of defining the boundaries of the *commons* forced different spheres of law, both learned and popular, into confrontation with one another and created a tension between the analysis of the particular case and the universal classification (which is why jurists and anthropologists paid it so much attention[67]); a similar hermeneutic short circuit arose every time the judicial body was faced with actions that referred to the complex world of the "vendetta".[68] The succession of acts of violence, which took on a ritualistic character, forcing those involved into a spiral of vengeful actions, called for the intervention, through its magistracies, of the *summa potestas* of the republic. As we have already noted, the machinery of the *ius commune* also functioned in these cases as a regulatory instrument for apparently irreconcilable judicial questions. Erasmo's local acquaintances helped him to weave a web of relations that ended up stretching from the city of Udine to the entire region, the "Patria del Friuli" and, from there, to Venice.

65 Giuseppe Occioni-Bonaffons, *La scuola d'"Instituta Iuris", fondata in Udine nel secolo XV* (Udine: Tipografia G.B. Doretti e Soci, 1884).

66 Lorenzo Freschi, *I sudditi al governo: Società e politica a Cividale e Gemona nel Friuli del Rinascimento veneziano* (Bologna: Il Mulino, 2021).

67 *Le risorse collettive nell'Italia settentrionale, sec. XII–XVIII*, ed. by Guido Alfani, Riccardo Rao (Milano: Franco Angeli, 2011).

68 Edward Muir, *Mad Blood Stirring: Vendetta and Faction in Friuli during the Renaissance* (Baltimore: Johns Hopkins University Press, 1993).

Part II

Ius Commune and England

6 The Invisible Border between *Ius Commune* and Common Law

Traditional Interpretations and New Prospects

Dolores Freda

Beyond the Tradition

In a famous essay written at the beginning of the twentieth century, the great English legal historian Frederic William Maitland spoke of the healthy "resistance" of common law to the penetration of Roman-canon law into England and the ability of local law to remain immune from foreign "contamination".[1] This point of view, which was wholeheartedly embraced by English legal-historical scholarship for a long time to come, was an expression of the European legal tradition's common assumption of the existence of a marked contrast between common law and continental law. The former was understood to be a customary law developed through the accumulation of judicial precedents from the twelfth century onwards and the latter the product of the interpretation of Roman-canon law texts by the *doctores* of the medieval universities, then codified, rationalized, and formalized in the nineteenth century. Codification itself – with its legalistic and positivistic ideologies – and, above all, the elaboration of the concepts of "system" and "law as science" by the German *Pandektistik* contributed to creating and reinforcing this contrast.

This division reflected that traditionally made by comparatists in the post–World War II period, in which what the West called the "civil world" was split into two big legal families: that of the countries of Roman-Germanic law and that of the countries of Anglo-American law.[2] This assumption was

1 Frederic W. Maitland, *English Law and the Renaissance* (Cambridge: Cambridge University Press, 1901), repr. in *Selected Historical Essays* (Cambridge: Cambridge University Press, 1957), at 141.

2 See, in particular, these fundamental texts: Renée David, *Les Grandes Systèmes de droit contemporains* (Paris: Dalloz, 1964); John H. Merryman, *The Civil Law Tradition: An Introduction to the Legal Systems of Western Europe and Latin America* (Stanford: Stanford University Press, 1969); Konrad Zweigert, Hein Kötz, *An Introduction to Comparative Law*, vol. I, *The Framework*, trans. Tony Weir (Oxford: Clarendon Press, 1977). The distinctive features of common law and civil law were explored by Raoul C. Van Caenegem, in *Judges, Legislators, Professors: Chapters in European Legal History* (Cambridge: Cambridge University Press, 1987), 1–65. He reiterated this view in Id., *European Law in the Past and the Future: Unity and Diversity over Two Millennia* (Cambridge: Cambridge University Press, 2002).

DOI: 10.4324/9781003425069-9

influenced, on the one hand, by comparative legal scholarship at the beginning of the twentieth century, which began in the climate of legal positivism that dominated at the time, with its emphasis on formalism and a systematic idea of law, and, on the other hand, by theories in legal historiography at the end of the nineteenth century, which, inspired by romantic nationalism, had mostly concentrated on the peculiar features of the national legal traditions and, consequently, on the differences between them.

Following the anti-formalist direction taken by legal science between the 1930s and the 1960s, and the extensive renewal of legal academia from the 1980s onwards, both Anglo-American and continental European legal historians began to open up the study of the history of European legal culture to also include English law. This international historiographical renewal was marked by a growing interest in the early modern period. This led to the setting up of two book series: Studies in Comparative Legal History in Berkeley and the international comparative-historical collection of Comparative Studies in Continental and Anglo-American Legal History. The latter's intent, explicitly laid out by the editor Helmut Coing in the first volume, was and still is to encourage researchers coming from the continental European and Anglo-American legal traditions to exchange views and cooperate.[3]

This opening up was connected to a wider process of historical, geopolitical, and cultural developments at an international level. These included the breakdown of the socialist regime in the former Soviet Union and the consequent change in the global balance of power; the creation and enlargement of the European Union; the modernization and democratization of post-colonial countries; and the IT, commerce, and transport revolution, which gave rise to so-called globalization. These events encouraged comparatists to reconsider the relationship between continental law and Anglo-American law and, at the same time, to recognize some "closeness between them, emphasising their similarities above their differences and seeing them both as a part of a common European legal tradition".[4]

3 Helmut Coing, "Common Law and Civil Law in the Development of European Civilization – Possibilities of Comparisons", in *Englische und Kontinentale Rechtsgeschichte: ein Forschungsprojekt*, ed. by Helmut Coing, Knut W. Norr (Berlin: Duncker & Humblot, 1985), 31–41. See also: Id., "The Roman Law as Ius Commune on the Continent", in *Law Quarterly Review*, 89 (1973), 505–517; Id., "European Common Law: Historical Foundations", in *New Perspectives for a Common Law of Europe*, ed. by Mauro Cappelletti (Stuttgart: Klett-Cotta, 1978), 31–44, where Coing talks about "a common European heritage in law" (32).

4 An initial example of this change in perspective can be found in the essay by Gino Gorla and Luigi Moccia, "A 'Revisiting' of the Comparison between 'Continental Law' and 'English Law' (16th–19th Century)", in *Journal of Legal History*, 2 (1981), 143–156, which highlighted the similarities, rather than the differences, between continental European law and English law, seeing them as both part of a common and unitary European legal tradition. See also the essays collected in Gino Gorla's edited volume, *Diritto comparato e diritto comune europeo* (Milano: Giuffrè, 1981). The limits of the traditional view have also been discussed in the following works: Guido Alpa, *Il diritto privato nel prisma della comparazione* (Torino: Giappichelli,

Thanks to the sociological and anthropological approaches developed in the final decades of the twentieth century,[5] comparatists now commonly talk of a single great "Western legal tradition" or "Western legal culture",[6] in which the traditional opposition between common law and continental law appears to be totally meaningless.[7] At the same time, the debate on building a common European private law and the consequent renewed interest in European legal history has involved both comparatists and legal historians, and it has also contributed to the current understanding of the relationship between common law and *ius commune.* Various comparatists and comparative-Romanists have in recent decades made ambitious and often questionable attempts to recover a European legal tradition Roman law, *ius commune* – in order to historically legitimize the harmonization of the various European national legal systems, theorizing a modern *ius commune europaeum* (described as a "re-Europeanization of legal science" aimed at overcoming the current "legal nationalism"[8]). However, from the 1990s onwards, these attempts have posed new questions that have redirected the debate towards the relationship between the two legal traditions. More often the emphasis is on their "convergence", excessively

2004); Alessandro Pizzorusso, *Sistemi giuridici comparati* (Milano: Giuffrè, 1998); Antonio Gambaro, Rodolfo Sacco, *Sistemi giuridici comparati* (Torino: Giappichelli, 1996), 41–59; James Gordley, "Common Law v Civil Law: Una distinzione che sta scomparendo", in *Scritti in onore di Rodolfo Sacco: La comparazione giuridica alle soglie del terzo millennio*, ed. by Paolo Cendon, vol. 1 (Milano: Giuffrè, 1994); and Mark Van Hoecke, Mark Warrington, "Legal Cultures, Legal Paradigms and Legal Doctrine: Towards a New Model for Comparative Law", in *The International and Comparative Law Quarterly*, 47 (1998), 501–502, which argues that "common law and continental law are very close to a point where there will no longer be *paradigmatical* differences. What will be left is some difference of degree, not of a fundamental nature" and that "the whole "legal families" division is now collapsing".

5 See especially anthropologist Clifford Geertz's fundamental work, *The Interpretation of Cultures: Selected Essays* (New York: Basic Books, 1973); and the studies by the sociologist Boaventura de Sousa Santos, "Law: A Map of Misreading: Toward a Postmodern Conception of Law", *Journal of Law and Society*, 14 (1987), 279–302.

6 The notion of a common "Western legal tradition", including English and American legal history, was elaborated in a famous work by Harold J. Berman, *Law and Revolution: The Formation of the Western Legal Tradition* (Cambridge: Harvard University Press, 1983).

7 In "Three Patterns of Law: Taxonomy and Change in the World's Legal Systems" (in *The American Journal of Comparative Law*, 45 (1997), 5–44), Ugo Mattei emphasized the need to re-map the world's contemporary legal systems and their fundamental features.

8 Reinhard Zimmermann, "Civil Code and Civil Law: The 'Europeanization' of Private Law within the European Community and the Re-emergence of a European Legal Science", *Columbia Journal of European Law*, 1 (1994–95), 63–105; Id., "Roman Law and European Legal Unity", in *Towards a European Civil Code*, ed. by Arthur S. Hartkamp, Gerrit Betlem (Dordrecht–London: Art Pub., 1994), 65–81; and Id., "Diritto romano, diritto contemporaneo, diritto europeo: La tradizione civilistica oggi: Il diritto privato europeo e le sue basi storiche", *Rivista di diritto civile*, 47:6 (nov./dic. 2001), 703–763. On this theme, also see Klaus Luig, "The History of Roman Private Law and the Unification of European Law", *Zeitschrift für Europäisches Privatrecht*, 5 (1997), 405–427.

stressing their similarities,[9] while in other cases there is a no less radical reemphasis on the differences between them.[10]

Recent scholarship critically highlights our path dependency on the foundational assumptions and concepts developed during the birth of European legal history in postwar Europe, arguing for a de-Europeanization of research traditions, allowing European legal history to be seen from a transnational or global perspective and thus rejecting a purely Eurocentric (or Western-centric) perception of the law. It has also emphasized the need to reconsider the relationship between different regions in Europe, properly taking into account areas traditionally considered to be "special cases" (for instance, Scandinavia, England, and Southeastern Europe) that are usually pushed to the peripheries, at the borders of what is traditionally considered to be the core of European legal culture.[11]

9 Reinhard Zimmermann, "Der europäische Charakter des englischen Rechts: Historische Verbindungen zwischen civil law und common law", *Zeitschrift für Europäisches Privatrecht*, 1 (1993). See also, among his many works on the matter, Id., *The Law of Obligations: Roman Foundations of the Civilian Tradition* (Cape Town: Juta, 1990), vii–xvi; and Id., "Savigny's Legacy: Legal History, Comparative Law, and the Emergence of a European Legal Science", *Law Quarterly Review*, 112 (1996), 576–605. Other works sharing this view include Patrick Glenn, "La civilisation de la common law", *Revue International de droit comparé*, 45:3 (juillet–septembre 1993); Basil S. Markesinis, *The Gradual Convergence: Foreign Ideas, Foreign Influences and English Law on the Eve of the Twenty-First Century* (Oxford: Oxford University Press, 1994); Id., *The Coming Together of the Common Law and the Civil Law* (Oxford: Oxford University Press, 2000); and Maurizio Lupoi, *Alle radici del mondo giuridico europeo: Saggio storico-comparativo* (Roma: Istituto poligrafico e zecca dello Stato, 1994). For a strong argument against this perspective, see Pier Giuseppe Monateri, Tomasz Giaro, Alessandro Somma, *Le radici comuni del diritto europeo: Un cambiamento di prospettiva* (Roma: Carocci, 2005). Douglas Osler, "The Fantasy Men", *Rechtsgeschichte*, 10 (2007), criticizes Zimmerman's view, defining as a "*historia fantástica*" and a "chimaera" the theorizing of a modern *ius commune europaeum* grounded on a supposed European legal unity (and on a uniform continental and English legal culture) embodied in the *ius commune* until the various national codifications of the nineteenth century. He argues that it fails to consider the historical reality of the religious, political, and juridical conflicts of the modern period.

10 See Oliver Remien, "Illusion und Realität eines europäischen Privatrechts", *Juristenzeitung*, 47 (1992), 277–284; and Eugen Bucher, "Recht, Geschichtlichkeit, Europa", in *Vers un droit privé européen commun?: Skizzen zum gemeineuropäischen Privatrecht*, ed. by Bruno Schmidlin (Basel: Helbing & Lichtenhahn, 1994), 7–31. Particularly important are works by Pierre Legrand: "Legal Traditions in Western Europe: The Limits of Commonality", in *Transfrontier Mobility of Law*, ed. by R. Jagtenberg, E. Örücu, A. J. De Roo (The Hague–London: Kluwer, 1995), 63–84; and "European Legal Systems are Not Converging", *International and Comparative Law Quarterly*, 45 (1996), 52–81. Legrand assumed the existence of an irreducible epistemological gulf between common law and civil law – seen as the expression of opposite legal "cultures", "mentalities", and "representations" – which would prevent real mutual understanding and reciprocal knowledge between lawyers educated within the two different legal traditions.

11 See, in particular, the recent work by Thomas Duve, "European Legal History – Concepts, Methods, Challenges", in Id., *Entanglements in Legal History: Conceptual Approaches* (Frankfurt am Main: Max Planck Institute for European Legal History, 2014), 29–66; and Id.,

So Far Yet So Near?

For different reasons and in different ways, this change in perspective involving both comparatists and legal historians has led to a gradual "opening up" and an increasing "dialogue" (in the well-known words of the great comparatist Gino Gorla[12]) between English and continental European law, which has revealed that the difference between them was smaller than had previously been thought. The traditional paradigm of the marked contrast between common law and *ius commune*, and of the completely "insular" character of English law, certainly cannot be applied *tout court* to the medieval and early modern periods.

As is well known, Roman-canon law was studied in both continental and English universities, leading to a wide circulation of students, law books, and lawyers across Europe. In England, the fundamentals of the Roman legal tradition spread from the sixth century onwards thanks to liberal arts teaching in diocesan and monastic schools, while Roman-canon law officially reached the country in the twelfth century[13]: around 1140, Vacarius, a distinguished glossator from the Bolognese school, was called to England by the Archbishop of Canterbury during a complicated ecclesiastical dispute which required reference to Roman-canon law texts. It appears that Vacarius subsequently settled in Oxford and, around the middle of the twelfth century, set up a centre for legal studies that would go on to attract a huge number of students.[14] In the 1280s he compiled a digest of the *Codex* and the *Digestum* in nine books containing the glosses from his teaching (thus introducing the *Corpus Juris* to England), which was called the *Liber pauperum* because it was a summary of Justinian work and was thus also available to less wealthy students.[15]

It was in Oxford, at the end of the twelfth century, that England's first university was founded and, during the first half of the following century (probably around 1209), the Cambridge *Studium* was also established. In addition to theology, the two universities taught Roman-canon law, with the

"Global Legal History: Setting Europe in Perspective", in *The Oxford Handbook of European Legal History*, ed. by Heikki Pihlajamäki, Markus D. Dubber, Mark Godfrey (Oxford: Oxford University Press, 2018), 116–140.

12 Gino Gorla, "L'origine e l'autorità delle raccolte di giurisprudenza", *Annuario di Diritto Comparato e di Studi Legislativi*, 44 (1970), 4–26, at 12.

13 On the presence of Roman law in England during the twelfth and thirteenth centuries, see Peter Stein, "Roman Law, Common Law and Civil Law", *Tulane Law Review*, 66 (1992), 1591–1603; John L. Barton, *Roman Law in England* (Milano: Giuffrè, 1971); and Ralph V. Turner, "Roman Law in England before the time of Bracton", *Journal of British Studies*, 15:1 (Autumn 1975), 1–25.

14 See Richard W. Southern, "Master Vacarius and the Beginning of an English Academic Tradition", in *Medieval Learning and Literature: Essays Presented to Richard William Hunt*, ed. by John G. Alexander, Margaret T. Gibson (Oxford: Clarendon Press, 1976), 257–286; and Leonard E. Boyle, "The Beginnings of Legal Studies at Oxford", *Viator*, 14 (1983), 107–132.

15 The *Liber Pauperum* has been edited by F. de Zulueta, *The Liber Pauperum of Vacarius* (London: Selden Society, 1927).

aim of preparing their students for roles not only in the Church but also in secular government.[16] This resulted in *ius commune* spreading across England throughout the Middle Ages and allowed for links to be made with the academic community in continental European universities. Many English students went to Bologna, the main medieval centre of legal studies, to study Roman-canon law. This led to the circulation and exchange of students, *doctores*, and legal texts between the island and the continent. Although Henry VIII abolished canon law teaching at Oxford and Cambridge in 1535, he maintained civil law, which, of course, included canon law, creating a Regius Professorship in that field.[17]

Furthermore, the late twelfth-century text *Tractatus de Legibus et Consuetudinibus Angliae*, which has been attributed to Ranulf de Glanvill, Chief Justice and diplomat during the reign of Henry II, is considered by some to be the first attempt to lay out English law in a theoretical manner. It was mostly concerned with real and feudal rights and was widely based on Roman-canon law.[18] More than that, the broader *Tractatus de Legibus et Consuetudinibus Angliae*, apparently dating back to the first half of the thirteenth century and traditionally attributed to Henry de Bracton, was also a systematic exposition of English law within the Roman law dogmatic structure. The author made much use of Roman legal concepts and vocabulary, with particular reference to the Gaius tripartition and to the *Corpus Iuris*, the

16 On Roman-canon law teaching at the Universities of Oxford and Cambridge between the Middle Ages and the modern period, see John L. Barton, "The Study of Civil Law before 1380", in *The History of the University of Oxford*, ed. by John I. Catto, Ralph Evans (Oxford: Oxford University Press, 1992), 281–313; James McConica, *The History of the University of Oxford*, vol. I., *The Early Oxford Schools* (Oxford: Clarendon Press, 1984); and Damian R. Leader, *A History of the University of Cambridge, I. The University to 1546* (Cambridge: Cambridge University Press, 1988), 192–201. More generally, among the many other works on the matter, see Alan B. Cobban, *The Medieval English Universities: Oxford and Cambridge to c. 1500* (Berkeley: University of California Press, 1988).

17 Leonard E. Boyle, "The Curriculum of the Faculty of Canon Law", in *Oxford Studies Presented to Daniel Callus* (Oxford: Oxford University Press, 1962), cit. in Mark Hill, "Canon Law: The Discipline of Teaching and the Teaching of the Discipline", in *Studies in Canon Law and Common Law in Honor of R.H. Helmholz*, ed. by Troy L. Harris (Berkeley: The Robbins Collection, 2015), 337–353, at 340. Boyle emphasized the central role of canon law university teaching, arguing that "competence in canon law was the goal, expertise in civil law the means". See also Id., "Canon Law before 1380", in *The History of the University of Oxford*, ed. by Catto and Evans, 531–564; and Dorothy M. Owen, *The Medieval Canon Law: Teaching, Literature and Transmission* (Cambridge: Cambridge University Press, 1990).

18 See G.D.G. Hall, "Introduction to Glanvill", in Id., *The Treatise on the Laws and Customs of the Realm of England Commonly Called Glanvill* (London: Nelson & Sons, 1965), 36–40. For a different point of view, see John Hudson, *The Formation of the English Common Law: Law and Society in England from King Alfred to Magna Carta* (New York: Routledge, 1996), 150. Hudson held that Roman law's influence on Glanvill was limited to its structure and some vocabulary. Glanvill was edited by George E. Woodbine, *De Legibus et consuetudinibus Angliae* (New Haven: Yale University Press, 1932).

Decretum, and the Azo *Summa*.[19] It is thus a further demonstration of the Roman legal presence influence in England during this period.

In relation to the courts, between the Middle Ages and the early modern period the Great Tribunals were at work both in Great Britain and on the continent, while the collections of their decisions circulated widely between European countries. John Baker has written that "by the sixteenth century there was more law reporting on the Continent than in the home of the common law".[20] On the one hand, the existence of a "judicial" element (in a broad sense) in the *jus commune* tradition has been emphasized, with legal historians alleging that the continental supreme courts' decisions were binding and spread through Europe by the prestigious and widely circulated collections of *decisiones*. On the other hand, a "doctrinal" element (again, in a broad sense) has been recognized within medieval and early modern English reports, seen as the product of the "commen erudycion", the common learning shared by all members of the legal profession.

It is also clear that in England Roman-canon law was known not only by civilians, but also by common lawyers. Even Edward Coke himself had a collection of *ius commune* books in his library[21], and there are references to Roman-canon law and to civilians' opinions in some medieval and early modern reports of cases discussed before the common law courts at Westminster and in the readings debated at the Inns of Courts and in the statutes. This proves some familiarity with or, at least, some opening towards *ius commune* by common lawyers.

The Role of Canon Law

From the 1970s onwards, various scholars, mostly Americans or continental Europeans, have highlighted the points of contact between canon law and

19 See these classics: Frederic W. Maitland, *Select Passages from the Works of Bracton and Azo* (London: The Selden Society, 1895); Paul Vinogradoff, "The Roman Elements in Bracton's Tratise", *Yale Law Journal*, 32 (1923), 751–756; George E. Woodbine, "The Roman Element in Bracton's de Adquirendo Rerum Dominio", *Yale Law Journal*, 31:8 (Jun. 1922), 827–847; Hermann Kantorowicz, *Bractonian Problems* (Cambridge: Cambridge University Press, 1941), 58–78; and Samuel E. Thorne, *Introduction* to Henry de Bracton, *On the Laws and Customs of England* (Cambridge: Harvard University Press, 1968). More recently, see John L. Barton, "The Mystery of Bracton", *Journal of Legal History*, 14:3 (1993), 1–142; and David J. Seipp, "Bracton, the Year Books, and the Transformation of Elementary Legal Ideas in the Early Common Law", *Law and History Review*, 7 (1989), 175–217. That Bracton knew canon law and was influenced by William de Drogheda, a professor at Oxford who was his contemporary (and possibly his teacher), was proved by Henry G. Richardson, "Azo, Drogheda and Bracton", *English Historical Review*, 22 (1944), 22–47.

20 John H. Baker, *Judicial Records, Law Reports and the Growth of Case Law* (Berlin: Dunker & Humblot, 1989), 6.

21 William O. Hassall, *A Catalogue of the Library of Sir Edward Coke* (New Haven: Yale University Press, 1950).

common law.[22] They have argued that the former was pervasive within some branches of English law, and not only in the Middle Ages.[23] Administered by the ecclesiastical courts from the end of the twelfth century onwards, they pointed out that canon law was the first international rational and scientific legal system involving every aspect of human life, both private and public, as well as the structure of society itself, and it was characterized by the same dynamics everywhere. It formed a vital part of the Western legal tradition – common law included – thanks to the fundamental doctrinal work of the canonists at a time of intense intellectual and legal activity.[24] It played a central role in regulating many aspects of everyday social and economic life all over Europe, and the regulation of many fundamental legal principles and institutes of English law developed within this legal culture, retaining strong traces of the role played by *ius commune*. Thus, canon law, taught in all European universities and applied in the ecclesiastical courts of all European countries, was part and parcel of the English legal system.

There are many examples of this common legal culture, especially in the Middle Ages: between the twelfth and thirteenth centuries, there was increasing interest in Gratian's work in England; from the twelfth century onwards, several collections of papal decretals circulated through the kingdom; and there were canon law schools not only in Oxford, but also in Exeter, Northampton, Lincoln, London, and, probably, Durham and York.[25] At the same time, canon lawyers, within an autonomous and productive law school, appeared to

22 Already at the end of the nineteenth century Frederic William Maitland had highlighted the importance of canon law for the medieval English church in an essay that would lead to a famous dispute between him and William Stubbs. See Frederic W. Maitland, *Roman Canon Law in the Church of England* (Cambridge: Cambridge University Press, 1898); and William Stubbs, *The History of Canon Law in England* (Oxford: Oxford University Press, 1900). For a re-reading of his view, see Charles Donahue, "Roman Canon Law in the Medieval English Church: Stubbs vs. Maitland Re-examined after 75 Years in the Light of Some Records from the Church Courts", *Michigan Law Review*, 72:4 (Mar. 1974), 647–716.

23 I refer, in particular, to an essay by William W. Bassett, "Canon Law and the Common Law", *Hastings Law Journal*, 4 (1978). The author took inspiration from a study by the American legal historian George E. Woodbine, "The Origins of the Action of Trespass", *Yale Law Journal*, 33–34 (1924–25).

24 In "Canon law", 1385 Bassett writes: "Common law and its institutions owe an incalculable amount to an international legal culture that developed in the Middle Ages and to the creative genius of the canonists who were a significant part of that culture". Recalling Berman, Bassett also argued that "it would be a serious distortion of historical facts to imagine that the common law developed within the feast of the island fortress tutored by a supposedly singular English genius" (1386--88).

25 See Charles Duggan, *Twelfth-Century Decretal Collections and Their Importance in English History* (London: Athlone Press, 1963); Id., "The Reception of Canon Law in England in the Later-Twelfth Century", in *Proceedings of the Second International Congress of Medieval Canon Law*, ed. by Stephan Kuttner, Joseph J. Ryan (Civitate Vaticana: Biblioteca Apostolica Vaticana, 1965), 359–390; Id., *Canon Law in Medieval England: The Beckett Dispute and Decretal Collections* (London: Variorum, 1982); Stephan Kuttner, Eleanor Rathbone, "Anglo-Norman Canonists of the Twelfth Century", *Traditio*, 7 (1949–51), 279–358; and the older,

play a significant role in developing and diffusing knowledge of canon law in the country. It was impossible to ignore canon law's contribution to constitutional law, criminal law, and private law, even to the point that it was stated that "noone can understand either medieval society or the medieval formation of the common law without a familiarity with the work of the canonists".[26]

Traditional English legal historiography usually held that common lawyers were hostile to the *ius commune*: they argued that "Roman law was by Tudor time an unintelligible and outlandish thing, perhaps good enough law for half-starved Frenchmen",[27] while the typical common lawyer "knew nothing and cared nothing for any system but his own".[28] However, studies of the printed law reports (*Year Books* and *Reports*) between the fourteenth and the seventeenth centuries show they contain plenty of references to Roman-canon law and to civilians' and canonists' *opiniones*, not to mention the frequent use of Latin maxims and definitions coming from *ius commune* sources. This has revealed that common lawyers "were neither 'wholly ignorant' of civil law and canon law, nor 'completely insular' in their professional outlook".[29] This undermines the so-called enemy theory, in which English judges and lawyers considered canonists and civilians to be enemies with which to fight for legal and political supremacy in the kingdom, despising Roman law for its association with continental despotism and canon law for its connection to the papacy and the Catholic hierarchies.[30]

In fact, common lawyers knew Roman law's norms, often exchanged views with civilians in doubtful cases which required extensive knowledge of

but still important, Samuel E. Thorne, "Le droit canonique en Angleterre", *Revue historique de droit français et étranger*, 4s., 13:3 (1934), 499–513.

26 Bassett, "Canon Law", 1419.

27 Frederic W. Maitland, Francis C. Montague, *A Sketch of English Legal History* (New York: Putnam, 1915), 110.

28 Frederic W. Maitland, "Why the History of English Law Is Not Written", in Id., *The Collected Papers*, vol. I (Cambridge: Cambridge University Press, 1911), 488.

29 See David J. Seipp, "The Reception of Canon Law and Civil Law in the Common Law Courts before 1600", in *Oxford Journal of Legal Studies*, 13:3 (Autumn 1993), 388–420. He writes: "English common law practitioners and judges borrowed much of the conceptual structure of their body of legal knowledge from the legal culture of Continental Europe over the centuries", 388.

30 According to Mario Caravale in his essay "Lo spartiacque tra *ius commune* e *common law*" (in *Relations between the ius commune and English Law*, ed. by Richard H. Helmholz, Vito Piergiovanni (Soveria Mannelli: Rubbettino, 2009), 55–64, at 56), common lawyers did not understand the *ius commune* as opposed to English law. He argues that the English legal doctrine of the early modern period appears to be fully aware of its validity in the kingdom, although it was applied by different courts from those in Westminster. Similarly Paul Brand, in a study of the *reports* of the thirteenth and fourteenth centuries ("The Common Lawyers of the Reign of Edward I and the Canon Law", *Studies in Canon Law*, 28 (2007), 27–40, at 35), stressed that, despite the different education, skills, and language of common lawyers and canonists they were not completely separate: "even if these were different worlds, they were not, and could not be, worlds hermetically sealed from one another".

Roman-canon law, and quoted Roman and canon law printed texts. Far from being distrustful or contemptuous, their attitude was respectful and open.[31] In fact, although they never considered Roman-canon law a binding authority or a superior legal model, common lawyers often made reference – more frequently than was traditionally thought – to the continental legal tradition when it could help to support their arguments or clarify their thought. They thus adapted it to the local needs at the time, creating what has been called "a fruitful interaction between the two systems".[32] This is argued to have contributed to the entry into England of new forms of legal thought, which were the typical forms of the learned and prestigious law in force across the continent, that would go on to affect common law's organization and system, paving the way for the treatises of the seventeenth and eighteenth centuries, up to the *Commentaries on the Laws of England* by William Blackstone.[33]

These first studies, however well documented and detailed, appeared "eccentric" and isolated from the traditional interpretation based on the dichotomy between common and continental legal traditions. Among these studies, of particular note are those of Richard Helmholz, an American legal historian, who, interested in the comparison between common law and *ius commune*, from the 1990s onwards, began to pose the question as to whether *ius commune* and common law should be considered "historical strangers" or "companions".[34] He argued that despite the dogmas of traditional scholarship, there were never any "absolute barriers" between the two legal systems, and "*ius commune* (…) ha[d] undoubtedly played a role in the history of England and in the development of Anglo-American law" within a common European legal tradition.[35] Although they were not experts in it, common

31 According to Seipp, "The Reception", 414, there was "greater receptivity to civil law and canon law than legal historians' accounts of English insularity and hostility would predict".

32 See Brand, "The Common Lawyers": "the justices and lawyers did indeed approach the canon law and the procedure of the canon law courts not with total ignorance or hostility, but with some degree of understanding and, on occasion, a willingness to incorporate ideas and concepts from the canon law when they could be useful", 40.

33 See Seipp, "The Reception", 419. Also see Peter Stein, "English Civil Law Literature", in "*Ins Wasser geworfen und Ozeane durchquert", Festschrift für Knut Wolfgang Nörr*, ed. by Mario Ascheri, Friedrich Ebel, Martin Heckel (Köln: Böhlau Verlag, 2003), 979–992, here 990.

34 Richard H. Helmholz, "Continental Law and Common Law: Historical Strangers or Companions?", *Duke Law Journal*, 6 (1990), 1207–1228. The author considered the imminent admission of the United Kingdom into the European Union as giving hope for further unity in the future, a hope that has today been crushed by Brexit. He argued that it would have influenced law and the courts, creating a revival, although in a different form, of a reality that had existed in the past.

35 Richard H. Helmholz, *The Ius Commune in England: Four Studies* (Oxford: Oxford University Press, 2001), 3. According to Javier Martínez-Torrón, *Anglo-American Law and Canon Law: Canonical Roots of the Common Law Tradition* (Berlin: Duncker & Humblot, 1998), the "time factor" played an important role in avoiding the reception of *ius commune* in England, as common law had already reached an advanced state of development by the twelfth century, following the early centralization and modernization of the English legal system, while *ius*

lawyers knew of continental law and referred to it when the need arose. The difference between the two systems thus never appeared to English lawyers as "an absolute and unbridgeable gulf".[36] In conclusion, although "in many areas there was always a divide between the English common law and the *ius commune*, it was never so wide that lawyers could not look across it".[37]

This led Helmholz to wonder if canon law could be considered the main means of connection and integration between the English and continental legal traditions. It is true that canon law and common law had their roots in different sources: the former in the *Corpus iuris canonici* and the latter in custom. They were engaged in different jurisdictional spheres *ratione materiae* and were administered by different categories of lawyers: the former by civilians and the latter by common lawyers, who acted in the ecclesiastical courts and in the Westminster courts, respectively. They were also taught in different places in different ways: the former at the universities, through the study of Roman-canon law texts,[38] and the latter at the London Inns of Court, through training mostly centred on practical exercises – readings and moots – and on law reporting in Westminster courts.[39] Their language was

commune in the same years was just starting to be elaborated in the medieval continental universities and could thus not yet have any great influence over English legal practice. This was also before the ecclesiastical legal courts adopted Roman-canon law procedure, which was developed between the twelfth and thirteenth centuries (this is the famous thesis by Raoul C. Van Caenegem, *The Birth of the English Common Law* (Cambridge: Cambridge University Press, 1989), 108), "the Anglo-American legal tradition has more elements in common with continental law than is frequently believed".

36 Helmholz, "Continental Law", 1226.

37 Helmholz, *The Ius Commune*, 6.

38 Richard H. Helmholz, "The Education of English Proctors, 1400–1640", in *Learning the Law: Teaching and Transmission of Law in England, 1150–1900*, ed. by Jonathan A. Bush, Alain Wijffels (Rio Grande: Hambledon Press, 1999), 191–210. Helmholz argued that civilians' education, with particular reference to proctors working in the ecclesiastical courts, consisted not only of study of Roman-canon law texts but also of treatises and of practical training in court, which differed less from common lawyers' education than was traditionally thought. See also Thomas Morrisey, "The Art of Teaching and Learning Law: A Late Medieval Tract", *History of Universities*, 7 (1989), 28–74.

39 The origins, organization, and workings of the Inns of Court and Chancery have been studied in these fundamental works by John H. Baker: *The Third University of England, The Inns of Court and the Common-Law Tradition* (London: Selden Society, 1990); *The Legal Profession and the Common Law: Historical Essays* (London and Ronceverte: Hambledon Press, 1986), 3–74; *The Common Law Tradition: Lawyers, Books and the Law* (London and Rio Grande: Hambledon Press, 2000), 29; and, with a more general *excursus* on legal education in London between the thirteenth and fourteenth centuries, *Legal Education in London, 1250–1850* (London: Selden Society, 2007). See also Walter C. Richardson, *A History of the Inns of Court, with Special Reference to the Period of the Renaissance* (London: Baton Rouge, 1978). In relation to the Inns of Court during the Tudor and Stuart ages, see Wilfred R. Prest, *The Inns of Court under Elizabeth I and the Early Stuarts, 1590–1640* (London: Longman, 1972); and, for the period between the end of the seventeenth century and the first half of the eighteenth century, see David Lemmings, *Gentlemen and Barristers: The Inns of Court and the English Bar, 1680–1730* (Oxford: Clarendon Press, 1990).

also different: Latin for the canonists, Law French (or Anglo-Norman, a mix of French, English, and Latin) for the common lawyers. On the other hand, with time the common law courts expanded their jurisdiction into areas that were traditionally the exclusive competence of the ecclesiastical courts (such as defamation, wills, and dowries). And, as we have already pointed out, there were frequent professional contacts between civilians and common lawyers, and English lawyers were familiar with Roman-canon law texts. What is more, the procedure followed by the Court of Chancery was based on Roman-canon law, and the lord chancellors were all churchmen until 1529 (when Thomas More was appointed) and, consequently, experts in canon law. In conclusion, an objective examination of the two legal traditions reveals not only a connection between canon law and common law, but also – and more importantly – the former possibly acting as "a unifying link (...), a force working for unity between England and the Continent".[40]

Canon law had a long history in England: there were frequent exchanges with the continent and a mingling between secular and spiritual powers even during the Anglo-Saxon period; it became part and parcel of the English legal system from the thirteenth century; and it played a central role between the thirteenth century and the reign of Elizabeth I thanks to the establishment of university teaching along the continental model. The continued validity of canon law was evident in the founding of the Doctors' Commons – the society of English civilians – at the end of the fifteenth century, the increase in the activity of civilians and the extension of and specialization in ecclesiastical jurisdiction.

Neither did the Reformation's breach with Rome sweep away "the heritage of the *ius commune* in England". The Church legal system, far from being abandoned, remained stable[41]: most of the canon law norms inherited from the Middle Ages continued to be applied in the spiritual courts, while only the rules affirming papal authority or contrary to the statutes enacted by Parliament were eliminated.[42] Despite the abolition of papal jurisdiction following Henry

40 Richard H. Helmholz, "Canon Law as a Means of Legal Integration in the Development of English Law", in *Die Bedeutung des Kanonischen Rechts für die Entwicklung einheitlicher Rechtsprinzipien*, ed. by Heinrich Scholler (Baden-Baden: Nomos Verlagsgesellschaft, 1996), 49–68, here 51.

41 Richard H. Helmholz, "Ecclesiastical Lawyers and the English Reformation", *Ecclesistical Law Journal*, 3:17 (July 1995), 360–370, at 369. See also Id., *The Oxford History of the Laws of England*, vol. I, *The Canon Law and Ecclesiastical Jurisdiction from 597 to the 1640s* (Oxford: Oxford University Press, 2004), 147; Id., *The Ius Commune*, 9.

42 Richard H. Helmholz, "Canon Law in Post-Reformation England", in Id., *Canon Law in Protestant Lands* (Berlin: Dunker & Humblot, 1992), 203–221; and Id., *Roman Canon Law in Reformation England* (Cambridge: University Press, 1990). The latter pointed out, through an examination of ecclesiastical law treatises, case reports discussed in the ecclesiastical courts and civilians' opinions, that "substantial numbers of Englishmen continued to make frequent use of the canon law even after the breach with Rome", 204.

VIII's prohibition on appealing cases in Rome,[43] canon law continued to have a broad influence in the kingdom, its norms were sanctioned by custom and considered to be in accordance with the Holy Scripture.[44] The connection between English civilians and lawyers on the continent was never broken, rightly placing the former in the European tradition of *ius commune*.[45] This made possible a reciprocal relationship and exchange between canon law and common law, allowing English lawyers to draw from the valuable normative background of *ius commune*, thus affecting common law's own development.[46] Finally, contrary to what is held by some scholars – according to whom canon law lost all importance in England after the break with the papacy[47] – its role

43 *Statute 24 Henry VIII*, c. 12, 1533; and *Statute 25 Henry VIII*, c. 19, 1534, both in *The Statutes of the Realm*, vol. III (London, 1810–28), 428 and 460.

44 James A. Brundage, in *Medieval Canon Law* (London: Longman, 1995), argued that in England "medieval canon law remained a notable force long after the break with Rome", in a process of "remarkable continuity", 182. Brian Outhwaite is of the same opinion in *The Rise and Fall of the English Ecclesiastical Courts, 1500–1860* (Cambridge: Cambridge University Press, 2006), 15.

45 Helmholz, *Roman Canon Law*, 195. Helmholz, "Canon Law in Post-Reformation England", 209, claimed that "most changes were less than revolutionary". See similar positions in Ralph Houlbrooke, "The Decline of Ecclesiastical Jurisdiction under the Tudors", in *Continuity and Change: Personnel and Administration of the Church in England 1500–1642*, ed. by Rosemary O'Day, Felicity Heal (Leicester: Leicester University Press, 1976), 239–257; Outhwaite, *The Rise and Fall*; William R. Jones, "Relations of the Two Jurisdictions: Conflict and Cooperation in England during the 13th and 14th Centuries", *Studies in Medieval and Renaissance History*, 7 (1970), 77–210; Seipp, "The Reception", 391. According to Robert E. Rodes, *Ecclesiastical Administration in Medieval England: The Anglo-Saxons to the Reformation* (Notre Dame: University of Notre Dame Press, 1977), xi–xii; and Id., *Lay Authority and Reformation in the English Church: Edward I to the Civil War* (Notre Dame: University of Notre Dame Press, 1982), 107, "the Church of England after the Reformation was the same institution as the Church of England before the Reformation".

46 Richard H. Helmholz, *Canon Law and the Law of England* (London and Ronceverte: Hambledon Press, 1987), 1–20, defined the *ius commune* as "a source of continued interchange of thought and practice" (11), highlighting the presence of "a movement back and forth, to the enrichment of both the canon and English common law" (20). See also Martínez-Torrón, *Anglo-American Law*, 185, who talks about a real "legal osmosis" between the English and continental legal traditions.

47 According to Richard J. Schoeck, "Canon Law in England on the Eve of the Reformation", *Medieval Studies*, 25 (1963), 125–147, the break with Rome resulted in a sudden interruption in the usage of canon law in England and a rapid decline in its importance. Christopher Haigh also argued that this schism caused the ecclesiastical courts' decadence in "Anticlericalism and the English Reformation", in Id., *The English Reformation Revised* (Oxford: Oxford University Press, 1987), 391–407; and Id., *English Reformation: Religion, Politics and Society under the Tudors* (Oxford: Clarendon Press, 1993). On the fight against the church courts, see Geoffrey R. Elton, "The Commons' Supplication of 1532: Parliamentary Manouvres in the Reign of Henry VIII", *English History Review*, 66:261 (Oct. 1951), 507–534. See also, for a more general picture, John J. Scarisbrick, *The Reformation and the English People* (Oxford: Basil Blackwell, 1984). A milder position can be found in Ralph Houlbrooke, *Church Courts and the People during the English Reformation, 1520–1570* (Oxford: Oxford University Press, 1979).

in English legal culture remained unchanged, with most of its norms applied up until the nineteenth century.

Conclusions and Prospects

According to the most recent historiographical interpretation of canon law in England, it had an undeniable impact on the elaboration of some common law branches. These include constitutional law, private law, and criminal law and procedure, and it even influenced some aspects of property law and contract law traditionally considered autochthonous. There are thus strong traces of the role played by canon law in the development of all of these branches. There is a partial overlap in many areas of common law and *ius commune*, which would be more clearly revealed through a comparative study free from historiographical prejudice. Whereas continental law clearly affected the law of testaments and of marriage in England – the similarities here are, in fact, widely accepted and easily identifiable – in other common law branches its influence is less immediately evident. However, a closer look reveals a common approach and some parallels [48]: even in these cases. For instance, some institutes that were traditionally considered to be typically English (such as sanctuary[49]) have unexpected points of contact and analogies with continental law, offering legal historians a potentially enormous field of research. Of course, this does not mean that English fundamental legal concepts did not have their own peculiar characteristics autonomous of the *ius commune* tradition, or that there were no differences between them. It simply shows that there were points of intersection, exchange, communication, and borrowing between the two systems. In conclusion, the many examples of connection, overlap, and similarity between English common law and *ius commune* weaken the role of the apparent differences. The more we go back in time, the more

48 For references to *ius commune* norms, see Richard H. Helmholz, "Origins of the Privilege against Self-Incrimination: The Role of the European 'Ius commune'", *New York University Law Review*, 65 (1990), 962–990; Id., "The Roman Law of Guardianship in England, 1300–1600", *Tulane Law Review*, 52 (1978), 223–257; Id., *Marriage Litigation in Medieval England* (Cambridge: Cambridge University Press, 1974); Charles Donahue, "Proof by Witnesses in the Church Courts of Medieval England: An Imperfect Reception of the Learned Law", in *On the Laws and Customs of England: Essays in Honor of Samuel E. Thorne*, ed. by Morris S. Arnold, Thomas A. Green, Sally A. Scully (Chapel Hill: University of North Carolina Press, 1981), 127–158; and Id., "Lyndwood+s Gloss *propriarum uxorum*: Marital Property and the *Ius commune* in Fifteenth-Century England", in *Europäisches Rechtsdenken in Geschichte und Gegenwart: Festschrift für Helmut Coing zum 70. Geburtstag*, ed. by Norbert Horn, Klaus Luig, Alfred Söllner (München: Beck, 1982), 19–37.

49 On the origins, discipline, and evolution of sanctuary, with particular reference to the role played by canon law in its development, see Dolores Freda, "Il diritto d'asilo in Inghilterra tra medio evo ed età moderna: una ricognizione critica", *Rivista internazionale di diritto comune*, 31 (2020), 293–320.

the differences (undeniable, but very often overemphasized) appear to get weaker, while the (frequently overlooked) similarities get stronger.

Nevertheless, the traditional assumption of a division between the two legal traditions had serious and long-lasting effects. One of the drawbacks of this presumed dichotomy was the rise – until recently and with a few well-known exceptions – of a sort of mutual distrust and a lack of interest by continental European legal historians in English law and by their English colleagues in *ius commune*. This attitude has greatly influenced research, discouraging studies on their points of contact. At least up until the end of the twentieth century, legal historians mainly focused on the history of their own legal tradition, without considering the system at the other side of the Channel. On the rare occasions when this has happened, they have often assumed polemical tones against the other legal system: English legal historians have praised the autonomy of common law from *ius commune*; and their continental European colleagues have emphasized the "insularity" and atypical and eccentric character of English law in respect to the European legal tradition.[50]

Some of the assumptions arising from the traditional view have still not really been challenged by the new approach. Indeed, over time, the emphasis on the differences between the two traditions has become so deeply rooted in the European legal consciousness that it has been projected backward, prejudicing the evaluation and the understanding of their peculiar features and giving rise to misleading oversimplifications. Taking for granted the opposition between common law and *ius commune*, legal historians have often made recourse to the category of "influence" to try to understand which tradition conditioned (or even prevailed over) the other. Finally, the traditional assumption of a deep and irreducible distance between the two traditions, which was completely taken for granted, has framed the reconstruction and narration of the history of European law,[51] simplifying the picture and preventing European normative pluralism and jurisdictional complexity from being properly taken into consideration.

There has clearly been an exponential growth in comparative legal history in the last two decades, with the creation of the European Society for Comparative Legal History in 2009 and its journal *Comparative Legal History* in 2013, signalling the emergence of comparative legal history as an autonomous discipline. But this approach needs to be expanded still further. It could be argued that the continental legal education of the author of this chapter necessarily affects the interpretation of the past, leading to an overestimation

50 See Luigi Moccia, "English Law Attitudes to the 'Civil Law'", *Journal of Legal History*, 2 (1981), 157–168.

51 For example, in *Judges, Legislators, Professors,* Van Caenegem stresses these differences, writing: "no half measures prevailed: the differences are fundamental", 2; "their very substance was different", 113; "common law was so different", 119; and "these legal systems [...] always remained alien to each other" (Id., *An Historical Introduction to Private Law* (Cambridge: Cambridge University Press, 1992)).

of the role played by Roman-canon law within the common law tradition. That is certainly possible, but, at the same time, although the lenses of the legal tradition in which we are educated are impossible to throw off completely, a civilian perspective could help to throw light on legal assumptions that are invisible to or taken for granted by the common lawyer as a result of their own education.

Further research, emancipated from the ideological distortions and biases of the tradition, is needed to have a more correct, complete, and balanced interpretation of the history of European law and the law of its different regions. Only through an approach that critiques the traditional view[52] can English legal history be placed within a genuinely European dimension, opening up new and exciting avenues for research. As has been argued in this chapter, a correct study of European legal history requires a "de-ideologization of the historic problem of the relationship between the two traditions",[53] and European legal history must be freed from the suffocating historiographical layers which ended up concealing its real scope and genuine meaning. At present this task is no longer about finding already ascertained contact points between the two legal traditions, but, in times of dramatic legal and political transition when centrifugal forces seem to threaten the very foundations of the European edifice (the *vulnus* of Brexit being only the most obvious example), about critically deconstructing the traditional narratives, which are affected by ideological biases and prejudice, in order to achieve a more balanced historical interpretation and to enhance European legal culture.

52 On the myth of English law's "splendid isolation", see Kenneth Pennington, "Learned Law, Droit Savant, Gelehrtes Recht: The Tyranny of a Concept", *Rivista internazionale di diritto comune*, 5 (1994), 205–215. He questions Maitland's view on the insularity and exceptionality of common law, the absence of any recourse to *ius commune* by English lawyers, and its irrelevance to the development of law beyond the Channel.

53 Mario Ascheri, "*Common law/ius commune* tra dottrina e storia", in Helmholz and Piergiovanni, *Relations*, 52 (author's translation).

7 Legal Pluralism in the Law Courts of Early Modern England

Sir John Baker

Dr Arthur Duck's treatise *De Usu et Authoritate Iuris Civilis Romanorum* contains (perhaps surprisingly) a section on England. In that section, Duck – a practising civilian advocate who died in 1648[1] – took issue with French authors who had written that the civil law was not used in England. He pointed out that it *was* used in England, in the Admiralty and the ecclesiastical courts, and he also noted that it had influenced early writers on the common law such as "Glanvill" (in the late twelfth century) and "Bracton" (in the early to mid-thirteenth century).[2] But he was careful to add the major qualification that, in his own time, "Judgments given according to pure English law have nothing in common with the *ius civile* of the Romans", and that when *casus omissi* or ambiguities were found in English law, recourse was not had to the *ius civile* – as elsewhere in Europe – but to the judges' own gut feelings ("suo arbitrio et conscientiae").[3]

Before going any further, it should be explained that the term "civil law" in sixteenth- and seventeenth-century England was understood to include not only ancient Roman law and the later *ius commune*, but also (and most often) the canon law. The explanation is that in England no degrees in canon law were awarded after 1540. The advocates in the ecclesiastical courts were

1 See R.H. Helmholz, *The Profession of Ecclesiastical Lawyers: An Historical Introduction* (Cambridge: Cambridge University Press, 2019), 145–150. The treatise *De Usu* was published posthumously.

2 The historical Ranulf de Glanvill and Henry de Bracton (Bratton) are no longer considered the authors of the books which bear their names. Duck thought Bracton was a professor of Roman law ("*juris Caesarei*") at Oxford, but the supposed connection with Oxford was probably the result of misreading Exonia (Exeter) as Oxonia, an error which may be traced back to John Bale (d. 1563).

3 Arthur Duck, *De Usu & Authoritate Juris Civilis Romanorum* (London, Richard Hodkinsonne, 1653), fols. 146v–147 (free translation by the present writer).

DOI: 10.4324/9781003425069-10

almost always known as civilians,[4] their doctorates being in civil law,[5] but in their daily practice they were mainly concerned with canon law.

It should also be explained that classical canon law remained current in England after the Church of England's break with Rome in 1533–34. It was not received without qualification, but the supremacy of Parliament over papal canon law was not a change brought about by Henry VIII. It was, no doubt, contrary to canon law as perceived in Rome for any part of it to be adjusted by secular authority; but that had long been the practice in England. There were several medieval acts of Parliament contradicting particular points of canon law, and English kings had exercised various functions in relation to the English Church[6] which in other countries were exercised by the pope. For instance, a statute of 1351 had accused the pope of "accroaching" to himself a power of presenting clergy to benefices, contrary to the law of England, and giving them to aliens who never set foot in England.[7] Likewise a statute of 1393 had complained of interferences by the papal curia "to the open disinheritance of the crown, and the destruction of the regality of our said lord the king, his law, and all his realm, if a remedy is not provided".[8] Encroachments by Church courts, whether or not they were acting in accordance with the canon law, were routinely restrained by the king's common law courts through writs of prohibition. However, although canon law emanating from Rome was seen as being in some sense foreign, no one questioned the general proposition that papal decretals and the *Corpus Iuris Canonici* were a principal source of canon law throughout Christendom. And that remained true after 1534, even though their study was dropped from the curricula at Oxford and Cambridge. It was enacted that commissioners should review the former provincial canons and constitutions and prune away those which were no longer worthy to be obeyed, with the express proviso that until the revision was carried out all those which were "not contrariant nor repugnant to the laws, statutes, and customs of this realm, nor to the damage or hurt of the king's prerogative

4 A rare exception is *Lewis* v. *Rochester* (1608) in London, British Library [BL] MS. Harley 4817, fol. 192 ("jour fuit done al Civillians et cannonists destre icy"). The civilians and canonists were, nevertheless, the same people.

5 In Oxford the doctorate in law is still called the D.C.L. (Doctor of Civil Law). In Cambridge it has for the last century or two been abbreviated as LL.D., which echoes the old doctorate of both laws; but in the university statutes it is Doctor of Law in the singular, and the words of admission are "ad gradum doctoris in iure".

6 The *ecclesia anglicana* mentioned in Magna Carta (1215), clause 1, and subsequent statutes, had always been distinguished from the *ecclesia romana*. But both were part of the one catholic Church, and to this day the Church of England considers itself part of the catholic Church in parallel to the Roman Catholic branch.

7 Statute of Provisors, 25 Edw. III, stat. 4. Printed English statutes and law reports (other than modern scholarly editions) are cited in this chapter using the standard legal abbreviations. A guide may be found in P. Osborn, *A Concise Law Dictionary for Students and Practitioners*, 12th ed. by M. G. Woodley (London: Sweet & Maxwell, 2013).

8 Statute of Winchester (Statute of Praemunire), 16 Ric. II, c. 5.

royal" should continue in use.[9] Since the revision never was carried out, the old law remained in force under the terms of the proviso. The wording of the proviso applied only to provincial and synodal canons and constitutions, but, in practice, a similar approach was taken to papal decretals, in as much as the law embodied in them remained in force except where it was held contrary to English law.[10] There was no alternative: it was the only ecclesiastical law there was, and the Church of England was part of the catholic (universal) Church. The jurisprudence could be seen after 1534 as having achieved an intellectual independence from the authority under which it was first created, just as the authority of Roman law could be accepted as an autonomous body of jurisprudence without acknowledging the supremacy of the Holy Roman Empire.[11] At any rate, the ecclesiastical courts continued to function in the same way as before, following much the same law, though they were now in a sense the king's courts applying the "king's ecclesiastical laws of this realm".[12]

The sense of foreignness nevertheless persisted. As was said in 1587, "There is yet another law in England but none of England, or at least not proper to England: I mean the Civil and canon laws".[13] According to Robert Hitcham, king's serjeant at law, "the common law, being the general law of England, has power to control the ecclesiastical law, which – though it be the law of England – is still only the particular law of England and brought in by permission, and therefore subject like a younger brother to the control of the common law, which is the elder brother".[14] As was foreseen in 1534, the old law was increasingly overtaken by legislation, both from Parliament and from Convocation, so that by 1700 it could be said by a lord chief justice that half the law in Lyndwode's *Provinciale* – the principal commentary on the canon law as it operated in late medieval England – was no longer the law of the land.[15] It will be noticed that the lord chief justice considered the other half of Lyndwode still to be the law of the land. The waning of its authority since the fifteenth century had little if anything to do with the jurisdictional schism, still less with the theological Reformation; rather, it was the result of the natural

9 Submission of the Clergy 1534 (25 Hen. VIII, c. 19). Cf. 3 & 4 Edw. VI, c. 11, which empowered the commissioners to review the "ecclesiastical laws" generally, but without a similar proviso; this was also ineffective. The Act of Supremacy 1559 (1 Eliz. 1, c. 1) was held not to have taken away or altered the canon law: *Cawdrye* v. *Atton* (1595) in *Reports from the Notebooks of Edward Coke*, ed. by Sir John Baker (London: Selden Society, vols. 136–142, in progress), vol. 3, 619.

10 Sir Edward Coke (d. 1634) understood the proviso to refer to all pre-1534 canon law: *The Fourth Part of the Institutes* (London: W. Lee and D. Pakeman, 1644), 323.

11 R.H. Helmholz, *Roman Canon Law in Reformation England* (Cambridge: Cambridge University Press, 1990), 149–157.

12 *Caudrey's Case* (1595) 5 Co. Rep., part 1, fols. 9, 32v.

13 Anon., "De Legibus Angliae", in BL MS. Harley 5265, fol. 198 (translated).

14 *Case of Commendams* (1616) in *Calthorpe's Reports*, BL MS. Hargrave 386, fol. 14 (translated).

15 *R.* v. *Raines* (1698) 1 Ld Raym. 368, *per* Holt CJ.

process of evolution and adaptation to which all mature systems of law are subject. It would have been equally true to say that less than half the content of the medieval books of common law was still the law of the land. The canon law had survived as law in England; and it had done so because it was administered as a living entity by a separate profession.

How, then, should Dr Duck's assertion be understood? He was quite right to state that recourse to the *ius civile* was not a normal feature of the common law itself. However, he understated his case when he said that recourse was *never* had by common law judges to Roman law. Like all lawyers, judges liked to find legal authorities, even if (*faute de mieux*) they happened to be Roman, to reinforce their innate sense of what was right.[16] In that very limited sense, Roman law had a residuary role – albeit not a peremptory or an extensive one – in filling gaps. This approach was not fundamentally different from that in continental countries, according to the contemporary observations of Sir Edward Coke,[17] Lord Ellesmere,[18] and John Selden.[19] The difference was only one of scale. If recourse to Roman doctrines and procedures was more limited in England than elsewhere, the reason was that common lawyers were not formally trained in Roman law and were not familiar with its intricacies. Most of the substantive Roman law they encountered came via the canon law, typically mediated by *Bracton* (printed in 1569), though there are also occasional examples of direct citation of continental literature. For instance, when Coke invented a doctrine that the ownership of funeral monuments set up in churches belonged to the heirs of the person commemorated, he relied on a passage in Barthélemy de Chasseneuz treatise on the customs of Burgundy (1528), which, in turn, discussed the *actio iniuriarum*.[20] Though atypical, it is an interesting example for two reasons. First, it shows that one of England's greatest early modern jurists saw nothing incongruous in citing continental and Roman law when it suited him. Second, and more importantly, it shows

16 Roman law can still be cited in English courts in very rare cases where there is no English authority in point: e.g., *Tucker* v. *Farm and General Investment Trust Ltd* [1966] 2 QB 421 (as to ownership of the lambs of leased sheep); it was, however, discovered that there was an English authority (of 1586) which agreed with the Roman law.

17 Coke's autograph note (1604), in *Coke's Notebooks*, vol. 6, 1458: 'Note that in Spain, France, Scotland etc. they are governed principally by municipal laws and customs, but in cases omitted they are governed by the Civil law'.

18 Speech in *Calvin's Case* (1608), printed as *The Speech of the Lord Chancellor … touching the Post-Nati*, London, printed for Society of Stationers, An. 1609, at 43 (spelling modernized): 'Neither in *Spain* nor in *France* (those two great monarchies) it is not generally received nor allowed as a concluding and binding law. They take there the reason of it only as a direction to their proceeding and judgment. But to produce or allege it as a concluding or binding law was no less than *capitis poena*.'

19 David Ibbetson, *Common Law and* Ius Commune (London: Selden Society, 2001), 3–4.

20 J.H. Baker, "Funeral Monuments and the Heir" (1970), reprinted in Sir John Baker, *Collected Papers in English Legal History* (Cambridge: Cambridge University Press, 2013), vol. 3, 1398–1413.

that either he did not understand the law that he was citing or he hoped that no one else would know enough to challenge him. This was not a reception of Burgundian law, but a device used by Coke to suggest that he had not made up the law from nowhere, and it incidentally added a veneer of learning to his argument. A similar function was served by the Latin tags of which Coke and his contemporaries were noticeably fond.[21] Indeed, when Coke referred to the civil law it was usually by citing a Latin aphorism rather than a juristic text.[22] Coke has often been accused of inventing Latin maxims to suit his arguments. It is often difficult to tell, since he did not usually vouch a source; but he certainly adapted some Roman tags for English use by adjusting the wording. They had a mnemonic rather than a juristic value. Any fuller references to Roman civil law in the books of common law were made only to point out general similarities or differences,[23] not to explore different lines of reasoning or modes of conceptual analysis from which new principles of English law could be derived.[24] It hardly qualified as comparative law, let alone true legal learning.

Of course, different legal systems often arrived at similar results, as they still do. It would be surprising if societies existing in proximity did not share general attitudes to wrongdoing, commercial practices and expectations, the protection of assets, and so forth. Since all mature systems of law were founded on reason, experience of life, and cumulative wisdom, there was enough general conformity for it to be expressible in broad maxims which everyone could understand.[25] Lord Chancellor Ellesmere acknowledged this in 1608:[26]

21 J.H. Baker, "Roman Law at the Third University of England" (2002), reprinted in *Collected Papers*, vol. 1, 367, 374–375, 378, 391–393; Ibbetson, *Common Law and* Ius Commune, 12–13, 14, 16–17; Ian Williams, "The Role of Rules: Legal Maxims in Early-Modern Common Law Principle and Practice", in *Law in Theory and History: New Essays on a Neglected Dialogue*, ed. by Maksymilian del Mar and Michael Lobban (Oxford: Hart Publishing, 2016), 188–205. Over 300 Latin maxims or epigrams are cited in Coke's notes between 1572 and 1616: see the index in *Coke's Notebooks*, vol. 8, 2056–2062. There is also an alphabetical collection of maxims in Coke's commonplace book, BL MS. Harley 6687D, fols. 907–914.

22 In *Lewis* v. *Goddard* (1605), in BL MS. Lansdowne 1062, fol. 40, he actually cited the maxim *Expressum facit cessare tacitum* as "un text de Civill ley".

23 For some early examples, see David Seipp, "The Reception of Canon Law and Civil Law in Common Law Courts before 1600", *Oxford Journal of Legal Studies*, 13:3 (Autumn 1993), 388–420, at 402–404.

24 A notable exception was *Coggs* v. *Barnard* (1703), in which Holt C.J. suggested a remodelling of the law of bailment in line with Roman legal categories, though he was careful to derive the Roman ideas at secondhand via *Bracton*: see David Ibbetson, "Coggs v Barnard (1703)", in *Landmark Cases in the Law of Contract*, ed. by Charles Mitchell, Paul Mitchell (Oxford: Hart Publishing, 2008), 1–22.

25 So wrote Sir John Doddridge, *The Lawyers Light* (London: Benjamin Fisher, 1629), 10; quoted in Baker, *Collected Papers*, vol. 1, 379. Doddridge was (unusually for a common lawyer) an Oxford graduate (B.A. 1577) and became a judge in 1612. The book was written before 1607.

26 Speech in *Calvin's Case* (1608), above, n. 18, at 42–43 (spelling modernized).

> I acknowledge [the Civil law] to be ancient, and general in many parts of the world; and I reverence the professors of it as men of great learning, wisdom and judgment. I profess it not. I have learned little of it. But in that little I have found that, in the real and essential parts of justice, the Civil and common law do in many things concur, though they differ much in the form and manner of proceeding.

The differences were not, however, merely confined to procedure. Superficial similarities in terminology could disguise conceptual differences. Francis Bacon made this point in his Gray's Inn lectures (1600) on the Statute of Uses.[27] He said:

> for the conception and progression of uses, I have for a precedent in them other laws, because states and commonwealths have common accidents ... I find in the Civil law that that which cometh nearest in name to the use is nothing like in matter, which is *usus fructus*[28] ... but that which resembleth the use most is *fidei commissio.*

Bacon did not then draw on the learning of *fidei commissio* to inform and augment his treatment of the trust. He was merely pointing out a similarity, which he acknowledged was not an exact one, before going on to explain the English law. And he was incidentally drawing attention to the dangers caused by parallels in vocabulary when comparing different legal systems. Similar pitfalls had been noticed in the twelfth century by the author of *Glanvill* when discussing the difference between the English understanding of *dos* (dower) and its meaning *secundum leges romanas* (dowry).[29] They also caused a French jurist of the sixteenth century completely to misunderstand Sir Thomas Littleton's fifteenth-century account of the common law estate in fee simple, much to the irritation of Coke.[30] The *ius commune* depended to some extent on legal words having a universal signification; but that was an aspiration beyond the capacity of mere vocabulary.

Even if it were possible to borrow words without changing their meaning, borrowing the law itself, that is, absorbing different legal ideas and reasoning, would have required a technical knowledge of other systems which English judges and practising lawyers lacked. It is true that a handful of them added a few continental law books to their libraries, but they were not acquired for use as working tools. Coke, an exceptional bibliophile, owned more books of Italian literature than of Roman law. The lack of interest in such books among common lawyers resulted from their having no professional need for

27 *The Learned Reading of Francis Bacon upon the Statute of Uses*, London, printed for Mathew Walbancke, and Laurence Chapman, 1642.

28 John Selden, who would not have heard Bacon's lecture, did make a connection between uses and usufruct in his commonplace book of *c.* 1608: BL MS. Harley 1674, fol. 179.

29 The author of *Bracton* was in places less careful. See John Baker, "The Three Languages of the Common Law", reprinted in *Collected Papers*, vol. 2, 515–536, at 521.

30 *Coke's Notebooks*, vol. 1, cxxvii.

the mountains of detailed learning which they contained and no inclination to take the considerable trouble of absorbing it. If they went to university at all, they left after a few years reading arts and went on to the common lawyers' university known as the Inns of Court and Chancery. Coke and Bacon both left Cambridge without even taking an arts degree. That was perfectly normal: only the clergy found degrees needful. And of the two common lawyers in a century who went on to become bachelors of law, neither took the doctorate. The degree they needed was that of barrister at law, conferred by the Inns of Court. That was the indispensable qualification for practising as an advocate – and then for becoming a judge – in the higher ordinary courts of law. The doctorate of law, which took longer to achieve, was the required qualification for advocates and judges in the highest ecclesiastical courts, including the High Commission,[31] and in the Court of Admiralty. The doctors practising in the province of Canterbury kept chambers in the London college called Doctors' Commons, not far from St Paul's cathedral and the Court of Arches.[32] Their society had the collegiate attributes of a common hall and an impressive library, with books of the canon law and the *ius commune* – a collection probably begun in the fifteenth century[33] – though unlike the Inns of Court it did not have students because its members learned their law at Oxford or Cambridge. Membership was convenient, but it did not confer a right of audience in the ordinary royal courts at Westminster or at the assizes.[34] Similarly, the lesser practitioners in the ecclesiastical and admiralty courts, known as proctors, had no right to practise as attorneys in the common law courts.[35]

Coke's *Fourth Institute*, written in the 1620s, listed seventy-four species of court in England: almost as many as in Venice. But at the heart of the system were the king's two ancient courts of common law in Westminster Hall, namely the King's Bench and Common Pleas. The common lawyers believed the legal system centred on Westminster Hall to be immemorial, at any rate in its fundamental features, and that this gave it a special authority and

31 The commission was set up by Act of Parliament in 1559 but was considered to derive some of its authority also from the queen's supremacy. It included lay members, but its jurisdiction was purely ecclesiastical. The only reports known to the writer of arguments in the court (dating from 1631–32) show that the advocates were entirely Civilian: BL MS. Harley 4139, fols. 50–93; Bodleian Library, Oxford, MS. Rawlinson A.128, fols. 27–45. The court was subjected to frequent challenges from the common law courts.

32 The Court of Arches was the highest ecclesiastical court in England, taking its name from the church of St Mary-le-Bow ('super arcubus"), where it sat. There had been a community of "doctors of the Arches" since the fifteenth century: J.H. Baker, *Monuments of Endlesse Labours: English Canonists and Their Work* (London: Hambledon Press, 1998), 43.

33 Ibid., 44. The doctors' original premises were in Paternoster Row, from whence they moved in 1568 (with the assistance of Trinity Hall, Cambridge) to a house in Knightrider Street: G. D. Squibb, *Doctors' Commons* (Oxford: Oxford University Press, 1977), 5–6, 59–65.

34 Strictly speaking, it did not confer any rights of audience at all, since admission as an advocate in the Court of Arches required a rescript from the archbishop of Canterbury. Nearly all advocates belonged to Doctors' Commons, but out of convenience rather than legal compulsion.

35 A few of them acquired dual qualifications; but they were a small minority.

superiority.[36] It meant that it was coeval with (or even anterior to) the monarchy, whose powers it conferred and whose prerogatives it controlled, that it preexisted the Church in England, which was thought by some to be over a thousand years old[37], and was far older than the papal usurpation, which had lasted only a few hundred years. English lawyers had once claimed that it was older even than Roman law.[38] That now seems absurd; but it had legal implications at the time because of the various parallel jurisdictions which the King's Bench and Common Pleas sought to control. Whatever the true chronology, it was considered important that the common law had been there from the beginning and enjoyed the primacy.

There were, however, a number of different kinds of court operating legitimately outside the common law system. The ecclesiastical courts dealt with matters of marriage and divorce, probate of wills, intestate succession to movables, and defamation. After 1534, when Parliament abolished appeals to the pope, they became (in a sense) the king's courts, though "exempted from the jurisdiction of the common law by the king's laws ecclesiastical".[39] Then there was the Admiralty, which purported to follow the civil law[40] or, perhaps more exactly, the *ius gentium*,[41] the common law of the sea – and there were a few other courts which followed the civil law.[42] In those courts, the doctors, not the barristers, formed the practising bar. Besides these there were courts of equity (most importantly the Court of Chancery) and various courts set up under the royal prerogative, such as the Star Chamber, the Court of Requests (supposedly for poor people), and the provincial councils in the North and in the Marches of Wales. All these newer courts followed inquisitorial procedures influenced historically by canon law, though no one thought of them as Roman. Their principal characteristic was that they did not use juries but collected written evidence in the form of answers to interrogatories. The

36 Cf. the contention in *Necton* v. *Company of Wax-Chandlers* (1591) BL MS. Add. 35950, at fol. 94v, that "nostre ley est universall per tout le realme ... et per ceo avera le preheminens".

37 This false calculation was based on a supposed letter from Pope Eleutherius to a king of England in the second century. The medieval forgery was not exposed until the seventeenth century.

38 Sir John Baker, *The Reinvention of Magna Carta 1216–1616* (Cambridge: Cambridge University Press, 2017), 85–86. In the fifteenth century it was the orthodoxy. Even in the early 1600s Coke was unwilling wholly to give it up: ibid., 445 n. 14.

39 *Caudrey's Case* (1595) 5 Co. Rep., part 1, fol. 48.

40 William Fleetwood, in the mid-sixteenth century, said that the court followed the civil law because "for the most part of the world [it] is used in all matters or causes", and he pointed out that the lord admiral's patent gave power to proceed *iuxta leges civiles et maritimas*: 108, Selden Soc. 151.

41 See A. Wijffels, "*Ius gentium* in the practice of the Court of Admiralty around 1600", in *The Roman Law Tradition*, ed. by A. D. E. Lewis and D. J. Ibbetson (Cambridge: Cambridge University Press, 1994), 119–129.

42 The Court of Chivalry and the university courts at Cambridge and Oxford, which were still active in the seventeenth century.

Chancery had developed those procedures in the fourteenth century, when the chancellor and his staff were clergy, and they were copied later by the other "English courts".[43] But none of them applied Roman civil law or the *ius commune* in their decisions. Indeed, in the Chancery and prerogative courts the doctors of law had no rights of audience. Their services were not required.[44]

These miscellaneous courts each had their defined jurisdictions, and practitioners on both sides thought it best to keep the definitions sharp. As an unnamed civilian, probably Sir Thomas Crompton, argued in 1605:[45]

> I do not here deny but in some generalities the common law and Civil law, like two Graces, have their hands linked together and their faces directly turned one to another; yet in the application and distribution of these generals to justice in particular cases, I may truly say that like the two faces of Janus they seldom look one towards another. For the common law professeth to itself the literal and strict meaning of contracts and businesses, and the Civil law (like a regular and settled Court of Chancery) professeth to itself equity and the true meaning of men's affairs; yet both the Civil and the common law in their several offices and ends are the sinews of the state and worthy instruments and levels of the happiness of this government. It were a great happiness to the state and no small enrichment to the subject if both the common and Civil law contained themselves within their several jurisdictions and subjects of their learning ... [The] intermixtion and confusion of the Civil law with the common is so great that no man knoweth where to begin or the leastwise where to end a suit.

In theory there was no overlapping. At any rate, the secular and ecclesiastical courts moved in separate channels: "The judges of the common law ought not to intermeddle with matters ecclesiastical, nor the judges ecclesiastical with matters temporal, but each of them ought to have their proper and natural jurisdiction".[46] The common law courts drew the boundary line and stopped the civilian courts from straying over it; and, in return, the common law courts restrained themselves from trespassing directly on the Civilian jurisdictions. For instance, if a dispute turned on the validity of a marriage or a will, the question was sent to the bishop to make a certificate to the

43 "English" here referred to the language of the pleadings and evidence. The Chancery had both a Latin side (for common law business) and an English side (for equity). The prerogative courts did not have Latin sides.

44 This had been true even when chancellors were doctors of law, as was often the case in the fourteenth and fifteenth centuries. Cf. *Bayne* v. *Moone* (1593) in *Coke's Notebooks*, vol. 3, 541 ("the lord chancellor is assisted by canonists and Civilians [as masters of the court], and therefore in the Chancery there are competent judges" in tithe cases).

45 *Bottelio* v. *Younge* (1605) in Bodleian Library, Oxford, MS. Eng. misc. f. 473, fol. 36 (spelling modernised). The advocate was objecting to the inclusion of common lawyers in commissions to hear appeals in admiralty cases. The case is dated 1605 in BL MS. Lansdowne 1075, fol. 167v, which mentions Dr Crompton (the king's advocate) as counsel.

46 *Burton's Case* (1605) in *Coke's Notebooks*, vol. 7, 523, at 524.

lay court, and the bishop's decision would usually be accepted without challenge provided it was certified in the correct manner.[47] Likewise, if a convicted prisoner claimed benefit of clergy, the question of clerical status (including any counter-allegation of canonical bigamy) was, in theory, determined by an ecclesiastical authority.[48] But some purely ecclesiastical matters had belonged since the twelfth century to the courts of common law. Litigation about the landed property of ecclesiastical bodies was within the exclusive province of the lay courts. The right to choose a cleric to fill a vacant benefice was (and still is) treated in England as secular property, though a proffered candidate could be refused by the bishop if canonically unsuitable. Litigation about benefices, including questions of lapse and plurality, was therefore appropriated to the common law. Disputes about tithes, the principal income of benefices, also came in many cases to the lay courts, especially if the tithes were in lay hands.[49] Although marriage was a matter for the Church, questions of inheritance and dower (which necessarily depended on marriage and legitimacy) were litigated in the secular courts even if the decisive issue had to be referred to a Church court. In any particular case the common law court always had the last word, using the machinery of the writ of prohibition to stop proceedings elsewhere or the writ of *habeas corpus* to release parties imprisoned by the process of other courts.

As Sir Thomas Crompton indicated, the practice was less straightforward than the theory. The boundary between jurisdictions was not determined simply by subject matter and it was not always sharp. How far canon law might have to be considered, or whether a reference was needed to the bishop's court, might depend on the way the case arose and how the parties framed their legal disagreement. For instance, an issue whether a person was legitimate had to be sent to the Church court, since it might turn on canon law; but an issue whether he was born before or after his parents' marriage ("special bastardy") was a question purely of fact and therefore triable by jury.

47 For the difficulties which might arise see *Mynne* v. *Grey* (1572–80) in J. Baker, "Some Elizabethan Marriage Cases", in *Studies in Canon Law and Common Law in Honor of R. H. Helmholz*, ed. by Troy L. Harris (Berkeley: Robbins Collection Publications, 2015), 181–211, at 189–193. In that case, an action of dower, three successive certificates from the bishop of Norwich were rejected by the judges after conflicting advice as to the wording was given to the bishop by numerous civilians. At one stage the defendant procured an opinion signed by fourteen doctors of law.

48 This was usually perfunctory, the only test (by the middle of the fifteenth century) being the prisoner's ability to read. This was decided by the bishop's representative, present in court; but he could be fined by the lay judge if his decision seemed perverse. Things were different in the fourteenth century, when a royal judge might cite a decretal at the Old Bailey to confound the claim: Baker, *Collected Papers*, vol. 2, 983 n. 90.

49 Many benefices were appropriated in the medieval period by monasteries, and after the monasteries were dissolved in the 1530s the benefices (that is, the tithes) were granted out by the crown as "lay rectories". As before the dissolution, the cure of souls in such parishes was exercised by an ordained vicar.

Likewise, the question whether parties were joined in lawful matrimony had to be referred to the bishop, whereas "marriage in possession" (*de facto*) was for the jury.[50] In other cases the two laws were so intertwined – *ius mixtum*, as a fifteenth-century judge put it – that "we are obliged to know their law of Holy Church, and they are obliged to know our law".[51] Coke cited that remark in 1583 to show that the judges were still bound in various cases to take notice of the civil law.[52]

The cases of 1583 and 1605 both concerned the Admiralty jurisdiction, though border disputes with the Admiralty were chiefly geographical. The Admiralty was limited to matters arising on the high seas, of whatever kind they were, such as prize, collisions, or seamen's wages earned at sea. On the other hand, a maritime contract (such as a charterparty to hire a ship) was usually made on land and therefore fell to the ordinary courts. The jurisdiction over contracts made or torts committed on land overseas was disputed. One view was that the common law had jurisdiction because the foreign place could be pleaded fictitiously as being in an English county;[53] but in 1625 the King's Bench allowed the Admiralty to have jurisdiction because the applicable law would either be the *lex loci* or the *ius gentium* and not the common law.[54] A marine insurance contract might cause difficulties, since it was made on land but covered a risk at sea. But the common lawyers won that one as well: jurisdiction followed the *lex loci contractus*. Jurisdiction overlapped only on the beach, between high and low watermark. In practice, however, there was much recourse on both sides to fictions, pretending that matters arose on the high seas or in England when they did not. Here, too, the machinery of prohibition gave the upper hand to the common law.[55]

How, then, were the judges to know "their law"[56] when it was necessary to their decision, given that they had not made it their study? The common law-

50 Baker, "Some Elizabethan Marriage Cases", 194–195.

51 *Bohun* v. *Broughton* (1456) Y. B. Pas. 34 Hen. VI, fol. 38, pl. 9, at fol. 40, *per* Tyrwhit J. and Prysot CJ. (translated).

52 *R.* v. *Lacy and Lacy* (1583) in *Coke's Notebooks*, vol. 2, 219 (concerning Admiralty jurisdiction); and see *Necton* v. *Company of Wax-Chandlers* (1591) BL MS. Add. 35950, fol. 94v, *per* Coke ("les judges del spiritual court doient prender notice de nostre ley ... et nostre ley prendra notice de le spiritual ley"). Cf. *Weekes' Case* (1605) BL MS Harley 1679, fol. 50, *per* Walmsley J. ("si lour ley soit tiel, nihil ad nos"; but that was because the question was outside the purview of the common law).

53 *Anon.* (1610) 2 Bro. & Golds. 10; *Palmer* v. *Pope* (1611) ibid. 16; Hob. 79, 212.

54 *Tucker* v. *Cappes and Jones* (1625) 2 Rolle Rep. 497.

55 For a full account, see the introduction to *Fleetwood and Hale on Admiralty Jurisdiction*, ed. by M.J. Prichard and D.E.C. Yale (London: Selden Society, vol. 108, 1993).

56 Making a contrast between *nostre ley* and *lour ley* was common in the medieval period: Baker, *Reinvention of Magna Carta*, 113; *An Introduction to English Legal History*, 5th ed. (Oxford: Oxford University Press, 2019), 140. It was still a common form of expression in Coke's time: *Coke's Notebooks*, vol. 1, 135; vol. 3, 559, 619. And it remained common (in English) in the eighteenth century. A late example is *Barker* v. *May* (1829) 9 B. & C. 489, 492. Yet those who

yers did not usually delve deeply into canonical learning. The lectures in the Inns of Court on subjects such as wills or tithes generally ignored the canon law completely.[57] A few lecturers on tithes ventured to quote the standard *ius commune* authorities, but another (in 1631) confessed that it was beyond his capacity: "My comfort is", (he said), "I have robbed no man's barn, but that which I have comes from the market of Westminster Hall". This language is typical. Canon law was "their law" in the sense that it was a different field of expertise, and it was not polite for common lawyers to plough into it. Nevertheless, "their law" was the law they sometimes had to apply, and so they had to ascertain what it was in a disputed case. If the case was thought straightforward, they might grapple with it unaided or even disregard it.[58] But that was unusual.

In most cases the obvious course was to take expert advice from civil lawyers, and this was done frequently.[59] There were at least six ways of obtaining help. Formal certification from a bishop was available in those cases where the issue was determinable by his authority, and it was conclusive of the issue referred.[60] Such a certificate—for instance, that persons were joined in lawful matrimony—was conclusive as to fact as well as law, though in rare cases a bishop might consult doctors of law and certify the law alone.[61] Second, the common law court might call for a written opinion from a panel of doctors of law, who acted like arbitrators and were chosen in the same way as arbitrators.[62] For instance, in 1586 when a problematic case concerning marriage was

spoke of "our law" were not being chauvinistic or dismissive of "their law" but acknowledging the difference in legal culture: Seipp, "The Reception of Canon Law and Civil Law", 394.

57 See J. Baker, "Roman Law at the Third University of England", reprinted in *Collected Papers*, vol. 1, 367–393.

58 See, e.g., *Mrs Havars' Case* (1628) BL MS. Add. 35957, fol. 214, where Serjeant Ashley said of a point, "serra in vaine pur les Civilians [de] escrier tiels grand tractes de ceo". But Edward Henden (a barrister) cited in reply "Corruvius" (presumably Covarruvias, i.e. Diego de Covarubias) and "lour institutes". See also *Case De Modo Decimandi* (1609) 13 Co. Rep. 37, at fol. 46, where Coke C.J. countered an argument by Dr Bennet by citing a passage in Lyndwode.

59 For more detail on this subject, and an analysis of the kinds of case in which civilians were brought in, see Seipp, "The Reception of Canon Law and Civil Law", 406–409; R.H. Helmholz, "Civilians in the Common Law Courts, 1500–1700", in *English Legal History and Its Sources*, ed. by David Ibbetson, Neil Jones, Nigel Ramsay (Cambridge: Cambridge University Press, 2019), 342–357; and see Ibbetson, *Common Law and* Ius Commune, 16.

60 In case of fraud, the affected party could bring an action to recover damages for the deceit, but he could not upset the certificate itself: *Anon.* (1605) BL MS. Lansdowne 1062, fol. 81v.

61 E.g., in *Turnor* v. *Andrews* (1579) on the equity side of the Exchequer, the meaning of *alteragium* and *mansus competens* in the endowment of a vicar was certified by the bishop of London "upon conference had with [six] doctors in law": *Coke's Notebooks*, vol. 4, 797.

62 E.g., *R.* v. *Bishop of St David's* (1570) Dyer, 287 ("by the opinions and subscriptions of Yales, Jones, Dale, and Lloide, doctors of the Arches"); *Hunt* v. *Bushey* (1586) in *Coke's Notebooks*, vol. 2, 310 ("the Civilians certified the court under their hands that ..."; this is also mentioned sub nom. "Bashly" in 1 Leon. 128); *Jeffrey* v. *Kenshley* (1591) in *Coke's Notebooks*, vol. 3, 423 ("Various Civilians have certified their opinion that ..."); *Gayton's Case* (1594) Owen 12, 13

first argued by the common lawyers, this was (in the words of the chief justice) "but little to the purpose, for the point and matter of the case will depend upon the canon law"; the court, therefore, invited the parties to choose two doctors each, who were not retained of counsel, to hear the arguments and agree on a conclusion.[63] Third, and most commonly, doctors of law were invited to argue at the bar on both sides. They had no right of audience, but they were admitted by leave of the court, usually after a demurrer had been argued by common law counsel. The initiative to invite them to argue seems usually to have come from the court itself: they were not supposed to proffer themselves spontaneously.[64] Once invited, however, they argued on the same terms as common law counsel, and the latter might reply to their arguments.[65] There is some evidence that they were permitted to argue in Latin.[66] Occasionally only one doctor argued, but this may be because the other side did not or could not retain one.[67] Fourth, doctors might be conferred with in open court as *amici curiae*, though it is not clear how they were chosen or summoned for this purpose.[68] Fifth, counsel might report the opinions given to them out of court by civilians,[69] and one with the confidence and standing of Coke might assert a position simply as being held by "the Civilians" in general, as if it was

("arguments given in writing by the Civilians to the judges"). Cf. *Prynce* v. *Sympson* (1599) in *Coke's Notebooks*, vol. 5, 1020 ("this was not resolved but referred to the Civilians"). Probably of the same character were the six "doctors of the Arches" who reported in *Grendon* v. *Dean of Worcester* (1575) in *Reports from the Lost Notebooks of Sir James Dyer*, ed. by J.H. Baker (London: Selden Society, vols. 109–110, 1994), vol. 2, 319. For a written opinion by a single doctor, see *Bedingfield* v. *Archbishop of Canterbury* (1570) *Dyer* [old ed.], 292, 293.

63 This course was adopted in *Morrys* v. *Webber* (1586) after the case had been argued at the bar by doctors: Baker, "Some Elizabethan Marriage Cases", 203–204; discussed further below.

64 In *Offley* v. *Best* (1666) 1 Sid. 293, Dr Turner came into the King's Bench prepared to argue, but the court would not hear him before demurrer, and leave given. Cf. *Smith's Case* (1599) Owen 87, 88 ("if the parties would not [*sic*] demur they would hear the doctors upon this matter").

65 E.g., *The Case of Commendams* (1615) 1 Rolle Rep. 453, in which Serjeant Mountague responded to Dr Martin.

66 Baker, "Some Elizabethan Marriage Cases", 204. Their written opinions, however, were in English.

67 E.g., *Sir Henry Goodier's Case* (1590) 1 Leon. 135 (where it is said that no doctor could be found to argue the contrary position); *Hitching* v. *Glover* (1615) 1 Rolle Rep. 227 ("2 civilians fueront appoint d'arguer et ore vient solement Dr Talbot pur le plaintiff et nul pur l'auter parte"); *R.* v. *Raines* (1699) 1 Ld Raym. 360 (argued by Dr Walker and two common lawyers).

68 E.g., *Pigot* v. *Gascoigne* (1598) in *Coke's Notebooks*, vol. 4, 844 ("Thereupon the court conferred openly in court with various doctors of the Civil Law ..."); *Ambrosia Gorge's Case* (1600) ibid., vol. 5, 1058 ("upon conference had with the Civilians it was agreed that ..."); *Ward* v. *Britton* (1621) Palm. 220 (similar).

69 Helmholz, "Civilians in the Common Law Courts", 346 n. 18.

axiomatic,[70] or even as being common to "all laws".[71] Reporting opinions like this was not objectionable as hearsay, since it was evidence of law, not of fact. Lastly, judges might themselves engage in informal discussion with doctors out of court.[72] In none of these cases, it will be noted, were the Civilians called to give evidence as to the principles of canon law. It was not foreign law in that sense, to be treated—as foreign law is treated in common law courts today—as fact, proved by witnesses on oath.[73] It was law which actually operated in England and which the judges were obliged in appropriate cases to know and apply directly. But where doctors had argued on both sides, it was for the judges to decide which argument was right.[74] Even if the doctors agreed, the judges were at liberty to reject their opinion.

The intricate interrelationship of jurisdictions may be illustrated by looking at the long-running case of John Bury.[75] It was admittedly unusual, but for that reason instructive. John Bury (or Berry) married in 1553, but in 1561 he was divorced *a vinculo matrimonii* on grounds of impotence, at the suit of his wife. The definitive sentence found that he and his wife had slept in the same bed, desiring to have children, but that the wife remained a virgin by reason of her husband's impotence—a problem of which they were unaware at the time of marriage. The husband's condition was found by medical experts to be one which neither medical science nor the passage of time could remove. Well, the next year John remarried, and in 1564 his new wife gave birth to a son (Humphrey). One hopes it was a pleasant surprise for both of them. No suggestion was made in any of the subsequent legal proceedings that Humphrey might have been born out of wedlock. It might seem to our

70 *Stransham* v. *Collaton* (1591) in BL MS. Add. 35945, fol. 305, *per* Coke ("Jeo ay parle ove les Civilians ... que disont ...'.) The question was whether parishes were known to, and triable by, the common law. Cf. BL MS. Add. 25228, fol. 9v (*c.* 1610): "per touts les doctors des Arches inter Palmer et Brownelowe".

71 E.g., *Davenant* v. *Hurdis* (1599) in BL MS. Add. 25200, fol. 145, at fol. 152 ("Monopolies sont abhorre nient solement in nostre ley mes auxi in toutes auters leies, pur que il cite le texte del Civill ley, *Statuit imperator ut monopolia excercentes bonis omnibus spoliarentur*"). This is a reference to Cod. 4: 59, also cited in *Coke's Notebooks*, 4: 926 (1598); *Case of Monopolies* (1602) 11 Co. Rep. at fol. 87.

72 See, e.g., Dyer CJ's note on the case of the bishopric of Winchester (1565) in *Reports from Dyer's Lost Notebooks*, vol. 1, 107 ("Enquire about this from Civilians and canonists"); *Bunting* v. *Leppingwell* (1585) in BL MS. Harley 4562, fol. 34 ("Wray chief justice dit que il ad conferre ove Doctour Dale et Doctour Abry [Aubrey], Civilians ..."); *Morrys* v. *Webber* (1586) in Baker, "Some Elizabethan Marriage Cases", 204; *Smith's Case* (1599) Owen 87 ("Williams said that the doctors of the Civil law informed him ...").

73 Cf. Frederic W. Maitland, "Canon law", in *Collected Papers of Frederic William Maitland*, ed. by H.A.J. Fisher (Cambridge: Cambridge University Press, 1911), vol. 3, 65–77, at 74, contra. Maitland's assumption was questioned by Helmholz, "Civilians in the Common Law Courts", 355.

74 Coke wrote in 1606 that "where doctors and judges differ, judges prevail": *Coke's Notebooks*, vol. 7, 1602, citing a case of 1443.

75 See Baker, "Some Elizabethan Marriage Cases", 201–210.

suspicious minds an obvious possibility, and sixteenth-century minds were no less suspicious. But the courts never considered it. The mother did not volunteer the information, and she could refuse to answer questions on oath which might incriminate her. The legal conundrum which obviously arose was this. If the child was indeed John's, then the reason given for the divorce had been scientifically disproved. And if that was an error which invalidated the divorce, John had not been free to marry Humphrey's mother, whence it followed that Humphrey was illegitimate. On the other hand, it was not wholly impossible that John had indeed been impotent in 1561 but had somehow recovered after marrying a different woman. A mistaken prognosis by the medical doctors might not upset the decree of divorce: at any rate, not without further judicial proceedings to reverse it.

Litigation began in 1586, after John's death, when Humphrey (now aged 21) claimed his inheritance in the father's landed property.[76] A dispute arose with his uncle Hugh as to which of them was the heir at law. This was indisputably a question for the common law. But, as Chief Justice Anderson of the Common Pleas pointed out, it depended on whether a definitive sentence of divorce could be treated as *ipso facto* void for an apparent error of fact, without being reversed by the Church court; and that, he said, was a question of canon law. He had already consulted "many learned in the canon law", who were of opinion that a decree could in some cases be treated as void; but he invited the parties to retain one doctor each to argue the point in court. Several doctors were engaged and argued the case in the Common Pleas. One advocate said the facts could not be reopened while the sentence was in force. Another said that, although that proposition was generally correct, it did not hold true where the soul was in danger and the Church had been deceived, because the parties would otherwise be compelled to live in adultery. A third said that the original sentence was not properly a divorce anyway, since the parties were never married in the first place, but was only a declaration of the errors of the parties. Various other points of canon law were raised—including the medical possibility of selective frigidity and the canonical concept of impotence by reason of witchcraft—until the court in desperation appointed a panel of doctors of law to thrash it out and report back. They duly reported that the plaintiff was legitimate, since the divorce remained unrepealed and the impediment did not in itself prevent marriage with a subsequent wife. The Common Pleas gave judgment accordingly.

But that was not an end of it. When the matter arose again in 1595, another group of canonists gave their opinion that whoever was fit for one woman must be fit for another, and therefore the procreation of Humphrey proved

76 *Morrys* v. *Webber* (1586–88) Moo. K.B. 225; 2 Leon. 169; 1 And. 185; Noy 72; BL MS. Lansdowne 1087, fols. 255–257v; sub nom. *Buries Case* (1588) in BL MS. Lansdowne 1104, fols. 104–105. The record is in London: Public Record Office [PRO], CP 40/1461, m. 1711.

the first marriage to be valid and the divorce void. One could not, in their view, be selectively frigid. This new opinion encouraged uncle Hugh to bring another action in the Common Pleas in 1598 to try to recover different lands from Humphrey. This time the extensive process in the Church court back in 1561, with all the written testimony of the witnesses, was incorporated in the jury's special verdict and by that means entered on the record of the Court of Common Pleas. This in itself is remarkable, since the common law courts kept no record of evidence given in their own trials. The medical testimony, which had not previously been available to the Common Pleas, was now on the record; and it provided uncontested proof that John Bury's impotence, caused by an accident with a horse, had been physical, permanent, and incurable. This not only supported the sentence of divorce, but seemed to rule out the question of relative frigidity. So the judges this time went against the latest panel of canonists and held once again that Humphrey was legitimate. This seems bizarre, since the decision rested on his father's inability to procreate him. But the legal logic was inescapable. The divorce *a vinculo* had freed both parties to remarry, and so the second marriage was valid. The second marriage might perhaps be voidable, but the principle of comity between courts meant that nullification could be achieved only by a decree of the Church court, and since this had not happened in the lifetime of the husband and wife, their issue was legitimate. A writ of error was brought in the King's Bench to reverse the judgment, but after many more arguments the decision was affirmed in 1599.[77] Even that was not the end. There was, finally, an attempt by uncle Hugh's son to revoke the divorce in the Church court. The saga reached its final conclusion in 1610, with a prohibition to stop the proceedings in Canterbury on the grounds that a marriage could not be annulled after the death of both parties, so as to bastardize the issue retrospectively.[78] The last word, therefore, went to the common law—and, as it happened, to Sir Edward Coke, who had reported the 1598 decision when he was still at the bar.[79]

Bury's case is an elaborate example of the way conflicts and conundrums were managed in practice between the secular and ecclesiastical jurisdictions. A knotty question, on which the canon law was unclear, was debated on both sides by doctors of civil law, but—since it affected title to land—it had to be decided by the common law judges. In arriving at their decision, the judges had deferred to the ecclesiastical court in treating a divorce decree as conclusive unless and until it was reversed on appeal. Coke himself accepted and restated that principle of comity in a number of cases.[80] The common law

77 *Berrie* v. *Webber* (1599–1600) in PRO, KB 27/1355, m. 393.

78 *Hugh Berry* v. *Humphrey Berry* (1610) in BL MS. Add. 9844, fols. 119v–120v, and other MSS.

79 The 1610 prohibition was granted by the Common Pleas, of which Coke was chief justice from 1606 to 1613. For Coke's 1598 report see the next note.

80 *Bunting* v. *Lepingwell* (1585) in *Coke's Notebooks*, vol. 2, 277; *Cheyney* v. *Frankwell* (1587) ibid., 334; *Cawdrye* v. *Atton* (1595) ibid., vol. 3, 617; sub nom. *Caudrey's Case* in 5 Co. Rep.,

judges would stop ecclesiastical judges from exceeding their jurisdiction by prohibition, as they did in 1610; but they would not question the correctness of decisions made within the Church's jurisdiction, even if they seemed *prima facie* to be mistaken, misinformed or unconvincing.

The corollary was that civil lawyers should not pronounce on the common law, which (for Coke) included the interpretation of statutes touching on ecclesiastical jurisdiction.[81] This was a controversial area, and Coke could be tetchy with individual Civilians who displayed professional arrogance. Civilians were perhaps inclined to regard themselves as superior by virtue of their higher academical degrees in the "learned laws": an expression which, even today, feels like a calculated insult to common lawyers. A colourful interchange in Chief Justice Coke's court was reported in 1615. A Puritan layman was charged with refusing to kneel to receive holy communion and with the offence of attending Bible readings. The Church authorities tried to make him incriminate himself in answering questions on oath, which he refused to do, and so they imprisoned him. When he brought *habeas corpus*, the King's Bench allowed a prominent Civilian—the king's advocate, Dr Martin—to argue against releasing the prisoner. He argued that courts should show no favour to fanatical schismatics, or there would be religious confusion. And he defended examination on oath upon a penal law, saying it would "open up a gap" if it could not be done. Coke was not best pleased by the argument, or at least by the manner of its presentation, and said the doctor had taken upon himself the persons of three men: he had behaved like a statesman, in declaring the inconveniences which schismatics caused and why they should be suppressed; he had taken upon himself to be a judge to censure the parties; and he had acted the part of an advocate. Only in the third role had he behaved properly, though his argument was wrong. In the other two, according to Coke, he had transgressed the rules of good manners. It did not become him to instruct judges and statesmen what they should do. The judges were wholly against schism and faction, but in the present case the question was simply whether someone could be imprisoned for refusing to incriminate himself on oath. The answer to that was clearly "No", and so the prisoners would be released on bail.[82] Here, it will be noticed, the common law court did not defer to the ecclesiastical court because personal liberty was at stake, and that was a matter for the common law. It was lawful to force clergy to answer questions on oath about their religious practices, even about their beliefs, because they owed canonical obedience. But laymen were protected by the secular law. No supposed principle of canon law could prevail against Magna Carta.[83]

part 1, fol. 7; *Webber* v. *Bury* (1598) in *Coke's Notebooks*, vol. 5, 942.

81 Likewise on the Admiralty jurisdiction: *Waltham* v. *Geere* (1605) in BL MS. Add. 35955, fol. 19, *per* Popham C.J. ("Le construction de les statutes appent a nostre ley").

82 *R.* v. *Dighton and others* (1615), discussed in Baker, *Reinvention of Magna Carta*, 373–375.

83 Ibid., 354–374, 429–430, 517–530.

Despite such occasional hints of friction, the relationship between the two systems and the two professions was not one of constant animosity: indeed, it depended on cooperation. A notable embodiment of the comity could be seen in the person of Sir Julius Caesar, whose father was a doctor of the University of Padua.[84] Doctor of law, advocate, master of requests, and chief judge of the Admiralty, he was in 1590 elected a bencher of Coke's Inn of Court (the Inner Temple), later becoming its senior bencher. And in 1614 he was appointed Master of the Rolls, the second senior judge in the Court of Chancery.[85] Caesar was, admittedly, untypical. Less exalted Civilians sometimes complained of being unduly restricted in their spheres of practice and deprived of sources of income which they saw as legitimately theirs, particularly in relation to tithes and Admiralty work. The common lawyers, on the other hand, thought the doctors were constantly trying to grab more than their due. But the civil lawyers, as a much smaller profession with limited competence, were hardly a threat; and they lingered on, as a specialist enclave, until the later nineteenth century. The profession was dealt a death blow in 1857, when matrimonial and probate cases were taken away from the Church courts and the Admiralty court was opened to barristers. The beleaguered advocates accepted defeat. Doctors' Commons, including its library, was sold in 1861; and the last practising doctor of law in England died in 1912. The Probate, Divorce, and Admiralty Division of the High Court, established on the creation of the High Court in 1875, perpetuated the memory of the Civilian spheres of practice and itself somehow managed to resist extirpation until 1971.[86] But it was served by the common law Bar, which included divorce and admiralty specialists, once the last doctors were gone. The ecclesiastical courts still remain, with a heavily curtailed jurisdiction limited to Church matters, but they are likewise addressed nowadays by barristers rather than doctors of law. In those areas in which the doctors once specialized, as Dr Duck pointed out, canon law and the *ius gentium* did have a lasting influence on the development of English law as a whole. Their learning was folded into it and became subject to the common law's methodology, turned into English case law, and (eventually) overtaken by legislation. But their influence on the other core aspects of English law—on the law of real property, trusts, contract, tort, and crime, and the public law remedies—was negligible.

84 Cesare Adelmare MD (d. 1569) immigrated to England and was court physician to Mary I and Elizabeth I.

85 He was the first bencher named in the grant of the freehold of the Temple by James I to the benchers of the two societies in 1608.

86 When it was broken up in that year, probate business went to the Chancery Division, admiralty to the Queen's Bench Division, and matrimonial causes to a new Family Division.

8 Roman Law in Sixteenth-Century England

Professor Thomas Smith

David Ibbetson

In 1540, the King of England, Henry VIII, endowed professorships of Roman law in the two English universities, Oxford and Cambridge.[1] To the Cambridge chair, he appointed one of Cambridge's finest up and coming young intellectuals, Thomas Smith.[2] Smith was in many ways ideally suited to the position. He was respectably Protestant, something that mattered in the years after the English Reformation. He was loyal to the Crown. He was fearsomely intelligent and had attracted notice, in particular, for his theories about the proper way to pronounce classical Greek. There was only one way in which it might have been thought that he was not an ideal candidate. He knew no law.

We may be sure that there were men in Cambridge, men who had obtained their doctorates in civil law, who were not especially pleased by the appointment, and probably some who were thoroughly jealous, having had aspirations to win the well-endowed professorship themselves, with the possibility of further royal patronage to come.

In a sense Smith had got the second prize: his friend John Cheke, with whom he had developed the theories of Greek pronunciation, was appointed to the newly created professorship of Greek.

In preparation for his duties, Smith resolved, hardly surprisingly, to learn some law. In his lectures he spoke of adding works of the humanists Zasius, Alciatus, and Ferrarius to his library; those of Zasius and Alciatus, given by him to Queen's College Cambridge, were published between 1537 and 1541, and his purchases presumably date from this period.[3] In May 1540[4] he travelled

1 F. Donald Logan, "The Origins of the So-called Regius Professorships", in *Renaissance and Renewal in Church History*, ed. by D. Baker (Oxford: Blackwell, 1977), 271–278.

2 For a useful summary of Smith's life and work, see Peter G. Stein, "Sir Thomas Smith, Renaissance Civilian", in *The Character and Influence of the Roman Civil Law* (London: Hambledon Press, 1988), 186–196; Mary Dewar, *Sir Thomas Smith: A Tudor Intellectual in Office* (London: Athlone Press, 1964).

3 The books have English bindings, so may well have been bought in England before his continental travels, as he hints in his lectures.

4 The dates at this period in his life are derived from his own notebook, printed by John Gough Nichols, "Some Additions to the Biographies of Sir John Cheke and Sir Thomas Smith",

DOI: 10.4324/9781003425069-11

to France, "passing through almost all the universities", he tells us, before moving on to Italy, where it is said that he studied at Padua, though there is no trace of his having obtained a degree there.[5] In 1542, he returned to Cambridge, was admitted to the degree of Doctor of Laws (perhaps by incorporation from Padua, though this seems unlikely), and entered into his professorship, giving a pair of inaugural lectures. This brief paper is based largely on the text of those lectures, which survive in manuscript in the Cambridge Uiversity Library.[6] These lectures, revealing how Smith saw his task ahead of him, cast light on the way in which the study of Roman law might have been seen in mid-sixteenth-century Cambridge.

Not unexpectedly, Smith began his first lecture with a reference to his apprehensiveness as he entered into his professorship. A degree of self-deprecation, even protestations that one was unfitted for the office to which one had been called, was not unusual at the time, and Smith had more cause to be apprehensive than most. His expected audience would have been made up both of scholars who had heard him lecturing or disputing on philosophy, rhetoric, dialectic, and history, on the one hand, and of lawyers, who would naturally have been suspicious of his lack of qualification, on the other. It was this second group which he feared, and we cannot think that they would have been comforted by his saying that some years previously he had bought a copy of the Pandects and Codex and dipped into them occasionally during his leisure hours. Instead, he went on the attack with what we would now want to describe as a broad humanist agenda for legal study. He spoke approvingly of Alciatus and Zasius and was highly critical of Accursius and Bartolus, who, he said, "had made monstrous and scandalous mistakes in explaining many of their laws, and wrote down without shame absurd old wives tales instead of true and certain history, simply because they had neglected humane studies and good literature". He spoke negatively of the execrable Latin of the medieval commentators and, by implication, of those who taught the civil law in his own day. He repeated the common criticism of the medieval *mos italicus*, which involved the amassing of more and more citations without trying to penetrate into the ideas at the heart of the texts. He was critical of the lawyers in his expected audience, who had devoted themselves narrowly to the study of the law rather than the broader field of humane letters. If they were inclined to disagree with him, he said, he would produce 600 passages from the Pandects in which poets or philosophers were prayed in aid.

Archaeologia, 38:1 (1860), 98–127, at 116–120.

5 Dewar, *Thomas Smith*, 22 n.2.

6 Cambridge University Library MS Mm 1.48, ff. 394–430 (formerly Baker MS 37). I have relied on the transcription and translation, believed to be by Professor P.W. Duff, now in the Squire Law Library, Cambridge. The lectures are summarized in James Bass Mullinger, *History of the University of Cambridge*, vol. 2 (Cambridge: Cambridge University Press, 1884, reprinted 1969), 129–132.

From all this, we can see him aligning himself with the current of legal humanism which was then prevalent in France and parts of Italy. It may well be that in appointing him to the professorship the King himself was concerned to foster this humanist form of scholarship. At least this seems to be what Smith had thought. He praised Henry VIII for his love of theology, philosophy, and the like, as well as for the way in which he had given patronage to the most able men in these fields.

It is more likely, though, that the King had more practical objects in mind.[7] There had been plans to set up a school of civil law in London, parallelling the Inns of court which brought together common lawyers, though these plans had come to nothing.[8] To the King's mind, the civil law provided the framework for diplomatic negotiations, and if England was to hold its own in this European world its ambassadors and other diplomatic representatives needed to be expert in this civil law world. There were, it is true, some highly placed individuals within the English state who might have favoured the adoption of a form of Roman law in place of the traditional English common law, but we have no good reason to think that the King himself would have favoured any such transformation.

If the King's purpose in setting up the professorship was to encourage the study of civil law, Smith would be able to succeed at that only if he could get students. However much he was a humanist by inclination and by his own educational background, this in itself would not have attracted students. Legal study was arduous. It required hard work and long hours. Why else, he asked, would there be so many teachers drawing such handsome stipends? Smith could say as much as he liked that the study was pleasant, that one could learn much about Roman society from the situations detailed in the text of the Pandects, but this would hardly inspire prospective students to take up the study of the civil law unless there was the promise of more worldly benefits. Much of his second lecture was taken up by his describing these benefits. He could point to men who had gained high office in the English state, such as Thomas More, after studying civil law, but we may doubt whether two or three examples would have been sufficient to attract many young men to the subject. He repeatedly spoke of the honour, or honours, and advantages which awaited the civil lawyer, without always being able to describe with any detail what those honours and advantages were. Clearly, the most successful might aspire to become ambassadors, who could speak to their continental European counterparts in their own terms; they might become bishops, and Smith was able to give examples of men who had studied civil law and achieved these positions. Even the Chancellor of England, Thomas Wriothesley, had

7 John Strype, *The Life of the Learned Sir Thomas Smith, Kt, Doctor of the Civil Law* (London: A Roper, 1698), 24.

8 D.S. Bland, "Henry VIII's Royal Commission on the Inns of Courts", *Journal of the Society of Public Teachers of Law*, 10 (1969), 178–194.

been a student of the civil law, though in 1542 Smith could not know that he was in a few years to be dismissed from his office allegedly because he was too partial to the civil law at the expense of the common law. But beyond this it was hard for him to proceed except in stating these generalities of honour and advantage. There would be work for some in the courts in England where civil law was practised, such as the court of Admiralty or the ecclesiastical courts, but there would be far fewer opportunities for civil lawyers to make a living in legal practice in England than there would have been in most of continental Europe. The only crumb of comfort he could offer was that there had been of late so few students of the civil law that, even though there were few positions, there was a dearth of people who could fill them.

It is here that we can see Smith's biggest problem. The true alternative to the study of civil law for many young men would be the study of the common law in the Inns of Court in London. The common law courts were seeing a real increase in business, particularly it seems in business arising out of commercial disputes.[9] The number of men seeking entry into the Inns of Court was beginning to rise, and even for the less successful students of the common law there were many openings in local administration in England.[10] So it was here that Smith had his hardest task. He could point to the barbaric half-French, as he put it, in which the English law books were written, contrasting it with the elegant Latin of the classical Roman jurists – although we might think that he had rather exaggerated just how elegant this Latin was. But to say that English law was written in barbaric half-French was no more than the humanistic commonplace, a cheap jibe at the language of English law. He could say too that English law was messy and disorganized, but so in truth, he admitted, was the civil law once the student had moved from the Institutes, needing a teacher as a guide through the tortuous intricacies of the law. No English lawyer would have disagreed about the imperfections of the common law, but that did not mean that the study of English law was more arduous than the study of the civil law, even if it did mean that English law might be thought to have less intellectual coherence than Roman law. Smith was at pains to say that English lawyers might be very skilled in rhetoric and dialectic, arguing their points with clarity and tenacity, showing a high level of competence in debate and disputation. Thomas More had said much the same thing in *defence* of the common law. The real question for Smith was whether studying the civil law would be of advantage to someone intending to practise common law. And his argument here strikes me as rather weak. It may be, as many in the sixteenth century would argue, that all laws ultimately derived from God, but that was hardly an argument for studying the civil law as a

9 C.W. Brooks, *Pettyfoggers and Vipers of the Common Law* (Cambridge: Cambridge University Press, 1986), 81.

10 Wilfrid R. Prest, *The Inns of Court under Elizabeth I and the Early Stuarts* (Harlow: Longmans, 1972), 6.

preparation for practising common law. Lawyers, he said, would be familiar with the ideal and fictitious legal systems described by ancient philosophers, Plato, Aristotle, Cicero. How much more valuable to study a real legal system, especially one which underpinned the law practised in continental Europe! I am not sure how many English lawyers would have been that familiar with the ancient philosophers' thinking about law, but I am certain that they would not have spent many years of heavy toil in the study of these idealized systems. Why should they spend years studying the civil law?

I have some sympathy with Smith's quandary, as someone who held the same professorship as Smith held, having to teach Roman law to students studying the English common law and having to justify the utility of Roman law in the curriculum of the modern law school. My task is easier than Smith's was, since from the eighteenth century English legal thinking has been structured along the lines which are in effect the lines of the Institutes of Gaius and Justinian. But in the sixteenth century English law was framed in terms of forms of action dating from the twelfth or thirteenth century and bore little relation to the categories with which Roman lawyers would have been familiar.

Smith seems not to have had great success in attracting students to the study of the civil law (his tenure as professor saw the creation of eight Bachelors of Laws and one doctor, his successor Walter Hadden[11]), but I fear that his high sounding rhetoric in favour of legal humanism was soon left behind in favour of a more traditional curriculum based on the *mos italicus*.[12] I do know that his successors for many centuries were men of relatively little ability in the civil law, suggesting that it had not obtained a central position in the intellectual life of the university. Nor did it attract men who were destined to practise the English common law. Although it became more common for common lawyers to have attended university, they did not go there to study civil law but, rather, the broad humanistic learning which Smith had lauded. This is not to say that English lawyers were unfamiliar with Roman law – we know that some of them, including the most eminent, had more than a passing acquaintance with the Justinianic texts, though hardly an expertise in them. Some English lawyers at the end of the sixteenth century used Roman law to explain quintessentially English law, though the Roman law they relied upon was rarely more than could have been found in the Institutes. Even the most English of English lawyers, Edward Coke, had his copy of the Institutes and we can tell from his marginal annotations that they had not simply sat in his library unread.[13] And English lawyers might plagiarize abstract legal ideas from books written in continental Europe, though this was simple copying rather than engaging in debate with the German, Dutch, French, or Italian lawyers,

11 Mullinger, *History*, 132.

12 This appears to have been laid down in the Statutes and Injunctions of the University in 1540: Mullinger, *History*, 111, 132–138.

13 The volume survives in Holkham Hall, Norfolk.

and the works copied were commonly legal dictionaries. A later holder of Smith's professorship, John Cowell, attempted to squeeze English law into the framework of Justinian's Institutes; however, the attempt was a failure and really showed only how different the systems were.

But there are occasional hints that in the later sixteenth century there were some in England willing to use a more sophisticated understanding of Roman law as a way to shape or reform English law. In his *Maxims of the Law*, Francis Bacon, as much a lawyer as a statesman and philosopher, brought together Roman and English materials to produce for English lawyers a modern equivalent of the Digest title *De Regulis Iuris*, though it was perhaps too advanced methodologically to gain success as a work of practical utility.

It may be that the most important contribution of Roman law to legal practice came from Thomas Smith himself. After stepping down from the professorship he had a successful career as an ambassador, no doubt pleased that he had a good enough knowledge of the civil law to debate with his continental European friends, and later he became Secretary of State to Queen Elizabeth I and an active member of the English Parliament. He was surely involved in the enactment of an important statute dealing with fraud, whose details seem to have been inspired by the Romans' *actio pauliana*. Here in the library of Queen's College Cambridge we still have his copy of the Pandects, perhaps the one he had bought and perused in his leisure hours at the start of his career, with his neat marginal annotations to the Justinianic texts on the *actio pauliana*.

Smith's ambitions to have revived the study of the civil law in England came to nought; his enthusiasm for the new legal humanism fell on deaf ears. But his tenure as professor was not a complete failure as it led to him immersing himself in Roman learning, enabling this intellectual star of the University of Cambridge to bring at least some civilian learning into the English common law.

9 Common Lawyers and Civilian Lawyers in England

Barriers and Connections

R. H. Helmholz

The English legal profession was divided into two distinct groups. On one side were the common lawyers. The more numerous of the two, their natural home was in the royal courts. On the other side were the civilians. Their natural home was in the courts of the church. The distinction between the two groups was also more fundamental than the courts in which they served. Their education and the sources of law upon which they relied for authority were markedly different. English civilians were taught the law in a university law faculty, normally at Oxford and Cambridge. The common lawyers learned their law at the Inns of Court in London. Their paths to promotion and judgeships were also distinct, and the laws they applied in practice were not the same. The common law was derived from the combination of immemorial custom, the evolving case law of the royal courts, and the statutes enacted by King and Parliament. The law English civilians applied came primarily from what they found in the European *ius commune*, the learned laws contained in the ancient Roman law and the church's canon law.[1] Taking these differences into account, the dominant view among English legal historians has been that both from the start and in their ongoing development, these two legal professions proceeded along separate, in fact, divergent paths.

This was certainly the view of F.W. Maitland, the greatest of English legal historians. He recognized the initial appeal which Roman law had held for twelfth and thirteenth century common lawyers, some of whom were also clerics who had been trained in the ways of thought derived from the *ius commune*. Attracted by the sophistication of that source of law, some civilian influence appears in the earliest treatises on English law – *Glanvill* and *Bracton*.[2] At length however, English common lawyers aimed to take a divergent tack.

1 For a learned and readable introduction to the subject, see Manlio Bellomo, *The Common Legal Past of Europe, 1000–1800*, trans. by Lydia Cochrane (Washington, DC: Catholic University of America Press, 1995).

2 See, e.g., Thomas J. McSweeney, *Priests of the Law: Roman Law and the Making of the Common Law's First Professionals* (Oxford: Oxford University Press, 2019); Anne Duggan, "Roman, Canon and Common Law in Twelfth-Century England: The Council of Northampton (1164) Re-examined", *Historical Research*, 83:221 (2010), 379–408, at 402–403.

DOI: 10.4324/9781003425069-12

They determined to resist the siren call of the civil law. The early contact with Roman law thus worked something like a smallpox vaccination, that is, acceptance of a small dose as a way of preventing a full and fatal infection. As a result, the two groups of lawyers went their own ways thereafter. Maitland also saw the later history of English law as something like a contest between two rival powers, one in which common lawyers rejected the application of the civil and canon laws in favor of the development of their land's own legal institutions.[3]

Subsequent legal historians have softened but not overturned this view.[4] Professor Paul Brand's excellent book on the subject, for example, concluded that the two professions had "developed along separate lines".[5] This divergence mattered. It was evident in the authorities they recognized as applicable, and it became important more dramatically in the constitutional controversies of the seventeenth century. Then, the tendency among the civilians was to favor the claims of the royalists; that among the common lawyers was just the opposite. As a matter of principle, most common lawyers resisted those claims. Their law stood contrary to many of the monarchical claims. Those of the civilians did not. The same split also occurred in many aspects of their professional lives. The division between them was made most visible (and most painful for the civilians) by the development and expanded use of writs of prohibition, royal writs which restricted the jurisdiction of ecclesiastical courts in order to keep them from encroaching upon common law subjects – a restriction that, in time, allowed the common law courts to expand the scope of their own jurisdiction at the expense of the courts in which the civil law was applied.[6] In other words, the history of the two professions was a contest between rivals,

3 Evidence on this subject is laid out at greater length in R.H. Helmholz, "The Learned Laws in 'Pollock and Maitland'", *The History of English Law: Centenary Essays on 'Pollock and Maitland'*, *Proceedings of the British Academy*, 89 (1996), 145–169. A slightly later date for the divergence in the Court of Chancery, but one equally based upon a general dislike of Roman law among common lawyers, is described in George Spence, *Equitable Jurisdiction of the Court of Chancery* (Philadelphia,: Lea and Blanchard, 1846, repr. 1981), 345–349; and W.J. Jones, *The Elizabethan Court of Chancery* (Oxford: Oxford University Press, 1967), 10–12.

4 T.F.T. Plucknett, "The Relations between Roman Law and English Common Law down to the Sixteenth Century: A General Survey", *University of Toronto Law Journal*, 3:1 (January 1939), 24–50; S.F.C. Milsom, *Historical Foundations of the Common Law*, 2nd ed. (London: Butterworths, 1981), 41–42; J.H. Baker, *Introduction to English Legal History*, 5th ed. (Oxford: Oxford University Press, 2019), 34.

5 Brand, *The Origins of the English Legal Profession* (Oxford: Blackwell, 1992), 156.

6 See Charles Gray, *The Writ of Prohibition: Jurisdiction in Early Modern English Law* (New York: Oceana Publications, 2004), https://catalog.lib.uchicago.edu/vufind/Record/5145823 ; W.R. Jones, "Relations of the Two Jurisdictions: Conflict and Cooperation in England during the Thirteenth and Fourteenth Centuries", in *Studies in Medieval and Renaissance History*, vol. VII, ed. by William Bowsky (Lincoln: University of Nebraska Press, 1970), 78–210; G.B. Flahiff, "The Writ of Prohibition to Court Christian in the Thirteenth Century [Part One]", *Mediaeval Studies*, 7:1 (January 1944), 261–313 ; Flahiff [Part Two], *Medieval Studies*, 8:1 (January 1945), 229–290.

one in which the common lawyers held the stronger and the ultimately prevailing hand.

Support for this way of thinking about these two English legal professions clearly exists. There is good evidence to support it. However, there is also evidence which suggests that this view is overly one-sided. It leaves out too much. It should be balanced, in my view, by acknowledging the existence and importance of the many things these two kinds of lawyers shared. In fact, the history of these two groups of legal professionals was not all competition and opposition. There were many areas of the law in which the interests and the legal practices of these two groups coincided. My intent in this chapter is to put some of them on the record, together with the addition of a word or two about the possibility of influence by one legal system on the other. This is a project worth undertaking, although it runs contrary to a strong view to the contrary. Historians seem naturally drawn to studies of crisis and conflict.[7] Study of relations between civilians and common lawyers is one example of this approach. I believe we should also pay attention to cooperation and common interests. For present purposes I will concentrate on evidence from the early modern period – roughly between 1450 and 1640, attempting to show that common lawyers and civilians were not inevitable rivals. It will be the object of his chapter to show that they had a great deal in common.

Common Allegiances

It is a mistake to ignore the obvious, even though we often do just that. Basic allegiances and the assumptions that went with them have often made a difference in the practice of law, and among the most obvious of factors that drew civilians and common lawyers together were several shared ties not directly connected to litigation but nonetheless influential in law's reach. Three of them are relevant in this chapter: allegiance to the monarchy, religious belief, and acceptance of the existence and utility of the law of nature and the law of nations. We can take the acceptance of all three for granted as an attitude characteristic of that held by the English civilians.[8] Their education and law practice depended upon application of the European *ius commune*. They accepted the legitimacy of the English monarchy, and acceptance of natural law was a given for all English civilians. All three were parts of their education and their practice.

The common lawyers are another matter. A prominent and representative example of apparent dislike of civil law is Sir Edward Coke (1552–1634). He is a fair choice because he has the reputation of skepticism towards all three

7 A Google search on 12 September 2022 for the inclusion of the term "crisis" in a book title produced 51,444 "hits".

8 Evidence on this point is found in R.H. Helmholz, *Profession of Ecclesiastical Lawyers: An Historical Introduction* (Cambridge: Cambridge University Press, 2019), 59–67.

of the continental institutions. J.G.A. Pocock's influential book on the subject of English law described his mind as being "as nearly insular as a human being's could be".[9] In fact, however, he does not deserve this awkward tribute to English exceptionalism. Coke accepted the existence and the importance of natural law, as did virtually every lawyer in his day, putting it to use most famously in Bonham's case. In that case he applied the law of nature's principle -- no man may serve as judge in his own cause – in invalidating action taken by the College of Physicians. Dealing with a statute of Edward VI, Coke asserted that "[n]o person ecclesiastical or temporal ought in any ecclesiastical court shall be examined upon the cogitation of his heart, or what he thinketh".[10] Coke's most famous biographer asserts that this was a departure from what Coke could and would have said as Attorney General under Elizabeth. That "would have been near to treason", she asserts.[11] In fact, however, that sentiment was itself a commonplace of the classical canon law. *De occultis non judicat ecclesia.*[12] Coke did not provide a canonical reference for what he wrote, but that is what it was in substance. The principle applied in both temporal and spiritual tribunals, and Coke could have found it stated in many of the canonical treatises he kept in his own well-stocked library.[13]

As for religion, Roger Williams, the founder of the State of Rhode Island, had served as Coke's clerk as a young man. He described him as "a lover and great admirer of the Church of England. . . . He was constant to it both in his life and at his death".[14] That rings true. It has been shown that, contrary to what many of us suspect from what has been written about Coke as a convinced Erastian, on Sundays at the Inner Temple, his Inn of Court, he attended both morning and afternoon services at the Temple Church, taking careful notes of what he heard in the sermons of Richard Hooker and Walter Travers.[15] He described the removal of a Bible from a parish church as "a sacrilege" not just

9 Pocock, *The Ancient Constitution and the Feudal Law* (Cambridge: Cambridge University Press, 1957), 56; a corrective is David Chan Smith, "Sir Edward Coke: Faith, Law and the Search for Stability in Reformation England", in *Great Christian Jurists in England History*, ed. by Mark Hill, R.H. Helmholz (Cambridge: Cambridge University Press 2017), 93–113.

10 2 Co. Inst. *658.

11 Catherine Drinker Bowen, *The Lion and the Throne: The Life and Times of Sir Edward Coke (1552–1634)* (Boston: Little Brown, 1956), 291–292.

12 See, e.g., X 5.3.33; Stephan Kuttner, "Ecclesia de occultis non iudicat: Problemata ex doctrina poenali decretistarum et decretalistarum a Gratiano usque ad Gregorium PP. IX.", in *Acta congressus iuridici internationalis, Romae 1934 III* (Roma, 1936), 225–246.

13 See W.O. Hassall, *Catalogue of the Library of Sir Edward Coke* (New Haven:: Yale University Press, 1950).

14 See "Letter of Anne Sadleir to Roger Williams, Winter 1652/1653", in *The Correspondence of Roger Williams: 1629–1653*, vol. 1, ed. by Glenn LaFantasie et al. (Providence: Brown University Press, 1988), 379.

15 David Chan Smith, "Sir Edward Coke: Faith, Law and the Search for Stability in Reformation England", in *Great Christian Jurists in England History*, ed. by Mark Hill, R.H. Helmholz (Cambridge: Cambridge University Press, 2017), 93–113, at 96.

a theft.[16] Coke may have rejected some of the conclusions of what we may anachronistically call the High Church position of ecclesiastical rights but that implied no rejection of the truths held within the Church of England itself. He never advocated the abolition of episcopacy. Indeed, the number of common lawyers found among the English regicides was negligible.

Personal and Professional Connections

One does not have to be an academic long enough to know that personal contact with other academics is no guarantee of mutual respect, let alone friendship. I also know, however, that it sometimes does lead to both. It provides the opportunity for both positive and negative reactions, particularly where a common endeavor joins participants from both sides together. Exactly that opportunity existed among English common and civil lawyers during this period. They knew each other. Indeed, some families produced both civilians and common lawyers.[17] Their professional centers were both in London. For the former this was in the Inns of Court and the Westminster tribunals. For the latter it was in Doctors' Commons near St. Paul's, the nearby Court of Arches, the provincial court of appeal for the southern province of Canterbury, and the Prerogative Court of Canterbury. Geographically, therefore, they were not far apart. However, it was not simply chance encounters on the street or at the theater that brought them together. Prominent ecclesiastics sometimes became honorary members of the Inns of Court,[18] and, for a time, Doctors' Commons also welcomed members from outside its own circle.[19] Some civil and some common lawyers would also have known each other from their experiences at Oxford and Cambridge.[20] They also met later on, as in their practice in the Court of Chancery, where some of the masters of the court were civilians.[21] Some of them served together as agents of the Crown in what has been called "educated public service".[22] They also sat together as judges in the so-called prerogative courts. The Court of Star Chamber, the Court of

16 "Bucksale v. Bucksale (1614)", in 81 Eng. Rep. 324, 1 Rolle 57.

17 E.g., the Fastolf family of Great Yarmouth in the 1320s; see J.H. Baker, "Dr Thomas Fastolf and the History of Law Reporting", in his *Collected Papers on English Legal History*, vol. 2 (Cambridge: Cambridge University Press, 2013), 569–582, at 575–576.

18 Robert Pearce, *History of the Inns of Court and Chancery* (London: Bentley, 1848), 354–355.

19 F. Donald Logan, "Doctors' Commons in the Early Sixteenth Century: A Society of Many Talents", *Historical Research*, 61:145 (June 1988), 151–165.

20 See Brand, *The Origins*, 154–156.

21 William Holdsworth, *A History of English Law*, vol. 5 (London: Sweet and Maxwell, 1924, repr. 1966), 257–258; Jones, *Elizabethan Court*, 110–111; Mark Beilby, "The Profits of Expertise: The Rise of the Civil Lawyers and Chancery Equity", in *Profit and the Professions in Later Medieval England*, ed. by Michael Hicks (Gloucester: Alan Sutton, 1990), 72–90.

22 Simon Walker, "Between Church and Crown: Master Richard Andrew, King's Clerk", *Speculum*, 74:4 (October 1999), 956–991, at 986; Ralph Turner, "Clerical Judges in English Secular Courts: The Ideal versus the Reality", *Medievalia et Humanistica*, n.s. 3 (1972), 75–98.

Requests, and the branches of the Court of High Commission all were staffed by civilian judges as well as by common lawyers.[23] This was a sensible, even natural practice. Many of the matters these courts took up involved ecclesiastical law and equitable considerations, as well as the settled common law. Of course, it is true that proximity did not guarantee perfect agreement. That would be too much to expect of lawyers. But in these courts common lawyers and civilians did not meet as enemies or strangers. They worked together.

A different sort of regular encounter between civilians and common lawyers also took place. It occurred in the common law courts themselves. When litigation in the Common Pleas or King's Bench raised a point related to the civil or canon laws, English civilians were sometimes invited to appear to provide information and help to the judges. They were "friends of the court" in that forum. So, in the period covered by this chapter, litigation involving the substantive law of tithes, last wills and testaments, clerical status, procedural irregularities, and a few others connected with the church's law came before the judges in Westminster Hall. These cases were often the occasion for hearing the views of English civilians, who appeared in person before them. It happened, for example, when the common law courts were called upon to pass judgment on whether a writ of prohibition should be issued to prevent a case in an ecclesiastical court from proceeding. This was long a sore point, a source of grievance among the English civilians, and it is right to recognize this. But it is also right to recognize that the common lawyers who made the decisions sometimes held back out of respect for the civilians they knew. Sir Daniel Dun, dean of the Court of Arches, was so treated on one such occasion, after he had committed a man to prison for having "saucily" introduced a writ of prohibition before him.[24]

Specific examples provide the most useful means of assessing the varied connections that existed between English civilians and common lawyers. One is that of Sir Arthur Duck (1580–1648), chancellor of the diocese of London from 1628 and author of a comparative and learned description of European and English law he called *De iure et authoritate iuris civilis*.[25] For purposes of this chapter, however, what matters is his relationship with common lawyers,

23 See, e.g., *Reports of Cases in the Courts of Star Chamber and High Commission*, ed. by S. R. Gardiner (Camden Society n.s. 39, 1886), 38; *The Ancient State and Authoritie and Proceedings of the Court of Requests by Sir Julius Caesar*, ed. by L.M. Hill (Cambridge: Cambridge University Press, 1975), 39; Roland Usher, *The Rise and Fall of the High Commission* (Oxford: Oxford University Press, 1913, reissued 1968), 42–63, 345–361; C.T. Allmand, "The Civil Lawyers", in *Profession, Vocation and Culture in Later Medieval England: Essays Dedicated to the Memory of A. R. Myers*, ed. by Cecil H. Clough (Liverpool: Liverpool University Press, 1982), 155–180, at 156–157.

24 "Bruistone v. Baker (1615)", in 81 Eng. Rep. 511, 1 Rolle 315.

25 See Peter Stein, "Duck, Arthur", in *Oxford Dictionary of National Biography* (Oxford: Oxford University Press, 2004), accessed 23 September 2022, https://doi.org/10.1093/ref:odnb/8128.

not his own accomplishments as a civilian. We can best assess it from the perspective of reported cases heard in the royal courts. They are available in the multivolume collection of English Reports and can now be uncovered by means of a word search. What that shows is that Duck appeared in several cases heard in the royal courts. He came not as a judge but as a learned friend of the court. In one example, in 1634 he appeared there, apparently by invitation in the judges in the Court of King's Bench. The case at issue involved the question of whether a writ of prohibition should be issued to the Court of Arches to prevent the judge from entertaining a suit for defamation. The slanderous words had been spoken in London, and the suit, brought in a court of the archbishop of Canterbury, was challenged as a violation of the settled rights of the bishops of London. For this reason, the party alleged, it should be prohibited as having been based on an erroneous venue. However, Duck appeared in the suit, explaining and justifying the existence of this venue as an accepted part of a general license granted time out of mind by the bishops of London. The archbishop was, Duck said, therefore acting under the applicable canon law.[26] Apparently in consequence of his intervention the justices of the King's Bench held that issuance of a writ of prohibition could not be justified. In other words, in this case the justices of the royal courts acted not to diminish the jurisdiction of the ecclesiastical tribunals, but rather to support them – this upon the submission provided by an English civilian.

Of course, there were cases that went the other way, particularly those in which the royal courts exercised their own jurisdiction at the expense of ecclesiastical interests. Where the royal courts offered a remedy, as they did for instance in the law of defamation where a crime had been imputed to the plaintiff, the availability of a writ of prohibition was established as a matter of course. It forbade the ecclesiastical courts from proceeding further in a case which had been brought before them by the choice of one of the litigants. Where a dispute belonged properly in their own courts, the common lawyers paid no heed to the objections of representative civilians.

For the most part, however, the important point is that the King's judges seem to have been open to intervention by English civilians where they had useful information that touched upon cases that had come before them. They used a process called "consultation" to submit questions to English civilians when a question like that of the validity (or invalidity) of a marriage contract had been raised. Civilians also sometimes came in person to inform the justices of the matters of common relevant interest.[27] They were invited to do so. In

26 "Gobbet's Case (1634)", in 79 Eng. Rep. 897, 898, Cro. Car. 339, 340: "Jones said that he was informed by Doctor Duck, Chancellor of London, that there hath been for a long time a composition betwixt the Bishop of London and the Archbishop of Canterbury ..., so as it is *quasi* a general license". For a later comment on the case, see "Ford v. Welden (1664)", in 83 Eng. Rep. 1165, 1 Keble 651.

27 See the examples and discussion in David Seipp, "The Reception of Canon Law and Civil Law in the Common Law Courts before 1600", *Oxford Journal of Legal Studies*, 13:3 (Autumn

another case involving the contents of the canon law, for instance, the King's Bench justices called upon Duck for help. This came in an action of ejectment involving a parcel of glebe land that belonged to the rectory of Molesworth.[28] Equally so did the justices find relevant what Doctor Duck had written on the subject in a case from much later, long after Duck's death, to establish the validity and universality of the rule that contracts were to be interpreted according to the law of the land where they had been entered into.[29] The variety and consistency with which interventions like these occurred is suggestive of the respect with which the English civilians were normally treated in the royal courts.[30] These encounters did not always include agreement, but the civilians were heard and treated with respect when they appeared.

Parallel Tracks

That the common law and the civil law were distinct entities is common knowledge. It is not my intention to challenge it. However, the language of competition between them, often put into quasi-military tones, occupies the pages of many treatments of the subject. That it is my intention to challenge. Much of it is based on the supposedly absolutist character of both the canon and the Roman laws. In the former, it was the pope who held unquestioned power. In the latter, it was the emperor, and, by logical extension, the lesser rulers of continental lands. Here I must ask readers to focus their attention on private law rather than large and constitutional questions. It is important for us to remember how small a part of the professional lives of lawyers political thought then occupied. When we do this, we will find ample evidence of legal institutions that the law the two systems shared. In fact, there were quite a few. I will leave aside questions of causation – attempts to prove that the *ius commune* influenced the growth of the common law.[31] That is a separate question. All I mean to say here is that both systems contained quite a few common ingredients. They gave lawyers much to think about, and even to talk about with each other.

One of the oldest of these shared subjects was the distinction between proprietary and possessory remedies. The Roman interdicts dealt with the two

1993), 388...420, at 406...412; and J.H. Baker, "Roman Law at the Third University of England", in his *Collected Papers*, vol. 1, 367–393, at 369.

28 "Dodson v. Lynn (1635)", in 79 Eng. Rep. 1011, Cro. Car. 475, 476.

29 "Robinson v. Bland (1761)", in 96 Eng. Rep. 141, 1 Black, W. 256, 257.

30 For other examples, see my "Civilians in the Common Law Courts, 1500–1750", in *English Legal History and Its Sources: Essays in Honour of Sir John Baker*, ed. by David Ibbetson, Neil Jones, Nigel Ramsay (Cambridge: Cambridge University Press, 2019), 342–357.

31 See, e.g., the careful weighing of evidence leading to a measured but positive conclusion in Carsten Fischer, "Cessavit per biennium – a 13th century example of a civilian transplant into English common law?", in *Rechtstranfer in der Geschichte*, ed. by Vanessa Duss et al. (Munich: Martin Meidenbauer, 2006), 399–417.

separately – they were distinct legal concepts. The first required physical control of property with an intent to hold it; the second required full ownership. This same division was also found in the common law in the distinction between seisin and ownership – the one protected by the assize of novel disseisin, the later by the writ of right.[32] These two laws concerning these similar ideas were not identical. They were similar, however, in that both offered recovery of possession of land without requiring that a possessor prove more than his ouster of possession, leaving the question of full ownership open for subsequent determination. The ecclesiastical courts in England made use of this distinction, most often in sorting out claims to ecclesiastical benefices.[33] The point is, then, that the subject would have been of interest to both civilian and common lawyers. Their laws were close enough in substance to encourage discussion.

It is remarkable how often this pattern recurred. It should be added, however, that the two sources of law rarely if ever used the same words to describe these similar institutions. They did speak the same language, or rather the same languages,[34] but they often chose different words to describe the similar if not identical legal concepts. The similarity was sufficient to have attracted the notice of at least one civilian commentator during the reign of Elizabeth.[35] The most obvious example was in the names given to the lawyers themselves. Both professions were divided into two. In the common law there were barristers and attorneys; in the civil law advocates and proctors. Roughly speaking, they performed identical functions. The same thing occurred in many areas of substantive law. It was a writ of *novel disseisin* in the royal courts; an action *unde vi* in the *ius commune*. In the royal courts an action to enforce a recurrent monetary obligation was called an annuity. In the ecclesiastical courts the same obligation was called an annual pension.[36] In the royal courts an action

32 The basic work on the English law is Donald Sutherland, *The Assize of Novel Disseisin* (Oxford: Oxford University Press, 1973), 40–42. See also Joshua Tate, "Ownership and Possession in the Early Common Law", in *American Journal of Legal History*, 48:3 (July 2006), 280–313.; but cf. David Seipp, "Roman Legal Categories in the Early Common Law", in *Legal Record and Historical Reality: Proceedings of the Eighth British Legal History Conference Cardiff 1987*", ed. by T.G. Watkin (London: Hambledon Press, 1989), 9–36. A convenient summary of the Roman law on the subject is found in W. W. Buckland, *Text-Book of Roman Law from Augustus to Justinian*, 3rd ed. by Peter Stein (Cambridge: Cambridge University Press, 1968), 196–208.

33 See, e.g., "Archbishop of York c. Dean and Chapter of Durham (ca. 1600)", in *Three Civilian Notebooks 1580–1640*, ed. by R.H. Helmholz (London: Selden Society 127, 2011), n. 8.

34 J.H. Baker, "The Three Languages of the Common Law", in Id., *Collected Papers on English Legal History*, vol. 2 (Cambridge: Cambridge University Press, 2013), 515–536.

35 British Library, Harl. MS. 4117, f. 80: "et denique nota quod in quibusdam casibus unum et idem crimen puniri potest in utroque foro, ..., sed non uno et eodem modo".

36 See R.H. Helmholz "Annuities and Annual Pensions", in *Law, Lawyers and Texts: Studies in Medieval Legal History in Honour of Paul Brand*, ed. by Susanne Jenks, Christopher Whittick, Jonathan Rose (Leiden: Brill, 2012), 69–85.

on the case to recover for harm to land by a tenant for life or less was called an action for waste. In the ecclesiastical courts, the virtually identical remedy, one brought for causing harm to glebe land held by the church and possessed by parsons, was commonly given the name of dilapidations.[37] The royal courts administered the law of wardship; the consistory courts the law of *cura* and *tutela*. Many aspects of the law of last wills and testaments were also shared in substance by both sets of lawyers, although normally not with the identical names. This phenomenon was not absolute, of course. It should be noted, for instance, that the term *res judicata* was used in the law of both.

A further and more consequential example is the law of defamation.[38] In the royal courts it was most often given the name of slander. In most but not all ways, it was the same thing. In the years that are the subject of this chapter, the common law courts began to offer a remedy for a wrong that had been a monopoly of the ecclesiastical courts during the Middle Ages. The original concept of defamation depended upon malicious imputation of a criminal act – "You are a thief, for you stole my wallet" for example. At some point around 1500 common lawyers had come to regard this as an illegitimate encroachment on their jurisdictional monopoly over secular crimes like theft. Their response was to allow suit to be brought in the royal courts – an action on the case for slander – where the crime imputed was a secular one. So it happened that the ecclesiastical courts gradually lost a large part of their medieval jurisdiction over defamation. Thereafter the two court systems continued along parallel paths, both gradually expanding the scope of their remedies slightly. A wider range of harmful language was brought within the jurisdiction of both legal systems. However, it remained true that the names they used in this equivalent process were different. What was called defamation in the ecclesiastical forum was usually called slander in the temporal forum. The point remains, however. The legal aspects of each remedy would have been natural subjects for discussion between common lawyers and civilians. Similar remedies invite discussion among those who make use of them.

This sort of correspondence in substance if not in nomenclature was the subject of a well-known treatise by William Fulbecke (1560–ca. 1603), commonly called Fulbecke's Parallels,[39] it took the form of a dialogue between a Romanist, a canonist, and an English common lawyer. They found many

37 John Rastell (d. 1536), *Les Termes de la Ley*, London, printed J. Streater, for the Company of Stationers, 1659, 554: "Waste by the Civil Law is call'd Dilapidation", See also James Elmes (d. 1862), *Practical Treatise on Ecclesiastical and Civil Dilapidations*, 3rd ed. (London: S. Brooke, 1829).

38 See the Introduction to *Select Cases on Defamation to 1600*, ed. by R.H. Helmholz (London: Selden Society 101, 1985).

39 William Fulbecke (d. ca.1603), *A Parallell or Conference of the Civill Law, the Canon Law, and the Common Law of This Realm of England*, London, for the Company of Stationers, 1602; a more modest example of this comparative literature from the early seventeenth century is found in Borthwick Institute, University of York, MS. Prec.Bk.6, folios 6–12.

points of substantive similarity although they were coupled with distinct names. So, for instance, Fulbecke's text took note that what was called an "action on the case" in English law was called an *actio iniuriarum* among the Romanists. In both situations, the same reasons for their adoption and use in law courts existed. The wide range of human activity they could cover, some of which could not be stated in advance, stood behind both. Also the inconvenience of finding a different name for each of the possible varieties factored it. As the common lawyer responded after hearing a description of the civil law's action, "so likewise an Action on the Case stretcheth as a remedy against many offenses".[40] They were parallel remedies all right, but they had different names.

Similarities in Practice without Similarities in Name

The most basic difference between the two systems of law discussed in this chapter lay in the procedural law of proof. They adopted distinct ways of resolving questions of fact. In the royal courts, it was by juries. In the ecclesiastical courts, the court of Chancery, and in other prerogative courts the outcome was determined by judicial evaluation of the testimony of witnesses. Those witnesses were normally called by the parties themselves, though they could be summoned by the judges themselves. In either case, their testimony was taken outside of court, making use of the questions and interrogatories that had been submitted by the parties. Answers to each of them were written down by a court official and later submitted to the court for judicial evaluation of their probative force. The evaluation was carried out according to a sophisticated system that had been worked out by European jurists.[41] In the sixteenth century, the basic work on this subject is one of those monster treatises that are usable only with the aid of its index.[42] The common law had no equivalent system. Sir Edward Coke took note that in criminal cases, the testimony of witnesses "is no part of the trial".[43] In civil cases, they sometimes appeared, but questions of fact were made by juries of laymen, and it is common ground among legal historians that for the creation of its own law of evidence, the common lawyers had to await the arrival of the eighteenth century.[44]

A disparity between the procedure used by these two systems was certainly real. It invited argument about which of the two was superior in content or authority, and argument there sometimes was. At the same time, however,

40 Fulbecke, *Parallell*, Pt. II, Dial. 2.

41 Jean Philippe Lévy, *La Hiérarchie des preuves dans le doit savant du Moyen-Age* (Paris: Sirey, 1939); Knut Wolfgang Nörr, *Ein geschichtlicher Abriss des continental europäischen Zivilprozesses* (Tübingen: Mohr Siebeck, 2015).

42 See, e.g, Josephus Mascardus (d. 1588), *Probationum Omnium quae in utroque foro quotidie versantur*, Francofurti ad Moenum, impensis Sigis. Feyrabendii, 1593.

43 3 Co. Inst. *26.

44 Baker, *Introduction to English Legal History*, 4th ed., 550–551.

this divergence was tempered because each also made some use of the other's method of proof. Both admitted the evidence of documents. Under some circumstances, as in actions of debt, the royal courts admitted proof by compurgation, although they called it by a different name – wager of law. The common law also sometimes admitted the presence of witnesses who were not jurors. They acted in aid of, or sometimes in opposition to, the verdicts reached by ordinary juries. This shows that the split between the two systems in determining the truth was not absolute. Even so, the evidence does not establish a necessary procedural connection. Historians have looked in vain for signs in the common law courts of adoption of the strict and elaborate civilian rules on the subject.[45]

More evidence of common usage is found for the courts where the civil law was used. The civilian system of proof left room for proof by notoriety or by common fame, although normally this amounted to only half proof. In substance, admitting its relevance in practice would have been very like what came from a presentment jury.[46] The church's own courts also made regular use of jury-like institutions. They did so in several circumstances by submitting questions to inquests of men who had knowledge of facts relevant to questions of guilt and liability. Questions involving taxation of parishioners, called church rates, were normally settled by convening groups of existing parishioners and asking them to testify about what past practice had been.[47] So were disputed questions in disputes about the holder of the advowson, the right to present the incumbent to a vacant benefice.[48] Finding facts in the church's law of dilapidations – that is in questions of the repair or restoration of churches themselves and of their property – was similarly put to inquests of local men.[49] Even in a matrimonial dispute, this sometimes occurred.[50] These were, at the

45 James B. Thayer, *Preliminary Treatise on Evidence at Common Law* (Boston: Little Brown, 1898, repr. 1969), 122–136; John Henry Wigmore, *Treatise on the System of Evidence in Trials at Common Law*, vol. 1 (Boston: Little Brown, 1904–05), § 575 (2) (describing an uptick in the use of witness testimony after 1400).

46 Lévy, *Hiérarchie des preuves*, 32–53.

47 Several examples are described in R.H. Helmholz, *Oxford History of the Laws of England*, Vol. I, *the Canon Law and Ecclesiastical Jurisdiction from 597 to the 1640s* (Oxford: Oxford University Press, 2004), 470–473.

48 Helmholz, *Oxford History*, 484–487.

49 Canterbury Cathedral Library, Sede Vacante Scrapbook III, n. 220: "Inquisitio facta in ecclesia de Broch per viros infrascriptos de parochia eiusdem ... super defectibus domorum rectorie eiusdem et cancelli". A sixteenth-century example in a dilapidations dispute is found in "Grene c. Mulis (Chester Archdeaconry 1514)", in Cheshire Archives and Local Studies, Chanter MS. 775, f. 45: the judge 'decrevit commissionem magistro Thome Nyson pro inquisitione facienda in ecclesia parochiali de Hunston'. The details of the procedure of the seventeenth century were given in a precedent book, now found in the Norfolk Record Office, MS. PCD/23, f. 29, under the heading "In Dilapidations what to be done".

50 See Lambeth Palace Library, London, Act book MS. 244, f. 54: the judge "auditis allegationibus et altercationibus partium predictarum decernimus inquirendum fore per Radulphum de

very least, jury-like institutions. They would have provided a subject of importance and interest to civilians and common lawyers alike.

Something like the same connection existed in the authorities drawn upon in the two court systems. It has been commonly assumed that a significant divide existed on this front. The common lawyers drew upon the precedent of decided cases in fashioning arguments, whereas the civil lawyers drew upon the authority of texts found in the laws of Justinian and the *Corpus iuris canonici*. For the civilians, prior cases were simply examples of the application of law found in the texts, not authorities in themselves. We now know, however, that the contrast was much less dramatic than had been supposed.[51] The civilians did make use of decided cases, arguing from collections of *Consilia* and *Decisiones* which contained the equivalent of English case law. The decisions of the Roman Rota, the highest court in the church's legal system, were authorities in themselves. *Consilia*, contained in the opinions of learned civilians in response to requests for aid in formulating legal arguments in specific cases, became authorities in themselves,[52] and both civil laws and papal decretals were interpreted with a freedom that is inconsistent with the strictures of legal positivism. We also know that by the late Middle Ages at the latest, English common lawyers also possessed a body of learned legal doctrine, some of it contained in the Readings at the Inns of Court in London and some of it found in treatises written by the common lawyers themselves. Here again, there was a lasting difference between the worlds of common lawyers and civilians, but it amounted to much less in practice than has most often been asserted by historians of the common law.

Conclusion

This has been a summary of the relevant evidence found in the sources, one drawn from court records compiled prior to the eighteenth century. Most of the specific examples have come from the records of the ecclesiastical courts. The evidence shows that, contrary to the assumption of the existence of a strict separation, one fueled by actual enmity between common lawyers and civilians, in fact the two legal professions had quite a bit in common. They

Cumbe et tresdecim vel duodecim de fide dignioribus vicinis dicti Johannis neutri partium predictarum suspectis".

51 A valuable summary of recent developments in this field, together with citations to relevant publications, is found, together with additions to it, in J.H. Baker, "Case-Law in England and Continental Europe", in Id., *Collected Papers*, vol. 2, 602–610; see also David Ibbetson, "Law Reporting, Authority and Precedent: The Common Law Paradigm", in *Authorities in Early Modern Law Courts*, ed. by Guido Rossi (Edinburgh: Edinburgh University Press, 2021), 84–97.

52 Peter Riesenberg, "The Consilia Literature: A Prospectus", *Manuscripta*, 6 (2015), 3–22; Guido Kisch, *Consilia: Eine Bibliographie der juristischen Konsiliensammlungen* (Basel: Helbung & Lichtenhan, 1970); J.A. Clarence Smith, *Medieval Law Teachers and Writers: Civilian and Canonist* (Ottawa: University of Ottawa Press, 1975).

shared many interests, and it is certainly thinkable that they would have shared ideas with each other. That there were significant differences and disagreements between the two there is no doubt. But these two professions were not separated by a Berlin Wall. If anything, it was a quite soft border that separated them, one that both groups of lawyers were sometimes willing to cross. Both groups of lawyers could admire the other's legal system even while they remained convinced of the superiority of their own.[53] In assessing the evidence that supports this conclusion, it is worth saying again that the men discussed in this chapter were all lawyers, and lawyers can disagree about many things and still have good reason to respect each other. In fact, they can even learn something from their experiences together.[54] It appears to this student of the subject that this kind of learning was a regular and important feature of the history of both parts of the legal profession in medieval England. It appears to be a mistake to portray them as natural and inevitable enemies.

53 Howard Nenner, *By Colour of Law: Legal Culture and Constitutional Politics in England, 1660–1689* (Chicago: University of Chicago Press, 1997), 9–15.

54 See Donald Sutherland, "The Brotherhood and the Rivalry of English Lawyers in the General Eyres", *American Journal of Legal History*, 31 (January 1987), 1–8.

10 Gerard Malynes and the "Ancient Law-Merchant"

A View on the *ius commune* from the Borders*

Stefania Gialdroni

Borderlands

In 1622, the Dutch merchant Gerard Malynes published in London a treatise devoted to the "Ancient Law-Merchant", which, according to the subtitle, was "Necessarie for all Statesmen, Iudges, Magistrates, Temporall and Ciuile Lawyers, Mint-men, Merchants, Marriners, and all others negotiating in all places of the World".[1] It stated:

> the *Law-Merchant*… doth properly consist of the Custome of Merchants in the course of Trafficke, and is approued by all Nations, according to the definition of Cicero, *Vera Lex est recta Ratio, Natura congruens, diffusa in Omnes, Constans, Sempiterna.*[2]

* The original research for this chapter was funded by the European Research Council: ERC CoG MICOLL – "Migrating Commercial Law and Language. Rethinking Lex Mercatoria" (11th–17th Cent.)", 2021–2026, Grant Agreement 2020 101002084.

1 Gerard Malynes, *Consuetudo, vel Lex Mercatoria, or The Ancient Law-Merchant*, London, Printed by Adam Islip, Anno Dom. 1622. This first edition, which was used for writing this chapter, is available online: https://quod.lib.umich.edu/cgi/t/text/text-idx?c=eebo;idno=A06786.0001.001. Two other editions followed in 1636 and 1686 (if we consider the 1629 and 1656 versions to be simple reprints). See Stefania Gialdroni, "Gerard Malynes e la questione della lex mercatoria", *Zeitschrift der Savigny-Stiftung für Rechtsgeschichte, Germanistische Abteilung*, 126 (2009), 38–69, at 48–49. In the last edition, designated as the third in the frontispiece, three other treatises followed that of Malynes. These were *Lex Mercatoria: The Jurisdiction of the Admiralty of England Asserted* by Richard Zouch, Doctor of the Civil Laws, and late Judge of the Admiralty; *The Ancient Sea Laws of Oleron, Wisby, and the Hanse-Towns, still in force: Rendered into English for the use of Navigators* by G. Miege, Gent; and *The Sovereignty of the British Seas, proved by Records, History, and the Municipal Laws of this Kingdom* by Sir John Buroughs, late Keeper of the Records of the Tower of London. The 1686 edition is also available online: https://archive.org/details/consuetudovellex00maly.

2 Malynes, *Lex Mercatoria*, 1622, *To the covrteovs rerder*. The quotation is taken from: Cicero, *De re publica*, 3.6.

DOI: 10.4324/9781003425069-13

And that:

> the *Law-Merchant* hath alwaies beene found *semper eadem*, that is, constant and permanent without abrogation, according to her most auncient customes, concurring with the law of nations in all countries.[3]

In 1697, about ten years after the publication of the third and last edition of Malynes's *Lex Mercatoria*, Daniel Defoe expressed an opposite opinion about mercantile law:

> The Affairs of Merchants are accompanied with such variety of Circumstances, such new and unusual Contingencies, which change and differ in every Age, with a multitude of Niceties and Punctilio's [sic]; and those again altering as the Customs and Usages of Countries and States do alter; that it has been found impracticable to make any Laws that could extend to all Cases.[4]

Although better known as the author of *Robinson Crusoe* and other masterpieces of English literature, Defoe was also a merchant who travelled around Europe, dealt in many commodities, and became an economic theorist.[5] Defoe and Malynes had at least three things in common: they both had Flemish origins (Malynes was born in Antwerp, and Defoe's father, James Foe, was a successful tallow-chandler of Flemish descent who devoted his later years to overseas trade[6]); they are both considered to be mercantilists[7]; and they both had bad luck in their commercial activities, despite their shared passion for economics. However, their opinions on the diffusion and efficacy of mercantile customs were, as we have seen, very different.

Their contrasting points of view should not surprise us: few issues in the history of commercial law have given rise to such a variety of opinions as the

3 Malynes, *Lex Mercatoria*, 1622, *To the most high and mightie monarch Iames.*

4 Daniel Defoe, *An Essay Upon Projects*, London, printed by R.R. for Tho. Cockerill, at the Three Legs in the Poultrey, 1697, *Of a Court-Merchant*, 307. Available online here: https://quod.lib.umich.edu/cgi/t/text/text-idx?c=eebo;idno=A37427.0001.001. It was Defoe's first book, and his earliest major contribution to political and social thought: D.N. DeLuna, "The Publication of Defoe's *Essay upon Projects*", *The Papers of the Bibliographical Society of America*, 87:4 (December 1993), 503.

5 John J. Richetti, *The Life of Daniel Defoe: A Critical Biography* (Chichester: Wiley Blackwell, 2015), chap. 5.

6 Richetti, *The Life of Daniel Defoe*, 2.

7 John Richetti, reporting Maximilian E. Novak's opinion, affirms that Defoe cannot be considered a proto-capitalist as he supported the state control of commerce, and, thus, he should be defined instead as a mercantilist: Richetti, *The Life of Daniel* Defoe, 144–145. Malynes is, in fact, commonly known as one of the main English "early mercantilists". See, for example, *The Early Mercantilists: Thomas Mun (1571–1641), Edward Misselden (1608–1634), Gerard de Malynes (1586–1623)*, ed. by Mark Blaug (Aldershot: Elgar, 1991).

existence of a body of customary commercial laws uniformly and universally applied across medieval and early modern Europe.[8] This body of laws is usually defined as *lex mercatoria*,[9] even though that locution was unknown until the end of the early modern period[10] outside of England, where it first appeared in the title of a short treatise (*Incipit lex mercatoria*, 1280 ca.) included in the *Little Red Book of Bristol*,[11] reappearing about 340 years later in Gerard Malynes's masterpiece: *Consuetudo, vel, Lex Mercatoria: or, the Ancient Law-Merchant.*[12] According to Malynes, this expression described a customary law "approued by the authoritie of all Kingdomes and Commonweales", while *ius mercatorum* was a law established by the authority of a sovereign.[13]

Whereas it has been demonstrated that, as far as university education and practice in the courts of the Church, the Admiralty, and the courts of equity are concerned, "the amalgam of Roman and canon law now generally known as the *ius commune* … has undoubtedly played a role in the history of England and in the development of Anglo-American law",[14] up until now the role played by the *ius commune* in the development of English *commercial* law has been overlooked.

The aim of this chapter is therefore to analyze this neglected issue from the privileged point of view of "the standard English-language work on the law

8 For an intellectual history of the concept of *lex mercatoria* with a comprehensive overview of the literature devoted to this never-ending debate, see Dave De ruysscher, "La *lex mercatoria* contextualizée: tracer son parcours intellectuel", *Revue Historique de Droit Français et Étranger*, 90:4 (oct.–dec. 2012), 499–515, in particular Footnote 2. See also Stefania Gialdroni, "Il law merchant nella storiografia giuridica del Novecento: Una rassegna bibliografica", in *Forum Historiae Iuris* (14 August 2008): .

9 See, for example, Albrecht Cordes, "Auf der Suche nach der Rechtswirklichkeit der mittelalterlichen Lex Mercatoria", *Zeitschrift der Savigny Stiftung, Germanistische Abteilung*, 118:1 (2001), 168–184.

10 Maura Fortunati, "La *lex mercatoria* nella tradizione e nella recente ricostruzione storico giuridica", *Sociologia del diritto*, 2:3 (2005), 29–41, at 33.

11 The "Little Red Book of Bristol" is a collection of texts that were considered useful for the merchants of Bristol (such as statutes, privileges, and oaths) mostly dated between 1344 and 1410. It also includes mercantile laws such as the *Roles d'Olerón* (the eleventh century) and the short treatise *Incipit lex mercatoria*: D.R. Coquillette, "Incipit lex mercatoria, que, quando, ubi, inter quos et de quibus sit: el tratado de Lex Mercatoria en el Little Red Book de Bristol (ca. 1280 a.D.)", in *Del ius mercatorum al derecho mercantil, III Seminario de historia del derecho privado: Sitges, 28–30 de mayo 1992*, ed. by Carlos Petit (Madrid: Marcial Pons, Ediciones Jurídicas y Sociales, 1997), 145–228, at 145–146.

12 Paul R. Teetor, "England's Earliest Treatise on the Law Merchant: The Essay on *Lex Mercatoria* from *The Little Red Book of Bristol* (circa 1280 AD)", *The American Journal of Legal History*, 6:2 (Apr. 1962), 178–210, at 180.

13 Malynes, *Lex Mercatoria*, 1622, *To the covrteovs rerder.*

14 R.H. Helmholz, *The Ius Commune in England: Four Studies* (Oxford: Oxford University Press, 2001), 3. See also: Paul Vinogradoff, *Roman Law in Medieval Europe* (Union: The Lawbook Exchange, 2001, first ed. 1909), 104–105.

merchant",[15] one of the most famous treatises written for the use of merchants in early modern Europe. As both commercial law and England's common law were "at the borders" of the *ius commune*, Malynes's treatise provides a unique insight into two "borderlands".

About Gerard Malynes and His Works

Malynes's father was a mint master who immigrated in the 1550s (probably from Lancashire) to the Low Countries.[16] Gerard was born in Antwerp, although we do not know exactly when.[17] By 1585, he was in London, where he remained for the rest of his life, pursuing his (often disastrous) commercial adventures, writing his treatises, and working as a consultant for commercial matters for Queen Elizabeth I and King James I.[18] He maintained a strong relationship with his fatherland, being a member of the city's Dutch church, marrying Marie, the daughter of his Dutch business partner, Guilliam van Ameyden, and remaining registered in the list of foreign residents.[19] However, he was also strongly integrated in London, being very much engaged in the empowerment of England's monetary policy, working as an informer for the Crown, proposing a number of reforms, and writing treatises.

In 1586, he became Commissioner of Trade in the Low Countries,[20] but not long afterwards his personal economic problems began: "in the 1590s he became embroiled in a series of legal disputes which threatened to ruin him completely".[21] The most serious of these disputes seems to be that involving the Dutch merchant John Honger, who accused him and his father-in-law of having stolen a sum of money (£18,000) that he had entrusted to them as his factors in England. Although Malynes declared that, on the contrary, Honger owed him a huge amount of money, he still went to prison several times between 1590 and 1596. In 1600, thanks to his contacts in government (in particular

15 Perry Gauci, "Malynes [Malines, de Malines], Gerard [Garret, Gerald] (fl. 1586–1641), merchant and writer on economics", in *Oxford Dictionary of National Biography*, 23 September 2004, https://www.oxforddnb.com/view/10.1093/ref:odnb/9780198614128.001.0001/odnb-9780198614128-e-17912

16 See, for example, Gauci, "Malynes". Raymond de Roover thought instead that he was a Dutch merchant who immigrated to England for religious or business reasons, probably belonging to the family van Mechelen, who invented those English ancestors in order to appear as much as possible a loyal subject to the Crown: Raymond de Roover, "Gerard de Malynes as an Economic Writer: From Scholasticism to Mercantilism", in *Business, Banking, and Economic Thought in Late Medieval and Early Modern Europe: Selected Studies of Raymond de Roover*, ed. by Julius Kirshner (Chicago: University of Chicago Press, 1974), 346–366, at 347–348.

17 Gauci, "Malynes".

18 Gialdroni, "Gerard Malynes", 45–46.

19 Gauci, "Malynes"; de Roover, "Gerard de Malynes", 347.

20 William Holdsworth, *A History of English Law*, vol. 5 (London: Methuen, 1924), 131.

21 Gauci, "Malynes". See also: Andrea Finkelstein, "Gerard Malynes and Edward Misselden: The Learned Library of a Seventeenth Century Merchant", *Book History*, 3 (2000), 1–20, at 3.

Sir Robert Cecil), he obtained royal protection "for special considerations", which was renewed in 1607. In 1609, he was appointed Commissioner on Mint Affairs, but his projects and business initiatives continued to go so badly that, in 1619, the Privy Council prohibited him from using the royal protection from 1607, and he had to go to debtor's prison again. There is no further record of him after 1641, when he submitted a last petition to the House of Commons. According to Perry Gauci, his decision to become a writer was in part due to his personal misfortunes.[22]

The works *Saint George for England, Allegorically Described* and *A Treatise on the Canker of England's Commonwealth* were published in 1601, and the treatise *England's View on the Unmasking of two Paradoxes* in 1603.[23] But his golden years came about two decades later. In the same year in which he published his treatise on the Law-Merchant (1622), he also published his most famous economic treatise, *The Maintenance of Free Trade*, which was a reply to Edward Misselden's *Free Trade, or the Means to Make Trade Florish* (1622). In 1623, he published *The Center of the Circle of Commerce*, which again was a reply to a work by Misselden published earlier that year: *The Circle of Commerce: Or the Balance of Trade.*

Lex Mercatoria was edited three times (1622, 1636, and 1686) if we consider the 1629 and 1656 versions to be simple reprints. Only the first two could have been published while Malynes was still alive. His first printer was Adam Islip, who was also responsible for the 1629 reprint and the second edition of 1636. In this edition, the bookseller, Nic(h)olas Bourn(e), was also written on the frontispiece. In 1656, the printer was William Hunt and the bookseller still Bourne. In 1686, four booksellers were specified but no printer. In 1667, Samuel Pepys still recommended this book as an excellent present for a young man that had to start a career as a merchant (in this case in the East Indies),[24] providing evidence for William Letwin's statement that it was "the most popular merchants' handbook of its time".[25]

During his long life, Malynes worked as a merchant, an interpreter, a writer, and a spy, but he never became a jurist. Nevertheless, one of his most influential works was devoted to legal issues, and although he focused on legal issues

22 Gauci, "Malynes".

23 Other works circulated only as manuscripts, such as "A Treatise of Tripartite Exchange" (1610). More information on Malynes's works can be found here: Lynn Muchmore, "Gerrard de Malynes and Mercantile Economics", *History of Political Economy*, 1:2 (1969), 336–358.

24 Sunday, 15 December 1667: "her son Francke being there, now upon the point of his going to the East Indys, I did give him "Lex Mercatoria", and my wife my old pair of tweezers, which are pretty, and my book an excellent one for him": https://www.pepysdiary.com/diary/1667/12/15/. This website makes available online the following edition: Samuel Pepys, *The Diary of Samuel Pepys*, transcribed by Mynors Bright, edited with additions by Henry B. Wheatley (London: Bell and Sons, 1893–1899), 8 vols.

25 William Letwin, *The Origins of Scientific Economics. English Economic Thought 1660–1776* (London: Routledge, 2003, first ed. 1963), 101.

peculiar to merchants, on several occasions he had to contend with the wider and international legal context in which merchants operated. He thus could not completely avoid the *ius commune.*

On the "Doctors and Learned of the Ciuile Law" and Their Doctrines

In his masterpiece *Consuetudo, vel, Lex Mercatoria: or, the Ancient Law-Merchant*, Malynes repeated over and over that the law-merchant was a universal and eternal customary law that had nothing to do with civil law (i.e., the *ius commune*). His mistrust and contempt for the "doctors and learned of the ciuile Law" is evident from the beginning of the treatise. He threw together, in no particular order,[26] Justinian, Roman jurists (e.g., Ulpian, Paulus, Papinian, Julianus, Pomponius, Celsus), glossators (Azo, Accursius), commentators (e.g., Bartolus, Baldus, and Jason of Mayno), humanists (e.g., Alciatus and Budeus), and some of the first commercial law writers (such as Benvenuto Stracca and Pedro de Santarém). They were all guilty of writing "many long discourses and volumes of bookes", which had nothing to do with the mechanisms of mercantile transactions, and of losing themselves in:

> quillets and distinctions ouer-curious and precise..., full of *Apicis* [sic] *iuris,* which themselues haue noted to bee subtilties, saying, *Apicis* [sic] *iuris sunt quae subtilitatem quandam respiciunt magis quam facti veritaetem.*[27]

He could rely on prestigious precedents: for example, by the second half of the fourteenth century, the famous commentator Baldus De Ubaldis had already noted that, when it came to mercantile affairs, it was necessary to keep to the truth of the facts and customs of merchants, putting aside the *apices iuris.*[28] Malynes often repeated his critiques, for example, when discussing monopolies, accusing civilians of making the Latin word *monopolium* (which they borrowed from Greek) difficult to understand by giving it so many different

26 Malynes, *Lex Mercatoria*, 1622, Part I, Chap. I: "An induction to *Lex Mercatoria*, or the Law-Merchant, and the antiquitie thereof", 5: *Bartolus, Baldus, Iustinian, Vlpian, Paule the Iurisconsulse, Papinian, Benvenuto Straccha, Petrus Santerne, Ioannes Inder, Balduinus de Vbald, Rodericus Suarez, Iason, Angell, Andrias Tiraquell, Alciatus, Budeus, Alexander Perusius, Pomponius, Incolaus Boertius, Azo, Celsus, Rusinus, Mansilius, Sillimanus, Accursius, Franciscus Aretinus, Grisogonus, Lotharius, Iulianus.*

27 Ibid.

28 Baldus De Ubaldis, *Consilia*, vol. V, cons. 400, n. 10: *inter mercatores non convenit de iuris apicibus disputare, sed de mera veritate et consuetudine mercantie*; see also cons. 466, n. 4: *item in causis mercatorum, ubi de bona fide agitur, non congruit de iuris apicibus disputare.* Both *consilia* quoted in: Umberto Santarelli, *Mercanti e società tra mercanti*, 3rd ed. (Torino: Giappichelli, 1998), 58.

definitions.[29] He implied that the ambiguity of the term was a result of the stubbornness of the civil lawyers, whom he treated almost as a single entity throughout the treatise: there was no need to specify who said what and when, it being better to use "the ordinary name of Ciuilians in generall, without naming any particular Author, to auoid ambiguitie and vncertaintie".[30]

However, although he argued that their "determinations" could "giue but little satisfaction to instruct merchants"[31] and despite claiming to be the first to provide really useful information for those eager to thoroughly understand mercantile activities, he still added the civilians' opinions to his account of merchants' customs. The only explicit reason he provided was to "giue satisfaction to the learned and judicious",[32] but this is clearly unsatisfactory. We will return to this in the conclusion.

Continuing his critique of the civil lawyers, he stated that: "They doe more regard certaine subtilties than the trueth of the fact or matter".[33] In particular, as we already underlined, they focused a lot on definitions, which were completely useless to Malynes's aims,[34] or, at least, this is what he claimed. They asked, for example,[35] what a merchant was and what "merchandising" (*mercatura*) was; whether someone who had bought and sold something just once should be considered a merchant; whether "merchandising" and "negotiating" were the same thing; whether a usurer could be considered a merchant; whether retail sales should be considered merchandising; whether clergymen and gentlemen who bought and sold should be considered merchants; in what cases a merchant could become a usurer; whether horse-sellers should be considered merchants; whether a "shop-keeper trading beyond the seas and at home" was a merchant; and whether a young man dwelling with a merchant should also be considered a merchant. And the list of questions went on: Could a merchant trade and perform promises with "Turkes, Heathens, Barbarians, and Infidels"?; Could a merchant lie?; Was education a requisite for becoming a merchant?; Could a merchant deal with prohibited commodities?[36]

As mentioned above, even though he judged those questions "unnecessarie", he reported what seemed to him to be the civilians' opinions on many issues, starting from their basic definitions. A merchant, for example, was someone who continually dealt in buying and selling commodities (also by

29 Malynes, *Lex Mercatoria*, 1622, Part I, Chap. XVLL: "Of Associations, Monopolies, Engrossings, and Forestallings, 213.

30 Malynes, *Lex Mercatoria*, 1622, Part I, Chap. I, 8.

31 Ibid., 6.

32 Ibid., 8.

33 Ibid., 5.

34 Ibid.: "And other the like questions which I hold to be vnnecessarie to trouble Merchants braines withal".

35 We have not reported the complete list of Malynes questions and have not respected the exact order of the questions: ibid., 5–6.

36 Ibid., 5–6.

way of permutation), both at home and abroad, and should be honest and trustworthy. However, other categories were excluded from being merchants:

> Clergie men, Noblemen, Gentlemen, Souldiors, Counsellors at the laws both Ecclesiasticall and Temporall, publicke officers and magistrates, franticke persons and mad men, youthes vnder yeares, orphanes, lunatickes and fooles, all these are exempted to be merchants: But sonnes and seruants may deale in merchandise with their fathers and masters.[37]

Furthermore, the civilians also specified that those who went bankrupt, gave up their commercial activities, or were prohibited from trading because of offenses they had committed would cease to be a merchant.

After having reported what a merchant was, Malynes referred to Plato and Cicero in order to define "merchandise". In general, his treatise is full of references to philosophers and writers from antiquity.[38]

> *Plato* saieth, That merchandise is two fold, namely, *ad victum & vestitum*, of things for the backe and for the bellie, as belonging to the bodie of man; and of things concerning the mind of man, as learning of musicke, and other arts bought for money, and sold againe to others for money; and this distinction is in regard of man, but farre from that matter of trafficke and commerce which is comprehended vnder Commutatiue iustice, whereof *Cicero* speaketh.[39]

He added that the civilians argued that merchandise is made up of movable things, with the exception of holy things, prohibited wares, and weapons for enemies and infidels. However, this was not the information that a merchant really needed. There was a gap in the literature on merchants and merchandise and he would fill it. He thus made a list of twelve things that a merchant should *really* know[40]:

1. Arithmetic (including the correct computation of time and the "mystery" of numbers);
2. weights and measures;
3. geometry, cosmography, and mathematic;

37 Ibid., 6.

38 For example, Cicero is quoted eleven times, Aristotle ten, Pliny six, Plato five, Seneca four, Pythagoras and the Pythagoreans three, Plutarch two and Virgil one. The erudition shown by Malynes in his works was analyzed here: Finkelstein, "Gerard Malynes", 5–8.

39 Malynes, *Lex Mercatoria*, 1622, Part I, Chap. I, 6. Plato, *Sophist;* see, for example, George Grote, *Plato, and Other Companions of Sokrates*, vol. 2 (London: John Murray, 1865), 404. When quoting Cicero, Malynes probably refers to *De Inventione*, 2.160.

40 Malynes, *Lex Mercatoria*, 1622, Part I, Chap. I, 6–7.

4. the "three Essential parts of traffick": "Commodities, Money, and Exchange for money by Billes of exchange";
5. the characteristics of the principal commodities of all countries;
6. the customs used for buying and selling;
7. the delivering of money at interest "or vpon Botomary, or vpon liues, annuities, or pensions in nature of rent, &c.";
8. the sea-laws;
9. the tolls and "all kinds of impositions to be paid for the import and export of commodities";
10. "insurances";
11. accounting; and
12. the Rules to be Applied in Cases of Dispute between Merchants.

Although civil law did not explicitly appear in this list, the civilians' opinions were often considered relevant, for example, when it came to analyzing commodities, promises, usury, and disputes resolution.

About Commodities

The opinion of the "Doctors of the Ciuile Law" was mentioned to describe the different kinds of commodities typical of several countries. Without making any direct reference to a specific author, Malynes clearly quoted Pomponius when he proposed the distinction between things that are "contained of one spirit" (*Quod continetur vno spiritu*), like a man or a stone; things that are made of several things joined together (*Quod ex pluribus inter se, coherentibus constat*), like a building or a ship; and things that are made up of several things that are distant from one another (*Quod ex distantibus constat*), like a people or a legion.[41] But he considered this distinction to be incomplete and of no particular use to merchants.

However, when it came to bartering, Malynes referred to the opinion of the civilians again. He attributed to them the definition of permutation, and he pointed out that they also called it a permutation in cases in which there was a scarcity of gold and silver and, as a result, the value of the commodities exceeded the money paid for them: "they do call that a permutation, and denie the same to be an emption by their distinctions".[42] He again referenced their opinions in relation to buying and selling.[43] Evidently this issue was (and

41 D. 41.3.30 (Pomponius *libro 30 ad Sabinum*) pr.: *tria autem genera sunt corporum, unum, quod continetur uno spiritu et Graece henomènon vocatur, ut homo tignum lapis et similia: alterum, quod ex contingentibus, hoc est pluribus inter se cohaerentibus constat, quod synemmènon vocatur, ut aedificium navis armarium: tertium, quod ex distantibus constat, ut corpora plura non soluta, sed uni nomini subiecta, veluti populus legio grex.*

42 Malynes, *Lex Mercatoria*, 1622, Part I, Chap. VIII: "Of Commutation or Bartring of Commodities", 83.

43 Ibid., Chap. IX: "Of ordinarie buyings and sellings of Commodities".

is) of particular importance for commerce, and so Malynes took it seriously. Among the eleven necessary conditions he listed, there were: consent; power to buy and sell; honesty; lawfulness; irrevocability; and the goal of buying in order to resell.[44]

As in many other cases, morality (which often overlapped with the concepts of divine law and natural law) was absolutely central for Malynes.[45] For example, a sale was unjust in cases in which the buyer was not an expert in the commodities, in cases in which they were in need or were obliged to buy, and, it seems, in cases in which they were persuaded to buy at a higher price than the merchandise was worth, if this is the correct interpretation of the following sentence: "that persuasiue reasons be ommitted, which cause the partie to buy deerer".[46] And it is on this last issue that the civilians were again referred to: according to them, by common estimation it was unjust to sell something for more than it was worth. Or better, they stated that there were two just options, either to buy at the right price or to buy at a very cheap price (bargain), but, in the latter case, the commodities had to be sold in an open market or a shop; thus, we could say, in broad daylight. Furthermore, the civilians argued that the seller could not increase the price but could decrease it if the buyer satisfied him sooner.[47]

About Promises

When writing about the efficacy of a *nudum pactum*, i.e., an agreement made without consideration, which was therefore unenforceable, Malynes called the civilians into play again. Bare covenants were not binding, but there were exceptions: *Nudae pactio obligationem non parit, exceptionem parit.*[48] In the case of suretyships, for example, a merchant could guarantee the obligation of another merchant "without quillets or titles of the law, to auoid interruption of trafficke".[49] This was true to such an extent that a "merchant may also be come in the nature of a Suretie vnawares, or vnknown vnto him"[50] as

44 Ibid., 92.
45 Finkelstein, "Gerard Malynes", 6.
46 Malynes, *Lex Mercatoria*, 1622, Part I, Chap. IX, 92.
47 Ibid.: "The Ciuilians ... do admit that a man may sell deerer vnto an expert man, than vnto a simple man; and to sell deerer than the thing is worth by common estimation, is adiudged by them to be alwaies vniust: as also to vse reasons and inducements to sell wares the deerer, neither is the seller to demand or expect any thing aboue the price agreed vpon. And intreating hereof, they make large discourses, which I do admit to handle for the reasons aforesaid".
48 Malynes is quoting the Digest again, this time Ulpian: D.2.14.7.4: *nuda pactio obligationem non parit, sed parit exceptionem.*
49 Malynes, *Lex Mercatoria*, 1622, Part I, Chap. X: "Of Suretiship and Merchants Promises", 93.
50 Ibid., 94.

happened to a friend of his at the famous Frankfurt fair.[51] Malynes's account paints a very interesting picture of merchant activities abroad.

The story goes like this: Malynes's friend went to a merchant's warehouse to do some business and there met another merchant whom he knew, who was negotiating to buy a parcel of silk from the owner of the warehouse. As the owner did not know the buyer, he asked Malynes's friend "whether he were a good man and of credit, and he answered he was".[52] So the bargain was concluded, but, instead of paying cash, the buyer presented a "bill obligatorie" (a promissory note) to be paid on the occasion of the next fair. However, the buyer did not show up and Malynes's friend was asked to pay for him, even though he did not remember acting as a guarantor. He replied, in his defense, that no claim could rise from a bare covenant: *nudum pactum ex quo non oritur actio*. To solve the dispute, other merchants' opinions were asked, but they differed so drastically that, in the end, they decided that "the Ciuile Law was to determine the same".[53] According to what Malynes calls the "title *de mandato consilij*" of the said (civil) law, his friend had to pay on the spot. In theory, he then became the payee, although in practice he did not recover anything because the fraudulent merchant became insolvent. The moral of this story, according to Malynes, was that his friend should have said something like: "He is taken or reputed to be a good man of credit, or, I take him to be so". This way, he would have been "cleered by the law, and the custome of merchants".[54] However, another question remains open. Where can we find the title *De mandato consilij*? If it were a title belonging to Justinian's *Corpus Iuris Civilis* it would be a very interesting case of *ius commune* playing a resolutive role in a merchants' dispute. But this is not the case. The Digest and the Institutions make reference to a particular kind of mandate (*mandatum tua gratia*) made in the sole interest of the agent, only to state that it has no binding force.[55] This is exactly the opposite of what happened at the Frankfurt fair. On the other hand, we can find this kind of mandate in the Statutes of Lübeck, which was the law adopted in the towns belonging to the Hansa and which worked as a kind of mercantile common law in northern Germany.[56]

51 Michael Rothmann, *Die Frankfurter Messen im Mittelalter*, Frankfurter Historische Abhandlungen, 40 (Stuttgart: Steiner, 1998).

52 Malynes, *Lex Mercatoria*, 1622, Part I, Chap. X, 94.

53 Ibid.

54 Ibid.

55 The fragment to be found in the Digest is taken from Gaius's Institutions: D.17.1.2.6. The passage of Justianian's *Institutiones* is almost identical: Inst. 3.26.6. See Gialdroni, *Gerard Malynes*, 2009, 56–57.

56 Lib. III, Tit. X, Art. I des Lübischen Rechts: *De Mandato Consilii. Vom Befehl, welcher Rechtsweise geschieht: Wil jemand einem Fremden sein Gut nicht verkauffen, und ein ander steht dabey und sagt: Ihr möget es ihm wol vertrauen, die Bezahlung wird euch wol: Wird der Verkäuffer von dem Käuffer nicht bezahlt, so muß der derjenige zahlen, welcher den Frembden loben that, dadurch der Verkäuffer verühret worde.* More details, especially about the *mandatum tua gratia*, can be found in Gialdroni "Gerard Malynes", 56. On the use of the Lübeck law in the

This story tells us at least three things: that Malynes's "civilians" could apparently use a municipal (written) law rather that the *Corpus Iuris Civilis* to solve a dispute; that a German law referring to mercantile transactions was unknown in England (therefore denying that universality of mercantile customs that Malynes so enthusiastically sustained); and that ultimately the law-merchant was not so informal, for if only his friend had used the right words, if only he had said "I take him" to be a man of credit, he would have been safe.

About Usury

Malynes, who was clearly concerned about moral issues, was particularly troubled by usury, and he devoted four chapters of the second part of his treatise to the matter.[57] Here he really had the opportunity to demonstrate his erudition.[58] He started with the Bible[59] and with an etymological analysis of the Hebrew word *Neshech*. Then came a list of saints and their opinions about usury: Jerome ("There is no difference betwixt Vsurie, Fraud, and violent Robbing"); Augustine ("An Vsurer is he said to be who doth demand more in money, or any other thing else, than he hath deliuered"); Ambrose ("If any man take Vsurie he doth commit extortion, rapin and pillage, and shall not liue the life"); and Bernard ("the Vsuror is a theefe in law, because the Ciuile Law telleth him before hand what it is that he must rob from others, as who should say, such Lawes as permit Vsurors are lawfull theeueries").[60]

After the Bible and the Church fathers, came canon[61] and civil law. With reference to the last, he quoted the opinion of the greatest commentators of the fourteenth century and of one of the leading canon law scholars of the fifteenth century. Malynes claimed that according to Baldus, "Vsurie is a gainefull piracie, contrarie to nature, vpon the loane of any thing that consisteth vpon Number, Weight, and Measure", while Bartolus said that "all Vsurie is

whole area of the Hansa, see Albrecht Cordes, *Spätmittelalterlicher Gesellschaftshandel im Hanseraum* (Köln: Böhlau, 1998); Albrecht Cordes, *Der Bardewiksche Codex des Lübischen Rechts von 1294, Band 3. Rechtshistorischer Kommentar*, ed. by Natalija Ganina, Albrecht Cordes, Jan Lokers (Oppenheim am Rehin: Nünnerich-Asmus Verlag & Media, 2022), 9.

57 Malynes, *Lex Mercatoria*, 1622, Part II, Chap. X: "Of the Lawes and Prohibitions against Vsurie"; Chap. XI: "Of vsurie politicke, and moneys deliuered at interest"; Chap. XII: "Of intollerable Vsurie, and Lombards"; Chap. XV: "Of vsurious Contracts".

58 Finkelstein, "Gerard Malynes", 5.

59 Exodus 22:25 and Leviticus 25:35.

60 Malynes, *Lex Mercatoria*, 1622, Part II, Chap. X, 325.

61 "Decretals and Clementines, made by diuers Popes, are directly against Vsurie. *Alexander* the Pope doth straightly forbid all Vsurie, not onely vnto the Clergie, but also vnto the Layitie. In the booke *Sextus Decretalium*, *Gregorie* the tenth Bishop of Rome of that name, saieth, We (being desirous to stop the gulfe or whirlepooles of Vsurie committed, which doth deuoure soules, and vtterly wasteth wealth) do command vpon the threatnings of Gods curse, that the constitution of the latter Concile set forth against Vsurors be without any violation at all, fully & wholly obserued: and therupon a prohibition is made, That no Corporation, Colledge, or Vniuersitie shall let any house or dwelling place to any stranger Vsuror": Ibid., 326.

vtterly forbidden, and offensiue to God and man". This opinion was also confirmed by "Panormitane", i.e. Nicolò de' Tudeschi.

At this point Malynes went back in time, reporting the opinion of Greek philosophers (Plato and Aristotle) and legislators (Lycurgus and Solon), as well as of the "Romans": from the Twelve Tables to authors, such as Tacitus, Cato, and Cicero, to emperors, such as Antoninus Pius, Alexander Severus, and Vespasian. This digression into antiquity is suddenly interrupted by a reference to Emperor Charles V, who:

> at an assembly at Augusta in Germanie, did conclude with the assent of the whole Empire, That no manner of contract that had any fellowship with Vsurie should be allowed; but rather that all Vsurie should be auoided for euer, and be neuer more vsed, and if any were found to haue made any such contract, the same man to forfeit to the Magistrate or ordinarie Iudge, the fourth part of his principall summe.[62]

The conclusion was that usury, meaning the lending of money at *any* interest, was:

> condemned and forbidden by the holy Scripture, the Imperiall Lawes, Ciuile and Canon Lawes, ancient Fathers, Decretals, learned Philosophers, eloquent Orators, Historiographers, and Law-giuers.[63]

However, in the following chapter, Malynes had to admit that "the practise of it is most vsuall in many Kingdomes and Common-weales, and the Lawes are also made accordingly", in particular English law admitted a rate interest of 10%, even though:

> the preamble of the said Statute Law in the narratiue part saith, That whereas Vsurie is against all Diuine and Humane Lawes, yet tenne vpon the hundreth is tollerated to be taken for the yeare, which by way of forfeiture in the nature of a punishment may be sued for by the Law: but if there bee neuer so little taken aboue the said rate of tenne vpon the hundreth for the yeare, the principle is lost and treble damages.[64]

He continued his analysis of the problem and his list of examples (from Justinian Law to the national laws of countries such as the Republic of Venice, the Low Countries, Poland, Lithuania, and Prussia), but it is important to note that Malynes also included Thomas Wilson within the category of the

62 Ibid. 327.
63 Ibid.
64 Malynes, *Lex Mercatoria*, 1622, Part II, Chap. XI, 329.

"civilians".[65] Wilson was a politician and a statesman who also served as a diplomat in Portugal and in the Low Countries during the reign of Queen Elizabeth I, as well as a religious reformer, a humanist educated at Eton College and at King's College (Cambridge), the translator of Demostenes' orations from Greek into English, an economist, and a civil lawyer. After a period spent in Padua studying Greek (1555) and one year of imprisonment for heresy in Rome (1558–59), he went to Ferrara "where he stayed long enough to obtain from the university a degree in civil law".[66] He also published "A Discourse upon Usury by way of Dialogue and Orations" (1572),[67] which was considered "the standard anti-interest tract of his days"[68] and was based on the discourse that he gave on the matter to the House of Commons on 19 April 1571.[69] Following Wilson, Malynes excluded from the category of usury three Roman law contracts: *mutuum* ("where my goods are made thine"); *locatio* ("where a thing is put forth or letten to hire, the propertie still remaining in the owner"); and *commodatum* ("to be a letting or lending without alteration of the propertie also, but free without any gaine at all").[70] In those cases, he said, there was no lending and where there was no lending there was no usury. Wilson was a layman writing on an issue considered to be pivotal by theologians and canon lawyers. His awareness of the various facets of the problem of usury was evident in his dialogue involving a merchant, a preacher, and a (civil) lawyer.[71] Wilson's writing style is incredibly redundant and almost nonsensical to the modern reader. Malynes took what he thought was essential from the chapter devoted to the "Ciuilians or Doctours oration".[72] Not just one definition but many, even though the first one that Wilson provided summarized them all: "Usurye is whatsoeuer is taken for lone aboue the principall".[73] However, Malynes preferred to provide concrete examples, such as the following:

65 Albert J. Schmidt, "Thomas Wilson, Tudor Scholar-Statesman", *The Huntington Library Quarterly*, 3 (1957), 205, 2018, at 205–209.

66 Ibid., 208.

67 See, for example, the 1925 edition: Thomas Wilson, *A Discourse upon Usury (1572)*, edited with a historical introduction by R.H. Tawney (London: Bell, 1925). The text is now available online: https://quod.lib.umich.edu/cgi/t/text/text-idx?c=eebo;idno=A15541.0001.001.

68 Finkelstein, "Gerard Malynes", 5.

69 Russel H. Wagner, "Thomas Wilson's Speech against Usury", *Quarterly Journal of Speech*, 38:1 (1952), 13–22, at 13.

70 Malynes, *Lex Mercatoria*, 1622, Part II, Chap. XV, 349.

71 The seventh paragraph of Wilson's "Discourse" is entitled: "A Communicacion or Speache betvvene the riche worldly merchant, the godly & zealous preacher, the temporal and ciuile lawyers, towchynge vsurie, or the lone of money for gayne".

72 This is the title of the twelfth paragraph of Wilson's "Discourse".

73 Wilson, "A Discourse", 84.

> I doe sell commodities vnto a man for six moneths at a reasonable price, and afterwards he payeth me in readie money, deducting the interest for the time after the rate of ten in the hundreth, this is Vsurie.
>
> I doe deliuer old Wheat to receiue new; if I doe deliuer the same for gaine, and assure my selfe of benefit, I am an Vsurer.I doe feare the fall of money, and therefore doe deliuer my money to another man, to haue as much at sixe moneths after, according as the money was then currant when I paied it; this is Vsurie.[74]

In conclusion, although he described the civilians' opinions, including those of Wilson, as "quillets and distinctions ouer-curious and precise",[75] he seemed obliged to take them into account.

On Dispute Resolution

Given that a reference to the "ciuilians" or the "ciuil law" is present in almost all chapters in which the customs of merchants were described, this was also the case when it came to controversies. In Chapter XIV, Part III,[76] Malynes listed the way in which merchants' disputes could be solved. Seafaring cases should be determined by the Admiralty Court, while other merchants' disputes could be resolved in three ways: by means of arbitrators chosen by the parties ("to end their differences with breuitie and expedition and auoid suits in law which vnto Mechants are inconuenient"); by merchants courts[77]; by means of "the ciuile or imperiall law" or by the laws of the different kingdoms, and therefore, one might infer, by means of ordinary tribunals.[78] Nevertheless, he argued that the law-merchant was "predominant and ouerruling for all nations do frame and direct their iudgement thereafter".[79] There were two main reasons for this widespread observance of the law-merchant: its antiquity and its rightfulness. And to support the latter point, he quoted the "three generall precepts of all

74 Malynes, *Lex Mercatoria*, 1622, Part II, Chap. XV, 350–351.

75 Ibid., Part I, Chap. I, 5.

76 Ibid., Part III, Chap. XIV: "Of the determination of Sea-faring Causes". Notwithstanding the title of the chapter, Malynes listed here how all merchants' disputes could be solved.

77 "The Ciuilians hauing considered of this Office of Prior and Consulls established in many places of France, Italie, and Germanie": Malynes, *Lex Mercatoria*, 1622, Part III, Chap. XVI: "Of the Merchants Courts, or office of Prior and Consuls", 451. And also: "Hereupon *Benvenuto Straccha* the Ciuilian maketh a treatise, *Quomodo procedendum sit in causis Mercatorum*, of the manner to proceed in Merchants affaires, wherein are many vniuersall things propounded which are easier, but particular things are commonly more truer, by his owne obseruation; and he concludeth that the decrees of Merchants need no other confirmation or approbation": Ibid., 452.

78 Ibid. Part III, Chap. XIV, 443.

79 Ibid., 443–444.

lawes", which he attributed to "Caius" and to "Tribonianus" rather than to Ulpian: *Honeste viuere, Alterum non laedere, & Ius suum cuique tribuere.*[80]

When describing the "imperiall lawes" and the "fundamentall Lawes of kingdoms and common-wales", Malynes suddenly erupts into an apologia for laws, displaying an unexpected faith in justice, if not in humanity:

> All lawes are tending in substance to the vpholding of trueth, maintaining of justice, to defend the feeble from the mightie, or the suppressing of iniuries, and to roote out the wicked from amongst the good, prescribing how to liue honestly, to hurt no man wilfully, and to render euerie man his due carefully, furthering what is right, and prohibiting what is wrong; summarily to be vnderstood according to the saying of our sauiour Christ What you will haue men to do vnto you, do the same vnto them.[81]

Only at this point, he specifies that there are three kinds of laws: the law of nature; the law of nations; and the civil law, "which is an abridgement, derogating many illicentious customes which grew by peruersnesse and corruptnesse of nature, and is termed Peculiar, vsed by one kind of people, called the Imperiall Law".[82] He then describes the laws and the rules applied to conflict resolution in England, Aragon, France, and Germany with the aim to demonstrate only that national laws were variable and that only the customary law-merchant was "constant and permanent".[83]

To sum up, as trade was "the sole peaceable instrument to inrich kingdomes and common-weales, by the meanes of *Equalitie* and *Equitie*", it was the best example of commutative justice. And, because of its stability, the best way to perform trade was by means of the law-merchant.[84]

Conclusion

In the 501 pages of Malynes's masterpiece, the word "ciuil(l)ian(s)" is used forty-six times in total, the words "ciuile lawyer(s)" two times, and the expression "ciuile law(es)" forty times. These numbers seem to reveal something more than simply giving "satisfaction to the learned and judicious",[85] as Malynes claimed at the beginning of his treatise. We will propose three theories that might explain those numbers.

80 D. 1.1.10pr.

81 Malynes, *Lex Mercatoria*, 1622, Part III, Chap. XVII: "Of the Lawes of seuerall Countries, whereby the Differences and Controuersies of Merchants are determined", 461.

82 Ibid., 461.

83 Malynes, *Lex Mercatoria*, 1622, *To the most high and mightie monarch Iames.*

84 Ibid.

85 Malynes, *Lex Mercatoria*, 1622, 8.

According to the first theory, which is the most *formal*, even though his experience in mercantile affairs was pivotal for his audience, Malynes had to make reference to the civilians and their doctrines to gain authority. This might be the reason why we can find citations of ancient philosophers and jurists also in other works aimed at a readership of merchants, such as the book on the "art of trade" written by the Ragusan merchant Benedetto Cotrugli in 1458 (but first published in 1573 under the title *Della mercatura e del mercante perfetto*), where we can find many citations of ancient philosophers (Aristotle and Cicero above all), the Bible, and both civil and canon law.[86] Ugo Tucci, in editing Cotrugli's treatise in 1990, noted that there is only an apparent plurality of references, as much of the material turns out to be "second-hand", due to the fact that in that period there was limited access to a wide range of texts and, in any case, it was common to quote them through the filter of systematic collections of *exempla* and other sacred and secular repertories.[87] The same could be supposed for Malynes about whose education we know nothing.[88] It has been assumed that as a child he attended the school of the Dutch church in London, where he would have been taught Latin, reading, writing, arithmetic, and accounting both in Dutch and in English, but after that he was probably self-taught.[89]

There is thus an important difference between Cotrugli and Malynes. The former studied law in Bologna before becoming a merchant in Venice, Florence, Barcelona, Aigues-Mortes, and finally Naples, where he was admitted to the royal court led by the Aragonese household and where he frequented a humanistic entourage.[90] Even if he interrupted his studies to devote himself to commerce,[91] he had a different background to Malynes and made explicit his aim of giving some order to such an important and useful subject as

86 Benedetto Cotrugli, *Della mercatura et del mercante perfetto*, Vinegia, all'Elefanta, 1573; see also the modern editions: Benedetto Cotrugli, *Il libro dell'arte di mercatura*, ed. by Ugo Tucci (Venezia: Arsenale, 1990); Benedetto Cotrugli, *Libro de l'arte de la mercatura*, ed. by Vera Ribaudo (Venezia: Edizioni Ca' Foscari, 2016), available online. As part of the same project that led to this online critical edition, the first English translation of the treatise was also created: Benedetto Cotrugli, *The Book of the Art of Trade*, ed. by Carlo Carraro and Giovanni Favero (Cham: Palgrave Macmillan, 2017).

87 Cotrugli, *Il libro*, ed. by Tucci, 1990, 52.

88 Andrea Finkelstein claims that Malynes declared that he used the *Noctes Atticae*, therefore admitting to using secondhand citations: Finkelstein, "Gerard Malynes", 6.

89 Ibid., 5.

90 Tiziano Zanato, *Premessa*, in Cotrugli, *Libro*, ed. by Ribaudo (2016), 1–12.

91 *diremo de l'arte di mercatura quello che per cotidiano exercitio mediante l'ingegno intrinseco sapemo e sentimo, possa che li fati e la fortuna permiseno che in sul più bello del nostro philosophare io fui raputo da lo studio e rimpiantato ne la mercatura. La quale per necesità mi convéne seguire, et abandonare l'amenità e la armonia dolcie de lo studi, a lo quale ero totalmente dedito*: Cotrugli, *Libro*, ed. by Ribaudo, 2016, *Prefatio*, 38.

the art of trade, which not only was in the hands of ignorant and undisciplined people, but was also neglected by the learned (or wise).[92]

The second theory is more *political*. It has been claimed that Malynes's aim in writing his treatise on the law-merchant was to demonstrate the existence of a body of customary, transnational commercial laws at a moment in which the functions of the Court of Admiralty were under threat from the common law courts. As Maura Fortunati has pointed out, in an attempt to persuade the common law judges to apply the rules that were in use at the Court of Admiralty, English merchants argued for the existence of a legal system that had been and remained in force in all countries and at all times, regardless of the wishes of individual national legislators.[93] This powerful court had become unpopular due to the struggle between the Stuarts and Parliament at that time, as well as due to the closeness of the Admiralty to the sovereign (a closeness that can be traced, among other things, to the fact that the proceeds deriving from fines, from the sale of goods that fell into the sea as a result of shipwrecks, and from taxes imposed on merchants had to be divided between the Lord High Admiral and the sovereign themselves).

England's exceptional commercial and maritime expansion during Queen Elizabeth I's reign had exaggerated the importance of the Admiralty, prompting a reaction from the common lawyers led by Sir Edward Coke. The reasons for this battle (finally won by the common lawyers at the end of the seventeenth century) are complex, and they are probably not limited to the desire of the common law courts to gain more economic power or the desire of Parliament to oppose a court so close to the sovereign, but should perhaps also be traced back to the suspicion the common lawyers had of a court steeped so heavily in Romanist principles.[94] If this theory is correct, then Malynes's many references to the civilians acquires another meaning: although he did not like them, in comparison to the common lawyers they were the lesser of two evils.

The final theory is, in a certain sense, the most *juridical*. It could be argued that even though Malynes was a merchant (and not a lawyer) and even though he was publishing his treatise in England (rather than on the continent) he could not ignore the opinion of the civilians. It could be that this continuous reference to civil law simply reveals what Francesco Galgano stated in his book devoted to the *lex mercatoria*: that commercial law is not, and has never been,

92 *dolsemi che questa arte tanto necesaria et tanto bisognosa et utille sia diventa in mano de li indocti et indisciplinati homini, et governata senza modo, senza ordene, con abusione et senza legie, et da li savii posposta et pretermisa*; Ibid.

93 Fortunati, "La lex mercatoria", 35. A similar interpretation can be found in: Karl Otto Scherner, "Lex mercatoria: Realität, Geschchtsbild oder Vision?", *Zeitschrift der Savigny Stiftung, Germanistische Abteilung*, 118 (2001), 148–167, at 160–161; Cordes, "Auf der Suche", 175–176.

94 "The Admiralty was watched by the common-law judges with that jealousy and suspicion which they bestowed on all jurisdictions tainted with Romanism": John H. Baker, *An Introduction to English Legal History*, 4th ed. (London: Butterworths LexisNexis, 2002), 123.

the law of commerce, as far as it does not regulate (and has never regulated) all mercantile transactions. In synthesis, contracts and obligations taken from civil law have always contributed to the regulation of commerce.[95]

According to Malynes, "the *Law-Merchant* hath alwaies beene found *semper eadem*, that is, constant and permanent without abrogation", while Defoe declared: "The Affairs of Merchants are accompanied with such variety of Circumstances …, that it has been found impracticable to make any Laws that could extend to all Cases". But although they had different opinions when defining the law to be applied to commercial transactions, they did have something in common: neither made any explicit reference to the *ius commune*. The latter was not something that merchants could acknowledge or even accept because it would have called into question the autonomy of merchants and of their law. However, the analysis of Malynes's treatise seems to reveal that even outside the borders of the *ius commune*, within the framework of commerce, Roman law, as transmitted through the medieval reflections on Justinian's *Corpus Iuris Civilis*, could not be avoided. Maybe the European *ius commune* (which included canon law, so important for some issues, such as in the case of usury) was the common legal background that allowed merchants to understand each other and that could not be ignored when it came to commercial transactions, which are, and have always been, transnational by definition.

95 Francesco Galgano, *Lex mercatoria* (Bologna: Il Mulino, 2001), 10. For a comprehensive list of the supporters and opponents of the idea of the autonomy of commercial law: Raffaele Teti, *Un diritto per gli imprenditori: Il diritto commerciale dalle codificazioni ottocentesche al Codice Civile del 1942* (Roma: Donzelli, 2018), 82–83.

Part III

Ius Commune and Scandinavia

11 *Ius Commune* at the Merchant Courts of the Hanse Kontor in Bergen?

Sören Koch

Introduction

The (rather anachronistic) claim of historians and politicians that the Hanse was a kind of first predecessor of a European trade organization seemed to have been based, at least in part, on the assumption that Hanse had developed a common legal framework for the involved merchants – a *lex mercatoria*.[1] Albrecht Cordes has proven that there was not a single corpus of substantive law governing the merchants' interactions, but that the early modern trade relations were characterized by pragmatic solutions and legal pluralism.[2] This raises the question of to what extent, if at all, did merchants solve conflicts

1 E.g., Ahasver von Brandt, "Die Hanse als mittelalterliche Wirtschaftsorganisation: Entstehung, Daseinsform, Aufgaben", in *Die Deutsche Hanse als Mittler zwischen Ost und West*, ed. by Ahasver von Brandt, Paul Johansen, Hans van Werveke, Kjell Kumlien, Hermann Kellenbenz, (Köln: Westdeutscher Verlag, 1963), 9–37; more recently, Klaus Peter Berger, *The Creeping Codification of the New Lex Mercatoria*. 2nd ed. (Austin: Wolters Kluwer Law & Business, 2010); Rolf Hammel-Kiesow, "Europäische Union, Globalisierung und Hanse: Überlegungen zur aktuellen Vereinnahmung eines historischen Phänomens", *Hansischen Geschichtsblätter*, 125 (2007), 1–44, at 38 ff.; and, more carefully, Rolf Hammel-Kiesow, *Die Hanse*, 6th ed. (München: C.H. Beck, 2021), 15; Paul Brood, "The German Hanse; a Medieval European Organisation?", in *The German Hanse in Past & Present Europe: A Medieval League as a Model for Modern Interregional Cooperation?*, ed. by Hanno Brand (Groningen: Hanse Passage, Castel International Publishers), 29–47, at 27 ff.; sceptical Albrecht Cordes, "Die Erwartungen mittelalterlicher Kaufleute an Gerichtsverfahren, Hanseatische Privilegien als Indikator", in *Eine Grenze in Bewegung: Öffentliche und Private Justiz im Handels- und Seerecht*, ed. by Albrecht Cordes, Serge Dauchy, Andreas Karg (München: R. Oldenbourg Verlag, 2013), 39–63, at 61 f.; Albrecht Cordes and Philipp Höhn, "Fernkaufleute", in *Handbuch zur Geschichte der Konfliktlösung in Europa*, ed. by David Mayenburg et al., *Band 3. Konfliktlösung in der Frühen Neuzeit*, ed. by Wim Decock (Berlin: Springer, 2021), 295–303, at 300.

2 Cordes 2013, see also Albrecht Cordes and Philipp Höhn, "Extra-Legal and Legal Conflict Management and Long-Distance Traders (1250–1650)", in *Oxford Handbook of Legal History*, ed. by Heikki Pihlajamäki et al. (Oxford: Oxford University Press, 2018), 509–526, here 512, 526; Philipp Höhn, "Pluralismus statt Homogenität: Hanse, Konflikträume und Rechtspluralismus im Vormodernen Nordeuropa (1400–1600)", *Städtebunde und städtische Außenpolitik, Träger, Instrumentarien und Konflikte*, ed. by Roland Deigendesch, Christian Jörg (Ostfildern: Jan Thorbecke Verlag 2019), 261–290.

DOI: 10.4324/9781003425069-15

according to the principles and rules of *ius commune*? We could assume that parties and judges would resort to the "learned law" when neither the local laws nor merchant customs and usages did provide sufficient legal mechanisms to handle a specific legal issue.[3] And, indeed, we find sporadic references to Roman law in distinct decisions of merchant courts and other organs of conflict management in commercial relations.[4] Especially, where legally educated actors were involved in conflict management, e.g., at commercial courts or other institutionalized forms of commercial dispute resolution, *ius commune* could function as an intellectual frame of reference and subsidiary source of law holding at least persuasive argumentative authority.[5]

In this chapter, I will provide an illustrating example of how the merchant court of the Hanse Kontor in Bergen (Norway) applied learned law, in particular Roman law, to decide a complex legal issue in the early 1700s.

Nevertheless, it needs to be emphasized from the outset that this case and the direct application of Roman law is a scarce exception rather than the rule. Most documented cases at the Bergen Kontor were decided based on either the Kontor's statutes or mere pragmatic considerations of justice and equity.[6] This seems to be true also for similar dispute resolution institutions or panels at other trading posts.[7] Still, in Bergen and other places where conflicts among merchants were administered, *inter alia*, by professionalised lawyers, constant references to Latin concepts and phrases coined by the learned law indicate that the clerks of the merchant court used their legal education and the *ius*

3 An illustrating example has been provided by Philipp Höhn, "Pluralismus statt Homogenität. Hanse", at 288 – references to Bartolus de Saxoferrato in the development of the normative frameworks on anti-piracy rules.

4 For many examples, see *Archiv der Hansestadt Lübeck* [hereafter: AHL], Findbuch 9, *Bergenfahrer* [thereafter: BgF], 1040–1046.

5 Albrecht Cordes and Philipp Höhn, "Extra-Legal and Legal Conflict Management and Long-Distance Traders", at 516.

6 Sören Koch and Geir Atle Ersland, "Rebranding or Creation – the Emergence of the 'Kontor'", *Hanseatic History Review*, 142 (2024), 1–32; Sören Koch, Ulla Kypta, and Johann Ruben Leiss, "Pluralistische Governance: Die Erforschung hanseatischer Kooperation", *Hansischen Geschichtsblätter*, 140 (2022), 59–91, at 88.

7 See, for similar dispute management regimes at the other Hanse Kontors and other trading posts, Volker Henn, "Das Brügger Kontor", in *Die Hanse: Lebenswirklichkeit und Mythos, Herausgegeben von Jørgen Bracker*, ed. by Volker Henn, Rainer Postel, 3rd ed. (Lübeck: Verlag Schmidt-Römhild, 1999); Philipp Höhn, *Kaufleute in Konflikt: Rechtspluralismus, Kredit und Gewalt im spätmittelalterlichen Lübeck* (Frankfurt am Main: Campus Verlag, 2021); Karl Engel, "Die Organisation der deutsch-hanseatischen Kaufleute in England im 14. und 15. Jahrhundert bis zum Utrechter Frieden 1474", *Hansischen Geschichtsblätter*, 1 (1913) 445–518, and 2 (1914), 173–226; Philipp Höhn, "Verflechtung und Streitschlichtung: Zur Austragung kaufmänischer Interessenkonflikte im Hanseraum (1365–1435)," in *Mit Freundschaft oder mit Recht? Inner- und aussergerichtliche Alternativen zur kontroversen Streitentscheidung im 15.–19. Jahrhundert*, ed. Philipp Höhn; Albrecht Cordes, "Die Erwartungen mittelalterlicher Kaufleute an Gerichtsverfahren"; Albrecht Cordes and Philipp Höhn, "Fernkaufleute"; Albrecht Cordes and Philipp Höhn, "Extra-Legal and Legal Conflict Management and Long-Distance Traders".

commune as an intellectual framework for their work at the borders of the realm of civil law.[8]

The Outline of the Chapter

Before we take a closer look at our model case, we need to amplify the historical context. Starting by explaining the establishment of the merchant courts and their function in the Hanseatic outposts labelled Kontor. In this regard, six aspects are crucial: (1) the establishment of institutional preconditions for the administration of justice at the Kontor, (2) the development and extent of the jurisdiction of these merchant courts, (3) the competences of the court and its organs, (4) the role and function of the court clerks secretaries, (5) the legislative and wider legal framework, in particular, and (6) the statutes and their relationship to other legal sources such as the Law of Lübeck, domestic Norwegian law, and *ius commune*. Having set the institutional scene, we will consider the primary source of the investigation into the court roles (*Protocollum*) of the Bergen merchant court at the Kontor.[9] These protocols are a highly interesting primary source that has been (with very few exceptions)[10] neglected by both historians and legal historians for centuries.[11]

The case concerns a regress and compensation claim in which questions of agency and distribution of economic risk and profit are of central importance. The case is an illustrative example of legal issues of exceptionally great importance for the practice of Hanseatic merchants' organizing their businesses

8 Illustrating in this regard is the formula used at the first page of the oldest surviving protocol from this court: *Incipit ipsum Prothocollum Civitatum Hansæ Teutonicæ Conthorij, quod isdem Bergis est in Regno Norwegiæ inchoatum Anno 1633.* Cf. AHL BgF no. 1040, 1. See also Philipp Höhn, "Pluralismus statt Homogenität. Hanse", at 288: "Da die Hanse mit solchen frühneuzeitlichen Territorialstaaten konfrontiert war, musste sie sich selber konsolidieren und zunehmend eine Verwaltungsstruktur aufbauen, die sich an Kategorien des römischen Rechts orientierte". For further references, see Philipp Höhn, "Pluralismus statt Homogenität. Hanse", at 288 n 109.

9 See n 4.

10 Justyna Wubs-Mrozewicz, "Traders, Ties and Tensions: The Interactions of Lübeckers, Overijsslers and Hollanders in Late Medieval Bergen", thesis (Hilversum: Verloren, 2008); Geir Atle Ersland, *Das Kaufmannshaus: Det hanseatiske kontorets rettslokaler og administrasjonhus i Bergen* (Bergen: Det Hanseatiske Museums Skrifter Nr. 30, 2011); Geir Atle Ersland, "Das Handelsgericht des Hansekontors in Bergen", in *Hanse und Stadt, Akteure, Strukturen und Entwicklungen im regionalen und europäischen Raum – Festschrift für Rolf Hammel-Kiesow zum 65. Geburtstag*, ed. by Michael Hundt, Jan Lokers (Lübeck: Schmidt-Römhild 2014), 89–102; Sören Koch et al., "Pluralistische Governance"; Sören Koch, "Dänemark-Norwegen", in *Handbuch der Geschichte der Konfliktlösung in Europa*, ed. by David Mayenburg et al., *Band 3. Konfliktlösung in der Frühen Neuzeit*, ed. by Wim Decock, (Berlin: Springer, 2021), 691–716, 221.

11 See for a brief historiography, Koch and Ersland, "Rebranding or Creation", see n 4, on p. 1 with further reference in n 1.

abroad.[12] It provides us with exceptional insights into a practice that has been established and little changed since the late medieval time.[13] I will briefly introduce the facts of the case and mention some additional contextual aspects. Furthermore, the judgment provides us with an excellent example of how the acting clerk (*secretarius*) used his knowledge of Roman law and his education at a German university to structure his argument in the verdict. However, the decision is rather unique and cannot be understood and explained without considering the specific institutional and intellectual context of the Hanseatic merchant court in the early modern period. I will therefore conclude this chapter with some reflections on the role and purpose of these courts in northern Europe and to what extent the *ius commune* was regarded as applicable law.

Contextual Reflections

In the first half of the fifteenth century, the Kontor in Bergen established a distinct dispute resolution organ, a court (*Handelsgericht*), with clearly defined jurisdiction, procedures, and legislative foundation. The term "Kontor" itself implies a special role and function. A Kontor was more than a mere settlement of foreign merchants or a trading colony. It has been characterized as a trade hub with an exceptionally high degree of institutionalization and administrative organization, including its own jurisdiction and bylaws, regulating the scope and application of this jurisdiction as well as merchants' rights and duties in the settlement.[14] In modern Scandinavian languages, *kontor* means administration office, and etymologically it derives from Middle Low German, from Dutch *kantor*, from Lower High German *Kontor*, and from French *comptoir* < latin *computare* (calculate).[15] Within the research community, it is common to refer to four Kontors as the main colonies of Hanse merchants residing abroad, that is, outside the German territories of the Holy Roman Empire.[16]

12 Regina Grafe and Oscar Gelderblom, "The Rise and Fall of the Merchant Guilds: Re-thinking the Comparative Study of Commercial Institutions in Premodern Europe", *Journal of Interdisciplinary History*, 40 (2010), 477–511, at 482 ff.

13 See Arnved Nedkvitne, *The German Hansa and Bergen 1100–1600*, (Köln: Böhlau Verlag, 2014), at 537 ff.

14 Knut Helle, "Die Rechtsstellung der Deutschen in Bergen während des Mittelalters", in *Beiträge zur hansischen Verfassungs- und Schiffahrtsgeschichte: Hansische Studien. Bd. 10*, ed. by Host Wernick, Nils Jörn (Weimar: H. Böhlaus Nachfolger, 1998), 315–322, at 316 ff.; Olav Brattegard, "Über die Organisation und die Urkunden des hanseatischen Kontors zu Bergen bis 1580", *Bergens historiske Forening Skrifter*, 38 (1932), 237–304, at 243; Schubert 2002, 2.

15 Hjalmar Falk and Alf Torp, *Etymologisk ordbog over det norske og det danske sprog: Opptrykk: Bjørn Ringstrøms antikvariat*, vol. 1 (Kristiania: Aschehoug, 1903); see also Koch and Ersland n 4, 5.

16 See *Hanserecesse von 1431–1476, Zweite Abteilung, Fünfter Band*, ed. by Goswin van der Ropp (Leipzig: Duncker & Humblot, 1888) [hereafter: HR], III, 4:79, in this Hanse recess from 1498, it is stated that no merchant of the Hansa doing business at one of the four Kontors or elsewhere where the merchants keep a staple should refrain from getting married outside the

However, as T.H. Lloyd has stated, the term "Kontor" has been used both anachronistically and for other communities of Hanseatic merchants abroad.[17] In addition, there seems to be no common understanding of when it is feasible to call a settlement a Kontor[18] and which characteristics distinguish a Kontor from other trading posts of the Hanse.[19]

In the fourteenth-century sources, the name "*Olderlude unde Copmans to Berghen*" was used, indicating that there already existed a *Genossenschaft* (*Copman*) represented by the aldermen (*Olderlude*). This *Genossenschaft* or *universitas* had been granted the right to manage internal conflicts.[20] The royal privileges documenting these rights were carefully preserved by the administrators of the Kontors. The emergence and legal recognition of the *Genossenschaft* can be regarded as a first and important step in the institutional development of the merchants' legal self-governance in Bergen.[21] Granting jurisdiction to manage internal conflicts was a core element of this right of self-governance. Accordingly, historians have often used the concept of Kontor already for this early form of institutional organization.[22]

Hansa. That there were four Kontors has been recognized also by the Diet in 1509 HR III, 5, Nr. 431 "*die vier Conthoir und stede*".

17 Terence Henry Lloyd, *England and the German Hanse, 1157–1611: A study of their trade and commercial diplomacy* (Cambridge, Cambridge University Press, 1991), 51 n. 3. See, e.g., Nils Jörn, *"With money and bloode" Der Lonodoner Stalhof im Spannungsfeld der englisch-hanseatischen Beziehungen im 15. und 16. Jahrhundert* (Köln: Böhlau Verl, 2000), 305 "und anderen kleinen Kontoren, die die Hanse zu diversen Zeiten in England unterhielt".

18 Yngvar Nielsen, *Bergen fra de aeldste Tider indtil Nutiden: En historisk-topografisk Skildring* (Christiania: C. Tønsberg, 1877), 227 and 231; *Bergen Fundas*, ed. by Mikkjel Sørlie (Bergen: Bergens historiske Forening, 1957), 47–56; Geir Atle Ersland, *Das Kaufmannshaus*; Geir Atle Ersland, "Das Handelsgericht des Hansekontors in Bergen"; Koch and Ersland, "Rebranding or Creation", 3ff.

19 Some historians use the concept of Kontor widely for all kinds of settlements of merchants in foreign cities or territories. They can refer to a degree issued by the Hanse diet of 1455 which speaks of all other Kontors; see Nils Jörn, "*With money and bloode*", 407 f., e.g., the Boston Kontor.

20 Knut Helle, *Bergen bys historie* (Bergen: Universitetsforlaget, 1982), 244 and 732; see also Knut Helle, "Die Rechtsstellung der Deutschen", 318 f. n 20 with reference to HR I, 1 Nr. 212, §§ 2 f, 233 § 6, 356 §§ 9, 18, 357 f. 384.

21 Regina Grafe and Oscar Gelderblom, "The Rise and Fall of the Merchant Guilds", 485.

22 See, e.g., Fridrich Bruns, *Die Sekretäre des Deutschen Kontors zu Bergen. Hanseatiske Foreningens Skrifter Nr. 13*, (Bergen: Grieg 1939), vii and cxi; Olav Brattegard, "Über die Organisation", at 243; Philippe Dollinger, *Die Hanse. Neu bearbeitet von Volker Henn und Nils Jörn*, 6th ed. (Stuttgart: A. Kröner, 2012), 136; Knut Helle, "Die Rechtsstellung der Deutschen", 316 ff.; Carsten Müller-Boysen, "Die deutsche Brücke in Bergen und die Niederlassungen in Tönsberg und Oslo", in *Die Hanse. Lebenswirklichkeit und Mythos, Herausgegeben von Jørgen Bracker*, ed. by Volker Henn, Rainer Postel, 3rd ed. (Lübeck: Verlag Schmidt-Römhild, 1999), 165–171; Schubert 2002, 2; Rolf Hammel-Kiesow, *Die Hanse*, 6th ed., 62; Arnved Nedkvitne, *The German Hansa and Bergen 1100–1600*, at 366. This is also true for the editors of the compilation of old Norwegian legal sources, *Norges Gamle Love, Annen Rælle, 1388–1604*, vol. 2, *1448–1482*, ed. by Oscar Albert Johansen, Oluf Kolsrud, Absolon Taranger

However, this view has recently been challenged.[23] The term "Kontor" (*Conthoir*, *Contor*, *Konthor*, etc.) did not emerge in the primary sources before the end of the fifteenth century.[24] When the term "Kontor" becomes more frequently used in the primary sources in the sixteenth century, reference is made to a specific institutionalized form of organization. According to a functional perspective, a Kontor is a governance institution, with an administration building, an archive, and, in our context most importantly, a court with judges (*aldermen*), assessors (*bisittere*) and a clerk (*sekretär*), who recorded important events in a protocol (*kopmansbok*).[25] The procedures of conflict management at the Kontor are thoroughly governed by a set of rules compiled in codified statutes (*Ordnung* or *statutes*).[26] Most of the norms in these statutes are based on older customary rules and written collections. However, in the second half of the fifteenth century, we can observe a systematic recodification and amendment of the statutes.[27] In addition, we recognize a significant increase in the manuscripts that have survived.[28]

In Bergen, these institutional reforms were the result of administrative changes that were adopted after the German merchants returned to the city in

(Oslo: Norsk Historisk Kjeldeskrift-Institutt, 1934), 2, which constantly speak about the Kontor even though the sources they are commenting on do not use this term.

23 Koch and Ersland, "Rebranding or Creation"; Geir Atle Ersland, "Das Handelsgericht des Hansekontors in Bergen", at 89 ff.

24 London: Karl Engel, "Die Organisation der deutsch-hanseatischen Kaufleute" (1913), at 466 with further reference; Antwerp/Bruges: Volker Henn, "Das Brügger Kontor", 163; Walter Evers, "Das hansische Kontor in Antwerpen", thesis (Kiel: Handorff, 1915), 17; Bergen: *Norges Gamle Love*, 2. R. II, No. 416, 677 sect. 14: 'Kopmans Kunthor'; sect. 21. 'kunthor'; according to the editors of the *Lagsraa for den tyske kjøbmand i Bergen* this codification of Bergen's Kontor Statutes (*vedtægter*) dates back to 1494.

25 Geir Atle Ersland, "Das Handelsgericht des Hansekontors in Bergen", at 95. These court roles were produced by professional clerks, which is a rather clear difference compared to, e.g., the Gerichtsbuch des Vogts in Schonen or the Revaler Ratsurteilsbuch; see Tobias Kämpf, *Das Revaler Ratsurteilsbuch, Grundsätze und Regeln des Prozessverfahrens in der frühneuzeitlichen Hansestadt* (Köln: Böhlau, 2013).

26 Ibid.; for a comparison between the statutes of the four Hanse Kontors, see Mike Burkhardt, "Die Ordnungen der vier Hansekontore Bergen, Brügge, Novgorod und London", in *Das Hansische Kontor zu Bergen und die Lübecker Bergenfahrer – International Workshop Lübeck 2003*, ed. by Antjekathrin Grassmann (Lübeck: Schmidt-Römhild, 2005), 58–77, at 59 ff.; on a general account of the importance of non-legislative codifications, see Nils Jansen, *The Making of Legal Authority: Non-legislative Codifications in Historical and Comparative Perspective* (Oxford: Oxford University Press, 2010).

27 For the Kontor in London, see Nils Jörn, "Die Herausbildung der Kontorordnungen in Novgorod, Bergen, London und Brügge im Vergleich – 12. bis 17. Jahrhundert", in *Prozesse der Normbildung und Normveränderung im mittelalterlichen Europa*, ed. by Doris Ruhe, Karl-Heinz Spiess, Ralf-Gunnar Werlich (Stuttgart: Franz Steiner Verlag, 2000), 216–235, at 217 has argued that the amendments of the statutes were the result of, and at the same time a reaction to, changed political and economic circumstances and aimed at reforming the organization of the Kontor in order to meet these challenges; see also Nils Jörn, *"With money and bloode"*, 5 f.; in the same direction, see Mike Burkhardt, "Das Hansekontor in Bergen im Spätmittelalter: Organisation und Struktur", *Hansischen Geschichtsblätter* 126 (2006), 21–70, at 53 ff.

28 Geir Atle Ersland, "Das Handelsgericht des Hansekontors in Bergen", at 95.

1432. They had left in 1427 because a coalition of Hanseatic towns became involved in a war with King Erik of Pomerania. The return of the Germans to Bergen and the peace accord between King Erik and the Hanseatic towns in 1435 paved the way for the emergence of the Kontor. The new institutional framework contributed to fundamentally changing the way internal conflicts were handled. This seems to have contributed to eventually changing the perception of the contemporaries, who, towards the end of the fifteenth century, started using the term *Kontor* instead of the previously used term *Nedderlag*. The guild-like structures which were in place before were gradually transformed into a more professionalized and institutionalized procedure for internal conflict management.[29] Some of the older organs and terminology were kept (*Aldermen*, *Ersamer Kaufmann*, etc.), but the nature of conflict management had changed.[30]

For the Stalhof in London, 'Duetsche Contor' is first mentioned in the peace treaty of Utrecht from 1474.[31] Bruges is referred to as a Kontor for the first time in 1476.[32] For Bergen, the term was in use in 1494 but might have been used already in the statutes of 1464.[33] For the purpose of this chapter, it is essential that, in contrast to other trading posts in which merchants applied at times similar dispute resolution mechanisms, the Kontors can be characterized by a comparably high degree of professionalization and established particular institutionalized procedures. This is, again, a feature that facilitated, or at least allowed for, the use of *ius commune*.

The court's clerks (*secretarius*) were of paramount importance in this regard. These secretaries were not just professional writers assisting the aldermen to draft letters to the Hanse Diet or the Hanse towns, but they had essential functions related to the administration of justice at the Kontor.[34] They prepared cases and decisions for the aldermen and their assessors and advised them in

29 Koch and Ersland, "Rebranding or Creation"; Mike Burkhardt, "Das Hansekontor in Bergen", at 68 ff.; Regina Grafe and Oscar Gelderblom, "The Rise and Fall of the Merchant Guilds", at 490.

30 For similar developments in the local courts of Denmark and Norway, see Sören Koch, "Dänemark-Norwegen", in *Handbuch der Geschichte der Konfliktlösung in Europa*, ed. by David Mayenburg et al., *Band 3. Konfliktlösung in der Frühen Neuzeit*, ed. by Wim Decock (Berlin: Springer, 2021), 691–716; Idem., "Consequences of Changing Expectations to Law and Its Institutions Illustrated by the Role and Background of Judges in Norway", 83 *Legal History Review*, 461–486.

31 Karl Engel, "Die Organisation der deutsch-hanseatischen Kaufleute" (1913), at 466 with further reference.

32 Volker Henn, "Das Brügger Kontor", at 163; Walter Evers, *Das hansische Kontor in Antwerpen*, 17.

33 *Norges Gamle Love*, 2. R. II, No. 416, 677 sect. 14: 'Kopmans Kunthor'; sect. 21. 'kunthor'; according to the editors of the *Lagsraa for den tyske kjøbmand i Bergen*, this codification of Bergen's Kontor Statutes (*vedtægter*) dates back to 1494.

34 Geir Atle Ersland, "Das Handelsgericht des Hansekontors in Bergen", at 91; *Norges Gamle Love*, vol. 2:2, 685 – statutes 1494 Art. 13 – same paragraph in the newer editions from respective 1572 and 1672.

legal matters, for instance, concerning the interpretation of the statutes.[35] They collected evidence, could question witnesses, and invited the respondents to produce counterpleas.[36] If they found a claim reasonably justified, they suggested the case be heard by the *Kaufmanns Rath / Senatu Emporico*, the merchant court at the Kontor later referred to as the *Handelsgericht*.[37] In many ways, their function can be compared to ceiling organs in modern jurisdictions protecting courts of higher instance from obviously ungrounded appeals and claims. Bruns, Brattegard, and Evers have extensively researched the background, appointment, function, and education of the secretaries.[38] They showed that the secretaries were, as a rule, handpicked by the heads of the Hanseatic towns and had received a specific education.[39] Most of them had studied law.[40] Furthermore, they were frequently sent abroad to the diets and to diplomatic missions representing the Kontor in negotiations with towns and foreign rulers.[41] Hinrich Stammel was appointed the first secretary whom we know. His service for the *Ersamen Kaufmann* is first documented in 1448. Therefore, the introduction of this office can be regarded as linked to the above-mentioned administrative changes in the 1430s and 1440s.[42] Hence, the establishment of this office can be regarded as an important step in the transformation of a settlement – *Niederlassung* or *nedderlage* – organized, in the form of a *Genossenschaft* or *universitas*, into an administrative headquarters and professionalized organ of conflict management.

The institutional framework that was established in the first half of the fifteenth century was sustained without major alterations until the abolishment of the Kontor in the second half of the eighteenth century. Admittedly, all institutions depend on the individual personality and skills of the human actors bringing them to life. Accordingly, we can observe a certain variation in the administration of justice at the Bergen Kontor throughout the years. However, studying the records of the court at the Bergen Kontor and comparing them with other surviving records of other Kontors provides evidence for

35 Ibid.
36 Ibid.
37 The term "Gericht" or "Gerichtstag" was used consistently in the oldest surviving manuscripts of the Bergen Kontor from 1633 onwards. The bibliographic reference to these protocols in the Bgf Fundbuch 9, note to no. 1040 has been given the title "Handelsgericht" (cf. index 195).
38 Fridrich Bruns, *Die Sekretäre des Deutschen Kontors zu Bergen. Hanseatiske Foreningens Skrifter Nr. 13*, (Bergen: Grieg 1939), at 12 ff.; Olav Brattegard, "Über die Organisation", 258 ff.; Walter Evers, *Das hansische Kontor in Antwerpen*, 47 ff.
39 Fridrich Bruns, *Die Sekretäre des Deutschen Kontors zu Bergen*, 14.
40 E.g., Hinrich Stammel 1448; Christian von Geren 1450–59; Hinrich Sommernat 1460–67, Dietrich Brandes 1478–81; Marcus Roterdes 1512–514. Nikolaus Repgenhagen 1515–20. See also Fridrich Bruns, *Die Sekretäre des Deutschen Kontors zu Bergen*, 14.
41 Fridrich Bruns, *Die Sekretäre des Deutschen Kontors zu Bergen*, 16, and with specific examples for such diplomatic missions, e.g., 35.
42 Geir Atle Ersland, "Das Handelsgericht des Hansekontors in Bergen", at 94–95.

a rather consistent practice. This allows for more general assumptions about the degree the merchant courts would refer to concepts and principles of *ius commune*. Empirical investigations of the surviving records, for four carefully selected sample years, show two general trends.[43] First, we find a constant and mostly consistent application of Latin terminology and, to a lesser degree, some phrases indicating that the clerks had at least some knowledge of the learned law. Second, direct quotations of Roman or canon law are very rare exceptions. This is not surprising as the most common conflicts arising among competing merchants were comprehensively regulated by the statutes.[44]

The following case study regards one of the few examples in which specific rules of the Disgests have been quoted explicitly, providing a unique insight into the functioning and legal expertise of the merchant court at the Hanse Kontor in Bergen and the skills of the court clerk who recorded the proceedings and issued the sentence.

The Case *Staman vs. Blumenthal*

The judgment that we will discuss here is one of the most comprehensive verdicts in the surviving protocols.[45] It contains 150 lines in the manuscript. Dated 24 April 1724,[46] the case falls in a period in which the Hanse had been in a constant decline both in its size and in its commercial importance for over two centuries. Nevertheless, the court's conflict resolution mechanisms were still functional. The clerk was Tobias Anthon Maysaal, born in Hamburg and educated at the faculty of law in Rostock (*Lizentiat der Rechte*).[47]

The case regards a claim for debt guarantee regress and compensation for economic loss. The plaintiff is Magarethe Staman, the widow of a merchant by the name of Hinrich Staman who had provided the respondent Joachim Christopher Blumenthal with a loan for pursuing litigation against a local Norwegian merchant. Blumenthal was the sales agent of a merchant by the name of Erdman Duve. Duve had his company headquarters in the northern German town of Lübeck, which was one of the political and commercial centres of the Hansa.

The question that the merchant court (*senatu emporico*) had to decide was whether the widow had to address her claim against the respondent Blumenthal or his principal Duve. The plaintiff's claim amounted to 522 riksdaler 2 mark and 10 schilling, a considerable amount of money at this time.

The background for the claim was that Blumenthal, as acting head of Duve's business in Bergen, had loaned money to pursue a litigation, which

43 Koch and Ersland, "Rebranding or Creation", 17 ff.
44 Ibid.
45 The proceedings started on 2 Decemberl 723, cf. AHL BgF Nr. 1046–13 54 12 (97).
46 AHL BgF Nr. 1046, 135.
47 Fridrich Bruns, *Die Sekretäre des Deutschen Kontors zu Bergen*, 110–111.

started in 1718. In the name of Duve, Blumenthal had provided a Norwegian merchant by the name of Christen Sörensen with a credit of 1127 riksdaler in exchange for the exclusive right to a certain amount of fish and other products to be delivered to Bergen and sold for a fixed price.[48] Upon the return of the Norwegian merchant from the most northern Norwegian province, Finmark, the parties got into a dispute about whether the conditions of the bargain were met. Blumenthal confiscated the goods of Sörensen in Bergen. The Norwegian merchant pressed charges using the appropriate jurisdiction of the Danish-Norwegian courts. Blumenthal, losing in the first instance, appealed through all instances up to the Danish-Norwegian Supreme Court in Copenhagen. To finance these court proceedings, Blumenthal convinced the Bergen-located merchant Staman to secure a loan. Despite all efforts to turn the verdict, the confiscation of the good was found illegal on all levels of the court hierarchy and Blumenthal was ordered to release the goods and pay damages. Not being able to do so, creditors took recourse at Staman's. His widow claimed regress for this amount, including interest.

In court, Blumenthal acknowledges the underlying facts but objects that he had acted as a sales agent only. Accordingly, he could not be held personally accountable. Duve counters that he never gave any direct order or consented to any of Blumenthal's actions related to the loan or the proceedings against the Norwegian merchant. Blumenthal maintains that he exclusively had acted in Duve's best interest and never exceeded the boundaries of his mandate. In a mostly written procedure, the court bases its verdict mainly on the testimony of the principal Duve and Blumenthal's responses as well as the evidence Blumenthal provides the court with. Among the documents presented to the court in Bergen is not only a written notice containing the contractual foundation of the mandate, but also letters exchanged between Blumenthal and Duve.[49]

The judgment is structured in concordance with a learned style of argumentation practised at continental European universities when providing legal advice "*Gutachtenstil*". After a brief but very concise presentation of the facts, and only the legally relevant ones, the clerk presents the crucial legal question. Has Blumenthal acted as a sales agent (*Handelsvertreter*) and consequently obliged his principal Duve? Or is he obliged to pay the debt himself?[50] The clerk presents arguments for both positions.

48 This was a common practice and for centuries an economic practice and credit system which secured the German tradesmen a monopoly-like position in the fish trade in Bergen; cf. Arnved inter, *The German Hansa and Bergen 1100–1600*; Justyna Wubs-Mrozewicz, *Traders, Ties and Tensions*, 148.

49 AHL BgF Nr. 1046, 136–138.

50 AHL BgF Nr. 1046, 138: "Scheinet H. Erdman Duve die allgemeine rechts-regal entgegen zu seyn: Wer den nutzen und profit aus einer Handlung ziehet, die sein Handelsgesell geführet hat, derselbe ist auch verpflichtet, seines gesellen obligationes mithin die Bezahlung über sich zu nehmen". Transl.: "The view of Duve can be objected by referring to the general rule:

Under the heading *Rationes Dubitandi contra H. Duve*, Maysaal argues with general principles of law that he deduced from the *ratio scripta* of Roman law. Blumenthal's legal position can be apparently based on the general rule (*allgemeine Rechtsregel*) that the principal is accountable for all actions of a sales agent (*Handelsgeselle*). The clerk refers to the Digest (D. 14, 3, 1 = l. æquum ff. de instit. action.) as a source of this rule;[51] stating that it is a general precept of justice that the principal who benefits from the actions of his agent is also obliged to bear the risks of the same actions.[52]

Blumenthal had proved that there existed a contractual agreement between him and Duve (*Dienst certer, oder contract*) that obliged him, the agent, to act in the best interest of the business (*staven*). This argument is based on D 14, 1, 4, 1 = 4. §. 1. ff. de exercit. act.[53]

Interestingly, the court implicitly assumes that the physical unit (*staven*) which Duve had rented in one of the warehouses (*garden*) was regarded as the residency of Duve's agent in Bergen. Staven was thus not only a section in a warehouse, but at the same time also a legal unit directly associated with the principal's business.

Another consideration in favour of Blumenthal's view is that Staman would most likely have relied on the economic capabilities and reputation (*Gutter Glaube*) of Duve and his store in Bergen (*Staven*) rather than his agent when agreeing to provide security for the loan.[54]

Even though Blumenthal has not received an explicit order to loan money for the litigation, nor to find a person who would provide security, one could argue, Maysaal continues to explain, that Duve still is obliged to cover the expenses as Blumenthal had acted in a situation of urgent necessity that required immediate action. According to a general principle of law, an emergency obliges an agent to take all necessary measures to prevent his principal from harm and allows him to exceed the limits of his mandate.[55]

Even if the actions of the agent were originally not covered by the mandate, subsequent approval by the principal could have transformed the unauthorized agency into an authorized one. Blumenthal claims that he had received such approval and provided evidence in the form of letters that indicate that Duve agreed to certain transactions made by Blumenthal. Again, specific rules in the Digests are referred to as the basis for this rule. *Rati habitio enim æqui*

A person having the benefit and profit generated by an action of another person, who acting as a sales agent, is obliged to pay for the obligations which have been stipulated by the agent".

51 Ibid.

52 AHL BgF Nr. 1046, 138.

53 AHL BgF Nr. 1046, 139.

54 Ibid.: "[D]er Cavent Staman seel. in ansehung des Principale und dessen stavens, also mehr auff den Principal und dessen gutter glauben, als auff den handels verwalter gesehen hat".

55 AHL BgF Nr. 1046, 140 "im Nothfall" – that is, in case of emergency.

paratur mandato.[56] Every consent given to what has already been done has a retrospective effect and equals a mandate. In addition, the clerk refers to the restatement of the principles by Ulpian in the context of unauthorized agency *negotiorum gestio* D 3, 5, (5), 6, 9, (11).[57] Both fragments contain a similar principle for unauthorized intervention into another's affairs.

Finally, one could argue that it is not even necessary that the money that the agent received in the name and for the account of the principal had been transferred to the latter. It would be unjust to impose all risks of an urgent and, for the principal, potentially highly beneficial intervention exclusively on the agent. This would mean punishing the latter for his vigilance.

Under the heading "*Ratio Dubitandi*", Maysaal thoroughly identifies, addresses, and legally refines all arguments put forward in the written defence submitted by Blumenthal.[58]

These arguments were, however, disregarded in the *rationes decidendi* of the judgment.[59] The clerk provides five distinct arguments for the opposite legal position, which he regards as decisive for this case.

First, the principal can be obliged by the actions of his agent only if the latter does not exceed the boundaries of the underlying contractual agreement which establishes the agent's mandate. In this case, the clerk refers to David Mevius's commentary on the laws of Lübeck (*ad Jus Lubeck Book 3, Title 6 art. 5 paragraphs 9 to 12*).[60] This precise reference indicates that the clerk had access to this book. Indeed, the inventory of the Kontor in Bergen made by Maaysal in 1724 provides evidence that this book was part of the archive of the court building (*Kaufmannshaus*) a few years later.[61] Mevius discusses in his

56 Ulpian D. 46, 3, 12, 4 *rati enim habitio mandato comparatur.* See also Ulpian D 50, 17, 60, 2: "And someone who endorses something which was done is bound by an action on mandate". Ulpian D. 50, 17, 152, 2. On the other hand, see Sabinus D. 3, 5, 8. For a comprehensive discussion of the different interpretations of the "parömie" *ratihabitio mandato comparatur,* see Sonja Dieckmann, *Die ratihabitio im klassischen ömischen Recht* (Berlin: Duncker & Humblot, 2023), 193 ff.

57 D. 3, 5, (5), 6, 9, (11) Ulpian Edict book 10 on Pomponius: "Thus the ratification makes the affair yours, which was not yours in the beginning, but only transacted on your account."

58 AHL BgF Nr. 1046, 110 ff.

59 AHL BgF Nr. 1046, 141 under the heading: Ratio decidendi, Maysaal states: "All dessen ungeachtet, ist das contrarium warhafter, und in rechten besser begründet". Translation: "Despite all of that, the opposite is more truthful and more in concordance with the law".

60 Mevius 1664 – David Mevius, Commentarii in Jus Lubecense libri quinque: ad explicationem ejusdem solidam, pro docendâ vera statutorum ratione, exponendis eorum recessibus, & informando fori usu, ante aliquot annos conscripti, nunc ex quibusdam notis, observationibus & additionibus multo auctiores, adjectis etiam quibusdam super controversiis istius juris responsis secunda editione in lucem emissi, Frankfurt am Main, Joachim Wilden, 1664; Regarding the impact of Mevius's commentary in the law of Lübeck and in particular the regulation of securities see Nils Wurch, David Mevius und das lübische Recht (Köln: Böhlau Verlag, 2014), 16 ff.

61 AHL BgF Nr. 536, published by Geir Atle Ersland, "The Archive of the Kontor in Bergen", in *Neue Studien zum Archiv und zur Sprache der Hanseaten. Det Hanseatiske Museum Skrifter*

commentary comprehensively the competence of sales agents, which he calls "*Mercatores ministri*",[62] which is the Latin word for the High German term *Handelsverwalter* that is applied in the judgment by Maysaal.[63]

In substance, Maysaal refers to the overriding principle that the principal can be bound by his agent only to the extent to which the latter's actions are in accordance with the provisions of the underlying mandate between them. In paragraph 12, Mevius states: "*Sed tamen inspiciendum est in his, sicut & omnibus, qui negocia aliena susipiunt, quid mandata corum contineant. Extra horum fines non obligatur dominus*".[64] He builds this argument not on any specific provision in the laws of Lübeck but cites Bartolus and other scholars.[65] Based on this rule, Maysaal interprets the contract between Blumenthal and Duve.

This contract contained an explicit clause (*ausdrücklich in formalibus*) stating that the agent was strictly prohibited from purchasing a bill of exchange, pledging the principal's property, or loaning money from anyone in Bergen. Blumenthal himself continuously admitted that he had acted without such an explicit order from Duve when he arrested the goods of Sörensen which started the proceedings. Consequently, Duve was not bound by Blumenthal's transactions. Once again, the Digests and secondary literature (Georg Adam Struve) are used to substantiate the legal opinion.[66]

Second, Duve had opposed, once he had received the knowledge of Blumenthal's actions, the continuation of the legal proceedings against the Norwegian merchant. This would imply that Duve did not approve that Blumenthal continued to appeal the decisions of the Norwegian court all the way to the Supreme Court in Copenhagen and to use the Staven's assets to do so.

Third, despite acting outside or even against the mandate contract, an agent's acts can oblige the principal only if they have been beneficial for the principal. In other words, if the principal was enriched by the action. Blumenthal did not manage to demonstrate that the money he had loaned was used to the benefit of Duve, meaning that Duve was enriched by the extraordinary measures of his agent. This argument is once again supported by legal treatises by Gail and Obherr, both works of learned lawyers and published in Latin.[67]

Fourth, Blumenthal did not act on behalf of Duve when negotiating with Staman. Evidence for this has been provided by the plaintiff, who submitted a written contract between Staman and Blumenthal containing the details of the

nr. 28, ed. by Geir Atle Ersland, Marco Trebbi (Bergen: Det hanseatiske museum, 2008), 11–46, here 25 ff.

62 David Mevius, *Commentarii in Jus Lubecense libri quinque*, book 3, tit. IV, art. 5 § 10.

63 AHL BgF Nr. 1046, 135 ff.

64 David Mevius, *Commentarii in Jus Lubecense libri quinque*, book 3, tit. IV, art. 5 §12.

65 Ibid.

66 AHL BgF Nr. 1046, 141.

67 AHL BgF Nr. 1046, 142.

loan. As the Roman lawyers had already established,[68] a person acting for his own account cannot bind a third party.[69]

Fifth and finally, Blumenthal cannot invoke that his appointment as Duve's sales agent would establish a legal presumption to be acting exclusively on behalf of his principal. This would require that the security would have been established according to the internal rules of the Kontor, that is, in concordance with the privileges issued by King Frederic III in the year 1654.[70] This privilege requires that the Kontor administration consisting of the Aldermen (*Alter Leüthe*), secretary, and assessors (*Achtzehnern am Comtoir*) need to sanction all transactions of these kinds. The reason for this kind of approval by the local community seemed to be regarded as necessary to protect the interests of the absent principal from the agent's competence to act in the name of the staven and, thus, the principal.[71] Therefore, the statutes require that the clerk needs to sign the contract with the Kontor's seal. This last rule distinguishes the legal situation at the Kontor from other trading posts and allows us to speak about a unique form of internal jurisdiction.[72]

Also, this requirement was not met in this case. Interestingly, this lack of formal requirements was explicitly referred to as a supportive argument (*in fernerer erwegung*).[73] This can indicate that this formal requirement was seldom upheld in practice and, therefore, would not provide the same persuasive weight as the more doctrinal considerations on which the verdict is based primarily.

The judgment's *sententia* contains the verdict. The court sentenced Blumenthal to pay the sum of 522 rigsdaler to Magarethe Staman, the widow of Hinrich Staman. The clerk summarizes the main arguments and points out that Blumenthal did not manage to prove that he acted according to a specific order from Duve. Disregarding the internal procedures of the Kontor when entering the contract with Staman releases Duve from all responsibility for the actions of his agent. Consequently, the respondent is personally accountable for the debt.

Concluding Remarks

The case shows many extraordinary aspects compared to other judgments we find in the protocols of the Bergen Kontor, and, therefore, it cannot be

68 D, 46, 3, 4 = L et magis 4. ff. de solut.

69 AHL BgF Nr. 1046, 142.

70 AHL BgF Nr. 1046, 143.

71 Statuta vetera, 1572 based on an older version of 1494, art. 38, cf. *Norges Gamle Love, Annen Rælle, 1388–1604*, vol. 2, *1448–1482*, ed. by Oscar Albert Johansen, Oluf Kolsrud, Absolon Taranger (Oslo: Norsk Historisk Kjeldeskrift-Institutt, 1934), 674 ff.; on 680.

72 Koch et al., "Pluralistische Governance", at 75; Koch and Ersland, "Rebranding or Creation", 12 f.

73 AHL BgF Nr. 1046, 143.

regarded as a typical example of the procedures and legal argumentation applied in the merchant court. Still, the verdict is also a brilliant example of the high degree of professionalization of the court clerk. Maysaal was, like most of his predecessors in the fifteenth and sixteenth centuries, a learned lawyer. Frequent references to Latin concepts and phrases in all court roles that have survived support this observation. The presented case indicates that they thought in terms of the *ius commune* when interpreting and applying the Kontors' statutes and privileges. In other words, at the very periphery or the borders of the civil law realm, learned law was less important as a body of substantive rules and principles; rather, it served as an important intellectual framework for those producing and applying the law.

The high quality of the legal reasoning in the merchant court and a thorough study of the types of cases that were solved in these courts, as well as the reasoning of the clerk, can provide us with highly interesting insights into the function and purpose of those institutions and their role in the overall organization of the Kontor.[74] Changing expectations had an impact on the institutions as well as the actors involved in conflict management both at the Kontor and at alternative dispute resolution regimes.[75] Much indicates that the traditional perceptions of the Kontor as a mere guild-like organized trading post need to be modified or adapted.[76] The Kontor was not just a cultural and commercial entity, but also a legal outpost.

Another interesting aspect of the judgment which I could not spend more attention to in this chapter is the use of Norwegian terms and their interpretation by the clerk. From a legal point of view, the concept of "*husbunde/hussbon*" has been applied when referring to economically *independent* tenants of a plot in Norwegian law. The clerk uses the same term here as a synonym for an agent (*Handelsverwalter*) with rather *limited* competences to freely dispose of the goods and assets of the principal. Is the etymology of the term indicating that the merchants' agents at the Kontor originally had a wider mandate or competences? This and many other highly interesting questions will need to be answered somewhere else.

74 Arguing for a focus on these organizational and administrative aspects in the Hanse research, see Stuart Jenks, "Die Hanse als kybernetische Organisation", in *Hansegeschichte als Regionalgeschichte*, ed. by Oliver Auge (Frankfurt am Main: Peter Lang), 59–84; Ulla Kypta, "Hansegeschichte als Organisationsgeschichte versus Hansegeschichte als Wirtschaftsgeschichte: Anregungen für eine diskussionsfähige Hanseforschung", *Hansische Geschichtsblätter*, 135 (2016), 133–165; Idem, "Aufstieg, Blüte, Niedergang – Entstehung, Krise, Übergang: Von der bürgerlichen zur postmodernen Hanseforschung?", in *Hansegeschichte als Regionalgeschichte*, ed. by Oliver Auge (Frankfurt am Main: Peter Lang, 2014), 413–428.

75 On the effects of the increasing control of territorial states, see Sören Koch, "Dänemark-Norwegen"; and Sören Koch, "Consequences of Changing Expectations to Law and Its Institutions. Illustrated by the Role and Background of Judges in Norway", *Legal History Review*, 83 (2015), 461–486.

76 In more detail, see Koch and Ersland, "Rebranding or Creation", 23 ff.

12 The Emergence of the Profession of Procurators

In Early Modern Denmark

Per Andersen

Introduction

On 9 September 1638, the Danish king Christian IV (1577–1648, r. 1588–1648) issued a statute with minor corrections to or specifications concerning Danish procedural and penal law. Among other subjects, the statute laid down rules for how to handle drunken priests, defamation of unfree persons, i.e., people bound by economic or working obligations towards squires, diets during imprisonment, poachers, and people carrying guns to church or court.[1] The largest chapter in the statute, though, contained the formal introduction of a new office or task within Danish procedural law, namely the role as "procurator". In the statute of 1638, the term – which nowadays can be translated as lawyer, counselor, attorney, or advocate depending on which legal tradition or system one is studying – clearly characterized a person representing or acting on behalf of another person, i.e., a party, in court. The medieval *ius commune*–inspired concept of learned advocates, who, as lawyers, trained in substantive law could give their clients legal advice, providing legal explanations to them (or to their in court performing procurators), was not mentioned.[2] The reason for this was not that the tasks of the learned lawyers and the trained procurators began to blur as was the case in, e.g., the late fifteenth-century German *Reichskammergericht*,[3] but the obvious lack of learned lawyers in early modern Denmark. There was simply no legal education at the country's only university in Copenhagen at the time as Danish legal education first occurred in 1736.[4] With the statute of 1638, though, the royal central

1 For the statute, see "Christian den Fierdes Forordning om Præste Druchenskab, ærrørige Domme, Kost oc Tæring, Arrest, Procuratorer, Lougfeldis Rettergang, Krybeskyttere oc Bøsser", in Palle Rosenkrantz, *Prokuratorerne i Danmark. Bidrag til den danske Prokuratorstands Historie*, vol. 1 (Copenhagen: Gyldendalske Boghandel–Nordisk Forlag, 1927), 9–14.

2 Christian Neschwara, "Lawyer", in *Encyclopedia of Early Modern History Online*, ed. by Graeme Dunphy, Andrew Gow (Leiden: Brill, 2015), consulted online on 28 June 2023 at https://dx.doi.org/10.1163/2352-0272_emho_SIM_016932.

3 Neschwara, "Lawyer".

4 Poul Johs. Jørgensen, "Retsundervisningen og Retsvidenskaben ved Københavns Universitet 1537–1736 – Forordningen af 10. Februar 1736", in *Festskrift i Anledning af tohundrede Aars*

DOI: 10.4324/9781003425069-16

administration for the first time recognized the wish for legal help in general for parties involved in a case in court.

In the 1638 statute's chapter on procurators, it is stated that "for some time, even though it is against the old and rightful customs", procurators have been acting within the legal system, raising and delaying cases to earn as much money as possible, exploiting especially poor and sick people who are not capable of acting in court themselves. To solve this unbearable situation, recognizing that some people might need skilled support and advice in court, it was, hence, decided by the king that from now on it would be possible to hire such professional procurators. These must, though, be approved by the king's local officer, or the mayors and councils of the individual market towns. The reason for this, the chapter tells, is to ensure that the acting procurators are "good, pious, unsullied, and sincere men". Thus, the requirements for the procurators are that they must not be related to any of the parties in the case; that they must swear to be fair and not to drag the case on for long; that they do not hand in too complicated submissions; and that they, without payment other than food and consumption, are willing to take cases for the poor, widows, etc., as the authorities are obliged to provide defense for everybody. It is also stressed that the once approved procurator does not hold the office for life, since he may lose it if he incites people, prolong cases, etc. The statute then states that the procurators must receive a salary if they are put in charge of tasks for the public sector, such as drawing up subpoenas, etc.; but if they, on their own initiative, introduce something unrelated to the case in such a subpoena (or for that matter in a pleading), it will be at their own risk. Finally, it is emphasized that the parties in a case must not use procurators for village matters, but only in town matters. In general, as a party in a case, it is stated that you are not obliged to use a representative in court, but, if you do, you are allowed to use a locally known person in both the countryside and in the town as long as he is sworn in by the local royal officer or the mayor of the town, while you also, as allowed with the statute, have the possibility to use a professional procurator in cases run at the courts in town.[5]

The statute of 1638 introduced professional procurators not only in Denmark, but also in Norway. Since 1536/1537, Denmark and Norway had formed a personal union under one king due to dynastic changes through the late Middle Ages, and, in 1638, the two countries were *de jure* a constitutional monarchy under the same king. A monarchy in which the king's power was somewhat limited as he had to consult the noblemen in the Rigsråd, i.e., the Royal Council, on more important matters concerning both Denmark and Norway.

Dagen for Indførelsen af Juridisk Eksamen ved Københavns Universitet, ed. by Erik Reitzel-Nielsen, Carl Popp-Madsen (Copenhagen: Nyt Nordisk Forlag–Arnold Busck, 1936), 84–114.

5 Rosenkrantz, *Prokuratorerne*, vol. 1, 10–13.

As mentioned, the statute of 1638 tells us that apparently professional procurators had already functioned within the Danish – and maybe also within the independent Norwegian – court system for a while. In that sense, the statute allowing the professional procurators did not introduce a new office or new players to the system, but just confirmed and formalized the existing role of such professional representatives. Almost contemporary sources support this, e.g., when in the summer of 1634 a litigant was granted permission to hire a procurator, as the litigant himself was not knowledgeable in procedural law, and when, in 1636, an aggrieved party summoned his procurator before the local royal officer for bad proceedings.[6] How far back in time we find the office of such professional procurators is uncertain, but if the historian Arild Huitfeldt (1546–1609), who was also King Christian IV's chancellor, and the lack of procurators in the historical sources is to be believed, professional procurators were not used in Denmark–Norway at the end of the sixteenth century.[7] Apparently, this seems to have changed during the first decades of the seventeenth century.

In another Scandinavian country, Sweden (and Finland which until 1809 was part of the Swedish Kingdom), it seems that the introduction of professional procurators was connected to the development of the legal system into a hierarchical system with courts of appeals beginning in the first decades of the seventeenth century and culminating with the Swedish law of 1734. The development also included changes within legal procedures, especially the introduction of procedures based on the parties' written briefs and a wish for finding the material truth in a case instead of just reconciling the two parties. These changes made it necessary to develop a professionalization not seen before in the Swedish legal system, making it necessary to introduce legal representatives of the parties in a case to help and support them.[8] It was not learned advocates as known in the early *ius commune*, but rather procedural advisors as the practical and procedure-oriented procurators known from sixteenth century Germany, the Netherlands, Scotland, Spain, France, and Italy.[9] The idea of legal representation was as old as Roman and Canon law, but in

6 *Kancelliets Brevbøger vedrørende Danmarks indre Forhold i Uddrag 1551–1660*, ed. by C.F. Bricka et al. (Copenhagen: Rigsarkivet, 1885–2005) [cited as KB in the following], 1633–34, 687; 1635–36, 531.

7 Rosenkrantz, *Prokuratorerne*, vol. I, 23–24.

8 Pia Letto-Vanamo, "On the History of Assistance in Conflict Resolution in Finland: The Emergence of Advocates in the 17th Century", *Scandinavian Journal of History*, 19 (1994), 193–200, at 194–197. On the development of professionalization in the early modern period, see Josef Ehmer, Ulrich Pfister, Markus A. Denzel, and Marita Hübner, "Professionalization", in *Encyclopedia of Early Modern History Online*, ed. by Graeme Dunphy, Andrew Gow (Leiden: Brill, 2015), consulted online on 28 June 2023 at https://dx.doi.org/10.1163/2352-0272_emho_COM_025950.

9 Steffen Schlinker, "Reception of *ius commune*", in *Encyclopedia of Early Modern History Online*, ed. by Graeme Dunphy, Andrew Gow (Leiden: Brill, 2015), consulted online on 28 June 2023 at https://dx.doi.org/10.1163/2352-0272_emho_COM_026699.

the sixteenth and seventeenth centuries it was revitalized and spread to more secular courts as a result of the second wave of *ius commune* hitting Europe and, among other new features, allowed people in general to be represented by a third party in court.[10]

As I will argue below, the introduction of professional procurators in Denmark in 1638 does not seem to have anything to do with major legal reforms as in Sweden since Denmark did not see any fundamental procedural changes from the High Middle Ages until the late eighteenth century. Even though, in the course of time, it also became possible to appeal a decision from a lower court to a higher court within the Danish legal system, this development ended already around the time of the Reformation, which officially was carried through in Denmark in 1536. And the goal to find the material truth in a case goes as far back as the thirteenth century in Denmark. Hence, the changes seen within the Swedish legal system cannot explain the formal introduction of procurators in the Danish legal system in 1638. The same goes for the introduction of a legal education, as this was not introduced in Denmark before 1736.

Thus, in the following, I will argue that the introduction of professional procurators in Denmark in 1638 happened not due to developments within the legal system itself, but due to developments within society, especially within trading and the concept of economy as a political tool. To do so, I will first introduce the Danish legal system as it developed from a horizontal structure in the thirteenth century towards a hierarchical organization prior to 1638. Second, I will show how the Danish legal procedure followed the scope and guidelines laid down in the High Middle Ages and continued doing so into the eighteenth century. Third, I will show how legal representation developed in Danish legal procedure from the thirteenth century to 1638. And finally, I will suggest that the emergence of professional legal procurators appearing in court was the result of a more complex private, but royal supported, development within economic transactions.

Focusing on the Danish tradition and organization of representation in court going back to the thirteenth century, I will omit the Norwegian development as Norway had other laws and another medieval tradition. Thus, the Norwegian development deserves its own investigation.

The Evolution of a Hierarchical Legal System

The Danish legal system that took form in the late twelfth and early thirteenth centuries did not consist of a hierarchy of courts in which a case could be appealed from a lower to a higher court. On the contrary, due to the existing

10 Mathias Schmoeckel, "Agency (law)", in *Encyclopedia of Early Modern History Online*, ed. by Graeme Dunphy, Andrew Gow (Leiden: Brill, 2015), consulted online on 7 July 2023 at https://dx.doi.org/10.1163/2352-0272_emho_COM_028252.

power structures, it never became possible for the Danish kings of the High Middle Ages to development a strong royal government forcing a hierarchical system through. Neither the king nor the magnates of the realm or the different regions of the kingdom had enough power to press the other part to accept anything they did not want.[11]

The earliest sources revealing something about the Danish legal system, the Danish provincial laws,[12] show that it was a horizontal system so that all courts could be courts of first instance depending on the nature of the transgression, and no matter whether it was a private or a criminal case. While most cases were probably conducted and decided by the nearest local district court in the countryside (*herredsting*), the provincial court (*landsting*) usually functioned as a first-instance court in severe cases such as manslaughter, etc. It could function as a kind of second-instance court in unusual cases, though, namely, when the defendant did not appear before the local court or did not comply with a sentence. In such cases, it was possible to conduct the case once more at the nearest of the provincial courts situated in Viborg (in the region of northern Jutland), Ringsted (on the island of Zealand) or in Lund, nowadays part of Sweden, to put more pressure on the parties to have the case settled. A sentence that had been passed was thus not appealed, meaning that another court scrutinized the evaluation of a case in a lower court; instead, a former district court case that was heard by the provincial court was always to be conducted as if it was a new case. Thus, the district and the provincial court were equal courts whose common aim was to guarantee that a sentence was passed and executed at all – and the power wielded by the magnates who were present at the provincial court probably put extra pressure on the convicted person to abide by the decision of the court. In addition, a sentence of outlawry passed by the provincial court covered a wider geographical area than a sentence passed by the district court.[13]

From the middle of the thirteenth century, two additional local courts appeared to supplement the existing system, namely the *birketing* and the town court (*byting*). The *birketing* can best be explained as a near equivalent of the English manor court, i.e., as a peculiar court under either a local magnate or belonging to the royal lands. We know of *birketing* from the beginning of the fourteenth century, and, around 1660, Denmark had approximately 120 such noble peculiar courts. The system was that the owner of a peculiar demarcated area (*birk*), which could also be the king himself, had the privileges of a provincial court, including fines to be paid. When a nobleman was

11 See the full argument unfolded in Per Andersen, *Studier i dansk proceshistorie: Tiden indtil Danske Lov 1683* (Copenhagen: Djøf Forlag, 2010).

12 See the introduction in *The Danish Medieval Laws: The Laws of Scania, Zealand and Jutland*, ed. by Ditlev Tamm, Helle Vogt (London: Routledge, 2016), 3–42.

13 Per Andersen, *Legal Procedure and Practice in Medieval Denmark* (Leiden and Boston: Brill, 2011), 84–191.

granted a *birk* from the king, he had to take care of all legal matters within it, focusing on law to be effective.[14]

From the beginning of the thirteenth century, we see the first laws for Danish market towns, differentiating them from the countryside, but it was not until the end of the century that the existence of market towns with their own laws multiplied. While we do not know how the provincial court and the local district court were managed in the beginning of the thirteenth century, it was obviously the town bailiff, appointed by the king or another owner of the town, who led the legal proceedings at the town court (*byting*). Beside the town court, the more closed and elitist court of the town council (*rådstueret*) developed throughout the fourteenth century. Whereas the town bailiff presided over the town court, the mayor(s) and the town council constituted the court of the town council, which functioned as both a court in civil cases and – in some cases – as a court running the second round of a case just as the provincial court could do with cases first time handled by the district court in the countryside. However, the sources do not reveal any structurally clear distinction between the two courts, i.e., the *rådstueret* developed differently in the individual market towns (if it developed at all).[15]

The beginning of the thirteenth century saw also the introduction of a legal institution which could challenge the other courts in the horizontal system. Through some of the provincial laws we learn about the possibility to initiate proceedings before the king instead of the *herreds-* or *landsting* in disputes over land. It seems that this possibility to let the king decide matters originally was on the same level as the district and the provincial court, at least in the first half of the thirteenth century when it was dealing only with disputes over land (probably of a certain size).[16] Later on, in 1282, the coronation charter of King Eric V Klipping (1249–1286, r. 1259–1286) stated that a case had to be completed at one of the ordinary courts before the king was allowed to become involved.[17] Hence, at that time, the magnates seem to have wished to limit the king's apparently growing competition to the established system of horizontal courts.[18] But this horizontal approach soon began to change.

The first instance of a clear sequence of courts – which appears to provide the possibility of appealing the decision of one court to another – is found in a decision from a provincial court in 1302 in which the case had been

14 Henrik Lerdam, *Birk, lov og ret: Birkerettens historie i Danmark indtil 1600* (Copenhagen: Museum Tusculanum, 2004).

15 Andersen, *Legal Procedure and Practice*, 356–398.

16 Henrik Lerdam, *Kongen og tinget: Det senmiddelalderlige retsvæsen 1340–1448* (Copenhagen: Museum Tusculanum, 2001), 39–40, and the discussion in Andersen, *Legal Procedure and Practice*, 220-221, and Thomas Riis, *Les institutions politiques centrales du Danemark 1100–1332* (Odense: Odense University Press, 1977), 55–59.

17 Andersen, *Legal Procedure and Practice*, 223–224.

18 Per Andersen, *Rex imperator in regno suo. Dansk kongemagt og rigslovgivning i 1200-tallets Europa* (Odense: Syddansk Universitetsforlag, 2005), 139–145.

"appealed to Zealand's provincial court since good men from the ... district pursued this appeal with the consent of both [parties]".[19] An amendment to the Law of Jutland, which dates from the same period, even provided the possibility for the culprit to appeal a sentence in semi-severe cases to the king if the appeal was made at the same court session that passed the sentence.[20] In the coronation charter of 1320, it was made clear to (or by) King Christopher II (1276–1332, r. 1320–1326 and 1329–1332) that a case went from the district court to the provincial court and from thence to the king before appearing in the final instance, namely the annual *Danehof*;[21] a parliament and court dating back to the coronation charter of Eric Klipping in 1282 at which the king and major magnates met and decided the most important political and legal matters. From now on, at least formally, the *Danehof* functioned as the highest court of the country as it became the forum in which the king defended his legal interests. Therefore, it was also often in connection with the *Danehof* (and later the so-called *Herredage*, taking over for the medieval *Danehof*) that the royal–initiated court met to decide the cases with which it was presented.[22] This sequence of courts was repeated in both King Valdemar III's (1314-1364, r. 1326-1329) coronation charter of 1326 and in King Valdemar IV's (1320–1375, r. 1340–1375) from 1354.[23] In the previous year, Valdemar IV had declared that an appeal from both the district and the provincial court had been conclusively decided when two judges from the provincial court in Zealand had testified to the royal court about the previous proceedings of the provincial court.[24] Nothing seems to have changed during the politically unsettled fifteenth century, but, around 1500, royal regulations began to pinpoint the necessity to pursue one's case at the right first-instance court, and, finally, with the coronation charter of Christian III (1503–1559, r. 1534–1559) in 1536, the possibility of appealing a case to the royal court held during the annual *Herredage* was not allowed before a sentence had been passed by one of the four first instances, i.e., the district court, the provincial court, the *birketing*, or the town court.[25]

The system of appeals was now a reality and, hence, it was confirmed in Christian III's royal recesses dating from 1537, 1539, 1547, and 1558,

19 *Diplomatarium Danicum*, ed. by C.A. Christensen et al. (Copenhagen: Det Danske Sprog- og Litteraturselskab, 1938–2000), 2. series, vol. 5, no. 229.

20 Cf. "Thords artikler", in *Danmarks gamle Landskabslove med Kirkelovene*, vol. 4, *Tillæg*, ed. by Erik Buus (Copenhagen: Det Danske Sprog- og Litteraturselskab, 1951), text 1, art. 82.

21 *Den danske rigslovgivning indtil 1400*, ed. by Erik Kroman (Copenhagen: Det Danske Sprog- og Litteraturselskab and Selskabet for Udgivelse af Kilder til dansk Historie, 1971), no. 13, § 4.

22 Anna Hude, *Danehoffet og dets Plads i Danmarks Statsforvaltning* (Copenhagen: Gad, 1893), 63–90.

23 *Den danske rigslovgivning indtil 1400*, no. 23, § 23; and no. 28, §§ 4 and 6.

24 *Diplomatarium Danicum*, 3. series, vol. 4, no. 39.

25 Andersen, *Legal Procedure and Practice*, 224–227.

repeating the rules for how to appeal from one court to another.[26] Thus, the development from a horizontal system of courts found in the medieval provincial laws towards a hierarchical system of courts, including the Royal Court founded after the Reformation in 1536, took a long time and was not confirmed as a common rule until after 1536. It began with the increased use of the king's possibility to settle land disputes in the thirteenth century, settled into a hierarchy during the fourteenth century, and found its conclusion at the beginning of the sixteenth century when an appeal of a sentence given at a lower court to the Royal Court became a common phenomenon.[27]

The Development of a Conservative Legal Procedure

When, in November 1215, it was decided by the Fourth Lateran Council to, among other things, make changes to the legal procedure used within the Church, it also influenced secular legal procedure across Christian Europe. The main problem in secular matters became the Church's prohibition against clerics' participation in the so-called Divine Judgements (c. 18) as this made it impossible for secular powers to maintain the procedure of, e.g., trial by fire or water as a tool to reach legal decisions. Since the Church rejected the rationality and possibility of Divine Judgement as an expression of God's just sentence, it made it impossible for secular princes to include such means of proof in valid procedural law, and, therefore, the secular sphere had to find alternative ways to determine the most serious legal disputes. Compared to this, some of the Lateran Council's other decisions were not as urgent to handle, but they still inspired the future development of secular legal procedure, not least the introduction of inquisitorial procedure (c. 8) and of written records of cases so that, if an appeal was made, it would be possible to evaluate previously produced proof and objections (c. 38).[28] While the latter augmented the idea of hierarchical legal systems with the possibility to appeal one's case to a higher court, the former supported the idea of finding and making the truth in a case visible for humans, just as was the aim with the prohibition against clerics' participation in the Divine Judgements.[29]

26 Andersen, *Legal Procedure and Practice*, 227–229.

27 For the later development, see Per Andersen, "Danish Courts of Appeal from Early-Modern to Modern Times", in *Suum Cuique Tribuere: Legal Contexts, Judicial Archetypes and Deep-Structures Regarding Courts of Appeal and Judiciaries from Early Modern to Late Modern Europe*, ed. by Kjell Å. Modéer, Martin Sunnqvist (Stockholm: Jure, 2018), 245–277; and Ditlev Tamm and Jens Chr. V. Johansen, "Kongens ting, byens ting og bondens ting – studier i det danske retssystem 1500–1800", *Fortid og Nutid*, 2 (1992), 73–100.

28 *Dekrete der ökumenischen Konzilien II: Konzilien des Mittelalters von ersten Laterankonzil (1123) bis zum fünften Laterankonzil (1512–1517)*, ed. by Josef Wohlmuth (Paderborn: F. Schöning, 2000), 227–271.

29 See Richard M. Fraher, "IV. Lateran´s Revolution in Criminal Procedure: The Birth of Inquisitio, the End of Ordeals, and Innocent III´s Vision of Ecclesiastical Politics", in *Studia in universitas Salesiana: Studia et textus historiae iuris canonici 7*, ed. by Rosalio I. Castillo Lara

Thus, inquisitorial procedure took its starting point with the Church's wish that legal procedure was about uncovering the truth, not just settling a dispute between two parties. Therefore, the judge or the court was no longer just to acknowledge a decision made based on fixed proof.[30] The aim of inquisitorial procedure was from now on not just to determine the accusation of one person against another, but to establish whether a crime or breach of law had been committed at all. While accusatory procedure – which, until now, had been used as the only procedure both in church matters and in secular law – depended on the judge's or the court's acknowledgement that the two parties had produced their proofs, the new form of procedure within the Church meant that the judge now enjoyed the right to single-handedly initiate a case if he suspected a transgression against the law and to question involved parties and witnesses to establish the truth. The development of the inquisitorial procedure thus coincided with a transfer of the burden of proof to the plaintiff, who was now to produce positive proof that the defendant was guilty, and an increased emphasis was placed on those proofs that concerned the facts of the case and not just the trustworthiness of the parties. In other words, an increased weight was placed on personal testimony, on written documents or legal records (which were taken to be irrefutable proof), and on confession. Circumstantial evidence was also included if it was of such quality that it could form the basis for a decision. Implicitly, this meant that the legal system increasingly distanced itself from the previously commonly used compurgators, who swore to the trustworthiness of the defendant rather than to the case itself.[31]

What happened in Denmark following the decisions of the Fourth Lateran Council was an adaptation of the new ideas, but in a form that did fit into the framework of the already existing Danish way of thinking about law. Before the Fourth Lateran Council, the Danish legal order was based on the accusatory procedure with its fixed proofs and its fundamental use of negative proof,

---

(Roma: LAS, 1992), 97–111, compared to Lotte Kéry, "Aspekte des kirchlichen Strafrechts im Liber Extra (1234)", in *Neue Wege strafrechtsgeschichtlicher Forschung: Konflikt, Verbrechen und Sanktion in der Gesellschaft Alteuropas. Symposien und Synthesen 2*, ed. by Hans Schlosser, Dietmar Willoweit (Köln: Böhlau Verlag, 1999), 241–297, at 276, n. 120, and R.C. van Caenegem, "Methods of Proof in Western Medieval Law", in *Legal History. A European Perspective*, ed. by R.C. van Caenegem (London: Hambledon Press, 1991), 71–113.

30 Winfried Trusen, "Der Inquisitionsprozess: Seine historischen Grundlagen und frühen Formen", *Zeitschrift der Savigny-Stiftung für Rechtsgeschichte. Kanonistische Abteilung* 74 (1988), 168–230.

31 Richard M. Fraher, "'Ut nullus describatur reus prius quam convincatur': Presumption of Innocence in Medieval Canon Law", in *Proceedings of the Sixth International Congress of Medieval Canon Law, Monumenta iuris canonici: Series C, Subsidia 7*, ed. by Stephan Kuttner and Kenneth Pennington (Roma: S. Congregatio de Seminariis et Studiorum Univ. and LAS, 1985), 493–506. See the full argument unfolded in Per Andersen, *Lærd ret og verdslig lovgivning: Retlig kommunikation og udvikling i middelalderens Danmark* (Copenhagen: Djøf, 2006), 59–66.

particularly symbolized in its most rarified form through that most difficult of proofs, namely, the carrying of hot iron. With the Lateran Council's final rejection of Divine Judgement, the frequently used carrying of hot irons was made obsolete and, as in the rest of Christian Europe, the Danes now had a pressing procedural problem that demanded an answer. This came in the form of juries, which were fundamentally intended to replace negative proof with a positive evaluation of material proofs presented by the parties, respectively. The jurors were picked from among the local men but had to be approved by the king and, hence, both the local or the regional magnates and the king could accept this solution.[32] At the same time, the procedure – as it became known in the royal promulgated Law of Jutland (*Jyske Lov*) in 1241 – became much more detailed with the same legal frame for summons, time limits, etc., as the learned law. Thus, as the learned law of procedure developed the principles of majority, subjective guilt, tighter time limits and a more extensive use of material proofs, it became clear to the king and to the Church that the Danish administration of justice had to be made more effective in order to create a legal order that satisfied the moral and ethical aims of the Church and which, in addition, provided the king with a role to play in the local administration of justice.[33]

Even though the new rules and ways of thinking about law were not accepted throughout the Danish realm from the beginning,[34] the goal to find the material truth in a case was still the aim. While this is not clear in all the Danish provincial laws, it becomes clear in the legal practice that is preserved from the fourteenth century onwards. This did not mean that legal decisions were forced upon the parties: the preferred option seems to have been to induce them to settle the matter or accept arbitration even if a jury had already decided. This indicates that local and regional courts preferred a settlement, but it cannot be denied that this may also have been a policy supported by the central administration because it would have meant a better foundation for future peaceful relations between the two parties.[35]

32 Per Andersen, "'The Truth Must Always Be Stronger: The Introduction and Development of Näfnd in the Danish Provincial Laws", in *New Approaches to Early Law in Scandinavia. Acta Scandinavica*, vol. 3, ed. by S. Brink, L. Collinson (Turnhout: Brepols Publishers, 2014), 7–36.

33 In general, Andersen, *Legal Procedure and Practice*.

34 Per Andersen, "Old Customs and New Trends: Legal Procedure between Ecclesiastical Ideology and Secular Practice in Medieval Denmark", in *Proceedings of the Fourteenth International Congress of Medieval Canon Law: Toronto, 5–11 August 2012: Monumenta Iuris Canonici. Series C: Subsidia*, vol. 15, ed. by J.W. Goering, S. Dusil, and A. Thier (Città del Vaticano: Biblioteca apostolica vaticana, 2016), 603–611.

35 Per Andersen, "The Use of Mediation and Arbitration in the Legal Revolution of 13th-Century Denmark", in *Law and Disputing in the Middle Ages: Proceedings of the Ninth Carlsberg Academy Conference on Medieval Legal History 2012*, ed. by Per Andersen, Kirsi Salonen, Helle Møller Sigh, Helle Vogt (Copenhagen: Djøf, 2013), 165–179.

Institutionally speaking, this conservative attitude to procedural law meant that, by and large, the institution of juries, which had been established by the provincial laws, was preserved. The fourteenth and especially the fifteenth centuries saw the introduction of the specific office of judge at the courts, but the judge seems to have served only the function of pronouncing the decision of the jury, at least until the time of the Reformation. During the sixteenth century, this changed so that the judge gained increased influence over the decision, although he rarely pronounced it on his own. Neither the judge nor the juries were given a general power to initiate cases, though, so the procedure remained accusatory with the two private parties producing their evidence, but, with the changes of the thirteenth century, inquisitorial traits supplemented the accusatory procedure in connection with the juries' investigation of the questions of fact and of guilt.[36]

Thus, Danish procedural law did not see large radical changes in the period between the late provincial laws of the thirteenth century and the end of the eighteenth century, when the inquisitorial process was implemented in criminal cases. Following the fundamental changes of the thirteenth century, the development was largely characterized by minor change: most comprehensive was the introduction of judges at local and regional courts and the institutionalization of the Supreme Court following the introduction of absolutism in 1660. While procedural law by and large was practiced as usual, except for the increased use of written documents, there was a development of the institutions of legal administration, as the royal central administration worked constantly to secure a certain measure of legal protection and uniformity of the administration of justice throughout the realm. This effort was in the end successful, so that from the second half of the sixteenth century it was possible to implement clearer guidelines that finally lead, also in practice, to the standardization of the institutions of legal administration as well as procedural law. This standardization was a hallmark of the Danish Code (*Danske Lov*) of 1683.[37]

Danish conservatism was probably not caused by the fact that the Danes did not follow developments outside the realm, so there must have been conscious choices to adapt or reject different international initiatives, possibly influenced by a lack of clarity in power politics that gave local and regional society a large measure of influence. It is clear, however, that where Danish procedural law in the thirteenth century had been a part of the common European way of conceptualizing and implementing the administration of justice – of the European *ius commune* – it remained unusual because of its conservative attachment to tradition during the early modern period.

36 This argument is unfolded through Andersen, *Legal Procedure and Practice.*
37 Andersen, *Studier i dansk proceshistorie*, 323–343.

Legal Representation and the Emergence of Professional Procurators

According to the Danish medieval provincial laws, it was possible to be represented by another person during court sessions, but only in two cases: In the first case, the defendant could let another person represent him at the third summoned court meeting if the defendant had not been able to attend the first two (for which he would be fined).[38] The representative seems not to have to do anything but to show up, acknowledging that the defendant knew about the ongoing case and the outcome. The second case was, in accordance with canon law, concerning the representation of the so-called *personae miserabiles*, who according to canon law counted, among others, the poor, widows, orphans, and deranged.[39] These categories were supposed to be unable to represent themselves in court, i.e., they were thought of as without formal legal status and, hence, needed a legal guardian. This could and, in most cases, probably was a close male relative,[40] but in one of the late provincial laws it is told that at that time, in the middle of the thirteenth century, it could also be the local royal officer, the *ombudsman*, acting as a guardian on behalf of the king for those who did not have one.[41]

Later, during the fifteenth and sixteenth centuries, unmarried women in the Danish market towns were allowed to choose their own legal guardian. Widows, though, on the one hand, also needed to have a male guardian as an official representative in legal matters, but, on the other hand, they often were allowed to handle things themselves to secure the necessary flexibility in an urban society focusing on economic transactions.[42] Thus, until the beginning of the seventeenth century, it seems to have been necessary to have another person representing you at court, if you were among the *personae miserabiles* or were not able to attend yourself, but this representative seems usually to have been a male person close to the party, not a paid procurator. The

38 For the Law of Scania, cf. chs 66, 83, and 146, in *Danmarks gamle Landskabslove med Kirkelovene*, vol. 1.1, ed. by Johs. Brøndum-Nielsen, Svend Aakjær Erik Buus (Copenhagen: Det Danske Sprog- og Litteraturselskab, 1933), text 1, and the corresponding ch. 91 in Anders Sunesons paraphrase in vol. 1.2, ed. by Svend Aakjær, Erik Kroman, text 1; ch. 213 in the old version and ch. 84 in the younger version of Valdemar's Law for Scania, cf. *Danmarks gamle Landskabslove med Kirkelovene*, vol. 8, ed. by Erik Kroman (Copenhagen: Det Danske Sprog- og Litteraturselskab, 1941), text 1, respectively.

39 A. Erler, "Miserabiles", in *Handwörterbuch zur deutschen Rechtsgeschichte*, vol. 3, ed. by Albrecht Cordes, Heiner Lück, Dieter Werkmüller (Berlin: Erich Schmidt, 2004–2015), 597–599.

40 Cf., e.g., Book I, article 43, or Book II, articles 20 and 32, in the Law of Jutland in *Danmarks gamle Landskabslove med Kirkelovene*, vol. 2, ed. by Peter Skautrup (Copenhagen: Det Danske Sprog- og Litteraturselskab, 1933), text 1; and Book III, article 36, in Eric's Law for Zealand in *Danmarks gamle Landskabslove med Kirkelovene*, vol. 5, ed. by Peter Skautrup (Copenhagen: Det Danske Sprog- og Litteraturselskab, 1936), text 1.

41 Eric's Law for Zealand, Book III, chs 48, 49, and 53.

42 Grete Jacobsen, *Kvinder, køn og købstadslovgivning 1400–1600: Lovfaste mænd og ærlige kvinder* (Copenhagen: Lindhardt og Ringhof, 2021), 64–102.

principal rule was, as it often was mentioned in laws and court rulings, that the parties themselves appeared and handled their own proceedings.[43]

During the late Middle Ages and the Reformation, things became more mixed, though. In the period from ca. 1300 to the beginning of the seventeenth century sources show that a party could entrust to another to run one's case if the party were indigent, subject to a lord, an outlaw, or already had lost a case and thus was recognized as untrustworthy.[44] The entrusted person did not necessarily know a lot about law, but since the procedure was conducted orally and under public auspices, rhetorical eloquence could probably influence the assessment of the jury and the judge, which could make it worth trying to get another person to run your case if you were not orally strong yourself. Therefore, in the beginning of the seventeenth century, we have examples of town clerks or even a local priest acting as such a legal representative in court.[45] We do not know whether they received money for their services, and, hence, we cannot reject the possibility that these people were among the apparently early professional procurators mentioned in the statute of 1638. However, the professional procurators that we meet in Supreme Court after its foundation in 1661 were often from the clergy and public legal officials.[46]

Whether the statute of 1638 refers to people like them or not, they found their way into or were dragged into a legal procedural model that had not developed in a revolutionary way since the beginning of the thirteenth century. Therefore, the introduction and public recognition of professional procurators is most likely not based on legal changes, at least not procedural ones, but rather on changed social conditions which made it beneficial for the parties to obtain help from people who were acquainted with law, at least with legal procedure. Following the statute of 1638, which made it clear that the professional procurators were allowed to act only in the market towns, it seems like the procurators were most often hired in cases of a special or particularly

43 E.g., *Den danske rigslovgivning indtil 1400*, no. 16, § 12; *Danske Domme 1375–1662. De private domssamlinger*, vol. 7, ed. by Erik Reitzel-Nielsen, Ole Fenger (Copenhagen: Det Danske Sprog- og Litteraturselskab, 1978–1987), 346–433, § 6; *Den danske rigslovgivning 1513–1523*, ed. by Aage Andersen (Copenhagen: Det danske Sprog- og Litteraturselskab and Selskabet for Udgivelse af Kilder til dansk Historie, 1991), no. 13, § 66; *Samling af gamle danske Love*, vol. 4, ed. by J.L.A. Kolderup-Rosenvinge (Copenhagen: Den Gyldendalske Boghandlings Forlag, 1821–1846), 214–236, § 8, and 237–246, § 4; *Corpus constitutionum Daniæ: Forordninger, Recesser og andre kongelige Breve, Danmarks Lovgivning vedkommende 1558–1660*, 6 vols, ed. by V.A. Secher (Copenhagen: G.E.C. Gad, 1887–1918), vol. 1, no. 1, § 12. For court practice, see, e.g., KB 1561–65, 77; 1561–65, 276; 1561–65, 299; 1561–65, 457, 468, 496, and 540–541; 1561–65, 580.

44 Thords Articles, Art. 82; *Danske Domme*, vol. 7, 346-433, § 24; *Den danske rigslovgivning 1513–1523*, no. 13, § 50; KB 1588-92, 203; *Corpus constitutionum Daniæ*, vol. 5, no. 143, 2:6, § 17.

45 KB 1624-26, 133; 1624–26, 629–630, and 663; 1633–34, 695, and 729. Also KB 1630–32, 483.

46 Rosenkrantz, *Prokuratorerne*, vol. 1, 52–61.

difficult nature, often for a party not familiar with Danish law.[47] Even though the royal administration was not always impressed with the procurators,[48] the parties seem to recognize the idea of using procedural experts and apparently began doing so increasingly in the years following 1638.[49] It is quite possible that there was usually only one sworn procurator in an ordinary market town, at least it seems to be an extraordinary situation that, in 1648, there were two procurators in the town of Odense.[50] But sometimes there were none, as, e.g., on the island of Bornholm in the autumn of 1650.[51]

The royal central administration repeated the rules on procurators both before and after the introduction of absolutism in 1660. King Christian IV's Great Recess (*Store Reces*) of 1643 and the Danish Code of 1683 repeated the regulations known from the statute of 1638, once again pinpointing that professional procurators were allowed to be active only in the towns.[52] Just as the two lawbooks repeated the legal procedure known from the High Middle Ages.

Money Makes the World Go Round...

If one is to understand why Danish law saw the introduction of professional procurators in 1638, the answer seems not to be found in the legal system itself, i.e., as a product of changes in the procedures used in court. Hence, Palle Rosenkrantz, who has written the most comprehensive account on the historical development of the profession of Danish lawyers, also concluded, without further explanations, that the professional procurators were introduced because of private interests, not public.[53] I will argue that it happened due to both private and public interests – not colliding interests, but common interests in developing and protecting stable marketplaces for both domestic and international trading. That was the reason why the central administration in 1638 accepted the use of professional procurators in the market towns and not in the countryside.

There are different possible explanations behind the development of towns in medieval Denmark, but two things are common for most of them, namely, the presence of a marketplace and, hence, trading, and a magnate, often the

47 E.g., KB 1640–41, 103–104; 1642–43, 317; 1647, 61, 213, 350, and 367–368; 1648, 197–198; 1653, 47 and 55. Cf. Rosenkrantz, *Prokuratorerne*, vol. 1, 43–50.
48 E.g., KB 1637–39, 665; 1642–43, 596; 1647, 350; 1648, 197-198. Cf. Rosenkrantz, *Prokuratorerne*, vol. 1, 40–43.
49 E.g., KB 1640–41, 103–104; 1642–43, 648; 1650, 125, and 170.
50 KB 1648, 226.
51 KB 1650, 329.
52 Rosenkrantz, *Prokuratorerne*, vol. 1, 40–43.
53 Rosenkrantz, *Prokuratorerne*, vol. 1, 20–23.

king, as owner of the land on which the town developed.[54] During the period ca. 1150–1350, these "town owners" – and especially the king – succeeded in centralizing most of the trading in Denmark in these towns, partly by collecting specialized crafts within the town walls, partly by handing the individual town its own town law. The aim with this was to let the town form its own jurisdiction focused on a more strict and effective enforcement for the benefit of, especially, trading.[55] Hence, the Late Middle Ages saw both growing domestic and international trading, but especially the international connections developed as the specialization of crafts increased.[56] This development continued after the Reformation, not least because of Denmark's position as a maritime society which supported international trading decisively.[57]

Denmark is not usually counted among the Western European countries that employed the idea of mercantilism in the seventeenth century, but as the country saw a strengthening of power by the royal central administration around 1600, the idea that the state should play a role in the country's economy, securing the functioning of the state through a progressive and protective economy, became part of the Danish state's *raison d'être* in the beginning of the century. The realization of this economic idea increased after the introduction of absolutism in Denmark, but it – and the idea about a progressive state in carrying this through – was already apparent before 1660. Hence, the idea of mercantilism – that a country should promote governmental regulation of the state's economy with the purpose of augmenting state power at the expense of rival national powers – began to grow before absolutism.[58] In that sense, economy became both a weapon in the international power struggle and a goal for the state itself. Trade balances had to be "favorable", meaning an excess of exports over imports, for a state that now was focusing on profit, just as one supporting capitalism later.[59] Thus, the interests of the state became equivalent to those of private players within trading.

It was against this background that the office of professional procurators was introduced. In the beginning of the seventeenth century, the Danish market towns had become the economic centers of the country, when it came to

54 Hans Krongaard Kristensen and Bjørn Poulsen, *Danmarks byer i middelalderen* (Aarhus: Aarhus Universitetsforlag, 2016), 36–40, 110–113.

55 Kristensen and Poulsen, *Danmarks byer i middelalderen*, 119–121, 149–151.

56 Kristensen and Poulsen, *Danmarks byer i middelalderen*, 359–363, 387–390.

57 Mikkel Leth Jespersen, Jørgen Mikkelsen, and Jakob Ørnbjerg, *Danmarks byer fra renæssance til enevælde* (Aarhus: Aarhus Universitetsforlag, 2023), 143–179; Per Boje, *Vejen til velstand – marked, stat og utopi: Om dansk kapitalismes mange former gennem 300 år: Tiden 1730–1850* (Odense: Syddansk Universitetsforlag, 2014), 52–54.

58 Boje, *Vejen til velstand*, 61–62; E. Ladewig Petersen, "Reformationstiden 1536–96: Modernisering – justering", in *Dansk forvaltningshistorie I: Stat, forvaltning og samfund: Fra middelalderen til 1901*, ed. by Leon Jespersen, E. Ladewig Petersen (Copenhagen: DJØF, 2000), 49–93.

59 Amy McKenna, "Mercantilism", in *Encyclopaedia Brittanica*, accessed 5 July 2023 at https://www.britannica.com/topic/mercantilism.

both specialized crafts and domestic as well international trading. People met and traded in the major market towns originally founded and owned by magnates, especially the king, who had been aware of the economic possibilities of controlling trading centers as early as the founding period in the Middle Ages. This awareness never disappeared, but only grew stronger during the centuries to come, later supported by a theory claiming that the state should have a say in economic development to secure its existence. And as crafts grew increasingly specialized, as trading became more internationalized, and as the economy grew in complexity, the need for somebody able to handle cases in court grew.

Summing Up: The Emergence of Professional Procurators

When, in 1638, professional procurators were allowed to act in Danish courts, it was not because Danish legal procedure saw major changes. As many European countries saw changes in the organization of courts, an increasing use of educated men within the system, and new elements in or clarification to the legal procedure used both in higher and lower courts, nothing that could have led to the use of procurators seems to have changed within the Danish legal system around 1638. On the contrary – the way legal procedure was handled in seventeenth-century Denmark, even following the introduction of absolutism in 1660, was the same as laid down in the younger provincial laws of the thirteenth century: One private party – who should meet at court himself – could, no matter whether it was private or criminal, raise a case against another. The plaintiff – who, with few exceptions, should also meet himself – should positively prove his case with documents, witnesses, etc., while the defendant could bring in his arguments and proofs to counter the accusations. The defendant would not, at least according to the procedural rules (and as far as we can see in the later legal practice), be convicted by the jury investigating the case unless the plaintiff was able to prove his case, just as the learned Roman-canonical procedural law of the thirteenth century prescribed. In that sense, Danish legal procedure followed the ideas of *ius commune* as it developed following the Fourth Lateran Council of 1215.

The Danish legal system saw some changes between the middle of the thirteenth century and 1638. During the Late Middle Ages and the century following the Reformation in 1536, the original horizontal court system developed into a vertical system in which it generally became possible to appeal a lost case to a higher court. At the same time, the juries were supplemented with a royal appointed judge to lead the procedure and make sure that a decision was reached. Although the judge gained increased influence on the decisions during the sixteenth century, he had not much knowledge of learned law, but he referred to the medieval Danish laws and the (new) regulations issued after the Reformation. From the end of the sixteenth century, the central administration appears to have tightened its supervision of the courts,and, therefore, we see an increased administrative uniformity, which – following the introduction of absolutism in 1660 – was given legal foundation in the Danish Code in 1683. The uniformity was both a consequence of equity and a prerequisite for the system of appeals that assumed its form after the Reformation.

Thus, the legal procedural and institutional changes in European neighbours as, e.g., Sweden in the seventeenth and early eighteenth centuries had already been part of the legal thinking in Denmark since the beginning of the sixteenth century (and maybe even since the thirteenth century). Due to unchanged power structures within the Danish realm, even after the Reformation, only minor adjustments were seen: The king did become more powerful after 1536, yes, but he could still not change the whole system – if he should have wished to do so at all – as his power was still, as in the Middle Ages, dependent on the support of the major landowners and squires of the realm. The unchanging context included the continuous lack of learned lawyers within the Danish legal system and the Danish central administration. Denmark did not acquire education in law prior to 1736 and, even though the central administration hired educated men from either the university in Copenhagen or foreign countries, they were probably only seldom learned in law. Thus, Danish conservatism was probably not caused by the fact that Danes did not follow developments outside the realm, because the royal central administration was aware of new economic trends and theories, etc., but because time was not up for changes within the legal system – or, rather, changes were not needed when it came to the legal procedure used at the Danish courts.

But what turned out to be usable during a period with more economic activity, especially specialization of crafts in the market towns and more international trading, was the professional procurators known from contemporary Europe and the *ius commune* of the sixteenth and seventeenth centuries. The historical sources do not give an answer to why the procurators were introduced in Denmark in 1638, but, as suggested, they would be able to support the focus on trading and solving disputes over trading in the Danish market towns, concerning both domestic and international agreements. This, the historical sources support. The inspiration to introduce professional procurators may very well have come from contemporary *ius commune*, but if the central administration scepticism mentioned in the statute of 1638 is to be believed, the wish for procurators probably came from private actors. But no matter what, the royal administration would also gain from implementing such an office as it could support the administration's wish for making it safe and profitable for international businessmen to trade with Danish merchants and craftsmen. At the same time, the royal administration could professionalize the representation in court for those, the *personae miserabiles*, whom the king was obliged to take care of.

Thus, the introduction of professional procurators in Danish law was probably seen as a win-win situation for all actors in the legal system. But it was introduced not because of defects or deficiencies within the legal system but due to the wishes of the business community.

13 Adjusting the *ius commune*

The Swedish Legal Procedure in the Early Modern Period

Heikki Pihlajamäki

Introduction

Ius commune came in many different forms. In the 1960s, German scholars started to distinguish between "full" and "partial" reception of Roman law. They referred to the differing amounts of normative material stemming from medieval and early modern scholarship of learned law that found its way into the different European jurisdictions. Italy and Germany were lands of the full reception, whereas other parts of Europe only partially received the learned laws, or not at all. Those that did not all take part in the reception were, according to this "classical" understanding, England, the Nordic countries, and large areas of Eastern Europe.[1]

The classical understanding of *ius commune*, however, slowly gave way to the notion of *ius commune* as a conceptual framework for norms or, rather, a collection of them. The Portuguese legal historian António Manuel Hespanha has emphasized how medieval European *ius commune*, both its secular and its ecclesiastic versions, formed a framework which served as the basis for different solutions enabling legal pluralism. *Ius commune* left "open and indeterminate legal spaces", which then would fill up with local laws, customs, or judicial decisions.[2] The *ius commune* provided default rules, which applied if the jungle of local norms or privileges did not state otherwise. In the early modern period they increasingly did, because so many levels of government started actively issuing legislation of their own (for instance, kingdoms, principalities, towns, religious authorities, and rural communities). In the absence of a suitable *ius commune* norm, the necessary norm of course also had to be found in another

1 On reception and its historiography, see Mia Korpiola, "Reception", in *Münster Glossary on Legal Unity and Pluralism* (Käte Hamburger Kolleg Münster, "Legal Unity & Pluralism", EViR Working Papers, forthcoming).

2 António Manuel Hespanha, "Porque é que existe e em que é que consiste um direito colonial brasileiro", *Quaderni Fiorentini*, 35 (2006), 59–81, at 59–60. For the different conceptions of legal pluralism in the premodern and modern periods, see Tamar Herzog, "The Uses and Abuses of Legal Pluralism: A View from the Sideline", *Law and History Review*, 42:2 (2023), 211–222.

DOI: 10.4324/9781003425069-17

source. A *ius commune* framework applied not only in Europe, but also in the overseas colonies of European colonial empires, such as France, Portugal, Spain, and the United Provinces of the Netherlands.[3]

Recently, scholars have emphasized the role of local communities in the early modern processes of legal globalization, of which the spreading of *ius commune* both as a framework and as a set of norms is an integral part. Customary law, for instance, was everywhere a concept of learned law and developed in close connection to *ius commune*. The romanticization of legal customs as something immutable, inherently communitarian, and good has long been overdue, and scholars generally acknowledge that legal customs, like any normativity, reflect social and political power. Therefore, legal customs also continually change. As Yanna Yannakakis has shown for colonial Mexico, they can also be negotiated and contracted upon.[4]

In the early modern period, *ius commune* was developing into several regional varieties. This happened for two reasons. First, the substantive rules of the European common law acquired local characteristics depending on which part of Europe one is considering. Second, national legislation was gaining increasing normative space everywhere, contributing to the different versions of *ius commune*. The school of *usus modernus pandectarum*, "the new usage of the pandects", and the Dutch elegant jurisprudence (*iurisprudentia elegantior*) were especially influential in arranging the new normative elements into the framework of *ius commune*. This way, Roman-Dutch law took shape in the Netherlands. In Germany, *gemeines Recht* was the local variety. In Spain, *derecho común* and, in France, *droit commun* were the local varieties that developed. The terms, although they are also direct translations of the original Latin, are not just that but, at the same time, different versions of the same theme.[5] The same applied to some extent to the English common law. Although the substantive rules of the *ius commune* had only partially penetrated the common law, by the seventeenth century it ruled as the general law of the land everywhere in England.

Ius commune has always been a delicate matter in national legal histories and ideologies supporting them. For some nations, it has been a matter of pride to trace their legal history to learned roots of Roman-canon law. For

3 See the articles in *The Oxford Handbook of Law in European Overseas Colonies, 1500–1800*, ed. by Tamar Herzog, Heikki Pihlajamäki, Airton Ribeiro (Oxford: Oxford University Press; forthcoming 2026).

4 Yanna Yannakakis, *Since Time Immemorial: Native Custom & Law in Colonial Mexico* (Durham: Duke University Press, 2023). The book of Yannakakis includes a good bibliography for recent English-language discussions on customary law. See also Tamar Herzog, "Immemorial (and Native) Customs in Early Modernity: Europe and the Americas", *Journal of Comparative Legal History*, 9 (2021), 3–55. For German-language historiography and discussions, for instance on the distinction between *Gewohnheitsrecht* and *Rechtsgewohnheiten*, see the *Debatte* section of *Rechtsgeschichte*, 17 (2010) and the *Fokus* section of *Rechtsgeschichte*, 24 (2016).

5 See H. Patrick Glenn, *On Common Laws* (Oxford: Oxford University Press, 2007).

others, it has been important to distinguish themselves from the European *ius commune* and to frame their national legal histories differently. The Nordic countries are among those which traditionally have opted for the latter alternative. However, *ius commune* is not an either/or type of a phenomenon. In the early modern period, all European normative laws were to greater or lesser extent marked by different features of the common European law. At the same time, *ius commune* was gradually waning away in all of them as its national variants were turning into national legal orders.

This chapter investigates one of the legal orders which traditionally, by both Nordic and non-Nordic legal historians, has not been considered part of the Europe of *ius commune*.[6] Part I of this chapter will show how, despite this traditional conception, the Swedish order nevertheless came to include many features which are typically counted as part of the *ius commune*. The examples cited in this chapter all come from the law of procedure: the institution of summons, the law of evidence, and the judicial system.

Ius commune and Swedish Legal Procedure: Summons, the Law of Evidence, and Judicial Organization as Examples

The Law of Summons: From Canon Law to Swedish Provincial Laws

In the late Middle Ages, the law of summons became an important part of the canon law of procedure. In the following, I will give a general picture of how summoning was organized. As to the details, canon law scholars differed wildly.[7]

Summons was an important part of the canon law proceedings because without a defendant in court, the trial could not start. This was equally true for Swedish legal procedure. I will now show how the canon law of summons gradually replaced the older layer of rules in the Swedish secular legal proceedings of the thirteenth and fourteenth centuries.

Summons (*citatio*) belonged to the preparatory phase (*praeparatoria iudiciorum*) of the canon legal procedure, leading to the actual court proceedings. The plaintiff obtained summons by presenting a libel letter (*libellus*) to the presiding judge. The plaintiff also needed to promise a guarantee (*cautio fideiussoria*). If the plaintiff lacked funds, he or she had to take an oath instead (*cautio iuratoria*).[8]

6 I do not mean that no other writer would not have noticed this. As I will show in this chapter, many have. The history of Roman-canon law in Sweden or the other Nordic countries has, however, not been written.

7 This part of the chapter is based on Heikki Pihlajamäki, "Summoning to Court: Ordines Iudiciarii and Swedish Medieval Legislation", *Scandinavian Journal of History*, 45:5 (2020), 547–572.

8 See Wieslaw Litewski, *Der römisch-kanonische Zivilprozeß nach den älteren* ordines iudiciarii (Kraków: Wydawnictwo Uniwersytetu Jagiellońskiego, 1999, 252–254.

If the case was deemed admissible and the summons issued, the judge himself or his bailiffs delivered it to the summoned party. The summons was usually written (*libellus citationis*), although some canon law scholars allowed for an oral summons as well. Some authors mentioned a minimum time for the summoned party to appear in court.[9]

How many citations would a court send in one case before taking recourse to harder measures? Medieval canon law courts were patient. Some scholars allowed for three citations, while others one or two was enough. Only the last citation was often peremptory, which meant that the absence of the summoned party led to contumacy. Again, however, some scholars were ready to admit two or three peremptory citations. A thirty-day period was typically required between the citations. Some canon law authors left the number of citations and the interval between them entirely to the judge's arbitration.[10]

The provincial laws have a complicated history, and we cannot go into details here. The provincial laws were put into writing during the period ranging probably from the 1220s to the 1320s, in other words, roughly the same period when canon law scholars were refashioning the old European law of procedure in a profound way.[11] At the same time, the Swedish provincial laws timewise coincide with the same trend of putting legal customs into writing, to which the Saxon Mirror, *Coutumes de Beauvaisis*, and other thirteenth-century legal texts belong. As these other laws, the Swedish provincial laws contained normative materials from both legal customs and learned laws.

Nine laws exist in part or in their entirety. These include the Laws of Gotland (*Gutalagen*), West Gothia (*Västgötalagen*, older and newer version), East Gothia (*Östgötalagen*), Uppland (*Upplandslagen*), Västmanland (*Västmannalagen*), Dalarna (*Dalalagen*), Hälsingland (*Hälsingelagen*), and Södermanland (*Sädermannalagen*).[12]

All provincial laws, except for the Law of Gotland, included a chapter on church law. They dealt with matters of canon law, such as church jurisdiction and marriage. The newer provincial laws also had a chapter on procedure (*rättegångsbalk*): examples include the Laws of Uppland, Dalarna, and Västmanland. The oldest laws, such as those of Gotland and West Gothia,

9 Litewski, *Der römisch-kanonische Zivilprozeß*, 259–261.

10 Litewski, *Der römisch-kanonische Zivilprozeß*, 282–284.

11 On this, see Heikki Pihlajamäki and Mia Korpiola, "Medieval Canon Law: The Origins of Modern Criminal Law", in *The Oxford Handbook of Criminal Law*, ed. by Markus Dubber, Tatjana Hörnle (Oxford: Oxford University Press, 2014), 201–214.

12 Several editions and translations to modern Swedish exist. Here, I refer to the edition of Carl Johan Schlyter, published in 1827–77 as *Samling af Sweriges Gamla Lagar I–XIII* (volumes I–II together with Hans Samuel Collin). The editions of Åke Holmbäck and Elias Wessén on the provincial laws, and Magnus Eriksson's Law of the Realm and Town Law (1933–66), are in modernized Swedish and widely used.

have procedural provisions appearing together with substantial norms in different chapters.[13]

The procedural chapters of the Swedish medieval laws, not surprisingly, must have looked outdated compared to the canon law. The courts were lay dominated, and there were no university-trained judges, scribes, or advocates. All members of the community were obliged to appear at the local assembly (*ting*).[14] Clearly, in these circumstances norms on citation would have been unnecessary. The oldest layer of provincial laws, such as the Laws of West Gothia, indeed, have no rules on summons.

Later in the thirteenth century, the duty to appear at the assembly later became increasingly burdensome. Consequently, the need to summons parties to the trials became evident. The Law of Dalarna (Chapter on Procedure, Art. 5) will serve as an example.[15] After the sheriff (*länsman*) or plaintiff himself had delivered the summons to the defendant, he or she was given three chances to appear at the *ting*. As explained above, this was one of the most typical solutions in canon law as well. If the defendant failed to appear altogether, he or she was fined but generously allowed three more chances. If the defendant failed to appear at the two following sessions, the case was tried at the third session whether or not he or she appeared in court. The defendant could thus ignore five sessions before the case was finally tried.[16]

The oldest surviving manuscript of the Law of Uppland dates to the late thirteenth century. The king promulgated the law in 1296, and the drafting commission is known to have included ecclesiastical representation as well. Being the law of the central region, where both king and archbishop resided, the Law of Uppland gained high status and was used as a model for other Swedish laws.

The rules regarding citation are in the Procedural Chapter of the Law of Uppland (Art. III). Also here, the defendant was first allowed three chances to appear in court. The source of this rule is beyond doubt. The rule of three citations occurs as early as Gratian's Decrete (*'debet autem illum citare tribus edictis aut uno peremptorio pro omnibus'*) of the early twelfth century.[17] Among many other variations to the theme, Gratian's solution became the dominant one, endorsed also by Hostiensis, the leading canonist of the thirteenth century. The origin of the Uppland law of summons in canon law becomes even clearer, as we observe the end of the passage cited above. If the defendant failed all the three of chances to show up in courts, the trial would be taken

13 The paragraphs on homicide, which typically mix procedural and substantive elements; the Older Law of Western Gothia (Chapter on Homicide, Art. 1; Schlyter I, 10–12) and the Law of Eastern Gothia (Chapter on Homicide, Art. 2; Schlyter II, 46–48).

14 This made sense because the medieval Swedish local assembly (*ting*) had political, administrative, and judicial functions.

15 Holmbäck and Wessén, *Dalalagen och Västmannalagen*, 102.

16 Holmbäck and Wessén, *Dalalagen och Västmannalagen*, 102–103.

17 C. XXIV, q.3, c.6.

"to his farm" (*till hans gård*).[18] The rule comes from canon law. According to *Liber extra*, the influential canon law compilation of 1234, if the defendant did not appear in court, the case was heard at his domicile ("*deferentur citationes ad domicilium eius*").[19] *Scientiam*, an *ordo* or procedural treatise from the late 1230s,[20] and *Summa Aurea* of Hostiensis have the same rule.[21]

There is more. If the defendant failed to appear even at the fourth session held at his homestead, the court would seize his property: "Now he fails to appear as before; then the judges shall in the same session order an seizure at his farm, every seizure according to the nature of the goods (*Nu þryzkæs han sum fyrre, þa a domæri a samu þingi mæt I garþ hans dömæ, hwart mæt æptir sinni sak.*)". The seizure did not, however, automatically turn the seized property over to the plaintiff. The defendant could still defend himself in one of the next three court sessions.[22]

Also here, the influence of canon law is easy to detect. *Scientiam*, for instance, had it that the plaintiff could "petition to the judge to seize the possession of the defendant ... distinguishing between real and personal actions" ("*actor debet petere a iudice, ut mittatur in possessionem causa rei servandae, habita tamen distinctione, utrum agatur reali aut personali*").[23] In canon law, as in the Law of Uppsala, the seizure did not automatically mean that the plaintiff became the owner of the goods. This happened only if the defendant did not appear within one year in court to defend his interests (" *qui missus est in possessionem causa rei servandae, non efficitur verus possessor, si reus infra annum venerit et noluerit comparare nec stare iudicio*").[24] In the first phase, according to both canon law and the Law of Uppsala, the goods were thus seized as a guarantee.[25]

The Uppland law of summons is thus remarkably like those of canon law. The differences are understandable, when considering the different procedural contexts of the two legal orders. Canon law was the playground of educated professionals, whereas in Swedish courts they did not exist. A telling example has to do with the way canon law, in the example above, distinguishes between real and personal goods. The distinction presupposes knowledge of legal theory, which the Swedish lay judges did not have. Therefore, the Law

18 Schlyter III, 260–261.
19 X. II. 14. 3.
20 Wahrmund, *Ordo iudiciarius 'Scientiam'*.
21 On Henricus de Segusio (Hostiensis), see Pennington, *Popes, Canonists and Texts, 1150–1550*, XVI.
22 Law of Uppland, Procedural Chapter, Art. 3; Schlyter III, 260–261.
23 *Scientiam*, 3; X.II.6.5.
24 *Scientiam*, 3; D. XXXIX. 2, 15 § 16.
25 The canon law of summons is similarly described in the *ordo iudiciarius* of Ricardus Anglicus, most likely of the Bolognese school and dated to 1196; and Wahrmund, *Ricardus Anglicus*, 107. It has been shown that contumacy could result in the seizure of goods also in North Italian town laws. See Carraway Vitiello, "Contumacy", 99–132.

of Uppland just states that the judge must consider the differences as to the "nature of goods".

The solutions based on canon law were also accepted into many other provincial laws and formed the basis of the citation paragraphs of the realm-wide Laws of Magnus Eriksson (mid-fourteenth century) and, finally, of those taken into the Law of the Realm of 1734. Canon law, adjusted to meet Swedish needs, thus had long-lasting influence.

Early Modern Procedure: Olavus Petri and the Law of Proof

I will now move from the Middle Ages to the early modern period and turn the focus from citation to the law of proof. As was the case with the rules on summons, the Swedish law of proof also followed *ius commune*. Also here, the *ius commune* rules were adjusted to meet the local procedural context. Again, the lay domination of the Swedish judiciary was the decisive factor.

In the twelfth and thirteenth centuries, European legal scholars and practitioners produced a revolution in procedural law. The transformation consisted of developing a distinction between adversarial and inquisitorial procedures, which then gave birth to public criminal law. The doctrinal bases of inquisitorial procedure were confirmed at the Fourth Lateran Council of 1215. The Council also prohibited ecclesiastics from contributing to the administration of ordeals. Until then, ordeals had served as the main method of deciding questions of truth in difficult cases. Ordeals prohibited, other ways of establishing procedural truth were needed. In the emerging statutory theory of proof, "full proof" consisted of two eyewitness statements or confession required for conviction in serious criminal cases. Part and parcel of this combination of inquisitorial procedure and legal theory of proof was judicial torture. Under strict prerequisites, defined in legal literature, torture could be used to extract confession.[26]

These medieval inventions constituted the kernel of *ius commune* criminal law and procedure, extending far into the modern period. In Sweden, the beginning of the modern era constituted a significant change, although continuities cannot be disregarded here either. As one of the results of the Protestant Reformation, the ecclesiastical courts of the Catholic Church lost their jurisdiction. Some of their powers were transferred to secular courts, and some to the Protestant ecclesiastical courts, now under state control.[27]

In this part of the chapter, however, I will emphasize the continuity between the medieval *ius commune* and early modern Swedish law. I will show how Olavus Petri, a sixteenth-century legal author but better known as Sweden's

26 See Pihlajamäki and Korpiola.

27 See Heikki Pihlajamäki, "'God's Eternal and Always Just Law': Swedish Criminal Law and Reformation", in Virpi Mäkinen (ed.), *Law and the Lutheran Reformation* (Leiden: Brill, 2006), 171–204.

Reformator, wished to modernize the Swedish law of evidence. I take up some examples of how the European *ius commune* influenced Swedish legal procedure in the sixteenth and seventeenth centuries.[28]

Olavus Petri (1493–1552) studied theology in Uppsala, Sweden, and continued his studies in Germany.[29] After holding several ecclesiastical positions, Olavus was,[30] in 1531, appointed Chancellor of the Realm. After a conflict with King Gustav Vasa, Olavus was deposed in 1533. He continued preaching and writing, and, sometime in the late 1530s, he finished the famous *Instructions for the Judge*.[31]

The *Instructions* continued the medieval *brocarda* (or *brocardica*) tradition, meant as advice for practicing lawyers.[32] With his *Instructions*, Olavus wished to modernize the unlearned Swedish procedure along the lines of the European *ius commune*, with which he certainly had familiarized himself while in Germany. The *brocarda* was an excellent mode of communicating some fundamental ideas of *ius commune* criminal procedure, however, in a simplified form, to lay judges of early sixteenth-century Sweden. The *Instructions* soon gained a significant place in court practice and often belonged to the collection of legal manuscripts that Swedish judges carried with them while sitting court.[33]

In the statutory theory of proof, judicial torture was thus designed to extract confessions in serious criminal cases in which "full proof" in the form of confession or two eyewitnesses was lacking. Having most probably acquainted himself with the theme in Germany, judicial torture worried Olavus. On the one hand, he thought that criminal convictions should no longer be based on oaths and compurgators, but, as in *ius commune*, on eyewitness statements and confessions.

Torture, however, was part of the *ius commune* criminal procedural, and that remained a problem for Olavus. He finally accepted torture, but only in cases of treason and homicide. The *Instructions* did not, however, succeed in establishing judicial torture even in these limited cases. In the 1560s, however, King Erik XIV's *High Court* (*Höga nämnd*), is known to have used torture in cases of high treason. However, torture was never accepted as a general,

28 This part of the article is based on my article "Olavus Petri (1493–1552): Transplanting Foreign Law in Reformation Sweden", in *Law and the Christian Tradition in Scandinavia: The Writings of Great Nordic Jurists*, ed. by Kjell Å. Modéer, Helle Vogt (London: Routledge, 2021), 90–104.

29 Gerhard Schmidt, *Die Richterregeln des Olavus Petri: Ihre Bedeutung im allgemeinen und für die Entwicklung des schwedischen Strafprozessrechts vom 14. bis 16. Jahrhundert* (Göttingen: Vandenhoeck & Ruprecht, 1966).

30 Gunnar T. Westin, "Olavus Petri", *Svenskt biografiskt lexikon*, 28 (1992–1994), 151.

31 For an English translation by Jarkko Tontti and Linda Augustine, see https://www.jarkko-tontti.net/blog/tieteilya-ja-filosofiaa/Olavus-petri-and-the-rules-for-judges-associations).

32 *Handwörterbuch zur Deutschen Rechtsgeschichte I*, 519–520.

33 On the influence of the *Instructions* on legal practice, see Henrik Munktell, "Domarereglerna i praxis fore 1734 års lag", *Svensk Juristttidning* (1939), 516–530.

accepted means of fact-finding, and, by the mid-seventeenth century, the little judicial torture that existed had vanished.[34] I have explained the reasons for this in another article and will not delve into them here. Suffice it to say just briefly that judicial torture poorly matched the Swedish system of oaths and compurgators, still dominant until the seventeenth century. Swedish criminal procedure was, furthermore, accusatorial and dominated by laymen, who could not be trusted with torturing their peers.[35]

There is still another reason for the fact that judicial torture never really gathered wind under its wings in Sweden. By the time *ius commune* criminal procedure replaced oath procedure in Sweden in the seventeenth century, torture was on the decline also in those parts of Europe where it had been entrenched since the late Middle Ages, such as France, Italy, and parts of Germany. Torture was in the process of being replaced functionally by the so-called extraordinary punishments. In cases of serious crimes, if when full legal proof was readily available, extraordinary punishment could be inflicted instead of death punishment. Extraordinary punishments came in many versions, such as different forms of forced labour. They had existed since the Middle Ages, but not until the early modern period did European polities possess infrastructures which extraordinary punishments typically required. The modern states were now able to organize, for instance, the gathering and transportation of convicts to galleys or mines. Now the medieval institution of extraordinary punishment could be fully brought into use, and, at the same time, the use of judicial torture – and death punishment – began their steady decline. Swedish criminal procedure, both as theory and as practice, joined this development.

Transferring ius commune *Judicial Institutions: Appeals Courts*

I will take one more example of *ius commune* influence, this time related to the institutional side of *ius commune*.

In 1495, the Diet of the Holy Roman Empire took important decisions to reform imperial justice. The Diet established the Imperial Chamber Court (*Reichskammergericht*) as the highest judicial organ. The Court would exist as long as the Holy Roman Empire itself, until 1806. The Imperial Chamber Court was a political compromise between the estates and the emperor, always understood as identified more with the estates than the emperor. During its over three centuries existence, the Imperial Chamber Court sat in several towns, most of which were rather unimportant, to reflect the Court's independence from the emperor. After continuous changes of location during its

34 Heikki Pihlajamäki, "The Painful Question: The Fate of Judicial Torture in Early Modern Sweden", *Law and History Review*, 25:3 (2007), 557–592.

35 This was also the point John Langbein made when discussing the lack of torture in early modern England. See *Torture and the Law of Proof* (Chicago: University of Chicago Press, 1977).

first decades, the Court moved to Speyer in 1527 and remained there until 1689. It was then relocated to Wetzlar, where it remained until its dissolution. The emperor, in turn, had his own highest court, the Imperial Aulic Court (*Reichshofrat*), which sat in Vienna.[36]

The Imperial Chamber Court came to exert great influence in many parts of Europe. First, of course, within the Empire itself, as one of its two supreme courts. Half of the judges at the Court were always university-trained legal professionals, while the other half had to noblemen. In practice, the nobles also had legal training. This made the Court one of the major vehicles of the so-called reception of *ius commune* in the Empire. Because of the so-called appeals privileges, the Court's jurisdiction was, however, also severely curtailed. Practically all major princes within the Empire acquired themselves an appeals privilege, as did many of the ruler of less significant territories as well. Appeals privileges could be either unlimited (*privilegio de non appellando illimitatum*), thus excluding all appeals from the territory, or the privilege could be partial and limited to certain kinds of cases only.[37]

At first sight, appeals privileges may seem as if they diminished the influence of only the Imperial Chamber Court, but that is not the entire truth. When an appeals privilege was issued, the prince receiving it agreed to organize an appeals system within his own territory. The territorial appeals instances were often arranged according to the model of the Imperial Chamber Court. They followed similar procedures, were staffed according to the model of the Imperial Chamber Court, and, finally, contributed to the reception of *ius commune* within their territories. As the founding of the Court led to an increasing separation of judicial power from the emperor, scholars often see the establishment of the Imperial Chamber Court as an important step towards the "judicial (or legal) revolution" of the early modern period. The term "judicial revolution",[38] following Gatrell, Lenman, and Parker, refers to a "tendency for local communities progressively to lose control of the content and the administration of criminal law to the agents of the expanding state".[39] Specifically for

36 The literature on the Court is enormous. See for instance, Ralf-Peter Fuchts, "The Supreme Court of the Holy Roman Empire: The State of Research and the Outlook", *Sixteenth Century Journal*, 43:1 (2003), 9–27. On both the Imperial Chamber Court and the Imperial Aulic Court, and their place within the imperial governance structure, see Peter Oestmann, "The Law of the Holy Roman Empire of the German Nation", in *The Oxford Handbook of European Legal History*, ed. by Heikki Pihlajamäki, Markus D. Dubber, Mark Godfrey (Oxford: Oxford University Press, 2018), 732–760.

37 On the appeals privileges, see Jürgen Weitzel, *Der Kampf um die Appellation ans Reichskammergericht: Zur politischen Geschichte einer Rechtsmittel in Deutschland* (Köln: Böhlau, 1976). Cases dealing with negation of justice were excluded from the privileges, also from the unlimited one. In these cases, a subject of the Empire could always appeal to the highest instance.

38 On the national versions of *ius commune*, see H. Patrick Glenn, *On Common Laws* (Oxford: Oxford University Press, 2007).

39 V.A.C. Gatrell, Bruce Lenman, Geoffrey Parker, "Introduction", in *Crime and the Law: The Social History of Crime in Western Europe since 1500*, ed. by V.A.C. Gatrell, Bruce Lenman,

Sweden, Korpiola has defined legal revolution as "the unification of Swedish law and legal practice which could only be achieved by centralizing the judiciary and by submitting it to monitoring from above, royal control".[40]

Similar high courts were established in other parts of Europe as well. In 1504, Duke Philip the Fair established the Grand Council of Mechelen (*Grote Raad van Mechelen*, *Grand Conseil de Malines*) as the permanent supreme court for the Burgundian Netherlands. All councillors, or judges, of the Grand Council needed to have a law degree.[41]

The European trend towards high courts spreading and consolidating national versions of *ius commune* did not leave Sweden untouched. Sweden's legal order, at the beginning of the seventeenth century, was based on medieval legislation of several layers, on the level both of provinces and of the realm. It circulated on manuscripts, which could differ from each other considerably. The situation was remedied under the reign of King Charles IX, when first the provincial laws of Uppsala and East Gothia were printed in 1607, and then King Christopher's Law of the Realm (1442) in 1608. The attempts to unifying the law were not limited to written legislation. From the point of view of the emerging centralized state that Sweden was, it was equally important to build an effectively functioning judicial machinery. On top of that, royal judicial powers needed to be reorganized.

Attempts and experiments to establish a royal high court had started during the reign of King Gustav Vasa in the first half of the sixteenth century, and they continued when King Erik XIV's High Council (*Höga nämnd*). The Council became known primarily for its harsh measures against suspects accused of lese-majesty and treason, and it was abolished during the reign of King John III. In addition to several other reform attempts, King Charles IX made the first attempt for a court of appeals in 1604.[42] That court also failed, but others soon followed, and the Svea Court of Appeal finally started its work in 1614.

Although the organizational model of the Svea Appeals Court is clearly the *Reichskammergericht*, the Swedish court has a founding history of its own. Korpiola has recently shown how the political and economic crisis led to the establishment of the Court. In addition, the continuous absence of the king during the many war campaigns abroad in the 1610s emphasized the benefits of organizing his judicial duties anew. The founding of the Court of Appeals occurred in haste, which was reflected in its somewhat unclear position in the judicial hierarchy: although meant to use royal judicial power, the Court

Geoffrey Parker (London: Europa Publication limited, 1980), at 6.

40 Mia Korpiola, "General Background: From Judicial Crisis to Legal Revolution through the Svea Court of Appeal?", in *The Svea Court of Appeal in the Early Modern Period: Historical Reinterpretations and New Perspectives*, ed. by Mia Korpiola (Stockholm: Institutet för rättshistorisk forskning, 2014), 23–54, at 29.

41 On the Grand Council of Mechelen, see L.Th. Maes, *Het Parlament en de Grote Raad van Mechelen, 1473, 1797* (Antwerpen: De Vries-Brouwers, 2009).

42 Korpiola, 44–47.

gradually became a middle instance between the lower courts and the king. In the first decades, the Svea Appeals Courts also adjudicated cases decided by other appeals courts on appeal. Finally, in the beginning it also held other duties, political and administrative rather than judicial, making its functions somewhat of a cross between those of the Imperial Chamber Court and the Imperial Aulic Court.[43]

Although the Svea Appeals Court was originally intended as a middle instance, after its early years its role thus consolidated as such. During the seventeenth century, a string of new high courts was established in different parts of the Swedish realm: Turku (1623), Dorpat (1629), Jönköping (1634), and Vaasa (1779). These courts, like the European high courts and the Svea Appeals Court after which they were modelled, had learned jurists as judges. This made it possible for new kinds of sources to gain wider authority in Swedish law. However, being "learned" in the Swedish high courts needs to be taken with a grain of salt: if often sufficed that a judge had some university studies, not that he had gained an actual degree.[44]

As in Germany, so also in Sweden the high courts contributed significantly towards transferring *ius commune* to the realm. Several studies confirm this, such as Inger's works on criminal procedural law,[45] Jägerskiöld's studies on private law,[46] Korpiola's monograph on marital law,[47] and the work of Trolle Önnerfors on the law of inheritance.[48] On the other hand, the "reception" never occurs without adjusting the object of transfer to the local circumstances. In Sweden, the *ius commune* could not be accepted in all its doctrinal niceties and finesses for the sheer reason that, in the seventeenth and eighteenth centuries, Sweden was a land practically void of lawyers. It would have made little sense for the appeals courts to introduce *ius commune* in any other form than of a kind which was accessible and understandable to the lay people active in the lower courts. This was how Olavus Petri had approached the

43 Mia Korpiola, "A Safe Haven in the Shadow of War? The Founding and the Raison d'être of the New Court, Based on Its Early Activity", in *The Svea Court of Appeal in the Early Modern Period*, 55–108, at 98–101.

44 On the studies of Swedish early modern laywers, see Marianne Vasara-Aaltonne, *Learning Law and Travelling Europe: Study Journeys and the Developing Swedish Legal Profession, c.1630–1800* (Leiden: Brill, 2020).

45 Göran Inger, *Das Geständnis in der schwedischen Prozessrechtsgeschichte I* (Stockholm: Institutet för rättshistorisk forskning, 1976); Göran Inger, *Institutet "insättande på bekännelse" i svensk processrättshistoria I* (Stockholm: Institutet för rättshistorisk forskning, 1976); Göran Inger, *Erkännandet i svensk processrättshistoria. 2, 1614–1948 I* (Stockholm: Institutet för rättshistorisk forskning, 1994).

46 Stig Jägerskiöld, *Studier rörande receptionen av främmande rätt i Sverige under den yngre landslagens tid* (Lund: Bloms, 1963).

47 Mia Korpiola, *Between Betrothal and Bedding: Marriage Formation in Sweden 1200–16* (Leiden: Brill, 2009).

48 Elsa Trolle Önnerfors, *Justitia et Prudentia: Rättsbildning genom rättstillämpning, Svea hovrätt och testamentsmålen 1640–1690* (Stockholm: Institutet för rättshistorisk forskning, 2014).

introduction of *ius commune* (in his case by simple *brocardica*). The appeals courts now continued in the same vein.

One more link uniting Sweden with *ius commune* must be mentioned. After the Peace of Westphalia in 1648, several territories in northern Germany became Swedish in the sense that the Swedish king became the emperor's vassal there (the Duchies of Bremen-Verden and Vorpommern, the Principality of Rügen, the town and the Barony of Wismar, and the Cathedral Chapter of Hamburg). In the newly acquired territories, the judiciary needed to be organized practically from scratch. The emperor also granted the Swedish king full appeals privilege (*privilegium de non appellando illimitatum*) in these lands. As in all imperial lands with an unlimited appeals privilege, the Swedish crown had to organize a high court for its territories.[49] An appellate court (*Oberappellationsgericht für die schwedischen Lehen im Heiligen Römischen Reich deutscher Nation*, or the Higher Appeals Court for the Swedish Fiefs in the Holy Roman Empire of the German Nation), in common for all Swedish fiefs, was indeed established and started functioning in Wismar in 1653.

Conclusion: *Ius Commune* as Norms and Structure

Reception, legal transplant, legal translation, or legal transfer? Scholars have developed these and many other concepts to refer to situations in which law and legal institutions move from one area to another. This is hardly the place to engage in conceptual discussions. In this chapter, I have used all these terms interchangeably. I have practical reasons for that. When they mean the wide-scale adoption of rules of *ius commune* in the Middle Ages and the early modern period, legal historians commonly speak of reception. Legal transplant, in turn, has been deeply entrenched in the language of comparative law since the 1970s. Legal translation and legal transfer, then, are both attempts at developing more sophisticated terminology, which would consider the changes that law always experiences when it moves and the cultural factors that influence the shape it takes.

With concrete examples, I hope to have shown how *ius commune* rules and institutions changed Swedish law in the Middle Ages and the early modern period. Examples could easily have been multiplied. The point I have been making with all my examples is that *ius commune* rules have served a purpose but that they have also been changed to meet the local circumstances while being accepted as part of Swedish law.

The citation rules, following models of canon law, made sure that defendants finally ended up in court. These rules gradually became necessary because people no longer automatically turned up at the local assembly meetings.

49 Heinz Mohnhaupt, "Organisation und Tätigkeit des 'Hohen Königlichen Tribunals zu Wismar'", in *Integration durch Recht: Das Wismarer Tribunal (1653–1806)*, ed. by Nils Jörn, Bernhard Diestelkamp, Kjell Åke Modéer (Köln: Böhlau, 2003), 215–237, at 217–225.

However, in the lawyerless society that Sweden was, canon law rules of citation could not be adopted in all their details but had to simplified.

In the case of Olavus Petri, the rules of evidence in the form of legal theory of proof replaced the medieval oath procedure. Scholars of canon and secular law had developed the legal theory of proof in the Middle Ages. Once ordeals had started disappearing fast after the decision of the Fourth Lateran Council of 1215 forbidding clerics to participate in them, new rules became needed. Moreover, the legal rules of proof better fitted the emerging hierarchical judicial structure, as appellate courts now could not also reevaluate evidence. The legal theory of evidence, together with inquisitorial procedure and a hierarchical judicial system with appeals courts, was an important piece in the construction of the modernized system of legal procedure. Olavus, however, was an individual legal writer and slightly ahead of his time. His *Instructions* did not change the Swedish law of evidence; instead, they marked the beginning of a gradual transformation that lasted until the Law of 1734 entered into force.

The slow transformation is difficult to imagine without the appeals courts, which were founded in Sweden, first in Stockholm (1614) and then in other towns of the empire. It is a matter of opinion whether high courts can be understood as part of *ius commune*. Since they came to form such an important institutional building block, which carried *ius commune* across the continent (and even beyond, to overseas colonies), I think it makes sense to consider them as part of the common European law. Again, as in the two first examples, the Swedish version of its *ius commune* had its own peculiarities. The early history of the first appeals court, the Svea Appeals Court, cannot be detached from the political and economic history of the early seventeenth century. First intended as the user of royal judicial power, the Court turned in some decades into a middle instance between the lower courts and the king, who continued using his judicial power despite the founding of the Svea Court. The Court was learned but learned in the Swedish more limited sense of the term. It contributed to substantive *ius commune* rules being transferred as part of the Swedish legal landscape. However, the foreign rules that Swedes adopted were always adapted to the particular lay-dominated environment of the country.

14 The Reception of the *ius commune* through German Law in Reformation Sweden (ca. 1530–1610)

Torture, Police, and Crime

Mia Korpiola

Introduction

In Stockholm in 1593, the Italian Niccolò Stagnole (orig. Niclaes Stangniole), having lost many items of foodstuff, accused six young men of theft. He attempted to have the culprits tortured but the attempt failed, and the Stockholm town court expressed disapprobation as it pronounced that Swedish law did not authorize torture.[1] This case exemplifies very well the clash of different legal traditions, each with their own expectations of the law. Niccolò Stagnole came from the learned Italian *ius commune* tradition, assuming that the court arrest the suspected thieves and torture them, while torture never became an established feature of the Swedish legal system even if it was exceptionally used.

Yet, during the sixteenth century, Swedish law was influenced by the *ius commune* via German law. Even if the role of canon law diminished through the Reformation, the importance of the *ius commune*, especially Roman and feudal law, was increasing. The new Vasa dynasty recruited German legal experts knowledgeable of the learned law. Many also possessed experience and skills in administration.[2] German norms and legal works, increasingly influenced by *ius commune* doctrines, found their way first to the libraries of Swedish kings and aristocrats, later also to high-ranking officials.[3] The new Swedish Protestant ecclesiastical norms, such as the 1571 Church Ordinance, were influenced by

1 23 Apr. 1593, in *Stockholms stads tänkeböcker från år 1592* 1: *1592–1595* [hereafter: *Stb från 1592* 1], ed. by Daniel Almqvist (Stockholm: Stockholms stadsarkiv, 1939), 117.

2 Mia Korpiola, "Desperately Needing Lawyers: Contacts in the Baltic Sea Region and the Rise of Diplomacy in Reformation Sweden", in *Migration und Kulturtransfer im Ostseeraum während der Frühen Neuzeit*, ed. by Otfried Czaika, Heinrich Holze (Stockholm: Kungliga biblioteket, 2012), 101–120.

3 E.g., Mia Korpiola, "On the Reception of the Ius Commune and Foreign Law in Sweden, ca. 1550–1615", *Clio@Thémis* 2 (2009), *Histoires des cultures juridiques: Circulations, connexions et espaces transnationaux du droit*, available online at: https://www.cliothemis.com/On-the-Reception-of-the-Jus .

DOI: 10.4324/9781003425069-18

German church ordinances.[4] German princely house laws (Ger. *Hausgesetz* or *Hausordnung*) – wills, contracts, and norms regulating succession, heirship and property in ruling families – also influenced the Vasa norms of succession and Swedish notions of royal and noble misalliances.[5]

This chapter explores this trend of the reception of the *ius commune* by investigating how elements of continental criminal law and the law of proof appeared in Swedish norms, law proposals, and legal practice roughly ca. 1530–1610. Earlier research has observed *ius commune* influences via Germany on the Swedish law of proof and criminal procedure via German law. I will discuss this especially first through an analysis of the Stagnole case, but I will also highlight the ambivalence towards the use of torture and the unwillingness to include it in the law. Moving on to criminal law, the appearance of police regulation in sixteenth-century Sweden will be analysed. Moreover, I will develop my argument on the influence of *ius commune* on Swedish law by focusing on some instances in which Swedish criminals were sentenced to harsh and unusual punishments that were not mentioned in Swedish law.

Based on case law and draft laws pertaining to a failed law reform in the early 1600s, I will argue that the influence on German law, especially the imperial criminal code (*Peinliche Gerichtsordnung*) of 1532, usually referred to as the *Constitutio Criminalis Carolina* after Emperor Charles V (r. 1519–56)[6] probably lay behind this development. Therefore, I suggest that Imperial legislation and especially the *Carolina* – as it will be referred to in this chapter – was known and actively used by the Vasa kings, their advisors, and learned lawyers who drafted laws and influenced policy and court cases in Sweden.

A Torturing Encounter: Different Expectations of the Law of Evidence

The Italian Niccolò Stagnole was outraged as his warehouse (*wisthus*) in Stockholm had been plundered. However, convinced that he knew the thieves, he went to the town court to denounce the offenders – six young men – and

4 E.g., Emil Färnström, *Om källorna till 1571 års kyrkoordning särskilt med hänsyn till tyska kyrkoordningar* (Uppsala: Almqvist & Wiksell, 1935), esp. 7–8, 280–282; Emil Färnström, "Inledning", in *Laurentius Petris Kyrkoordning av år 1571*, ed. by Emil Färnström (Stockholm: Samfundet Pro fide et Christianismo, 1932), xii–xiii; Hjalmar Holmquist, *Svenska kyrkans historia 3: Reformationstidevarvet*, vol. 1 (Stockholm: Svenska Kyrkans Diakonistyrelses Bokförlag, 1933), 211.

5 Mia Korpiola, "Affection or Ancestry? Royal Misalliances, German Legal Influences, and the Law in Reformation Sweden", *Zeitschrift der Savigny-Stiftung für Rechtsgeschichte, Germanistische Abteilung*, 129 (2013), 145–179.

6 Its official title is *Des allerdurchleuchtigsten großmechtigsten vnüberwindtlichsten, Keyser Karls des fünfften, vnnd des heyligen Römischen Reichs peinlich gerichts ordnung, auff den Reichsztägen zu Augspurgk vnd Regenspurgk, inn jaren dreissig, vnn zwey vnd dreisssig gehalten, auffgericht vnd beschlossen* [hereafter: *Constitutio Criminalis Carolina*], Gedruckt zu Meintz bei Ivo Schöffer, 1533.

have them arrested for the crime. When the case was first heard at the Town Court of Stockholm on 23 April 1593, Stagnole presented his accusations. As he did not have any evidence to support his claims that the six youths were guilty and the accused denied the charges, the case was postponed to be investigated further.[7]

Stagnole was also busy outside the town court. He had visited both the mayors as well as the town council several times requesting that the suspected thieves be tortured so as to obtain more evidence in the case.[8] In addition, Stagnole had visited Marshal (*hovmarskalk*) Hans Åkesson [Soop] (1552–1619)[9] several times to petition that the detained young men be tortured (*pijnlige förhördh;* lit. "tormentingly interrogated").[10] We do not know from which region or town Niccolò Stagnole originated. However, suspected thieves and burglars were in some Italian jurisdictions regularly tortured on suspicion without much ado.[11] It is unclear what Stagnole wanted to achieve by turning to Hans Åkesson, who as a marshal was a high dignitary in the royal court assisting with the administration. Could he perhaps have authorized torture in the name of the king? This seems unlikely. King Sigismund (r. 1592–99 in Sweden; r. 1587–1632 in Poland-Lithuania) had succeeded to the Swedish throne only the previous year and had not even visited Sweden as king. His coronation was to take place only in the autumn of 1593.

The larceny case took a sudden new turn on 21 May 1593, a month after the first court hearing, when Michel Andersson confessed in court that he and Jacob Tile(man)sson had stolen goods from "Niklas the Italian" (*Niclaes italiann*), that is Stagnole, in Norrmalm. His confessions meant that the six gaoled men were innocent of the crime and thereby freed from Stagnole's accusations. Michel Andersson seems to have been a habitual thief as he confessed to six other thefts, listing the stolen goods as well. He was sentenced to be hanged for his crimes in accordance with the Chapter on Theft in King Magnus Eriksson's Town Law.[12]

7 23 Apr. 1593, in *Stb från 1592* 1, ed. by Almqvist, 117. The stolen property was listed as two fox furs, two sheep furs, a sack of hops, a sack of bread, meat and pork, four cheeses, and three bags of peas.

8 23 Apr. 1593, in *Stb från 1592* 1, ed. by Almqvist, 117.

9 Hans Gillingstam, "Soop, släkt", *Svenskt biografiskt lexikon*, 32 (Stockholm: Riksarkivet, 2003-2006), 668–675, here 668–670. Few Swedish noble families used surnames in the Middle Ages, and most noblemen and -women were known by their first name and their patronym. Over the sixteenth century, the use of surnames increased, especially among men and abroad, while in the course of the seventeenth century, all Swedish noble families, including women, started to use family names that were often derived from their coat of arms.

10 23 Apr. 1593, in *Stb från 1592* 1, ed. by Almqvist, 117.

11 Trevor Dean, *Crime and Justice in Later Medieval Italy* (Cambridge: Cambridge University Press, 2007), 190–191.

12 21 May 1593, in *Stb från 1592* 1, ed. by Almqvist, 125–126; *Corpus Iuris Sueo-Gotorum Antiqui [CISGA] 11: Codex Iuris Urbici Magnæanus*, ed. by C. J. Schlyter (Lund: Berlingska Boktryckeriet, 1865), Chapter on Theft [*Thiuffwa balker*], art. 3, 384.

Michel's confession was good news for Niccolò Stagnole. Not only were the thieves, who had taken his property, identified, but also one of them was sentenced to the gallows as the lawful and just punishment for his many serious crimes. Simultaneously, the thief's admission of guilt landed Stagnole into a precarious and potentially life-threatening position vis-à-vis the accused innocent men. The matter was postponed until the incarcerated were freed, but the court reconvened two days later. The six men delivered from gaol attended the session. The court reiterated the case against Niccolò Stagnole: he had caused six innocent men to be gaoled for a month and had repeatedly insisted and implored that they be tortured for a crime they had not committed. This was against Swedish law. Now, the innocent six urged that Stagnole be punished in his turn. Stagnole was read "a hard text" (*enn hård tæxt*), the appropriate sections on the royal peace (*edzöre*) and town courts from the Town Law.[13] The court scribe noted "*poena talionis*" in the margin. Thus, Stagnole was threatened with hanging – the penalty for theft to which the men he had wrongly accused had risked to be condemned.[14]

Niccolò Stagnole was a foreigner who, as such, tended to be disadvantaged in early modern criminal law. They were less likely to find oath-helpers and more often executed for similar crimes than natives.[15] He might have already felt the noose around his neck. Instead, the court exhorted him to come to an agreement with the injured parties and to satisfy them apparently with pecuniary compensation. This Stagnole promised. We do not know the details of this extrajudicial reconciliation, but the bailiff and town servants (*kemner*) were to ensure that a fine was paid to the royal and municipal coffers.[16] The case demonstrates the expectations of an Italian, coming from a *ius commune* jurisdiction, in Sweden with a somewhat different legal culture. Yet, the Swedish legal system was not so different as the Stockholm town fathers suggested. In addition, the *ius commune* influenced Swedish law and practice significantly via Germany, filtered through its laws, during the long sixteenth century.

Creeping Reception of Judicial Torture in Sweden: The Romano-Canonical Inquisitorial Process through Germany

Even if the magistrates of Stockholm town court lectured Stagnole that Swedish law did not know torture, the situation was more complex than they stated. They were quite right in observing that torture was unmentioned and unauthorized in the royal laws from the mid-fourteenth century and 1442.

13 This probably referred to art. 30 in the Chapter on Town Courts (*Radstuffw Balker*) and to art. 21 in the Chapter on Royal Peace (Edzöris Balker) in King Magnus Eriksson's Town Law, in *CISCA* 11, ed. by Schlyter, 283, 313.

14 21 May 1593, in *Stb från 1592* 1, ed. by Almqvist, 125–126; 23 May 1593, ibid., 128–129.

15 On the proportionally higher execution rate of foreigners in general, see Trevor Dean, *Crime in Medieval Europe* (Harlow: Longman, 2001), 125–126.

16 23 May 1593, in *Stb från 1592* 1, ed. by Almqvist, 128–129.

Yet, we also have evidence from the account books of Stockholm that in 1462 the town acquired locks, manacles, and thumbscrews (*jonfrver*) "for the town's needs". We also know of late medieval instances when the town court of Stockholm had used judicial torture.[17]

As the Swedish secular court system was increasingly in royal hands during the Middle Ages, the powers of injured parties were reduced. No criminal cases were to be extrajudicially reconciled so that the Crown would lose control of the criminal jurisdiction and its portion of the fines. While according to some laws the catching and even the punishing of sentenced criminals had been the responsibility of the injured party in the thirteenth and fourteenth centuries, these tasks became increasingly the duty of the royal administration. In Stockholm, the population and town administration were partly German. Thus, the town obviously followed the practice – albeit tardively – of late medieval German towns that had been longer influenced by the Romano-canonical procedural law and the inquisitorial procedure. The first mentions from town laws date from the thirteenth and the early decades of the fourteenth century only to increase as the late Middle Ages ripened. For example, in Frankfurt am Main, suspected criminals were occasionally tortured by the town officials already in the later fourteenth century.[18]

Earlier research has identified several cases of the use of torture in the town of Stockholm during the sixteenth century. These took place especially during the reign of King John III (r. 1569–92), and the tortured persons were mostly suspected of murder, treason, and theft. A suspected thief was tortured so severely in 1591 – a couple of years before the Stagnole case – that it took

17 *Stockholms stads skattebok 1460–1468 samt strödda räkenskaper från 1430-talet och från 1460–1473*, ed. by Joh. Ax. Almqvist. Stockholm stadsböcker från äldre tid, ser. 3:1 (Stockholm: Kungl. Samfundet för utgifvande af handskrifter rörande Skandinaviens historia, 1926), 117. Despite the similarity of names, the "maiden" (*jungfru*) had nothing to do with the neo-medieval and mythical "iron maiden" of which there is no medieval or early modern reliable evidence. See also Lizzie Carlsson, "Bödelsämbetet i det medeltida Stockholm: En kulturhistorisk studie", *Samfundet Sankt Eriks Årsbok 1934* (Stockholm: Samfundet Sankt Erik, 1934), 95–118, here 113; Henrik Munktell, "Tortyren i svensk rättshistoria: Ett bidrag till straffprocessrättens historia", *Lychnos*, 4 (1939), 102–135, here 108; Göran Inger, *Das Geständnis in der schwedischen Prozessrechtsgeschichte, 1: Bis zur Gründung des Svea Hofgerichts 1614* (Lund: Institutet för rättshistorisk forskning, 1976), 103–105; Björn Åstrand, *Tortyr och pinligt förhör: Våld och tvång i äldre svensk rätt* (Umeå: Institutionen för historiska studier vid Umeå universitet, 2000), 101–102.

18 E.g., John H. Langbein, *Prosecuting Crime in the Renaissance: England, Germany, France* (Cambridge, Mass.: Harvard University Press, 1974), 147–155; Winfried Trusen, "Strafprozeß und Rezeption: Zu den Entwicklungen im Spätmittelalter und den Grundlagen der Carolina", *Strafrecht, Strafprozess und Rezeption. Grundlagen, Entwicklung und Wirkung der Constitutio Criminalis Carolina*, ed. by Peter Landau and Friedrich-Christian Schroeder (Frankfurt am Main: Vittorio Klostermann, 1984), 29–118; Alfons Vogt, "Die Anfänge des Inquisitionsprozesses in Frankfurt am Main", *Zeitschrift der Savigny-Stiftung für Rechtsgeschichte, Germanistische Abteilung*, 68 (1951), 234–307, here esp. 301–304.

three weeks for him to recuperate.[19] We also know that King Erik XIV's (r. 1560–69) high court, known as the "*Höga Nämnd*" (Eng. "High Jury"), functioning in the 1560s, occasionally used torture especially in cases of treason after the suspected traitor had already been condemned to death. This practice is known also from King Gustav I Vasa's reign (r. 1523–60).[20]

According to historian Jerker Rosén, German criminal procedural law and the *Carolina* inspired the Swedish practices.[21] The *Carolina* regulated criminal procedure and criminal law throughout the Empire even if its preamble observed that it did not encroach on the "established, just and equitable customs" of princely territories. It set the threshold for the use of torture and regulated its use, thereby granting the accused some rights against the unlawful use of torture. Yet, while limiting the use of torture, it somewhat paradoxically also spread it. The *Carolina* was naturally very authoritative throughout the Holy Roman Empire even if it did not override local territorial norms, which by the early sixteenth-century already were influenced by the *ius commune* and Roman law to a varying decree.[22] However, the influence of the *Carolina* radiated to countries many beyond the Reich, such as Poland, Denmark, and Russia.[23] Sweden was one of them.

Previous research has already shown that the *ius commune*, filtered through the *Carolina* and German law, influenced the Swedish criminal procedural law in the sixteenth and seventeenth centuries even if the Stagnole case suggests

19 Munktell, "Tortyren", 109–110; Jerker Rosén, "Pinligt förhör i Erik XIV:s rättskipning", in Jerker Rosén, *Studier kring Erik XIV:s Höga Nämnd* (Lund: Kungl. Humanistiska Vetenskapssamfundet i Lund, 1955), 41–64, here 46–48; Inger, *Das Geständnis*, 187, 193–204; Åstrand, *Tortyr*, 113–128 and passim. See also Bengt Ankarloo, *Satans raseri: En sannfärdig berättelse om der stora häxoväsendet i Sverige och omgivande länder* (Stockholm: Ordfront, 2007), 162–163.

20 Rosén, "Pinligt förhör", 41–64.

21 Rosén, "Pinligt förhör", 41–64.

22 E.g., Gerd Kleinheyer, "Tradition und Reform in der Constitutio Criminalis Carolina", in *Strafrecht, Strafprozess und Rezeption: Grundlagen, Entwicklung und Wirkung der Constitutio Criminalis Carolina*, ed. by Peter Landau and Friedrich-Christian Schroeder (Frankfurt am Main: Vittorio Klostermann, 1984), 7–27, here esp. 8–9, 21–25; Olav Moorman van Kappen, "Die Kriminalordonnanzen Philipps II. für die Niederlande im Vergleich zur Carolina", ibid., 227–252; Maria R. Boes, *Crime and Punishment in Early Modern Germany: Courts and Adjudicatory Practices in Frankfurt am Main, 1562–1696* (Farnham: Ashgate, 2013), 35; John H. Langbein, *Prosecuting Crime in the Renaissance: England, Germany, France* (Cambridge: Harvard University Press, 1974), 165–209.

23 E.g., L. Dargun, "Die Reception der peinlichen Halsgerichtsordnung Kaiser Karls V. in Polen", *Zeitschrift der Savigny-Stiftung für Rechtsgeschichte: Germanistische Abteilung*, 10 (1889), 168–202; George G. Weickhardt, "Probable Western Origins of Muscovite Criminal Procedure", *The Russian Review*, 66:1 (2007), 55–72; Morten Kjær, *Guds og øvrigheds straf: Centralmagt og sædelighed i Danmark-Norge 1536–1648* (Copenhagen: ExTuto Publishing, 2017), esp. 97–102; Poul Johs. Jørgensen, *Dansk stafret fra Reformationen til Danske lov*, ed. by Ditlev Tamm and Helle Vogt (Copenhagen: Jurist- og Økonomforbundets Forlag, 2007), 72–76.

otherwise.[24] How did the Stockholm town court resolve hard cases of serious crime in the years surrounding the Stagnole case, then?

For example, in 1594, the Stockholm magistrates were willing to resort to torture the "loose woman" (*löß quinne*) Ursula. Her suspected infanticide had put the Stockholm judicature in a quandary. The state of the infant's corpse and its cause of death supported Ursula's tale of the baby being still-born because a man had jumped on her stomach. She had also steadfastly denied infanticide although she had long been imprisoned. Yet, Ursula had concealed her pregnancy, given birth clandestinely, and hidden the infant's corpse. Thus, the truthfulness of her statements could be doubted. The king and the Council of the Realm had the previous summer already dealt with the case with some concern. Nobody was willing to order that she be freed, but, on the other hand, no one was prepared to take upon their conscience that she be sentenced and order her execution. Therefore, the town council had asked for advice and permission from the Council of the Realm whether they could let the executioner "somewhat sharply interrogate" (*nogot skarpt förhöre*) her.[25] The Stockholm town court records do not reveal whether she was actually tortured at the end or not, nor is there a final verdict in the case.

Yet, in another prolonged criminal case from Stockholm, there was no mention of torture even if the suspected witch, Brita, Jören the Piper's wife, was imprisoned for several years and "nobody wanted to take it on their conscience that they would have sentenced her to death, but no one wanted to free her of the accusations, either". When she first appeared in court, in September 1593, she had already been long in gaol. She was sentenced to be exiled from town with the threat of decapitation on her return, but she had been ordered to be kept in prison until further notice in December 1593.[26] In September 1595, she was still in prison, and she had denied her guilt of witchcraft all that time, but admitted to have used spells and incantations. At this point, she was released from gaol, but permanently banished from the town.[27] Thus, the use of torture in Stockholm was exceptional. Lengthy imprisonment while the matter was being investigated, banishment, and compurgation were considered preferable to the use of torture even in cases of serious crime with clear suspicions.

In addition to the fact that Swedish law did not refer to torture, there was another legal authority that distrusted torture-induced confessions. "The Judge's Rules" (Sw. *Domareregler*), a *brocardica* collection of legal maxims and principles, were one of the most popular additions to the Swedish laws

24 Munktell, Tortyr, 108–110, 112–114; Inger, *Das Geständnis*.
25 10 Apr. 1594, in *Stb från 1592* 1, ed. by Almqvist, 204–205.
26 17 Sept. 1593, in *Stb från 1592* 1, ed. by Almqvist, 156–159; 27 Oct. 1593, *ibid.*, 173; 12 Dec. 1593, ibid., 185.
27 1st Sept. 1595, in *Stb från 1592* 1, ed. by Almqvist, 342.

which circulated in manuscripts only until the early seventeenth century.[28] The author of the Rules was normally not named in the manuscripts, but they are attributed to the Swedish Reformer Olavus Petri (1493/7–1555). He was a clergyman, but he had ample practical courtroom experience as he had been the town scribe of Stockholm for many years from 1524 on.[29] "The Judge's Rules" were cited in early modern legal practice and courts used them in their argumentation, which also indicates that they were read and used by court staff.[30]

The "Judge's Rules" warned against confessions obtained through torture. "Torturing and tormenting" usually lead to false confessions and therefore, one could not base convictions on them. While Olavus Petri did not absolutely reject torture in connection to the most heinous crimes (*Högmäles ärende*), he emphasized that one had to be very cautious so that one did not torture innocents. It was always better to let a guilty person walk free than to torture innocents. Moreover, he preferred torture was not used because "injustice was so often done by it".[31]

Yet, there were attempts to introduce torture formally in Swedish law in the early 1600s. King Charles IX (r. 1604–11) proposed in the incomplete draft law bearing his name that torture could in some cases be introduced. If a suspected criminal, who had not been taken in the act but had – according to the community – a bad reputation, wanted to purge himself free from the crime with the help of oath-helpers who were either unknown in the community or of bad repute, such compurgation was not to be allowed. Instead, if the case involved serious crime (*Högmåle brått*), a breach of the king's peace (*Edzöris brått*) or theft worth at least 400 marks, the King or those adjudicating in his name would be allowed to "interrogate him with the executioner" (*med Bödelen fråga*). The following sentence reveals that torture was meant as it went on to discuss the question if he did not confess when tortured (*Bekenner han i pinorne eij annars än tilföredne*).[32]

28 E.g. Jan Eric Almquist, "Inledning", in *Domareregler från den yngre landslagens tid med inledning och kommentar*, ed. by Jan Eric Almquist (Stockholm: Almqvist & Wiksell, 1951), esp. 5–12; Henrik Munktell, "Domarereglerna i praxis före 1734 års lag", *Svensk Juristtidning*, 24 (1939), 516–530.

29 On Olavus Petri, see, e.g., Gunnar T. Westin, "Olavus Petri", *Svenskt biografiskt lexikon*, 28 (1992–94), 151–166; Heikki Pihlajamäki, "Olavus Petri (1493–1552): Transplanting Foreign Law in Reformation Sweden", in *Law and the Christian Tradition in Scandinavia: The Writings of Great Nordic Jurists*, ed. by Kjell Å. Modéer, Helle Vogt (Abingdon: Routledge, 2020), 90–104.

30 Munktell, "Domarereglerna i praxis", 520–522.

31 *Domareregler från den yngre landslagens tid med inledning och kommentar*, ed. by Jan Eric Almquist (Stockholm: Almqvist & Wiksell, 1951), nrs. 31 and 38, 33, 36; Inger, *Das Geständnis*, 188–190.

32 *Lagförslag i Carl den Niondes Tid*, ed. by J. J. Nordström, Handlingar rörande Sveriges historia, 2. serien, vol. 1 (Stockholm: P. A. Norstedt & Söner, 1864), Carl den Niondes lagförslag, Tingzmåla Balker 19, 248. See also Munktell, "Tortyr", 115–117.

King Charles's proposal (1604) for an ordinance for a new royal appellate court (*Förslag till Hofrättsordning*) also included the option of torture (*med tortura och Pinebenken*) in cases "full proof and evidence" was not available. Torture would be possible only if authorized by the court. Moreover, there had to be "conjectures", circumstantial evidence or *indicia* of the suspected criminal's guilt. The torturing proceedings had to be minutely recorded and the torture could be applied three times if the hardened and obstinate criminal denied the accusations. However, after the third round of torture, the tormented person was to be freed.[33] As the proposal was vague about the torturing threshold, and as it seems to have presupposed the guilt of the suspect to be tormented, it is not surprising that the reception of the Council of the Realm was wary. The Council could not accept the proposal's unspecified authorization to torture, but suggested that, in case of treason, there had to be manifest (*vppenbara*) evidence, a person's own letters, "full proof or lawful witnesses". Moreover, nobody was to be sentenced based on the torture-induced confession, but rather by virtue of the law of Sweden, witnesses and full proof.[34]

However, this did not become law, and the monarch or the Court of Appeal using delegated power could authorize torture only in individual cases. Torture without this consent was punishable. Accordingly, the chief procurator (*advokatfiskal*) of the Svea Court of Appeal accused Peder Olofsson, bailiff of Sunnerbo in Småland, of executing Elin of Hårsnäs, a suspected witch and practitioner of magic, without authorization or lawful trial and sentence.[35] Two priests had written a letter of Elin's suspicious behaviour. Moreover, the local people wanted her to suffer the punishment she had merited.[36] Elin had long had a reputation as a witch and was suspected of causing a local woman's death by her malevolent skills. She denied this under torture, but she confessed to killing her husband with arsenic. Master Håkan, the executioner of Jönköping, had obtained special expertise and renown in several provinces in southern Sweden as a witch hunter, pricking many suspected women for the witches' mark and swimming and torturing them at least between 1594 and 1618. Elin and two other women had been swum by him as suspected witches – Elin alone survived then, but not later.[37]

33 *Lagförslag i Carl den Niondes Tid*, ed. by Nordström, Förslag till Hofrättsordning, art. 8–11, 555–556.

34 Ibid., 562–563.

35 Riksarkivet [hereafter RA, Stockholm, Sweden], Svea hovrätt [hereafter SH], Huvudarkivet [hereafter HA], A Protokoll och föredragningslistor, I Egentliga protokoll, a Protokoll i civila mål, 1 Renskrivna protokoll 1614–1950, 1 1614 19/-11/11, 8 Oct. 1614, 119r–121v; RA, SH, HA, B Registratur och koncept, I Över utgångna skrivelser, a Registratur 1614–1802, 1 1614, 12 Nov. 1614, 69v–70r.

36 RA, SH, HA, AI a1:1, 119r–121v.

37 Ankarloo, *Satans raseri*, 165–167; Bengt Ankarloo, *Trolldomsprocesserna i Sverige* (Lund: Institutet för rättshistorisk forskning, 1971), 68–70; Annika Sandén, *Bödlar: Liv, död och skam*

Heikki Pihlajamäki has interpreted the appearance of swimming suspected witches and looking for the witches' mark as signs of the reception of German criminal law in late sixteenth-century Sweden. According to him, "the influential German law may well have acted as a bridge, spreading its own medieval [ordeal] alternative to other European regions in which that alternative [...] had never existed" – like in Sweden.[38] In the wider context of the reception of German criminal and procedural law in early modern Sweden that has been presented so far, his tentative results can be confirmed.

Returning to the torture of Elin, Jöns Jöransson Lilliesparre (d. 1623/24), one of the judges of the Court of Appeal ("*een af Konungz Nämpd*") testified that he himself had been presiding over the local district court when Elin had been accused of witchcraft. Lillieparre observed that nobody had been able to prove Elin guilty of the crimes and that she had consequently been able to free herself through the required number of oath-helpers. Thus, the investigation was unlawful. Elin had been induced to confess through unlawful torture, and she had been executed based on this confession.[39]

As torture was not mentioned in the law of proof, it was unclear who had the power to authorize it and how it was to be administered. However, the Court of Appeal was adamant that the local bailiff Peder Olofsson had no such authority. Olof Hård, whom Peder claimed had ordered, authorized, and incited the proceedings, had even less such authority as he was neither the governor nor royal deputy (*Landzherre eller Ståtthollere*) of Småland, but only led a group of foot soldiers. Consequently, both Peder Olofsson and Olof Hård were cited at the following court session for unlawful torture and execution.[40]

The reception of the *ius commune* criminal procedure was well on its way in sixteenth-century Sweden even if torture did not become a standard part of the Swedish variant of the inquisitorial procedure. As Heikki Pihlajamäki has argued, referring to John Langbein's research, the stance of Swedish law towards torture resembled that of England: judicial torture was not authorized by law in either country. Yet, in both it was occasionally administered in political trials or for serious crime until the practice disappeared during the seventeenth century.[41] Yet, as has been discussed above, the increasing use of the inquisitorial procedure and torture in Sweden in the course of the sixteenth

i svenskt 1600-tal (Stockholm: Atlantis, 2016), 182–185.

38 Heikki Pihlajamäki, "'Swimming the Witch, Pricking for the Devil's Mark': Ordeals in the Early Modern Witchcraft Trials", *Journal of Legal History*, 21:2 (2000), 35–58, here 46–47.

39 RA, SH, HA, AI a1:1, 119r–121v.

40 RA, SH, HA, AI a1:1, 119r–121v.

41 John H. Langbein, *Torture and the Law of Proof: Europe and England in the Ancien Régime* (Chicago: University of Chicago Press, 1977), esp. 129–139; Langbein, *Prosecuting Crime*; Heikki Pihlajamäki, "The Painful Question: The Fate of Judicial Torture in Early Modern Sweden", *Law and History Review*, 25:3 (2007), 557–592.

century can certainly be perceived as a result of the reception of German law and the *Carolina* more specifically.

The Language and Influence of German Police Norms in Sweden

Swedish secular criminal law – like other fields of law – had been codified in the mid-fourteenth century in King Magnus Eriksson's laws. The Town Law remained unaltered until 1736, but the law observed in the countryside was updated in 1442 by the Union King Christopher of Bavaria.

While some aspects of criminal law had been updated through statutes in the Later Middle Ages, the Swedish kings Gustav Vasa and Erik XIV quickly adopted the terminology of the German police legislation (*Policey*) in the sixteenth century and police legislation as a means to govern.[42]

King Gustav Vasa's Ordinance of 1540 appears to have been the first time the term was used, and it used the word repeatedly. In the preamble, the King lamented that there was a great lack of "peace, law, justice and good governance or police" weakening the crown daily.[43] Slightly later the King referred to the need to improve the situation that could take place only "through a good Christian, highly respected governance, peace, justice, good ordinances and policies". He added that "all secular authorities, the Empire (*keyseredöme*) and kingdoms" were built on such a fundament.[44] At the end, the ordinance again explained that the ordinance had been issued "to praise and honour God Almighty, to ensure the prosperous well-being, peace and calm of the Realm as well as for the formation and improvement of good order and police so that the common good can thereby be furthered".[45]

The reference to the (Holy) Empire is telling. Another feature adopted from Germany is the expression "*ordinantia* and *policia*" (or the same in the plural form) as, for example, the preamble of Emperor Charles V in the Imperial Police Ordinance of 1530 uses twice the expression "*ordnung vnd*

42 Gabriela Bjarne Larsson, *Stadgelagstiftning i senmedeltidens Sverige* (Lund: Institutet för rättshistorisk forskning, 1994), esp. 23–38, 41–44, 79–82, 108–129; Toomas Kotkas, *Royal Police Ordinances in Early Modern Sweden: The Emergence of Voluntaristic Understanding* of *Law* (Leiden: Brill, 2013), esp. 35–93.

43 Ordinantia eller landsordning, Lödöse, 9 Apr. 1540, in *Svenska riksdagsakter jämte andra handlingar som höra till statsförfattningens historia, series 1, Under tidehvarfvet 1521–1718, dept. 1, vol. 1:1*, ed. by Emil Hildebrand and Oscar Alin (Stockholm: P. A. Norstedt & Söner, 1879), nr. 138, 261–289, here 261: "*uti vort rige befunnit ett dråpeligt stort mangel och fell uppå frid, lag, rett och en godh ordinantia eller policia*".

44 Ibid., 262: "*alenest egenom et got christeligit och höglöfligit regimente, frid, retvise, gode ordinantier och policier*". See also ibid., 265: "*en god policia*", 275: "*en god ordinantia eller policia*"; 287: "*gode policier*".

45 Ibid., 288: "*alzmectig Gud til lof och äre, vort rige til licksalig välfgardt, frid och roligher och til en godh ordninanties och policies formering och forbättring, upå thet att thet menige beste*".

pollicey".[46] We can see the influence of the knowledge brought by King Gustav Vasa's German chief administrator, Royal Chancellor Conrad von Pyhy (ca. 1500–53) in recent Imperial norms behind this terminology. Pyhy (bef. 1536: Conrad Peutinger) was doctor of both laws (*Doctor der Rechte*) and had apparently served as councilor to Emperor Charles V before he entered Swedish service and became King Gustav's chancellor in 1538.[47] When King Gustav addressed the Swedish Estates in a very long speech at the Diet of Västerås in 1544, he referred several times to God-fearing "good governance and laudable ordinances and policies" and "good ordinances and policies".[48]

King Gustav Vasa's son and successor King Erik XIV's so-called Patent on Heinous Crime ("*Patent om Högmåhl Saker*") is a statute, given by the king and dated 1 May 1563 in Stockholm. The statute's arenga states the king's constant willingness to further the best interests and welfare of the inhabitants of Sweden. The king wanted – with the help of the Almighty – to maintain a "good *Politie* and skillful governance" (*god* Politie *och skickeligit Regimente*) – especially for the welfare and good of the common man. Then, King Eric observed that evil and wickedness increased in the world. Consequently, there were many evil and misbehaving people who neither cared for "God or His Holy Word and Commandment" let alone any other "good and Christian law or statute" that the King's late and illustrious forefathers (meaning Eric's predecessor and father Gustav Vasa) had given for the common good.[49]

The first article insisted that the King wished that all heinous crimes (*Högmåls Saker*) were to be punished with their "right punishments" instead of being atoned with money and silver. Therefore, the King insisted that all princes, noblemen, royal bailiffs, and others were not to accept fines for blasphemy, treason, murder, notorious adultery, incest, rape, bestiality, and similar crimes. These had always to be investigated by a court, adjudicated and the verdict executed in accordance with the sentence as God Almighty himself had order in his law. As people were often plagued for the sake of these sins with pestilence, hunger, bad harvests, and other scourges (*wedermöde*), and whole kingdoms were often punished by a single person's crimes. Therefore, to avoid God's wrath, it was necessary that notorious malefactors were not to be spared for money. Otherwise, wickedness and evil would grow and the

46 *ROmischer Keyserlicher Maiestat Ordnung vnd Reformation guter Pollicei im Heyligen Römischen Reich Anno M. D. XXX. zu Augspurg vffgericht* (Mainz: Johannes Schlöffer, 1531), 2.

47 Sven Lundkvist, "Conrad Pyhy, von", *Svenskt biografiskt lexikon*, 29 (Stockholm: Norstedts Tryckeri, 1995–1997), 533–537, esp. 533.

48 "King Gustav Vasa's speech to the Estates", in *Svenska riksdagsakter*, 1:1, ed. by Hildebrand and Alin, nr. 162, 339–378, here 339: "*gott regemente, loflige ordninger och politier*"; see also 340, 371, 373–374.

49 "Patent om Högmåhl Saker, 1st May 1563", in *Kongl. Stadgar, Förordningar, Bref och Resolutioner, Ifrån Åhr 1528 in til 1701: Angående Justitiæ och Executions-Ährender*, ed. by Johan Schmedeman, Stockholm, Tryckt med egen bekostnad af Johann Heinrich Werner, Kongl. May:tz så ock Upsala Acad. Boktryckiare Åhr 1706, 47–50, here 47–48.

criminals would be encouraged in their sin to offend God even more often with the same or other sins, which is why it would please God more that they would suffer the punishment they had deserved.[50]

While blasphemy was not a crime mentioned in the Swedish medieval laws, it received increased impetus in Europe in the later Middle Ages first through heresy processes and, later, by the reception of Roman law. The Bible had considered blasphemy against the Holy Spirit as the only unpardonable sin. In Roman law, Emperor Justinian's Novel 77 not only mentioned crimes against nature, incited by the devil, that caused God in his just wrath to destroy cities with their whole population. It also insisted on the death penalty for blasphemy for the same reason. However, Justinian's *Novellae* had not received as much scholarly attention by medieval jurists as the other books of the *Corpus Iuris Civilis*, and it circulated in manuscripts mostly as the *Epitome Juliani* and the *Authenticum*. With Humanism, the Novels were first printed in 1476 which helped spread its influence.[51] Several kingdoms (Sicily, Castile, France) had penalized blasphemy since the thirteenth century, and, for example, in late medieval France or the southern German lands, it was no "paper tiger", forming 1–5 per cent of criminal cases in some southern German towns, as Gerd Schwerhoff has observed. Yet, generally blasphemy has been perceived as a crime "overshadowed by heresy" (Nash). In Germany, especially the statutes of the Diet of Worms (*Reichsabschied*, 1495) and a royal mandate from 1497 threatened blasphemers with punishments.[52]

In learned jurisprudential classifications – like in that of the influential *Praxis rerum criminalium* by the Flemish jurist Joost de Damhouder (Jodocus Damhouderius, 1507–81) – blasphemy was listed among the offences of divine lese-majesty (*Crimen læsæ Maiestatis diuinæ*). Referring to Roman law, Damhouder observed that it was punishable with death. He also listed a range of different penalties for blasphemy in various secular jurisdictions – including the punishments enacted in the legislation of Emperor Charles V.[53] Blasphemy and its sanctions were some of the topics in several police ordinances (1530, 1548, 1577) of the Holy Roman Empire (*Reichspolizeiordnung*), and the *Carolina* also mentioned it, referring to the 1530 police ordinance. The punishments ranged from the death penalty to mutilation, imprisonment,

50 "Patent om Högmåhl Saker", in *Kongl. Stadgar*, ed. by Schmedeman, 48.

51 Novel 77, *Corpus iuris civilis, 3: Novellae*, ed. by Rudolfus Schoell and Guilelmus Kroll (Berolini: Apud Weidmannos, 1877). On the use of spreading of the Novels, see the useful overview of Timothy G. Kearley, "The Creation and Transmission of Justinian's Novels", *Law Library Journal*, 102:3 (2010), 377–397.

52 E.g., Gerd Schwerhoff, *Verfluchte Götter: Die Geschichte der Blasphemie* (Frankfurt am Main: S. Fischer, 2021), esp. 127–140, 199–250, quotation 133; David S. Nash, *Blasphemy in the Christian World: A History* (Oxford: Oxford University Press, 2007), quotation 42.

53 Jodocus Damhouderius, *Praxis rervm criminalivm, elegantissimis iconibvs ad materiam accommodis illustrata* (Antwerpen: Ioannes Latius, 1561), 180–181. Damhouder's *Praxis* also influenced Polish law and practice, see Dargun, "Die Reception", 198, 200–202.

fines, and penalties depending on the circumstances of the crime (*ad penam arbitrariam*).[54]

In sixteenth-century Sweden, some authors had frowned on the practice of people to swear "big and coarse" oaths on the body of God, on his torments, on his precious blood, and so on.[55] However, as blasphemy was not mentioned in Swedish medieval laws or practice, it is likely that the Reformation and the influence of the German imperial statutes combined influenced Swedish concerns. After the Reformation, the new influx of German influence, expressed also in the Imperial police ordinances that discussed thoroughly blasphemy and swearing, gave impetus to the mention of blasphemy in King Erik XIV's Patent.

The Swedish Reformer Olavus Petri (1493/7–1552) had published a sermon against cursing and oaths already in 1539. It dwelt upon human sin and God's punishment because of it. It also observed that Emperor Justinian, i.e., Roman law, punished blasphemers by death as did a statute issued by King Philip of France.[56] The Ordinance of Västerås of 1544 banned both swearing and intoxication possibly inspired by Olavus Petri's sermon and the 1530 Imperial Police Ordinance that not only targeted blasphemy, but also drunkenness.[57] Malefactors were threatened with royal punishment.[58] Like his brother, Archbishop Laurentius Petri (archep. 1531–73) considered unnecessary oaths in God's name "a wicked and frivolous custom". Oath-breaking, perjury and saying God's name in vain were reprehensible deeds for which God punished the whole country.[59] Archbishop Laurentius also translated a German treatise against drunkenness into Swedish.[60] Thus, several of the topical moral issues in the German lands became the subject of norms there. Blasphemy, swearing, and drunkenness found their way also to Swedish sermons and norms. This suggests German moral concerns and ensuing norms both ecclesiastical and

54 E.g., *Römischer Keyserlicher Maiestat Ordnung vnd Reformation guter Pollicei im Heyligen Römischen Reich Anno M. D. XXX. zu Augspurg vffgericht*, Gedruckt zuo Mentz durch Johannem Schöffer im jar 1531, 3–8; *Constitutio Criminalis Carolina*, art. 106, xxiii.

55 E. Linderholm, "Om norrländska kyrkostadgar från 1500- och 1600-talen", *Kyrkohistorisk Årsskrift*, 12 (1911), 1–51, here 37–38.

56 O[lavus] P[etri], *Een predican emoot the gruffueliga eedher och gudz försmädilse, som nw almenneliga brukas*, Stockholm, O.P., 1539, esp. Cii^{v}.

57 *Römischer Keyserlicher Maiestat Ordnung vnd Reformation guter Pollicei* (1530), 10–11.

58 Ordinance of Västerås, *Svenska riksdagsakter 1:1*, ed. by Hildebrand and Alin, nr. 164, 390–391, here art. 22, 391; Linderholm, "Om norrländska kyrkostadgar", 37.

59 Circular to the diocese of Uppsala 20 Oct. 1566, in *Skrifter Och Handlingar, Til Uplysning i Swenska Kyrko och Reformations Historien 5*, ed. by Uno Von Troil, Upsala, tryckt hos direct. Johan Edman, 202–230, here 213–215.

60 L[aurentius] Up[salensis], Emoot Dryckenskap: Några wigtiga orsaker, hwarföre alla menniskior sigh wachta skola för dryckenskap. [...] Aff Tydzkon uthsatt på Swensko. in *Skrifter Och Handlingar, Til Uplysning i Swenska Kyrko och Reformations Historien 5*, ed. by Uno Von Troil Upsala, tryckt hos direct. Johan Edman, 27–81.

secular authorities, their teachings, and occasionally even legal practice – as will be discussed next.

Swedish Criminal Practice and the Influence of the *Carolina*: "Nipping", Crushing, and Necessity

Even if legal cases demonstrating clear influences of German criminal doctrine and the *Carolina* are not plentiful, their existence is evidence of their influence in Sweden. An indication that the *Carolina* was known and occasionally influenced legal practice even in Sweden are the few references to tearing the condemned criminal's body with red-hot pliers. The *Carolina* mentioned it as an additional punishment before execution and instructed how the additional sanction was to be written in the verdict. This "nipping" was also applied in legal practice in various parts of the Reich, e.g., Münster, Frankfurt am Main, and Nuremberg, in the sixteenth century. In France, one of the penalties of the regicide François Ravaillac (1578–1610) in 1610 was also "plucking" with red-hot pincer.[61] However, it may have spread to Germany from Italian cities. For example, the punishment of tearing the flesh off with pincers before burning was meted out on a female slave who had poisoned her master in Bologna in 1379. A Bolognese street robber, who had robbed three German merchants, also had his flesh torn with pincers before hanging.[62]

The first reference I have discovered comes from 1541. This unusual case involved drunkenness on Easter during divine service, and the discussions of the suitable punishment can probably be explained through the German influence in the panel of judges. Royal Chancellor Conrad von Pyhy (ca. 1500–53) and superintendent Georg Norman (d. 1552~53), both learned Germans in the king's service, sat on the panel. When von Pyhy fell from power in 1543, Norman became the main royal advisor, but the "German period" of Swedish administration came to end.[63]

61 *Constitutio Criminalis Carolina*, art. 194, xlii^{v}: "*Von reissen mit glüenden zangen*". It was, e.g., used on January 22, 1536, as one of the punishments in the execution of the three Anabaptist leaders of the Münster Rebellion, Ralf Klötzer, "The Melchoirites and Münster", *A Companion to Anabaptism and Spiritualism*, ed. by John D. Roth, James M. Stayer (Leiden: Brill, 2007), 217–256, here 250; Sigrun Haude, *In the Shadow of "Savage Wolves": Anabaptist Münster and the German Reformation during the 1530s* (Boston: Humanities Press, 2000), 16; Joel F. Harrington, *The Faithful Executioner: Life and Death in the Sixteenth Century* (London: Vintage Books, 2014), passim; Boes, *Crime and Punishment*, 139; S.H. Cuttler, *The Law of Treason and Treason Trials in Later Medieval France* (Cambridge: Cambridge University Press, 1982), 116.

62 Dean, *Crime in Medieval Europe*, 128; Dean, *Crime and Justice*, 60.

63 Sven Lundkvist, "Conrad Pyhy, von", *Svenskt biografiskt lexikon*, 29 (Stockholm: Norstedts Tryckeri, 1995–1997), 533–537, esp. 533; Ivan Svalenius, "Georg Norman", *Svenskt biografiskt lexikon*, 27 (Stockholm: Norstedts Tryckeri, 1995–1997), 577–580, esp. 577–579. See also Ivan Svalenius, *Georg Norman: En biografisk studie* (Lund: Gleerupska univ.-bokhandeln, 1937).

The young male accused in the case, Matts Larsson, had appeared visibly intoxicated in church on Easter so that he had been exhorted not to make a spectacle of himself and take communion. Disregarding this, he had received the Lord's Supper. Later, he vomited in into a mitten, after which he had started to drink again. After he was imprisoned, he had uttered improper expressions that he belonged to the devil and was bound for hell. This was perceived as an indication of his unrepentance. The panel of judges, including von Pyhy, Norman, Archbishop Laurentius Petri, and Olavus Petri, adjudicating in the king's name, observed that Matts Larsson had "shamefully and in an unchristian way offended both God and the secular authorities through his misdeed". The sentence was harsh: the judges thought Matts Larsson ought rightly to be condemned to death through tearing with red-hot pliers until he died as a warning to others. Yet, now he was only hanged.[64]

The *Carolina* did not state explicitly that blasphemy or related crimes were to be punished by "nipping"; rather, it stated that judges could consider the circumstances of the crime, the blasphemy, and the person when punishing the blasphemous person to life or limb.[65] Even if Matts Larsson was not torn with red-hot irons in the end, the fact that it was discussed indicates the influence of the *Carolina* through King Gustav Vasa's German chief administrators, who were knowledgeable in recent Imperial criminal law.

Neither medieval Swedish law nor sixteenth-century statutes mentioned such a crime or the punishment of tearing the culprit with red-hot pincers. Yet, we find it being discussed and even used in a gruesome murder case from 1595. Bernt the Barrelmaker's wife Moicken and her lover, her late husband's master apprentice (*mester swen*) Hans Ladehoff, were convicted for the dastardly murder of Bernt. As the adulterous lovers wanted to get married, they had concocted a murderous plan. They had three times attempted to poison Bernt with arsenic and another strong purgative (*schafförnie*), but this had not succeeded because of his heavy vomiting. When even the third attempt proved a failure, Moicken summoned Hans, who had struck Bernt on the hands and head with an axe (*texle*), while Moicken had knifed her husband in the chest.[66]

The town court of Stockholm sentenced both for murder: Moicken to be burned at the stake and Hans to be decapitated and the body parts displayed in a wheel (*till stegl*; *stägledes*). As regent in the absence of his nephew, King Sigismund, Duke Karl of Södermanland (future King Charles IX) confirmed

64 *Uppländska konungsdomar från Vasatiden intill Svea hovrätts inrättande*, ed. by Nils Edling (Uppsala: Kungl. Humanistiska Vetenskapssamfundet i Uppsala, 1933), 4 May 1541, 116–117: "*medh glödende tenger leffuende sönderslites*".

65 *Constitutio Criminalis Carolina*, cvj: "*darumb an leib, leben oder glidern, nach gelegenheyt vnd gestalt der person vnd lesterung gestrafft werden*". On blasphemy in the Middle Ages and the Early Modern period, see e.g., Schwerhoff, *Verfluchte Götter*. 113–250; Leonard W. Levy, *Treason against God: A History of the Offense of Blasphemy* (New York: Schocken Books, 1981), 103–330; Nash, *Blasphemy*, esp. 42–71.

66 6 Dec. 1595, in *Stb från 1592* 1, ed. by Almqvist, 346–347.

the verdict. Nevertheless, using his ***arbitrium***, he added that the punishment was to be exacerbated "because of the heinousness of the crime", both were to be torn with red-hot pliers en route to the place of execution and prior to the execution, their right hands – with which they had committed their wicked crime – had to be amputated.[67]

This additional punishment was obviously influenced by the *Carolina*, and Duke Karl was interested in developments in Germany. He had been called the "entrepreneurial prince" who was busy developing the industries of his duchy, trade and the iron industry in modern research. He had married twice into German princely families, and he had travelled ten months in Germany in 1577–78 and returned later for shorter visits in 1579 and 1583.[68] The so-called Rosengren's Commission, drafting a new law in the early 1600s, would have introduced the tearing of the criminal with red-hot pincers (*medh heeta tänger tagen*) as an additional punishment to wheeling (*stegla*) for adult children for matricide or patricide (murdering or slaying in anger).[69]

Another sign of the influence of German criminal law was the appearance of breaking on the wheel in Sweden in the form of crushing the executed criminal with a wheel. The medieval Swedish laws knew the breaking on the wheel, in Old Swedish *stäghla* (Sw: *stegla*) for male criminals for severe crimes. For example, the Town Law prescribed explicitly breaking on the wheel as punishment for male murderers and witches.[70] However, breaking on the wheel has two meanings: one post-execution and another pre-execution. The former, which is believed to have been used in Sweden, meant that the body of the decapitated criminal was quartered and exhibited on wheels. However, the other was known from the early modern period as *rådbråkning*. The origins of wheeling and whether only post-execution but also pre-execution wheeling was practiced in earlier medieval Sweden or not are disputed.[71]

But when we start having cleared descriptions of executions, it is easy to perceive that wheeling in its crushing variant formed a new case of reception

67 6 Dec. 1595, in *Stb från 1592* 1, ed. by Almqvist, 346–347.

68 E.g., Herder Block, *Karl IX som teolog och religiös personlighet: Studier öfver utvecklingen af hans åskådning* (Gothenburg: Elanders Boktryckeri Aktiebolag, 1918), esp. 70–175; Lennart Hedberg, *Karl IX: Företagarfursten & enväldshärskaren* (Stockholm: Prisma 2009), esp. 58–71, 206.

69 *Lagförslag i Carl den Niondes Tid*, ed. by Nordström, Det Rosengrenska lagförslaget, Högmåla Balken 2, 475.

70 "King Magnus Eriksson's Town Law", in *CISCA 11*, ed. by Schlyter, Chapter on Heinous Crime [*Höghmæles balker*], art. 1–2, 4, 8, 320–324, 326.

71 E.g., K.F. Söderwall, *Ordbok öfver svenska medeltids-språket*, 2:1 (Lund: Berlingska Boktryckeri- och stilgjuteri-aktiebolaget, 1891–1900), 538. Cf. Poul Meyer, "Dødsstraf", in *Kulturhistoriskt lexikon för nordisk medeltid från vikingatid till reformationstid*, 3 (Helsingfors: A. B. Örnförlaget, 1958), cols. 455–459, referring to Folke Ström, supposes that crushing was practiced all through the Middle Ages in Sweden in addition to the quartering of the body and placing the body parts on display on the wheel, esp. 457–458. See also Ankarloo, *Satans raseri*, 153.

as also the new terminology indicates. Crushing, breaking the criminal's bones by a wheel or another heavy item such as a mallet or cudgeon, was a severe penalty, known in Germany as *radebrechen*, was mentioned as a punishment for example for arsons, traitors, and church robbers in the thirteenth-century *Sachsenspiegel*. It was occasionally used for severe crimes especially in Switzerland and southern Germany in the late Middle Ages and early modern period.[72]

Possibly the first case in which the punishment was used in Stockholm was in 1586. Anders Bengtsson had publicly beaten to a pulp one of his two young sons who had been making much noise on the roof of the house in the evening. Many persons had intervened by repeatedly shouting Anders to stop, but Anders had not done so but continued his senseless violence. Nothing could be done to save the life of the child. Anders had a history of violent behaviour, which had recently peaked as he had committed two homicides: a man had died of his injuries after Anders's assault and he had also killed his own apprentice. Neither of the two manslaughters had yet been in court. The Stockholm town scribe had recorded the horror felt by the court and townspeople for the unchristian, tyrannical and inhuman torture meted upon the child. The town court sentenced Anders Bengtsson to the wheel (*till hjul och stegel*) for the brutal killing of his own child, the two other unatoned homicides, and his other acts of violence. However, King John III specified – apparently exacerbating the usual mode of execution – that Anders's hand was first to be cut off, then both his legs were to be broken by hitting with an iron rod, then the thigh and knees, before moving on to crushing his back and ribcage. Only after this was he to be decapitated, his body placed on the wheel, and his head on a pole over the amputated hand.[73]

The crushing of Anders Bengtsson was perhaps intended to mirror the crime he had himself committed. The term *rådbråkning* was not used, but obviously the punishment differed from the normal death penalty through the wheel. In fact, the wheel did not play any part in the execution in itself and featured only as a display platform for the body. This also supports the notion that the two punishments were perceived to be different. An analysis of the draft of the so-called Rosengren's Commission, drafting a new law in the early 1600s, gives the same result. The proposal mentioned wheeling (*råbråkar*) as a possible punishment for the most severe crimes without specifying these offences. As it also talked about sentencing men to "the wheel" (*till stegel och hiul*), it must be referring to two different things.[74] Crushing is known to have

72 *Sachsenspiegel nach der ältesten Leipziger Handschrift*, ed. by Julius Weiske (Leipzig: Johann Friedrich Hartknoch, 1863), 2. book, art. 13:4, 47: "*Alle mordère un die den phlùg berouben oder mulen oder kirchen und kirchof, und verrètère und mortburnère, oder die ire botschaft werben […] die sal man alle radebrechen*".

73 Sandén, *Bödlar*, 134–138.

74 *Lagförslag i Carl den Niondes Tid*, ed. by Nordström, Det Rosengrenska lagförslaget, Högmåla Balken, cap. 17, 488, cf. ibid., cap. 10, 481–482.

been used on a few occasions in the seventeenth and early eighteenth centuries for treason or heinous murders. However, it was an extraordinary punishment and, as such, exceptional. In the second part of the seventeenth century and in the early eighteenth century, murderer and traitors were occasionally sentenced to be crushed (*rådbråkning*) for particularly heinous crimes.[75]

The influence of the *Carolina* probably also explains why the principle of extreme necessity found its way to the Swedish law proposal of the early 1600s. The rule that life-threatening hunger excused stealing a moderate amount of food if the circumstances were deemed to be of extreme necessity had been discussed widely in later medieval legal scholarship, especially canon law. While the Norwegian Code of the Realm of 1274 by King Magnus VI Lawmender (r. 1263–80) had accepted that starving deserving paupers who stole food to preserve their lives were not to be punished for larceny, this principle was accepted only in one of the Swedish provincial laws. When Swedish King Magnus Eriksson (r. in Sweden 1319–64, r. in Norway 1319–55) issued the first law for the whole of Sweden drafted after the Norwegian example, the exception of the starving thief of victuals was not included.[76] Thus, Swedish law apparently consciously rejected the equitable natural law right of self-preservation as an exception in larceny crimes.

However, German criminal law accepted the principle. It had been included in one of the most influential predecessors of the *Carolina*, the *Bambergische Halsgerichtsordnung*, and it came to be included in the *Carolina* as well. Both these works accepted that stealing food in a situation of real starvation for oneself, one's wife, or one's children was excusable, provided the stolen food was not worth very much or the theft was particularly harmful. It was stressed that the injured party was not to be penalized for the accusation even if the

75 Birger Wedberg, *Karl XII på justitietronen: Rättshistorisk-biografisk studie* (Stockholm: P.A. Norstedt & Söner, 1944), 83–84; J.E. Almquist, "Drottning Kristina, den första kvinnliga domaren i Sverige", *Svensk Juristtidning*, 26 (1941), 818–826, here 826; Rudolf Thunander, *Hovrätt i funktion: Göta Hovrätt och brottmålen 1635–1699* (Lund: Institutet för rättshistorisk forskning, 1993), 75; Sandén, *Bödlar*, 174–175; Mia Korpiola and Heikki Pihlajamäki: "Henrik Florinuksen rikos ja rangaistus: Näyttökysymykset hovioikeudessa 1700-luvun alussa", in *Turun hovioikeus 1623–1900 – ihmisiä, verkostoja ja oikeuskäytäntöä modernin kynnyksellä*, ed. by Mia Korpiola (Turku: Turun Historiallinen Yhdistys, 2023), 227–275, here 235–237.

76 See discussions and examples in Mia Korpiola and Jørn Øyrehagen Sunde: "The Influence of the Principle 'Necessitas non habet legem' on Nordic Medieval Laws on Theft", *Journal of the History of Ideas*, 85:4 (Oct. 2024), 681–711; *CISGA 1: Codex Iuris vestrogotici*, ed. by H.S. Collin and C.J. Schlyter (Stockholm, Z. Haeggström, 1827), Juris Vestrogotici codex recentior, 14, Þiufua bolker [Chapter on Theft], 164–165.

thief was left unpunished.[77] Moreover, learned jurists, such as Damhouder, accepted the principle in their widely read works.[78]

In the proposal of the Rosengren's Commission, the exception of the starving theft was introduced in a way that both suggests influences of the *Carolina*, but with important and very Swedish modifications. The proposition took from the *Carolina* the definition of "necessity of real starvation" (*rätt hungers nödh*) as well as the circle of starving family members: the thief, his wife, or children. Then, drawing from the Swedish threshold of pilfering certain agricultural produce, it limited the amount of the foodstuffs stolen to a load (*bördha*) that the thief alone could carry away. This property the thief was to repay or compensate – thus, this was no case of charity. If he was unable to do so, he had to work for the owner to pay for the stolen property as was the normal case if the criminal was unable to pay the fine. However, the proposal imposes on the owner of the property the duty to feed the working thief for the duration of the forced labour.[79]

Conclusion

This chapter has investigated the reception of *ius commune* doctrines of criminal law and torture in Sweden through Germany. Even if Swedish law did not know torture, the number of cases in which torture was used in practice increased in the second half of the sixteenth century. There were also failed attempts to institutionalize the practice and have it included in new legislation. The risk of torturing and condemning innocents was also expressed but yet, the practice continued. However, the authorization had to come from the monarch or his appellate court, and, in many difficult cases, no attempt to torture was made.

The terminology of Swedish police regulation was borrowed from imperial police ordinances. The concerns for blasphemy, swearing, cursing, and

77 *Bambergische halsgerichts ordenung* (Bamberg: Hans Pfeil, 1507), art. 192, lv[v]: "*Stelen in rechter hungers not. Jtem So yemant durch rechte hungers note, die er, sein weyb, oder kinder erlidten, etwas von essenden dingen zu stelen geursacht wurde, vnd doch derselbig diebstal nicht sunderlich groß geuerdlich oder schedlich were, Söllen abermals Richter vnd Urteyler (als ob stet) Rats pflegen, Ob aber derselben dieb einer vnstreflich gelassen wurde, So sol jne doch der cleger vmb die clage deßhalb gethan, nichts schuldig sein*"; *Constitutio Criminalis Carolina*, art. 166, xxxvii[r-v]. The text of the *Carolina* has more or less the same contents as the *Bambergensis*.

78 Jodocus Damhouderius, *Praxis rervm criminalivm*, cap. cx [*De furto*]:36–37, 412: "*Hoc tamen notandum est, Iudices non parvam debere observationem adhibere circa furum necessitate & inopiam an ex necessitate famis, non vero animo fraudulenter luctandi, furtum factum sit, excusari certe potest, c. Si quis, & ibis crib. ext. de furt. si non sit insigne & magnum, iuxta l.1.ff. de furt. Non enim factum quaeritur, sed caussa faciendi, l. Verum est, ff. eod. Et necessitas sane non habet legem; quum etiam ob extremam necessitatem aut alimentorum gratiam, filios suos vendiderint parentes, authore Paulo lib. 5. Sentent*".

79 *Lagförslag i Carl den Niondes Tid*, ed. by Nordström, Det Rosengrenska lagförslaget, Tjufva Balken, cap. 7, 533–534.

drinking that can be found in Swedish ecclesiastical texts and secular norms probably had the same German origin. We find mentions of severe new punishments, such as tearing with red-hot pincers ("nipping") and crushing/wheeling, in Stockholm in the 1580s and 1590s. We also find attempts to include them in new legislation together with references to the doctrine of necessity in case of stealing food. Especially the *Constitutio Criminalis Carolina* of 1532 but imperial police ordinances also influenced Swedish norms, legal terminology, and practice.

For example, it is known that King Erik XIV owned some law books dealing with Germany or the Holy Roman Empire.[80] The *Polithiæ Cesaris Caroli 5:tj* can with all likelihood be identified as Justin Göbler's (1504–67) *Diui Caroli Quinti politiae ac reipublicae imperialis constitutio.*[81] While it is possible that the "*Keiserlige Malefitz rætt*" referred to the Tirolean "*Malefizordnung*" of 1499, it is likelier that it is the *Constitutio Criminalis Carolina*. That such works spread even wider is likely as more and more Swedes studied in the continental universities. Later, ca. 1619, even the Cathedral Chapter (*domkapitel*) of Uppsala referred to a collection of imperial law (*Constitutiones Imperatorum et Principum*) containing the *Carolina*.[82] Thus, German and imperial law were some of the main channels of influence from which the Swedish kings, their lawyers, and their judges found inspiration, which they picked and chose from. The *ius commune* provided useful tools, but these had to be applied selectively and in moderation.

80 "Concept till Inventarium öfver Konung Erik XIV:s Böcker; upprättadt den 27 September 1568", ed. by L. O. Fägersten, in *Handlingar rörande Skandinaviens historia*, 27 (Stockholm, Kungliga Samfundet för utgivande av handskrifter rörande Skandinaviens historia: 1845), 380–390.

81 Justin Göbler, *Divi Caroli Qvinti Politiae Ac Reipvblicae Imperialis Constitvtio, in Clarissima Civitate Avgvsta Vindelicorvm, Anno Domini 1548: Germaniae publicata: nunc uero per Doctorem Iustinum Goblerum etc. Latine interpretata, & explicate*, Francoforti, apvd Haeredes Christiani Egenolphi, 1566.

82 Ankarloo, *Trolldomsprocesserna*, 91–92. Ankarloo observed that research has shown this to be Melchior Goldast's collection *Statuta Imperatorum, Caesarum Augustorum, Regum et Principum Electorum a Carllo Magno usque ad Carolum V*, impensis Ioannis Iacobi Porsii & Ioan. Theobaldi Schönvetteri, civium Francofurd., apud Iohannem Spiessium, 1617. However, the only norm in the collection that dealt with witchcraft that the Uppsala Chapter was writing about was the *Carolina*.

Epilogue

15 Re-reading Arthur Duck

Ius Commune and Insular Exceptionalism

Mario Piccinini and Chiara Maria Valsecchi

Our contribution to this volume focuses on Arthur Duck's work, *De Usu et Authoritate Juris Civilis Romanorum in Dominiis Principum Christianorum*[1], published posthumously in 1653.[2] We consider it to be particularly useful for three reasons: first, Duck's noteworthy position as an English civilian writing at a significant moment in the political and legal history of his country; second, the global reach of his investigation; and third, the opportunity it offers for a reflection on the borders of *ius commune*, not only the external borders that mark its geographical confines, but also those internal borders that lay out its limits in places where it is at the margins of the legal regime. Our analysis will also allow us to reflect on the nature of *ius commune* in a historical period in which its traditional role was fading. We will explore Duck's work through a close reading of a number of passages, paying particular attention to the textual references, which we believe are fundamental to a full understanding of Duck's point of view.

Roman Law in England: The View of a Civilian

There is a particular group of terms that recurs repeatedly throughout Arthur Duck's work, from his dedication to Harry Pierrepont, 1st Marquess of Dorchester, to his *Conclusio operis ad lectorem*: terms such as *nostratis* and *noster*. These words, which indicate belonging, sometimes refer to his own country, pointing to the specificity of English history (*reges nostri*) and particularly to that of the English jurists who studied and, above all, practiced *ius civile Romanorum*. However, precisely because of the marginal position of these jurists, Duck continuously reminds us that they not only operate within this history but also fully participate in a wider dimension, which he sets out

1 This text was jointly conceived by the two authors. The authors drafted the first part together (pp. 239–245), with Mario Piccinini writing the second part (pp. 245–282) and Chiara Valsecchi writing the third (pp. 282–298). The authors would like to thank Dr Luca Crisma and Dr Mattia Ruzzarin for their help.

2 Londini, apud Richardi Hodinksonne, 1653. Some copies have been corrected by hand to read 1652 [Hereinafter referred to as *DUA*].

DOI: 10.4324/9781003425069-20

to analyse. The sense of belonging evoked in Duck's language is marked by a series of differences of which he is aware, but which he refuses to see as oppositions. This prompts him to examine almost all of the legal regimes of Christian countries as a whole, looking beyond their now irreversible confessional disunity.

Much of the historiography has understood Duck's work as an early attempt at comparative analysis. But after this brief acknowledgement, he is usually relegated to the antiquarian tradition. However, although his efforts at documentation are significant, it is only one aspect of his work. It seems to us that, by beginning from the difference between the situation in England and that in continental Europe, Duck's main aim is to give an account of an internal difference within the former; thus to give an account of Roman law *in England*. He attempts a *comprehensive* definition of the Roman-canon law of his time from the perspective of a civilian in a common law country that stubbornly insists Roman law is foreign to it. This helps to explain why in the chapter on England limited space is given to *specific* institutes and their points of convergence and divergence in relation to these two legal languages. This demonstrates Duck's distance from prominent academics such as John Cowell, who at the beginning of the century was still striving to find a plane of translatability between these languages with a view to a possible rearrangement of *common law*, convinced that "legem nostram communem nihil aliud esse quam Romani et feudalis mixtionem".[3] It is unsurprising that the reformist tension of the sixteenth century was foreign to Duck, given that he was living in a different time.

Duck was explicit about where he was speaking from, what we might call his station. He studied civil law and practiced it *quam in Anglia habemus* for forty years, after which his career was interrupted by the ongoing internecine war. Although his royalism was not straightforward in doctrinal terms, he was a King's man. He was based at Oxford University, his alma mater, where he could use the Bodleian Library and take advantage of the academic community. He decided to spend his *otium sine die* on a subject that had always interested him: the fact that all the Christian princes, even if not all in the same way (*modo dispari*) admitted the civil law of the Romans in their dominions. His focus was on the reasons for and manner of this admission, thus on the authorization of the practice (*DUA*, A3r). This central theme of Duck's work can be seen in the division between historical narrative and law that organizes the descriptive development of both the first book and the various chapters of the second.

The English situation and his own specific situation are placed within this universalist reading, and both are in some sense saved by it. It is hard to find

3 John Cowell, *Institutiones iuris Anglicani, ad methodum et seriem institutionum imperialium compositae et digestae*, Londini, Ex officina Iohannis Legat, 1605, *Epistula dedicatoria*, no page numbers.

any "militant" position in the text of the *civilian* Arthur Duck, let alone any polemic against *common law*.[4] Instead, his work suggests the disillusionment and retreat of someone who already sees themselves as out of the game. He says that he wrote in the midst of the civil war, "ubi Leges minimum locum habent" (*DUA*, Z4v), which had overshadowed the old confrontation between English common law and English civil law that was mainly based on the role and position of the courts. The traditionally asymmetrical position of civilians had never been so clear, so much so that in the end of Chapter VIII of the second book he alludes to the words of Toulousian Forcadel, and before him René Choppin, on the death of English civil law. This was a scenario that Duck could not rule out, although, contrary to what is often believed, it is not a prognosis he shared.

In the *Conclusio operis* Duck gives the traditional *excusatio* to the reader, whether *exterus*, a foreigner, or *nostratis*. He apologizes to foreign readers for any shortcomings and errors because, although he had travelled in France, Italy, and the German territories[5] and had listened to important lectures and received precise explanations of Roman laws in the universities of those countries, he had not attended their courts and *curiae*. He had thus remained a guest, and as all jurisconsults know: "leges ex usu et praxi magis quam ex libris disci". He ends by quoting Baldo and his definition of *praxis* as *scientia digestiva* (*DUA*, Z4r). Once again, praxis is a fixed point. He makes fewer excuses to his British readers. Duck studied Roman law in his home country, and he was therefore a *doctor*, not a lawyer, thus not a man of the common law dominant in the country. However, he adds, "per multos annos exegerim in praxi Curiarum nostrarum, et Causarum Judiciis, quæ magnam Juris Civilis Romanorum Jurisque communis Angliæ communionem, et commixtionem habent" (*DUA*, Z4v). Praxis calls for the terms *communio* and *commixtio*, which prevent existing differences and conflicts from hardening into absolute otherness and antagonism.[6] From the perspective of practice, the legal system of England, although uneven and plural, is one. It requires an understanding that does not adhere to a doctrine, and so it necessitates the adoption of a different perspective. Although apparently paradoxical, what he calls the most difficult case, "the English exception", turns out to be a resource for his overall framework on a European level. Legal cultures and languages – *scientia juris* – must always also be understood in relation to concrete legal orders,

4 See the very useful essay by Francisco J. Andrés Santos, "Ius commune vs common law en el siglo XVII: el caso de Arthur Duck", *Anuario da Facultade de Dereito da Universidade da Coruña*, 7 (2003), 63–104, which has various merits, but whose title suffers from a misleading simplification.

5 In a letter dated 15 January 1612 to Sir Dudley Carleton, then English ambassador to Venice, John Chamberlain reported: "There one ... of college (I thinke his name be Ducke) hat ... hither from Padua where he lieth, that ..." (*Letters of John Chamberlain*, ed. by Norman Egbert McClure (Philadelphia: The American Philosophical Society, 1939), vol. I, 330).

6 The chapter by Helmholz in this book provides interesting observations on this.

the way they function in practice, and the various times and places of their jurisdiction, however problematic that relationship is. This is the focus of *De Usu et Authoritate.*

His final words in the *Conclusio* on the possible outcomes of civil law in England leave things more open than they had been at the end of the chapter on England, and they also challenge the idea that he thought civil law would disappear. The last two paragraphs of that chapter complain of the increasing restriction on civilians' sphere of influence. *Iureconsulti*, who had traditionally been involved in the drafting of international contracts and treaties, as well as being employed in ambassadorial occupations and in public affairs more generally, had now been replaced with untrained secretarial staff, resulting in their significant demotion: "Ita a publicis, et a privatis Negotiis undique excludimur". His most virulent critiques in these pages are not directed against common law, but rather against lawyers who aimed to exclude civilians: "Iuriconsulti nostri Municipales nos insectantur". These common lawyers proclaimed the uselessness of Roman laws, dismissing them as foreign laws from a foreign country, and joking, "quod Cives simus in aliena Repubblica. Hospites in nostra, cum meminisse potuissent quid in eos pro nobis retorserint" (*DUA*, 157v). But this was nothing new. Duck himself points out that the reduction in the use of *professores* dated back to immediately after the reign of Elizabeth I, thus indicating a relatively long-term trend, and the point that contested the rumours of the Municipales began with Alberico Gentili's *Laudes Academiae Perusinae et Oxoniensis*,[7] which had been published forty years previously (1605). Suggestions that opportunities for wealth and fortune were the exclusive prerogative of common lawyers can be found even earlier; for instance, Duck mentions the letter Erasmus wrote to Ulrich von Hutten more than a century before[8] and also the last chapter of Fortescue's *De Laudibus*, which Selden had recently re-edited and annotated, but which was first written between 1468 and 1471. Duck thus paints a general, long-term picture, although one that was coloured by the civil war in which he was writing. "Videtur Juriconsultos Gallicos, Stephanum Forcatulum, Renatumque Choppinum recte vaticinatos fuisse, nullum Juris Civilis Romanorum usum in Anglia aliquando quando futurum esse" (*DUA*, 158r). How, then, should

7 Hanoviae, apud Guilielmum Antonium, MDCV. The passage is as follows: "Apage, qui nec concedendum mihi censes ali quid veluti Anglo. Et sum tamen longissimo incolatu, annorum quattuor et viginti, Anglus certè. Civis sum Anglus sanè, qui in Anglia ius istud docendi, et istam cathedram teneo" (49). On this point, see G. Minnucci. "Da esule a civis anglus. Alberico Gentili e la difficile condizione dello straniero, tra vicende personali e riflessioni dottrinali", in *Soggettività contestate e diritto internazionale in età moderna*, ed. by G. De Giudici, D. Fedele, E. Fiocchi Malaspina, (Roma: 2023, Historia et Ius, Collettanee 9), 13–33.

8 This is the letter of 23 July 1519 in which Erasmus provides his famous portrait of Thomas More. The reference is based on an episode in the latter's life. See *The Correspondence of Erasmus: Letters 993 to 1121 (1519–1520) – Collected Works of Erasmus Volume 7* (Toronto: University of Toronto Press, 1987), 15–25.

we read these lines that close the chapter and in which there is no textual reference?

In fact, there is a reference, but it is in the first paragraph of the first part of the chapter on England, thus creating a kind of circularity. One of the premises of his argument is summed up as follows: "Britannia nostra, ut a toto Terrarum Orbe per Oceanum, ita a reliquis gentibus Europaeis per usum juris Civilis Romanorum divisa est, cum Principes nostri non tantam Legibus Romanis Authoritatem inter suas Leges, quantam reliqui Principes Europaei concesserint". From this difference stems the widespread belief that Roman law had been poorly received in England, which was found mainly in the French legal literature: "Scriptoresque magni nominis apud Gallos nobis vicinos nullus juris Civilis Romanorum usum esse apud Anglos asseruerunt" (*DUA*, 124r). Duck sees Etienne Forcadel and Choppin as epitomizing this historiographical position. Their names, albeit to varying degrees, recur as authoritative sources throughout *De Usu et Authoritate*, but in Chapter VIII are largely used to stress a disagreement in the idea of the relationship between the two countries. Duck makes unequivocal references to them in his citations. For instance, he quotes a passage in Book VII of Forcadel's *De Gallorum Imperio et Philosophia*, published posthumously in 1579: "Non enim Angli iure populi Romani lites dirimunt, sed municipali, et regiis constitutionibus" (and emphasizing the opposition between the English and the Scottish).[9] And he identifies the same misunderstanding in Book II, tit. 15 (*De Iudiciis, et ubi de Domanio agi oporteat*), n. 5 of Choppin's *De Domanio Franciae libri tres*: "Huius autem Romani Iuris nullus Anglis usus: sed ex vetere gentis instituto Britanni reguntur statutis municipalibus patria lingua propositis, quae illis maiorum Leges Moresque praescripserunt".[10] Thus summarized, and taken out of their respective contexts, the two passages speak of a past that is, in some sense, original, meaning that no prognostic value can be logically attributed to them.[11] What Duck alludes to in the last line of the chapter is thus

9 Parisiis, Apud Guilielmum Chaudiere, 473v.

10 Parisiis, Apud Martinum Iuvenem, 1574, 328–329 (with minor variations in the following editions).

11 The French edition of Duck's book, on the whole very loosely translated, is different, assertively stating: "Etienne Forcatule & René Choppin ont bien deviné, quand ils ont dit que le droit romain serait quelque jour entierement banni de l'Angleterre", *De l'Usage et l'Autorité du Droit Civil dans les Etats des Princes Chrétiens*, A Paris, chez Jean Guignard, 1689, 362. In the French title the word "Romanorum" is dropped. Similarly, John Beaver added an English version of Duck's chapter on England as an appendix to his translation of the French text by Claude Joseph de Ferrière, *The History of Roman or Civil Law* (1717), London, Browne and Clay, 1724. Beaver translates Duck as follows: "both *English* and *French Lawyers*, *Forcatulus* and *Choppinus*, were true Prophets; in foretelling, That one time or other, the *Civil Law* would be no longer in use in this Kingdom" (xxxviii). Beaver, in fact, added the word "English" to this sentence, indicating a restrospective attempt at assimilation. It is also worth noting the lack of the *Conclusio operis* in the French translation, as well as in Beaver's English version of Chapter VIII of the second book.

a feared outcome, namely that what the two French jurists imagined might indeed come to pass sooner or later, ultimately proving them right. He constructs the sentence in such a way as to leave it in the realms of possibility, a decision we could perhaps see as having an apotropaic function.

Whilst again pointing out the limits of his own work, in the *Conclusio operis* Duck emphasizes that it was written in the hope of helping to preserve Roman law in England. However, he adds that should Roman law then disappear from the country his work could serve as a kind of farewell, a rite due to its ancestors.[12] Furthermore, the preceding lines address other jurisconsults from across Europe, expressing the hope that they will take up the challenge posed by his work, which, he proudly points out, was unprecedented. Duck's desire for others to use their practical knowledge to more deeply analyse the realities of their own countries makes his plural affiliations clear.

Conatus and *voti* also reveal the difficult and risky connection between universalism and the concreteness of Duck's position as an Englishman. As we have already seen, his universalism is that of *scientia iuris* and of the transnational community of Roman-canon law jurists, collectively referred to as *ius commune*. It is clear that, from a continental perspective, Duck is what we might call a jurist of late common law, and he also perceives himself as such. However, he does not passively accept the *auctoritates*, never using them as merely authoritative texts or in an exclusively documentary way. Clearly an integral and important part of the text, he uses the *auctoritates* together and in relation to the sources, at times questioning them without any note of deference, even in the most authoritative cases, for example, those of Bartolus or of Alberico Gentili.[13] Similarly, his documentation is almost always well reasoned and the limits he inevitably encounters almost always coincide with the limits of the sources themselves (with a few conspicuous exceptions, which Scotland seems to be). By way of example, we will analyse the tools and references he uses when speaking of the Italian princes in Chapter III, Book II of the *dominia*, in which it is also important to note his references to Venice and its internal and complex differences that distinguish it from the rest of Europe. However, the way Duck uses the terms *scientia iuris* and *ius commune* are not immediately intelligible, and so it is worth taking a closer look at them. The fact that, as he stresses repeatedly, he belongs to the world of the *doctores* appears in the way he illustrates the interplay of different traditions

12 "Ubicunque demum in hoc Opere benignus Lector me errasse observaverit (sicuti in tot Gentium Legibus investigandis, me aliorum Authoritatem secutum sæpius errasse necesse est) igno, scet nimio meo Juris Civilis ornandi studio; cum hoc tantum in votis mei habuerim, ut possim Juri Civili Romanorum in Anglia retinendo inservire eidemve, si discessum paraverit, valedicere, justa persolvere, et parentare" (Z 4, IIr.).

13 On this matter the recent books edited by Focke Tannen Hinrichs have serious limits. His anastatic reprint of the 1668 Lipsian edition of Duck's text (Köln: Bohlau Verlag, 1990) does not include indexes or bibliographies of the *quotations*, and its German translation does not even include the attached references (Göttingen: Wallstein Verlag, 1993).

(*mos italicus, mos gallicus*), displaying an originality that also demonstrates moments of tension between the two traditions.

The Legacy of Duck

Duck was not forgotten after his death: numerous references to his book crop up years afterwards in various studies, particularly on some particular issues that touch on a wide variety of questions. For instance the question of civil law in England, to which Robert Wisemann, also a *doctor*, explicitly returned in *The Law of the Laws, or the Excellency of Civil Law above all other Laws* (1657) shortly after Duck's death. However, despite its apparent similarities in terms of subject matter, even the title indicates a position that is substantially removed from Duck's, not to mention Wisemann's republican leanings, which were completely foreign to Duck. The same can be said on the relationship between Roman law and the Germanic empire. A few years later, in the third edition (1665) of his *De Origine Juris Germanici*, Hermann Conring strongly criticized Duck, although not without praising his "summa industria" for having approved the legend of Lothair III who would replace Germanic customs with Roman laws.[14] Significantly, the index reads: "Arthur Duck, laudatus et reprehensus". More than a century later, Edward Gibbon cited Duck as an authority together with Heineccius at the beginning of Chapter 44 of *The History of the Decline and Fall of the Roman Empire*, a kind of monographic insert dedicated to the history of Roman law that, separated from the rest of the work, would play an important role in the early days of the *Historische Schule* via its German translation by Gustav Hugo.[15] A French edition of this chapter, translated by Leopold August Warnkönig on the basis of François Guizot's previous translation, included Hugo's notes. Warnkönig also added his own introduction and set of notes, often in open disagreement with Hugo's.[16] Two years later Gibbon's chapter was republished in the English original with Hugo's annotations translated by William Gardiner.[17] This is an interesting case of transmission, in which new structures are laid on top of old ones without completely covering them over, making it difficult for legal historians to avoid making associations with the way in which glossators worked. It is worth noting here that Gibbon's reference to Duck was the subject of a marginal but in some ways significant controversy. While Hugo clearly takes this part of the text seriously, adding his own notes, although without referencing Duck himself, Warnkönig critiques Gibbon's use of Duck (Beherends, 19), calling

14 Helmenstadii, typis & sumtibus Henningi Mulleri Academiae Typographi, 1665, 136 and 219.

15 Edward Gibbon, *Historisches Übersicht des Römischen Recht übersetz, eingeleitet und kommentiert von Gustav Hugo*, Göttingen, beim Johann Christian Dietrich, 1789, the new edition of which is edited by Okko Behrends (Göttingen: Wallstein Verlag, 1996).

16 E. Gibbon, *Précis de l'histoire du droit romain* (Liège: Collardin, 1821).

17 E. Gibbon, *A Survey of Roman or Civil Law* (Edinburgh: W. Aitchison, 1823).

the latter's work "assez insignifiant" while singing the praises of Savigny in a comparison that now seems completely nonsensical.[18] This judgement is transcribed literally in Henry Hart Milman's edition for Murray (1846), one of the most widespread and influential nineteenth-century editions of Gibbon, which helped to create a new ambivalent attitude towards Duck's book, in which it was considered legitimate to use it as a source (after all, Savigny had also used it), but only as long as it was treated with some suspicion.

We can even find traces of this ambivalence, albeit from a different point of view, in the period in which Duck's work was most widely discussed in Europe, in an intellectual context that is connected not only temporally but also thematically to that of Gibbon.[19] It is well known that Duck's writing on Southern Italy (II, 4) played an important role in the disputes on the subject of jurisdictionalism between Neapolitan jurists in the first half of the eighteenth century, *in primis* Francesco D'Andrea, Donato D'Asti, and Pietro Giannone, which led to a 1719 Neapolitan re-edition of *De Usu et Authoritate*.[20] His role in these events has been fairly well documented in the history of law, including in recent studies.[21] Years later, in his *Vita scritta da se medesimo*, written between 1736 and 1741 when he was a prisoner in Piedmont, Giannone pointed out the seminal role that *De Usu* had played in the project that had resulted in the *Istoria civile del regno di Napoli* in 1723, and he continued to show unreserved admiration for its author:

> Mi avea a ciò maggiormente spinto l'esempio di Arturo Duck inglese, il di cui aureo libretto, *De usu et auctoritate iuris Romanorum* etc., in Napoli allor rarissimo ed a pochi noto, mi avea mostrata la via, ciocch'egli fece esattamente nei regni della Gran Brettagna, di poter far io nel regno di Napoli, senza dilungarmi in altri remoti paesi. Poiché, se bene egli avesse scorso quasi tutti i regni e le provincie di Europa, nulladimanco l'opera sua stessa dimostrava che non era impresa d'un solo; ma che ciascuno dovea raggirarsi in quella provincia ov'era nato e, lungamente dimoratovi, avesse potuto minutamente avvertire le vicende ed i vari cangiamenti del suo stato politico e civile.[22]

18 E. Gibbon, *Historisches Übersicht* (Behrends) 19; E. Gibbon, *Précis*, 91–92.

19 See H. Trevor-Roper, "Pietro Giannone and Great Britain", *The Historical Journal*, 39 3 (1996) 657–675; J.G.A. Pocock, *Barbarism and Religion* 2 *Narratives of Civil Government* (Cambridge: Cambridge University Press, 1999) 29–71 (on Duck see 35 and 66).

20 Neapoli, Typis Dominici-Antonii, and Nicolai Parrino. However, the widely circulated Neapolitan edition should be used with caution due to the minor modifications made to the text and the reduction in the number of textual references, probably those that were not immediately familiar to the eighteenth-century reader.

21 D. Luongo, *Consensus Gentium. Criteri di legittimazione dell'ordine giuridico moderno* I (Napoli: Arte Tipografica Editrice, 2007), 459–539.

22 *Opere di Pietro Giannone*, ed. by Sergio Bertelli, Giuseppe Recuperati (Milano: Ricciardi, 1971), 53–54. He had said something similar in the introduction to *Istoria*, ibidem, 369–370.

On the one hand, Giannone took up the exhortation found in *Conclusio operis*, and, on the other, albeit without any malice, he turned Duck's assertions on the limits of his work against him, concluding that it was impossible for a single scholar to carry out a work of such magnitude. The understandably paradoxical nature of Giannone's position was symptomatic of a shift in which the core problematic of Duck's work was no longer fully understood.

Cores within *De Usu et Authoritate* (1): *Arma* and *leges*

While citations and detailed readings of Duck continue to appear in important studies,[23] alongside a recent increase in interest in his work which seems to have thrown off a previous trend for overly hasty judgements about him, there is no general analysis of the structure of *De Usu et Authoritate*. This task is also beyond the reach of this chapter, and so we will limit ourselves to exploring some aspects of his work that help identify the approach he uses, with the aim of clarifying what he meant by *ius commune*. We will thus attempt to "dig deep" into two chapters: that which opens Book I and that in Book II devoted to the *dominia* of the Italian princes. This will allow us to closely follow his argument and at least partially identify the way he weaves together the various threads of his references.

Book I, in particular, has been carelessly interpreted, largely because it has been overshadowed by later historiographical studies on Roman law. Not that the book lacks interesting historical observations, such as its focus on Byzantine law and the post-Justinian affair of the *Basilici*. On the latter, Duck, working on the recently published book by the Provençal Charles Hannibal Fabrot, shows a grasp of the available sources and an attempt at synthesis which is remarkable for his time.[24] But this is not the key point. Put crudely, Duck is not a historian, he is a jurist and a jurist of his time, for whom the partitions of normative knowledge are clearly defined (law, moral theology, and the historical narrative itself as an archive of *exempla*) and have few overlaps, operating in a different way than they would do in the following centuries. His relationship with history is thus entirely mediated by his identity as a jurist of his time. It is tempting to see hints of a modern conception of history in his work, but if there is any truth in this it is in relation to the juridical sphere and, perhaps, the theological sphere. However, his is an *image* of history, not

23 See, for example, Duck's references and uses by Sir William Holdsworth, who also devotes a whole paragraph to him in vol. 5 of his *History of English Law* (2nd edition, London: Methuen, 1924), 24–25, by Francesco Calasso in *Medioevo del diritto* (Milano: Giuffrè, 1954), 627–628, and Riccardo Orestano in his *Introduzione allo studio del diritto romano* (Bologna: Il Mulino, 1987), *passim*.

24 "Son livre ne manque pas de grandeur, mais le cadre est trop restreint" is the even-handed judgement of the nineteenth-century historian Jean-Anselme-Bernard Montreuil, *Histoire du droit byzantin*, vol. 1 (Paris: Guilbert and Thorel, 1863), xlvi.

a *conceptualization* of it. Let's explore this subject in relation to the opening of *De Usu et Authoritate*.

"Summa rei publicae tuitio de stirpe duarum rerum, armorum atque legum veniens vomque suam exinde muniens felix Romanorum genus omnibus anteponi nationibus omnibusque dominari tam praeteritis effecit temporibus quam deo propitio in aeternum efficiet istorum etenim alterum alterius euxilio semper viguit, et tam militaris res legibus in tuto collocata est, quam ipsae leges armorum praesidio servatae sunt". These are the opening lines of the *Constitutio Summa Rei Publicae* which is the second "preface" to the Codex (*De Iustiniano Codice Confirmando*).[25] The first chapter of Book I starts by paraphrasing this text, interpreting it in an unusual way. While the Codex closely connects *arma* and *leges*, Duck introduces a separation between them from the outset that at first glance seems to be at odds with Justinian. It does not seem, he argues, that *leges* and *arma* have equal glory, for while everyone acknowledges the equity and justice of the former, it would be very difficult to say the same for the latter. The Roman conquests as a whole, in all periods, are marked for the most part by inequity and injustice. Duck creates two separate registers for *arma* and *leges*, respectively, seeming to suggest that if they are interlinked then the usual reading of them should be inverted: it is the law that corroborates the injustice of Roman expansion and thus of the empire. This almost seems to imply that it is not history that justifies the law, but the law that can be used to judge historical events. Duck realizes that this is a difficult operation, not least because those whose reading he is inverting are precisely those jurists he tends to use and identify with. But it is also an operation that he considers necessary to his argument. "De legibus romanis igitur acturus, necessarium duxi aliquid de iustitia armorum et bellorum, cum in eam controversiam juriconsulti nostri in scriptis suis saepe incidant" (*DUA*, 1r–1v). It is worth noting that he does not allow the opposition between *arma* and *leges* to be reduced to a mere rhetorical game, perhaps to emphasize the excellence of the latter.[26]

Sources: Ancient Historians and the Roman Authors

The chapter proceeds in a kind of indictment, whose charges are drawn from three types of sources. The first source is the ancient historians and the Roman authors themselves (I, 1, 2–11) for whom his references begin from the wars against the Latin and Italic peoples and continue to the Punic wars and then on to Trajan's wars against the Parthians and the conquest of Britain. In

25 On the complexity of this passaage, see Paolo Garbarino, "Brevi riflessioni sui rapporti tra res militaris ed esperienza giuridica in età tardoantica e giustinianea", in *Civitas, iura, arma. Organizzazioni militari, istituzioni giuridiche e strutture sociali alle origini dell'Europa (secc. III–VIII)*, ed. by F. Botta, L. Loschiavo (Lecce: Grifo, 2015), 79–90.

26 Yves Mausen is of this opinion in his "Arthur Duck et le droit romain: *Ius Commune* ou *peregrinae leges*?", *Rivista Internazionale di Diritto Comune*, 20 (2009), 197–207, esp. 182.

the *De Officiis* (II, 8), Cicero argued that the Romans had taken over the world because they had a duty to defend their allies, but this was disproved by numerous other authors and texts. The humanist period revealed multiple sources that are still widely accepted today, which testify against the Romans by pointing out their predatory tendencies and their deceitful and disrespectful attitude to pacts, in brief, their *iniustitia*. These include Livy, Annio Floro and his *Epitomae* liviane, Eutropius, Polybius, Dionysius of Halicarnassus, Cassius Dio, Caesar and Tacitus, Ammianus Marcellinus, and, for the Jewish wars, the books of the *Maccabees*, as well as the Lusitanian Paulus Orosius, Augustine's collaborator, and two Byzantines: Joannes Xiphilinus, who had written an epitome of Cassius Dio, and the monk Joannes Zonaras. Duck also adds some notable modern authors. While on the conquest of Corsica he refers to a historian with some legal sensibilities, Carlo Sigonio[27] from Modena, on the complex case of the Carthaginian siege of Sagunto, one of the most controversial episodes even for the ancients,[28] he uses the jurists Hugo Grotius and Alberico Gentili to support his reading of Polybius, which is sympathetic to Hannibal. In the case of Grotius ("æquior jurisconsultis videtur sententia"), the question is *de iure* and is resolved by denying that a treaty between the Romans and Saguntines preexisted the agreements between Rome and Carthage and therefore denying that we are dealing with the breaking of a pact, in itself "res odiosa". This would have deprived the Carthaginians of the freedom to use arms against those who they felt had wronged them, a *libertas* that, in Duck's citation, Grotius calls *naturalis*.[29] The second case is only apparently more straightforward. "Licetque Saguntini essent foedere Romanorum comprehensi, eos Annibal justissime oppugnabat, quod hostes Carthaginensium reciperent et adjuvarent" (*DUA*, 3r). Duck takes what he needs from Gentili in order to validate his thesis. The citation he uses refers to Chapter 22 of Book I of Gentili's *De Iure Belli*,[30] which significantly bears the title "De uetustis caussis non excitandis". Here Gentili praises Hannibal for not using the "old" issue of Corsica as the reason for the war, which is the key point at the beginning of

27 "[I]n Corsicam insulam belli Romani nullam fuisse justam causam fatetur Sigonius". The citation references *De Antiquo Iure Provinciarum libri II* (Venetijs, ex officina Iordani Ziletti, MDLXVIII), lib. I, ch. iiii (15–17). On Carlo Sigonio, see the entry of Vincenzo Lavenia in the *Dizionario biografico degli italiani*, vol. 92 (Roma: Istituto della Enciclopedia italiana, 2018), 578–583.

28 On this point the great Italian historian Santo Mazzarino's short book *Introduzione alle guerre puniche* (1947) (Milano: Rizzoli, 2003) is still significant. Its entire last chapter is focused on *Sagunto* (119–156), attempting, among other things, to understand the thinking behind Book III of Ἱστορίαι by Polibio.

29 Chapter XVI (*De Interpretatione*), n. 13 of Book II of De *Jure Belli ac Pacis Libri Tres*, in the *Editio Nova*, Amsterdami, Apud Iohannem Blaev, 1646, n. 278.

30 The first edition of *De Usu et Authoritate* refers to Book II, but it is clearly an error that remains in the following editions. It was corrected in the French version of 1689.

the chapter. What is then said, including the citation, is actually secondary.[31] This is not an example of his imprecise use of references; on the contrary, his transcription here is accurate. What is striking is his work of selection, which is always there, but which in this case becomes obvious, demonstrating that the textual quotations are never neutral, but are the field in which the *controversiae* take shape.

Sources: Church Fathers and Theologians

After the historians, his next source is the Church fathers and theologians (I, 1, 12–15). This passage has not received much attention but is crucial for understanding the way in which Duck sees the empire, and also allows us to look into his intellectual background, further complexifying and deepening our understanding of him. The first he refers to are Jerome, Isidore of Pelusium, Cyril of Jerusalem, Cyprian, the *causidicus* Minucius Felix, Arnobius and his disciple Lactantius, and finally Augustine. Duck retrieves most of these sources from the extensive collection of patristic writings by the French theologian and preacher Marguerin de la Bigne, the *Sacra Bibliotheca Sanctorum Patrum*, which also included texts from the Greek tradition translated in Latin for the first time, and which, starting with the Paris edition of 1575, would be reprinted at various times in an ever larger size and with an increasing number of volumes. Duck uses the 1618 Cologne edition,[32] which differs from the previous editions in chronologically organizing the material by centuries. To support his reconstruction, he uses Jerome's *De Viris Illustribus* (which he refers to in the older and more properly Jeromian form of *De Scriptoribus Ecclesiaticis*) and the text of the same name by the Jesuit Roberto Bellarmino, in keeping with his tendency to place an ancient author and a modern author side by side where possible.[33] As he explains, these are authors who document the continuity and consistency of patristic thought on the empire "primis religionis Christianae temporibus", when almost all peoples were subject to it, and which can be divided up according to the various emperors (up to Valentinian II) and which was marked by the gradual weakening of the empire's hold. The lengthy direct quotations he uses in I, 1, 12 further enrich

31 See *Alberici Gentilis De Iure Belli libri tres*, Hanoviae, excudebat Guilliemus Antonius, 1598, 168–170.

32 *Magna bibliotheca veterum patrum et antiquorum scriptorum ecclesiasticorum, a M. de la Bigne coll., & tertiò in lucem ed., nunc verò plus quàm centum authoribus, & opusculis plurimis locupletata*, Coloniae Agrippinae, sumptibus Antonii Hierati, sub signo Griphi, 1618–22. For the identification, see Chapter IV of *De Bibliothecis et Catenis Patrum, variisque veterum scriptorum Ecclesiasticorum collectionibus Tractatus*, Lipsiae, sumptibus Hæred. Friederici Lanksit, 1707 on the German Lutheran Thomas Ittig.

33 Roberto, Bellarmino, *De scriptoribus ecclesiasticis: liber unus: cum adiunctis indicibus undecim, & breui chronologia ab orbe condito usque ad annum M.DC.XII*, Romae, Ex typographia Bartholomaei Zannetti, 1613, a work which Duck seems to make use of beyond his explicit references to it.

his exposition. He presents the Romans as villains and brigands who banded together for reasons of self-defence, went so far as to make a *parricida* (who murdered his family members) their first king, and whose marriages consisted in broken pacts of hospitality and cruel wars against their in-laws (Cyprian). The city of Rome, born from the slaughter of other human beings, subjugated an entire *innocuus*, blameless world (Arnobius). Its actions in the end seem to substantiate Augustine's famous question in the fourth book of *De Civitate Dei*: "Remota iustitia quid sunt regna nisi magna latrocinia et ipsa latrocinia quid sunt nisi parva regna?" (*DUA*, 5v).

All these passages refer, more or less explicitly and with the partial exception of Augustine, to the identification of the fourth kingdom of the Book of Daniel with the Roman Empire, contributing to the empire's definition on an eschatological level. It is no surprise that Duck's first reference is to Jerome's commentary on the second chapter of Daniel (2:40). From the second half of the fourth century, Jerome established the Christian interpretation of the biblical text, providing a reading that remained dominant for a long time afterwards. Nebuchadnezzar's dream tells of the enigmatic statue of a human figure whose head is made of gold, chest and arms are made of silver, belly and thighs are made of brass, legs are made of iron, and feet are made of iron mixed with clay. The enigma deepens when, in the king's dream, a stone detaches itself from the mountain without human intervention and strikes the statue, destroying it and then growing so large as to occupy all space. Daniel's interpretation is considered to be a prophecy: the four metals indicate the four kingdoms that will succeed one another in time, the stone announces the fall of the last of the worldly kingdoms and the messianic advent of the Kingdom of God. It is worth quoting the passage from Jerome's commentary that Duck attaches:

> Et regnum quartum erit veluti ferrum: quomodo ferrum comminuit et domat omnia, sic comminuet et conteret omnia haec, etc. Regnum autem quartum, quod perspicue pertinet ad Romanos, ferrum est quod comminuit et domat omnia. Sed pedes eius et digiti ex parte ferrei, et ex parte sunt fictiles, quod hoc tempore manifestissime comprobatur. Sicut enim in principio nihil Romano imperio fortius et durius fuit, ita in fine rerum nihil imbecillius: quando et in bellis civilibus, et adversum diversas nationes, aliarum gentium barbararum indigemus auxilio.[34]

He then melds two older exegetical traditions into a single framework, that which insisted on the origin of the stone as an allusion to Christ's conception by a virgin and that which connected the destruction of temporal kingdoms

34 This citation is from the Erasmian edition: *Omnium operum divi Eusebii Hieronymi Stridonensis*. T.V: *operum divi Hieronymi, commentarios in prophetas, quos maiores vocant* (Basileae: Ex Acuratissima Officina Frobeniana, 1516), 269v.

with the second coming: "In fine autem horum omnium regnorum auri, argenti, aeris et ferri, abscissus est lapis, Dominus atque Salvator, sine manibus, id est, absque coitu et humano semine, de utero virginali, et contritis omnibus regnis, factus est mons magnus, et implevit universam terram".[35] Jerome's Christological translation of the messianic figure of the stone worked in a dual sense: the Roman Empire was the setting of the Christian event, but it was also the last in the succession of the four great earthly empires evoked by Daniel. After the dashed expectations of the first centuries of Christianity on the imminent return of Christ, the empire is faced with its own insurmountable eschatological limit and becomes increasingly weak ("nihil imbecillius"), necessarily falling between the first advent of Christ and his final return. The Roman Empire is the reign of iron, and *ferrum* is the element that connects the successive references to the Fathers, almost seeming to be the thread that binds them. In the words of Isidore of Pelusium, the iron teeth and bronze paws connote the fourth nameless beast of Daniel's vision, in which Rome is recognized as having gathered together all peoples under its yoke.[36] And Cyril of Jerusalem, with some hermeneutical audacity, connects the messianic promise of the second Psalm ("he shall rule them with a rod of iron") to the "Roman" reading of Daniel, indicating the interweaving of Christ's incarnation, the imperial age, and the advent of the Kingdom of God.

The "Roman" Interpretation of Daniel's Prophecy

Duck limits his reference to Daniel to the patristics of late antiquity, but he must have been aware of its contemporary significance. This is confirmed by his choice of patristic references. The Reformation saw the return of the theme of the oldness of the world and the maturity of the times, which had also been clearly present in the medieval world.[37] The Book of Daniel, more or less connected with the Book of Revelation, acted as a screen on which to project messianic expectations and political necessities, soteriological needs, and hermeneutic demands. It was written about extensively with different emphases over the course of at least a century, not only by well-known figures from Luther to Melanchthon, from Calvin to Bodin and Grotius, but also by those who, outside the world of the learned, finally had access to the biblical

35 On this point, see Reinhard Bodenmann, *Naissance d'une exégèse: Daniel dans l'Eglise ancienne des trois premiers siècles* (Tübingen: J.C.B. Mohr, 1986), 309–310.

36 Useful on this point is Irena Backus, "The Beast: Interpretations of Daniel 7.2–9 and Apocalypse 13.1–4, 11–12 in "Lutheran, Zwinglian and Calvinist Circles in the Late Sixteenth Century", *Reformation & Renaissance Review*, 3:1 (2001), 59–77.

37 Also on later developments, see the useful essay by Gregorio Piaia, "Interpretazione allegorica e uso ideologico della prima profezia di Daniele agl'inizi del Trecento" in his *Marsilio e dintorni. Contributi alla storia delle idee* (Padova: Antenore, 1999), 136–163.

text and so a chance to speak on the matter.[38] In the seventeenth century, this process was particularly intense in England due to deepening radicalization during the civil wars and the collapse of the Cromwellian compromise. However, this does not mean we should lose sight of the preceding years in which Duck was educated and began to work.[39] Further on in the chapter it could seem at first that Duck wanted to keep out of this debate, in line with his image as a vocationally inclined jurist trying to temper the enthusiasm of theologians and preachers. However, this impression seems to be partly mistaken, and includes, among other things, an anachronism, which we will return to later. Here, too, Duck is aware that he is being highly selective and that important objections could be raised against him that he would have to confront, particularly in relation to the Augustinian reference. But for the time being he moves on with his argument, adding a passage of only a few lines (*DUA* I, 1, 14) on the *Theologi posteriores* to the section on the Church fathers, certifying that the Romans occupied the kingdoms and dominions of other princes *per vim et tyrannidem* in the same way that the three great world empires were built, that of the Assyrians with Ninus, that of the Medes and Persians with Cyrus, and that of the Greeks with Alexander the Great. Duck thereby confirms the idea that in Nebuchadnezzar's dream the Roman Empire is the fourth kingdom and accepts, against Calvin and against Bodin of the *Methodus*, the continued relevance of the "Roman" interpretation of the prophecy. However, those who expect to find a reference to the Protestant and Reformed debates will be disappointed and confused. The abundance of references acts as a counterweight to the brevity of this passage, and almost gives us a compendium of the School of Salamanca, from Domingo de Soto to Luis Molina and Juan de Salas,[40] to which he once again adds Bellarmino and, to be more precise, Bellarmino the controversialist.[41] Here he seems

38 On this subject Mario Miegge's book *Il sogno del re di Babilonia: Profezia e storia da Thomas Müntzer a Isaac Newton* (Milano: Feltrinelli, 1995) is indispensable. But also see the various essays collected in *Die Geschichte der Daniel-Auslegung in Judentum, Christentum und Islam: Studien zur Kommentierung des Danielbuches in Literatur und Kunst*, ed. by Katharina Bracht, David S. du Toit (Berlin: De Gruyter, 2007), particularly 219–371.

39 Katharine R. Firth, *The Apocalyptic Tradition in Reformation Britain 1530–1645* (Oxford: Oxford, 1979); Kenneth Fincham, *The Early Stuart Church, 1603–1642* (London: MacMillan, 1993).

40 At the end of the chapter 6, § 31, on Spain (*DUA*, 117rv), Duck gives a concise outline of the excellence of the Iberian jurists, adding to those indicated here the names of Antonio Agustin, of Diego de Covarrubias y Leiva, of Alfonso Acevedo, of Suarez, of Juan Gutiérrez and of Marcos Salón de Paz, as well as those of Martín de Azpilcueta and of Vazquez, which we find immediately afterwards.

41 The reference is to *caput sextum* of Book III (*De Laicis sive Secularibus*) of *De Membris Ecclesiae Militantis*. See *Disputationes Roberti Bellarmini Politiani, Societatis Iesu, De Controversiis Christianae Fidei, Adversus huius temporis Hæreticos, Primi Tomi Septima Controversia Generalis, De Ecclesia Triumphante, Tribus Libris explicata*, vol. 9, Ingolstadt, David Sartorius, 1587, 437–440, paraphrased by Salas.

to be almost blindly carried along by his citations, which is certainly more embarrassing for a non-papist Englishman than references to *De Scriptoribus ecclesiasticis*. They are all Catholic theologians, but above all theologians and lawyers, whose references are almost all ascribable to a specific genre, that of the treatises *de legibus* and *de iustitia et iure*.[42] His reasons for doing this go beyond simply providing a documentary supplement corroborated by authoritative scholars, with the usual transconfessional promiscuity of a jurist. It is true that his criticism of Rome and mention of the four kingdoms can also be found in these references, but in a less direct way. Let us look more closely at the first reference, which opens the sequence and makes no reference to the Roman Empire, but seems to be significant. In the fourth book of *De iustitia et iure*, in which Soto begins to look at commutative justice, the second article of the second *quaestio* is particularly important.[43] Under the more general question of what is included in man's *dominium*, this article is specifically concerned with whether and in what ways the *dominium* of men over other men is possible. In other words, its theme is domination, and its problem is posed from the outset in a form that would later become commonplace. The sacred books teach that man is born free and his freedom belongs inalienably to natural law. The *Ecclesiasticus* says that God made man *rectus*, leaving him in the hands of his own *consilium* and so placing him above all creatures, but not above other men. On the question of *dominium*, the analogical use of the Creator/creature relationship meets an insurmountable theological limit. Similarly, Roman jurisconsults recognized that it was *contra naturam* for one man to be subjugated to another man. At the same time, there is no doubt that the same passages in the *Corpus Iuris* support the possibility of slavery, as does Aristotle in *Politics*. De Soto aims to resolve this contradiction through separating the various levels, which he achieves by exploring the sources in which the different levels of the "multiplex species" of servitus can be identified and then declaring whether each one is legitimate or not. He proceeds *per viam specificationis*, indicating different legal registers whose hierarchy cannot be found in a single deductive process, but requires the identification of a plurality of principles that, albeit subordinate, reshape the relationships between eternal law, natural law, the law of nations, and legislation.[44] Soto's frame of

42 On this point, see José Barrientos García," Los Tratados *De Legibus* y *De iustitia et iure* en la Escuela de Salamanca de los siglos XVI y XVII", *Salamanca, Revista de Estudios*, 47 (2002), 371–415.

43 *Fratris Dominici Salamantiae, Soto Segoviensis, Theologi, ordinis Predicatorum, Cesareae Maiestati a sacris confessionibus, Salmantini Professoris, De Iustitia et Iure Libri decem*, Salamanticae, Excudebat Andreas a Portolariis, MDLIII, 288–291. On the central role of Soto for the School of Salamanca, at least equal to that of Vitoria see Merio Scattola, "Domingo De Soto e la fondazione della Scuola di Salamanca", *Veritas*, 54, n. 3 (2009), 52–57.

44 On this point see, Merio Scattola, "Natural Law and Natural Right in the Spanish Scholasticism", in Jörg Alejandro Tellkamp (ed.) *A Companion to Early Modern Spanish Imperial Political and Social Thought* (Leiden: Brill, 2020), 128–148, particularly 137–141.

reference is the *Secunda Secundae* of Thomas's *Summa Theologiae*, although he is also heavily influenced by the context of the conquest of the New World and the phenomenon of transoceanic trade. Whereas the new problems that the occupation of American land posed to European culture, including juridical culture, are clearly far from Duck's thoughts – he mentions it only briefly in *De Usu et Authoritate* in the chapter dedicated to Spain (VI, 7) – he nevertheless finds aspects of Soto's work that support his argument. We could say that whereas Soto writes with an eye on the imperial development of the Iberian world, Duck has his eye on the Roman Empire.

Of Duck Using De Soto

Of the four *conclusiones* put forward by De Soto, the first identifies two types of slavery: *natural* slavery, for which the reference is to Aristotle, but through a reading in which the opposition between autonomy and heteronomy foreshadows the division of labour (directive rational capacity vs. executive manual force); and *legal* slavery, for which the reference is partly to Justinian law and partly to the historical Jewish tradition as narrated in the Bible. Legal slavery is also *duplex* and is divided into two classes. The first includes those who, driven by subsistence needs, sell themselves to masters, "causa partecipandi pretium". God made men free, but the desire and the right (*Ius*) to preserve one's life is so innate in all living beings that the needy can accept slavery in return for it. This is certainly permissible (*Secunda conclusio*), since, De Soto argues, "Non bene pro toto libertas venditur auro: vendi tamen pro vita fas est, quae omni pretiosior auro".[45] With the caveat, however, that what *Leviticus* prescribes about the difference between a *pro tempore* servile condition for Jews and a perpetual one for Gentiles belongs to ancient law and no longer applies to Christians, and likewise that the sale of children, which the Roman *patria potestas* authorized, is now obsolete among European peoples, although it is still practised elsewhere. This is certainly not a new argument, but goes back as far as Bartolus. But, added Soto, it was said that it was customary for Ethiopians, the term generally used for African peoples, to sell their children. Thus when the Portuguese bought them it was not considered in itself a crime. "Quod si libere veneunt, non est cur mercatura illa crimine ullo denotet". Many instead believed that wretched people were forced into slavery by fraud and violence and sold by those who had no title to them. What is more, the buyers were completely aware of this, and they should have

45 Soto's argument is not easy to follow and shows the historical difficulty of maintaining a distinction between slaves and wage earners under the category of selling oneself. While they certainly do not overlap, the slave and the wage earner do have points of contact. This issue returned in the *Quaestio*, when Soto, having established that those who are subservient by nature must generally be treated in their own interest and not in the interests of their masters, would remark that cases in which the latter happens, when they are used as mere tools, must be limited according to natural equity and honesty, "nisi ubi essent mercede conducti."

restored freedom to those who were born free and *per iniuriam* forced into slavery. And, Soto concludes, this would not be done for the slaves' benefit in order to make them Christians, which is an offence against the faith and which God would not allow. Soto's argument in this passage risks hyperbole when, criticizing the slave trade, he compares it with the fraudulent sale of other people's goods; it is clear that for him there is always a connection between domination and *iniuria* that undermines domination's legitimacy. It is this point that Duck apparently wants to use for his own purposes. Another section of Soto's text should be analysed. The second class of *servitus legalis* takes us back to the etymology of the word: servants are those who have been spared in war (*servati*) and by virtue of this are enslaved (*mancipia*). This *servitus* is also lawful (*Tertia conclusio*); indeed, it can be said to derive from mercy. If one can give oneself to slavery to have access to the necessities of survival, it is even more reasonable to do so to save one's life. The changes in customs that came with Christianity had softened or made obsolete the harsher aspects of slavery, so much so that among Christians, prisoners of war no longer tended to be enslaved. However, a difference between the two classes of slaves remained and posed a general problem. Although the legal character of slavery makes the position of slave owners the same for both classes, this is not the case for the slaves themselves. Roman law certainly insisted on the unlawfulness of the slave escaping, which constituted a *furtum sui*, and, therefore, as a *res furtiva*, gave rise neither to usucapion nor to long-term prescription. But this did not apply to prisoners of war, given that it concerned only those who had justly been sold or had justly sold themselves, unless the captive slave had given their word that they would not escape, which would therefore be perjury, which was prohibited, especially for Christians. Soto does not agree with the claim that it is not permissible to escape slavery generated by war, and this applies to everyone, Christians and infidels alike, "quoniam ius gentium gentibus cunctis aequale est". Even though present in *De iustitia et iure*, the article of the *quaestio* significantly lacks any reference to the idea of a just war. There is mention of it in the gloss by Isidore of Seville on what Gratian says on the law of nations (D. 1. C. 9), but Soto explicitly strays away from this argument. Thus, he ends up identifying a domination that is not correlated with an obligation and it is this that seems to motivate Duck's argument that those who had the strength and historical opportunity to escape Roman rule (both princes *and* peoples – this hendiadys remains constant throughout his work) were completely legitimated in doing so, and that the Romans could not make any claim for their return. The reference to *furtum sui* reappears at the end of Duck's chapter, but the argument is turned on its head. In *Codex* (6.1.1), the matter of imprescriptibility instead applies to the Roman Empire, which cannot use the passing of time to render legitimate an originally unjust domination, just like in the case of *res furtiva*. "Quocirca gentes a Romanis iniuste debellatae possunt post quaecunque saecula, etiam post mille annos, se in libertatem restituere dominiumque earum est in aeternum revocabile, sicut in servo fugitivo qui sui furtum facit; et quae bello amiserunt, possunt iterum bello recuperare, in iis praeserim Provinciis, quas Romani non titulo oneroso, sed per vim acquisiverunt". Duck's reference to the law of *De servis fugitivis*, which is apparently extemporaneous and which created some interpretative problems for the editor of the French version in 1689,[46] can be explained in light of the passage by Soto he had attached, in which it becomes clear that Duck's position conflicts with the pro-imperialism that he attributes at the beginning of Book II (II, 1, 2) to most of the Italian and German jurists, who, in their literal interpretation of the imperial *constitutiones*, maintained a superstitious attitude towards the latter (*DUA*, 56v).

Jurisconsulti nostri juris utriusque interpretes

To explore this key point, let us return to the chapter as a whole. After calling upon the *theologi posteriores* to certify the thesis of the original injustice of the empire, he turns to the "jurisconsulti nostri juris utriusque interpretes". For the most part they extol the virtues of Roman laws and for this reason play a decisive role in Duck's work. In Paragraph XV Duck makes an astonishing number of references, spanning three centuries. Duck's references run from the thirteenth-century canonist Jean Lemoine (read with the *addictiones* of the sixteenth-century Philippus Probus) to Albericus de Rosate[47] and Giovanni d'Andrea,[48] from Sinibaldo Fieschi[49] to Niccolò Tedeschi[50] and Francesco Zabarella,[51] and from Antonio Roselli[52] to the Valencian Pere

46 *De l'Usage et l'Autoritè du Droit Civil*, 21.

47 See *infra*.

48 *Ioannis Andreae Iuris consultum bononiensis in tertium Decretalium librum Novella Commentaria*, Venetiis, Apud Haeredem Hieronymi Scoti, 1612, 173ra n. 12.

49 *Innocentii qvartii Pontificis Maximi in quinque Decretalium libros Commentaria doctissima*, Venetiis, Apud Bernardinum Maiorinum Parmensem, 1570, 256rb n. 10.

50 *Nicolai Abbatis Panormitani Commentaria super prima parte primi Decretalium libri*, Augustae Taurinorum, Apud haeredes Nicolai Bevilaquae, 1577, 156ra n. 18.

51 *Cardinalis Zabarella in librum primum decretalium*, Lugduni, Claude Servain, 1558, 179rb n. 6.

52 *De conciliis ac synodis generalibus libri sex* in *Volumen II Tractatuum ex variis iuris civilis interpretibus collectorum*, Volumen II, Lugduni, Thomas Bertellus, 1549, 65v, that in the most well-known collection on this theme by Melchior Goldast (*Monarchiae S. Romani Imperii, sive Tractatuum de Iurisdictione Imperiali seu Regia et Pontificia seu Sacerdotali*, Tomus Primus, Hanoviae, impensis Conradi Biermanni, 1611, appears with the usual title "Monarchia, sive Tractatus de Potestate Imperatoris et Papae" and is Chapter XII at the beginning of the fifth part (541). The composition and editing of Roselli's work have a complicated history that led to divided interpretations. J.H. Burns traces this history in "The Monarchia of Antonio Roselli (1380–1466): text, context and controversy" in *Proceedings of the Eighth International Congress of Medieval Canon Law*, ed. by Stanley A. Chodorow (Città del Vaticano: Biblioteca Apostolica Vaticana, 1992), 321–351. For a summary of this, see also the entry of Chiara Valsecchi in *Dizionario biografico dei giuristi italiani (XII–XX secolo)*, vol. 2, ed. by I. Birocchi, E. Cortese, A. Mattone, M. N. Miletti (Bologna: Il Mulino, 2013), 1734–1735.

Belluga y Donat.[53] He also cites later authors, such as "Senator Tholosanus" Guglielminus Maynerius,[54] the Orleanian Jean Feu,[55] and the Perugian Ristoro Castaldi,[56] as well as more recent jurists, such as the German Catholic Konrad Braun (Brunus)·,[57] Pierre Rat[58] from Poitiers, and the Spaniard Juan Bautista de Villalobos,[59] as well as Barthélemy de Chasseneuz, author of the successful *Catalogus gloriae mundi*,[60] and Charles Fabrot, whose *Ton Basilikon* Duck mentions the *epistula dedicatoria* to the Chancellor of France, Pierre Séguier.[61] It is a broad collection of diverse and sometimes conflicting authors in which a key position is given to canonists, confirming the persistence of

53 *Speculum Principum D. Petri Bellugae Valentini Iurisconsulti Famosissimi*, Venetiis, Expensis Iacobi Anielli Mariae, Bibliopolae Neapolitani, 1580, ff. 91v–92ra n. 13.

54 *Gulielmi Maynerii doctoris in utroque Commentaria in titulum Pandectarum De regulis iuris*, Ludguni, Apud Antonium Vincentium, 1545, 302va n. 20.

55 *Secunda pars Commentariorum viri Clarissimi Ioannis Ignei iuris utriusque doctoris... in titu lum de Senatoconsulto Sillaniano et Claudiano libro digestorum vigesimonono*, Ludguni, Apud Vincentium de Portonariis, Aureliae, in Aedibus Francisci Gueyardi, 1541, ff. 4v et seq.

56 *Restauri Castaldi Perusini Iureconsulti, Amplissimus tractatus de imperatore*, Romae, Antonij Bladi Asulani, 1540, ff. VIIIv n. 3 and CXXVr n.10. Although he is not in the *Dizionario Biografico dei giuristi italiani*, Castaldi had a certain renown among his contemporaries and his work is cited fairly frequently. Brief mentions of Castaldi can also be found in Agostino Oldoini, *Athenaeum augustum in quo Perusinorum scripta publice exponuntur*, Perusiae, typis, & exspensis L. Ciani et F. Desideri, 1678, 293–294, and with a few corrections in Giovan Battista Vermiglioli, *Biografia degli scrittori perugini e notizie delle opere loro*, t. I, p. II (Perugia: Bartelli e Constantini, 1828), 310–313.

57 *De seditionibus libri sex rationibus et exemplis ex omni doctrinarum et authorum genere locupletati, Authore Clariss. Et Doctiss. Viro Conrado Bruno*, Moguntiæ apud S. Victorem, ex officina Francisci Behem, 1550, 29. The reference text for this German jurist, author among other things of an important work on ambassadorships, is Maria Barbara Rößner, *Konrad Braun (ca. 1495–1563) – ein katholischer Jurist, Politiker, Kontroverstheologe und Kirchenreformer im konfessionellen Zeitalter* (Münster: Aschendorff, 1991). Also see Mario Sbriccoli's discussion of *De seditionibus* in his *Crimen Laesae Maiestatis: Il problema del reato politico alle soglie della scienza penalistica moderna* (Milano: Giuffrè, 1974), *passim*, above all the second chapter of Part III. See also Francesco Migliorino, "Materiali per l'immaginario del nemico interno: Il trattato *De Haereticis* di Konrad Braun", in *Tutto è grazia: In omaggio a Giuseppe Ruggieri*, ed. by A. Melloni (Milano: Jaca Book, 2010), 329–344.

58 *Petri Rat Pictavensis decurionis in Pictonum leges quas vulgus consuetudines dicit glossemata*, Augustoriti Pictonum, Ex officina Antonii Mesnier, 1609, 15.

59 *Antinomia iuris regni Hispaniarum, ac ciuilis, in qua practica forensium causarum versatum authore Ioanne Baptista a Villalobos Hispano ac Toletano*, Salmanticae, Excudebat Alexander a Canova, 1569, f. 1va n. 3.

60 *Catalogus Gloriae mundi, Laudes, honores, excellentias, ac Praeeminentias omnium fere statuum, plurimarumq[ue] rerum illius continens*, Quinta Pars, Cons. 28, Lugduni, per Dionysium de Harsy, 1529, fo. 19v–20r. A comprehensive survey of this comprehensive and boundary breaking jurist can be found in Giovanni Rossi, "Il mondo in un libro: cultura giuridica e sapere enciclopedico nel *Catalogus gloriae mundi*", in *Il Rinascimento giuridico in Francia*, ed. by Giovanni Rossi (Roma: Viella, 2008), 219–262.

61 *ΤΩΝ ΒΑΣΙΛΙΚΩΝ BIBLIA/ΒΑΣΙΛΙΚΩΝ Libri LX. Carolus Annibal Fabrotus Antecessorum Aquisextiensium Decanus Latinè vertit, & Græcè edidit*, Tomus I, Parisiis, Sumptibus Sebastiani Cramoysi et Gabrielis Cramoysi, 1547, fol. *IIIv.

their doctrine even after the Anglican schism.[62] Again, at first glance this long list seems to be at odds with his brief analysis, in which he repeats the same well-worn argument: the Roman Empire fought its wars through violent and tyrannical invasions made up of kidnaps and raids, its only title deriving from war and weapons. Thus, what it called *ius gentium* was, in fact, "protervitas et iniuria gentium", making it completely continuous, in line with Daniel's prophecy, with the empires that preceded it, and thus deserving of the same reproach. The dialogue between the text and the attached citations, however, goes beyond reading them in a strictly literary sense, which is in itself accurate but insufficient. It must be understood in the context of the further references made within the attached passages themselves. For instance, an important connecting role is played by the reference to the two decretals of Innocent III, *Per venerabilem* and *Venerabilem*, collected in the *Liber extra* and the subject of a long debate that eventually settled into the various layers of *utriusque iuris*.[63] Duck moves with ease not only between various time periods, but also between different positions and identities. In this way he touches on themes that still had some doctrinal, even if not strictly speaking political, importance, such as the claim to the universality of the imperial *dominium* or the emperor's presumption of a superordinate position vis-à-vis the princes of the various Christian countries.[64] This provides him with a starting point for the next steps of his argument. We should also note that Duck concludes the paragraph by introducing a notation of an almost anthropological nature, linking his criticism of the conquests with the denunciation of avarice (*avaritia*) and ambition as qualities of the Roman people. "Romam appellant avaritiae caput", he writes, taken from a passage by Philippus Probus in the *additiones* to Lemoine.[65] He also uses Salvianus of Marseilles and Jacques Cujas to confirm this, once again referring to both an ancient and a modern author (*DUA*,

62 See R.H. Helmholz, "Canon Law in Post-Reformation England" in *Canon Law in Protestant Lands*, ed. by R.H. Helmholz (Berlin: Duncker u. Humblot, 1992), 203–221.

63 The relevance of the decretalist reference in influential authors active in the University of Padova in the early fifteenth century (Fulgosio, Zabarella, Roselli, who all passed through Basel for various reasons) is clearly shown in Daniela Rando's text, "La forza vitale di un'idea: l'impero insegnato allo *Studium* di Padova nel primo Quattrocento" in *Emperors and Imperial Discourse in Italy c. 1200–1500*, ed. by Anna Hulbeck (Roma: École Française de Rome, 2022), 105–128.

64 The best example of this is the appended passage by Juan Bautista de Villalobos, a legal practitioner from the second half of the seventeenth century, who swiftly moves, in the course of a few lines, from the rape of the Sabine women to the affirmation that "Rex Hispaniæ non recognoscit superiorem, et est imperator in suo regno", also referencing Du Moulin straight afterwards. See *Antinomia Iuris Regni Hispaniarum*, 1r.

65 *Iohannis Monachi Picardi In Sextum Librum Decretalium Dilucida Commentaria Glossa Aurea Nuncupata, Additionibus Clarissimi I.C. Philippi Probi Biturici*, Venetiis, Apud Iuntas, 1585, f. 98v. On Probus see the contribution by Ennio Cortese, "Philippus Probus, canonista gallicano della prima metà del '500" in *Excerptiones iuris: Studies in Honor of André Gouron*, ed. by Bernard Durand, Laurent Mayali (Berkeley: Robbins Collection, School of Law, 2000), 125–145.

6v–7r). Whereas his references to the *Iulia de repetundarum* and *Iulia de ambitu* laws glossed by Cujas simply express the need to curb the widespread corruption of magistrates and those holding public office in the provinces,[66] his reference to the presbyter Salvianus (Duck gives him the title of bishop, although he was not in fact a bishop) is more significant.

The longevity of the argument certainly strengthens it, with one important difference between the two thinkers. Salvianus was writing in the mid-fifth century, a long time after the promulgation of the abovementioned *leges*, which dates back to the late republic. When Salvianus, in Duck's words, speaks of "avaritiæ inhumanitatem" as "proprium Romanorum poene omnium malum", he is talking about an empire that was almost entirely Christianized, and, in fact, Book VII of *De gubernatione Dei* to which Duck refers deals largely with the Church and the depravity that had taken hold among Christians in the Gallic and African provinces, contrasting them to the morality of the barbarians who were devastating the empire with fire and sword.[67] Although pagans and heretics, they are God's instrument, used to punish the Romans and it is they, once converted, who would be the possible future resource of Christendom. When in the eighteenth century Gibbon referenced Salvianus in *Decline*, he was used as a still somewhat reliable historical source, particularly on Latin Carthage in late antiquity, a subject that is poorly documented.[68] But between the sixteenth and seventeenth centuries things were different. Duck uses a specific edition, identifiable by the variant in the title, printed in Paris in 1615,[69] which reproduced that of 1580[70] by Pierre Pithou. An important jurist with a humanistic vocation, and a pupil and friend of Cujas, through the course of the Iron Century, Pithou, along with many others, shifted from an initial Calvinism to a more or less forced return to Catholicism, finally arriving at a convinced Gallican position.[71] Salvianus's publication places itself in this

66 Jacques Cujas, *Paratitla in libros quinquaginta Digestorum seu Pandectarum Imperatoris Iustiniani*, Coloniae, Apud Maternum Cholinum, 1570, 272–274.

67 On the related historical contexts, see *The Conflict between Paganism and Christianity in the Fourth Century*, ed. by A. Momigliano (Oxford: Clarendon, 1963), in particular the "Introduction" by Momigliano and the essay by A.E. Thompson ("Christianity and the Northern Barbarians").

68 J.G.A. Pocock, *Barbarism and Religion* 6 *Barbarism: Triumph in the West* (Cambridge: Cambridge University Press, 2015), 388.

69 *Salviani Massiliensis presbyteri, de Providentia et Gubernatione dei, et de iusto præsentique eius judicio libri VIII*, Parisiis, Apud Edmum Pepingué, in Aula majori Palatij, prope Aulam Delphin., 1645. Duck references this text as "*De Providentia*".

70 *Salviani Massiliensis De Gubernatione Dei & de iusto præsentique eius judicio libri VIII*, Parisiis, Apud Sebastianum Nivellium, sub Ciconiis, via Iacobea, 1580. On the history of Salviano's text reference should be made to the critical edition edited by George Lagarrigue: Salvien de Marseille, *Oeuvres*, tom. II, *Du Gouvernement de Dieu* (Paris: Cerf, 1975). On Pierre Pithou's edition the eighteenth-century biography by Pierre-Jean Grosley, *Vie de Pierre Pithou* I (Paris: Guillaume Cavelier, 1756), 183–186 is still essential reading.

71 See Donald R. Kelley, *Foundations of Modern Historical Scholarship: Language, Law, and History in the French Renaissance* (New York and London: Columbia University Press, 1970),

Gallican context, as testified by the long dedication to his friend and collaborator Nicolas Le Fèvre. Duck's focus on Salvianus also follows this Gallican line, without daring to say that the latter could be seen as a moment in a non-Roman genealogy of churches, which was a problem for those in seventeenth-century England in search of an ecclesiological background to the Reformation. Salvianus nevertheless provides Duck with useful tools for dismantling theological support for the legal justification of imperial rule, offering a different perspective to Orosius, but also to Augustine himself. Although Duck puts Salvianus into opposition with Augustine, it seems unlikely that the *De gubernatione Dei* contains direct criticism of the latter, also because Salvianus's knowledge of Augustine's texts, although chronologically plausible, is not supported by documentary evidence.[72]

From Paragraph XVI onwards, Duck adopts an openly controversialist tone, making explicit what was hidden in the attached citations and re-reading many of them in a different light, drawing attention to their ambivalence in relation to the very matter they helped determine. "Ex Theologis tamen et Jurisconsultis non pauci defendunt justitiam Romanorum in acquirendis Dominiis, asserentes, eos juste armis suis usos eorumque imperium justum et legitimum fuisse". Despite his assertive tone, we see a shift in his discourse: at this point justice and legitimacy concern the maintenance of acquisition and the stabilization of ownership, rather than how they were acquired, and therefore many who denounced the ways in which they were acquired believed there were nevertheless arguments in favour of the empire. Duck organizes his counter-argument into three parts, but already in the above quoted passage clearly sets out the terrain and goal of his argument. He mentions three people: the aforementioned Albericus de Rosate, the Modenese Fulvio Paciani, and Alberico Gentili. To the first two correspond two citations that are closely connected, so much so that the second acts as a summary of the first. The passage by Albericus de Rosate, from his commentary on the first part of the Codex (I, tit. *De summa Trinitate*, l. 1 *Cum cunctos populos*), is worth citing[73]: "Quicquid tamen sit, supra dictum videtur mihi suam veritatem dici posse, quod imperium Romanum initium habuit a violentia, et non a iustitia, ut ex superioribus satis patet. Et idem credo de omnibus aliis regibus, et potentibus, quia videamus, quod qui plus potest, plus rapit, nisi reperiantur vel a Deo processisse, vel aliquo iusto titulo". Duck had already used this citation in the past, but it is what follows it that interests him now:

241–270 ("The Historical School of French Law: Pierre Pithou Introduces Philology into Medieval Studies").

72 David Lambert, "The Uses of Decay: History in Salvian's *De Gubernatione Dei*", *Augustinian Studies*, 30:2 (1999), 115–130.

73 *Alberici De Rosate Bergomensis, Iurisconsulti Clarissimi Ac Summi Practici. In Primam Codicis Partem Commentarij*, Venetiis, Sub Signo Aquilae Renouantis, 1586, 8r n. 20. Albericus was an author that Duck returned to fairly often and this specific reference in the text appears a number of times.

> Credo tantum imperium Romanorum, et alia regna processisse permissione, et voluntate divina propter bonum commune, quia commodius est regi, per unum, quam per plures ut optime probatur *de potestate Papali et imperiali*, c. j. *quid sit regnum, et unde habeat ortum*, et credo quod per longissimum consensum provinciarum et populorum, qui voluntarie sussuerunt imperio[,] vitium violentiae fuisse purgatum, et dissensum transuisse, in consensum, ut infra *de his quae vi metusve* [Cod., II, tit. 19] causa gesta sunt l. II et IIII unde hoc considerato potest dici iustum imperium, et omnes nationes sibi obedire debere secundum quod probant iura praedicta, et opiniones praedictorum doctorum, et glossatorum.

The central point is thus the *purgatio* that redeems the empire from its original vice. This follows from two factors: first, the recognition of the divine concession that, as with previous empires, was given on the basis of the common good, which is always better governed by one than by many; and, second, enduring consensus by the subject peoples, which transformed resistance into acceptance. In this way, Albericus can consistently claim not only the *iustitia* of the empire, but also its excellence. Referring explicitly to Alighieri's *Monarchia*, he continues: "Et hoc est subtilissime, et per Philosophicas, et probabiles rationes probant ille valens [D]antes de Fiorentia, in quodam suo libello de civitate [Nardi reads 'necessitate'] monarchiae ubi querit, et disputat tres quaestiones. Primo an ad bene esse mundi, sit necessaria monarchia. Secundo an Romanus populus de iure monarchie officium assumpserit. Tertio an auctoritas monarchie dependat a Deo immediate, vel ab alio Dei ministro, seu vicario". Albericus then examines how the emperor derives his authority from election alone, referring back to Innocent III's decretal, Dante's text, and the *De potestate papali et imperiali*, "c. 7 et pluribus capitulis sequentibus", by Johannes Parisi, also known as Jean Quidort. In closing he makes reference to other titles of the Codex, *in primis* title 37.3 of Book VII, *Bene a Zenone*, in which the same references appear.[74] Albericus creates an unusual mosaic of an argument, having to reshape the various pieces to make them fit together, as so many of them pose serious problems to historical reconstruction. It is no surprise that Albericus's argument has been the subject of close analysis, with different readings focusing on different individual features of it, from the "juridical Danteanism", which provides its dominant tone, to the involvement of Quidort.[75] However, none of these readings seems to properly

74 *Alberici De Rosate Bergomensis, Iurisconsulti Clarissimi Ac Summi Practici: In Secundam Codicis Partem Commentarij*, Venetiis, Sub Signo Aquilae Renouantis, 1585, 107v–108r.

75 The earliest essay on Dante and Quidort is by Carlo Cipolla, "Il trattato *de Monarchia* di Dante Alighieri e l'opuscolo *De Potestate regia et Papali* di Giovanni di Parigi" (1892), now found in *Gli studi danteschi* (Verona, 1921), 175–300, which is certainly dated, but it does not merit the *damnatio memoriae* that he has been subject to due to the critiques of him by Hans Kelsen in *Die Staatslehre des Dante Alighieri* (Wien: Franz Deuticke, 1905). Many

grasp Albericus's argument as a whole. Furthermore, there is no *libellus* by Quidort with the title that Albericus gives it, and neither does it seem to appear in the manuscripts. However, a text called *De potestate regia et papali* (sometimes with the terms reversed) does exist, and Albericus's references seem to match it. In the substitution of *regali* with *imperiali* we see a shifting of the argument from one figure to the other, a shift in which Albericus seems to be fully invested.[76] Although there were constant transfers and annexations between the two registers of Roman-canonical law, this case is different: despite the fact that moments of contact, without proof of direct influence, can be found between Quidort's and Alighieri's reflections, Albericus's work tends to reduce the thought of the two men to a single position. This leaves little room for other lines of interpretation and is echoed in the way in which Quidort was first received. As Jean Leclercq points out: "C'est en Italie que nous rencontrerons le premier témoignage explicite de l'influence de Jean de Paris en matière politique: Alberic de Rosate, commentant le Code Justinien à Bologne vers 1340, invoque notre théologien comme une autorité en matière du droit civil; il lui emprunte des longues citations et il le loue avec insistance à l'égal de Dante; mais il applique à l'empereur tout ce que Jean de Paris a écrit du pouvoir royal".[77] More than three centuries later, Duck relies heavily on Albericus's interpretation of Quidort, which is interesting given that the proto-Gallican aspects of Quidort's thought clearly lent themselves to a more sympathetic reading by Duck. Duck must have had some knowledge of Quidort, at least from what Bellarmino says ("propensior … erga Regem, quam erga Pontificem"),[78] but also because the Parisian is frequently referred to in the texts Duck uses and often right next to the parts he cites. On the other hand, Albericus's position[79] seems to be supported by the fact that the

of these critiques, driven by a demand for systematicity, seem to be unfounded. Both texts ignore, or almost ignore, Albericus. Bruno Nardi's text "Fortuna della Monarchia nei sec. XIV e XV" in his *Nel mondo di Dante* (Roma: Edizioni di Storia e letteratura, 1944), 161–205, is focused on Albericus and his passages in the *Commentarii*, touching on Quidort somewhat in passing. A broader and more structured treatment is given in Mario Conetti's detailed essay, "La dottrina dell'Impero e la donazione di Costantino in Alberico da Rosciate", *Studi di Storia del diritto II* (Milano: Giuffrè, 1999), 305–405.

76 In the essay cited above (328), Conetti points out that in his will Albericus indicates the copy of Quidort that he owns with the same title used in the *Commentarii*. Conetti infers from this that that title pre-existed Quidort's interference. However, this argument is not particularly convincing.

77 Jean Leclercq, *Jean de Paris et l'ecclésiologie du XIIIe siècle* (Paris: Vrin, 1942), 152–153 (a seminal text, even though it contains an inaccuracy: Albericus, "Doctissimus Practicus" not only did not teach in Bologna, but also never taught at all). Leclercq's opinion is repeated by A.P. Monahan in the introduction to John of Paris, *On Royal and Papal Power: A Translation, with Introduction, of the* De Potestate Regia et Papali *of John of Paris* (New York: Columbia University Press, 1974), xlvii.

78 Roberto Bellarmino, *De scriptoribus ecclesiasticis*, 217.

79 On this, see l'*Epistula dedicatoria* to Massimiliano II that Schard includes in his collection *De imperiali jurisdictione, autoritate et praeeminentia Imperii atque juribus Regni syntagma*

first printed editions of *De potestate regia et papali* were to be found in pro-imperial collections such as that by the Lutheran Simon Schard (Schardius) and the Calvinist Melchior Goldast in which the contestation of the Constantinian donation was a key theme. Of course, this does not rule out the possibility that between the lines of *De Potestate* there is a very different use of Albericus. But as we have said, what matters to Duck and motivates his use of Albericus can be found in the following citation: "Attamen hodie imperium Romanum dicitur esse iustum, quia per longissimum consensum populorum, et provinciarum, quæ semper tacuerunt, et voluntarie Imperatoribus obedierunt, tenendum est, omne vitium violéntiæ fuisse purgatum, et dissensum transivisse in consensum accedente maximè approbatione Sanctæ matris Ecclesiæ, ut tradit Alber[icus]".[80] The tacit consent of peoples and territories is tied to theological approval. This is the doctrinal perspective, or at least its earliest version, that Duck intends to challenge. Duck adds the name of Alberico Gentili to those of Albericus de Rosate and Paciani, thus problematizing this perspective and giving it a more contemporary form.

Of Duck Using Gentili

He does not deal with a specific passage by Gentili, but with an entire work, *De Armis Romanis*, indicating its last chapter, Chapter XIII of Book II, on the "Fortuna Imperii Romani".[81] It is clear that this is not just one text among others, not only because of the author's importance among civilians, but also

tractatuum, Basileae, Johannes Oporinus, 1566: "Quam invictis argumentis, præter Parrisium, Babenbergium, et Dantem, Cusanus et Valla commenticiam Constantini donationem refellerunt? Quam solidis ac firmis rationibus Parrisius, et post eum Dantes, ordinis Politici ac Ecclesiastici potestate, et dignitate in utramque partem discussa, Thrasonicam pontificum, se Imperatoribus præferentium superbiam redarguit, ostendens potestatem politicam Ecclesiasticæ minimè subiectam: nec papam aliquod ius in Imperium habere, sed ei spiritualia, mundana soli Imperatori commissa esse?", 16.

80 *Tractatus Fulvii Paciani Mutinensis, comitis, d. et equitis, cui incumbat onus probandi, liber primus et secundus: opus noviter impressum, et tanta doctrina, tantaque praxi refertum, ut advocatis, procuratoribus, causidicis, & omnibus aliis in foro versantibus nihil utilius, aut magis*, Francofurti ad Moenum, Sumptibus Godefridi Tampachij, Typis Caspari Rotelii, 1631, 662 n. 55. The two-book treatise on the Modena born Paciani, known as *De Probationibus*, which is not really a doctrinal text, had been widely circulated in various editions in Venice and in Germany due to its practical leanings. For more on Paciani, see the entry by Raffaele Volante in the *Dizionario Biografico dei giuristi italiani* II, 1479.

81 *Alberici Gentilis IC. Clarissimi, Professoris Regii, De Armis Romanis Libri duo*, Hanoviæ, Apud Guilielmum Antonium, 1599. The chapter is not indicated in the contents page, but it is, in fact, included in pages 266–284. What drew attention to Gentili's work after its long absence (after the seventeenth-century editions it was reprinted a few times in the eighteenth century) was its reproposition within the new phase of international legal historiography. See Alberico Gentili, *The Wars of the Romans. A Critical Edition and Translation of* De armis Romanis, edited by B. Kingsbury, B. Straumann (Oxford: Oxford University Press, 2011), preceded by a book of essays with the same editors, *The Roman Foundations of the Law of Nations: Alberico Gentili and the Justice of Empire* (Oxford: Oxford University Press, 2011).

because of its title. Published by Gentili the year after *De iure belli*, *De Armis* is clearly complementary to the larger work, but differs from it in terms of structure and genre. Constructed as a diptych, it follows the model of a forensic dispute: in the first book ("De iniustitia bellica Romanorum Actio") an accuser, *Picenus*, insists on the injustice of Roman wars and their acquisitions, while in the second ("De iustitia bellica Romanorum Defensio") a defender, *Romanus*, claims their complete legitimacy and, rebutting the charges point by point, refers to the Roman Empire as an example of political wisdom, a model in which utility and justice, realism and virtue sit side by side and, in some way, influence each other. And so, in the chapter referenced by Duck, Gentili counterposes fortune and tyranny, the issue with which Chapter XIII of Book I, entitled *Tyrannis Romanorum*, concluded. Gentili resolves the opposition between fortune and virtue, a Machiavellian opposition of which he is well aware, with the idea that the good fortune of the Romans, which allowed them to govern situations to their own advantage, is due to the fact that their fortune was animated by *virtus* and thus capable of being understood juridically. On this basis, he can reject the accuser's recrimination of the fortuitous character of Roman conquests.

The centuries-long debate on the question of just war and justice in war is reexamined in Gentili through the lens of his own context, whose radical novelty and plurality of subjects left no room for anachronisms. In Chapter XXIII of the first book of *De iure* ("De regnorum eversionibus"), Gentili pointed out the continuity between the Roman Empire and its Franco-Germanic metamorphosis, in a strong version of the *translatio imperii*. However, he is clear that the latter cannot be used to make any demand or instigate any action, and does not lead back to the political vision underlying Albericus de Rosate's legal writing. Duck is completely aware of this Gentilian attitude and would resort to it a number of times to critique those who remained stuck in anachronistic positions that have almost become sacred. Thus, we could see *De Armis* as a model drawing its strength from the *exempla*, which, through the skillful use of historical narration and rhetoric, Gentili transformed into a normative repertoire usable in a new historical moment.[82] Duck has a remarkably different approach. In the list of names that Duck attaches, the empire

See also the more recent reading by Valentina Vadi, *War and Peace: Alberico Gentili and the Early Modern Law of Nations* (Leiden: Brill, 2020).

82 On this perspective, see Diego Panizza, "Alberico Gentili's *De Armis Romanis*: The Roman Model of the Just Empire", in B. Kingsbury and B. Straumann, *The Roman Foundations*, 53–84, and "Il *De Armis Romanis* di Alberico Gentili: Paradigmi imperiali, guerra e la 'moderna cosmopoli'", *Filosofia politica*, XXV 2 (2011), 215–226, that develop a long reflection on the Gentili, which began with the seminal *Alberico Gentili, giurista ideologo nell'Inghilterra elisabettiana* (Padova: La Garangola, 1981). On *De Armis*, see the detailed essay by Alain Wijffels, "Antiqui et Recentiores: Alberico Gentili – Beyond Mos Italicus and Legal Humanism", in *Reassessing Legal Humanism and Its Claims. Petere Fontes?*, ed. by Paul J. du Plessis, John W. Cairns (Edinburgh: Edinburgh University Press, 2016), 11–40.

as such is never the most important issue. He sees it as outdated, and he is apparently uninterested in its relation to the increasingly imperial dimension of seventeenth-century powers. He is however interested in denying that Roman law is dependent on its imperial contextualization, without, of course, denying that that imperial context exists. Gentili brings *arma* and *leges* together again, aware that to do so he must also let the criticisms against the empire be heard, even conceding some factual points to these critiques, but only in order to refute them. This is the complete opposite of what Duck claims to do and indeed does. It is hard not to see the argumentative structure of *De Armis* reproduced in Duck's text, especially in this chapter, making the latter appear as a counterpoint to the former, at times in a very pointed way. Their arguments are thus almost specular, even if they reach opposite conclusions. However, their sources are different, with Duck embracing those that Gentili tends to exclude with sarcasm ("obscuri illi monachi, id est tenebriones, nec modo exteri reipublicæ").[83]

Duck sees *De Armis* as an important point of comparison that lays out the contours of a significant controversy. His response to it deserves attention, if only because it is unusual in its engagement with Gentili's work, which had been poorly received. It is striking that Duck's treatment of Gentili has not been discussed in recent years by those revisiting Gentili's work, not even by those who are interested in both authors. But this does not tell the whole story of Duck's ambivalent relationship with Gentili's heritage (a comparison between natural law and *ius gentium* could be helpful here). Duck's encounter with Gentili is, in fact, rather awkward and should be contextualized within Gentili's reception among English *civilians* after King James I. This explains, at least in part, why his opposition to Gentili is never made explicit, instead remaining in the citations for those who know how to read them, first and foremost the Roman-canon law jurists whose unity as a community of discourse Duck aims to defend despite their differences. We find the second reference to *De Armis*, again in the chapter "Fortuna Imperii Romani" at the end of *De Usu*, as the last citation of the second book, just before the *Conclusio operis* (*DUA*, 181v). Its placing is important: Duck had just expressed admiration for the divine goodness and power that overthrew the rule of the emperors and ensured that the "legum Cesaraerum imperium" had remained in Europe to his day, so that, after shaking off the yoke of the Romans, the Europeans had spontaneously submitted to their laws. He makes particular reference to the situation in France by referencing Chapter 38 of the ninth book of *Les Recherches de la France* by Étienne Pasquier ("Du nouvel ordre de la Pratique iudiciaire que nos ancestres enterent sur le Droict Civil des Romains").[84] He also reminds us that even those who were not conquered by the Romans

83 *Alberici Gentilis IC. Clarissimi, Professoris Regii, De Armis Romanis*, 92.
84 Paris, chez Pierre Menard, 1643, 899–900. We use a complete edition that is as close to the original *De Usu* as possible.

embraced their laws. Duck references Gentili at this point, in an ambivalent cross-reference in which consent and dissent coincide or diverge in each passage according to the scale at which he is analysing them. There is also a more general reason why he does not express overt opposition to *De Armis*. Duck's text does not aim to be an Anti-Gentili, as his goal differs from Gentili's. Although necessary, the separation of arms from laws is merely preliminary to his main argument.

Roma domina mundi, magistra errorum: *The Issue of Consent*

Let's return to the last pages of the opening chapter of Duck's first book. Three lines of argument lay out the main topic that Duck intends to refute, based on what had been anticipated in the texts of Albericus de Rosate, Paciani, and Alberico Gentili. The first has a theological character, while the second and third are purely juridical. In this passage, Duck retraces the structure of the entire chapter, bringing it to a conclusion. Of those who defend the justice of the Roman conquests, some derive their reason ("causam petunt") from God's will, in continuity with the prophetic tradition that had attributed divine assignment to the Assyrian, Persian and Greek monarchs in the Bible. His objection here takes a hermeneutical form. How are the words of prophets to be understood? Duck borrows his interpretation not from theologians, but from a great fourteenth-century jurist, Andrea d'Isernia, who, precisely when speaking of "Roma domina mundi, magistra errorum", clearly distinguishes "a Deo praecipiente, et iubente" from "a Deo permittente, et sinente".[85] Rome achieved "talis dominium, talis potentia" due to a God who permits and tolerates rather than directs and commands, meaning that no legitimacy can be derived from its victories as such. Duck applies this distinction to the entire history of world empires, making it a general interpretative category, and, supported by other references, including the aforementioned Molina and Braun and the Monferrato-born Paolo Carraria,[86] it becomes the

85 *D. Andreae de Isernia In Usus Feudorum Commentaria*, Lugduni, Sumptibus Phillippi Tighi, 1579, 4rb, n. 30.

86 *De litterali ac mystica regularum iuris canonici interpretatione et veritate, etc. Auctore Fratre Paulo Carraria de Casali Montisferrati*, Bononiae, apud haeredes Ioannis Rossi, 1617, 268a n. 78. Carraria insists on the false universality of the empires. Despite their claims, their monarchs "non tamen totum potuerunt orbem sibijpsiis subijcere quin maior pars remaneret libera, et sub aliis potentatibus. Et quia violenter fuerunt introducti, nec perpetuo esse potuerunt. Quare effracti sunt, et ad nihilum redacti, ut patuit per figuram in illa Danielis statua". The point indicated by Duck (Quaest. iii, art. IX) is as follows: "Quare omnino dicendum et deducendum est, non esse de facto, nec de iure dari posse unum Imperatorem totius mundi". This is interesting because it demonstrates significant dissent within the Italian context in relation to the supposed pro-imperialist position, via Bartolus and Baldus, between jurists (on this point see Rodolfo De Mattei, "Il mito della Monarchia Universale nel pensiero politico italiano del Seicento", *Rivista di Studi Politici Internazionali*, 32:4 (Ottobre–Dicembre 1965), 531–550). But the whole course of article IX leads towards a conclusion on divine

foundation of his argument. Of these, Luis Molina provides him with the strongest doctrinal support. Speaking of Daniel's four empires, and agreeing that the last is the Roman Empire, Molina argued that empires were just if the wars through which they were acquired were just. If, on the other hand, the wars were unjust, then the empires were unjust. It is probable, he added, that these empires were largely acquired unjustly, as asserted by, among others, the French Dominican Durandus de Sainct Purcain (De Sancto Porciano), the Dutchman Albert Pigge (Pighius), and the Flemish Johannes Driedo. This is why Daniel referred to these kingdoms not as human beings, but as wild animals. Although it might be argued that the Holy Scriptures sometimes say that these kingdoms were granted by God, we must remember that God only granted them in the form of permitting them ("permittendo") and using them to punish the sins of men. If it is objected that Paul, in Romans 13, and Peter in Acts I, 2 spoke of the *potestates* of their time, thus those of the Romans, we must argue that they spoke of them in general, without considering or determining whether a specific *potestas* was legitimate. "Quoniam esto in se tales non essent non spectabat ad eos tunc id docere, neque expediebat".[87] Duck aimed to do away with any idea that retribution could legitimize imperial conquests. God admits these conquests only permissively, that is, so that they fulfill a punitive role for sins and certainly not as a rewarding element for the *potestates*, who are "ignorantes" and engage in these conquests in an economy that eludes men. As a result, throughout history there has been a transfer of empires and kingdoms from one people to another and from one prince to another.[88] Even tyrants and evil people can play a ministerial role in this sense, with God using them "ut Ministris suis in vindictam peccatorum". The story of the Roman Empire is no exception. Its successes were not granted to it as gratification for its "sanctissimae leges" and alleged virtues, but rather to counter and punish (*coercere*) the tyranny and wickedness of other peoples. On this point, Duck criticizes an important doctrine that suggested that the Romans had some moral superiority that justified their actions, even if this put him in conflict with the likes of Augustine, Jerome, and Aquinas.[89] In making Rome

permissio being insufficient to produce a legitimate title: "Nec valet dicere, quòd Deus hoc permiserit, et quòd ex hac permissione acquisiverunt sibi iustum titulum Dominij. Hoc certè nihil est dictum. Permissio namque non facit iustum titulum. Romani enim permissi erant habere potestatem in terris Iudæorum".

87 *R.P. Lodovici Molinae Primarii Quondam in Ebonensi Academia S. Theologiae, E Societate Jesu, De Iustitia et Iure Tomi VI*, Tomus Primus, Coloniae Agrippinae, sumptibus Hermanii Mylii, 1614, Tract. II, Disp. 24, n. 11, col. 122.

88 "Regnum a gente in gentem transfertur propter injustitias, et injurias, et contumelias, et diversos dolos" (*Ecclesiasticus*, 10, 8). Duck's biblical references are always according to the Clementine Vulgate, therefore according to the Catholic canon, which, however, was not unusual even in the Protestant area for those using the Latin version of the Bible.

89 Duck refers, following Castaldi (vedi infra), for Jerome to C. 28 q. 1., post c. 14, pars V § 2 ("c. omnes") (but it is an indirect source) and for Thomas to Chapter 5 of Book III of *De Regimine Principum* entitled "Qualiter Romani meruerunt dominium propter leges sanctissi-

homologous with other empires, Duck is aware of a possible objection that points to the Roman Empire's singularity as a messianic scene for Christians. He counterbalances this by comparing it ("eodemque modo") with another moment in sacred history, referencing Deuteronomy when Moses scorned the arrogance of the Israelites by reminding them that it was not for their virtues that God had granted them the Canaan, but as a punishment and torment for the Canaanites.

The insistence on divine *permissio* radically complicates the idea of legitimacy, shattering its unitary character. Our Lord commands, so the Apostles teach, that in Judea, as everywhere in the subject provinces, tribute must be paid to the Caesars and their magistrates, because they are their legitimate princes. The divine derivation of all *potestas* is undoubtable and those who dominate must be obeyed. And so it is too with the law of nations. But Duck insists that the Roman occupation of Judea is still illegitimate because it lacked *legitima causa*. And applying as it does to all similar cases, it takes on a paradigmatic character. Thus he concludes, in the very brief paragraph XVII, "permissionem vero divinam non esse justum belli inferendi Imperiique acquirendi titulum, Theologi et Jurisconsulti asserunt, et Deus videtur reprobasse Romanum imperium quod injuste inceperit" (*DUA*, 7v), to which he attached *ad hoc* a passage by the Venetian Pietro del Monte.[90] The conclusion

---

mas quas tradiderunt", which, as with everything that follows Chapter 4 of Book II, was written by Ptolemy of Lucca, who completed the text some forty years later. Also see the passage by Vazquez that he attaches straight afterwards, which, indicating how that chapter should be read, offers a more complex interpretation: "Unde ut aliquo tempore id Deus permisit propter eorum virtutem sic aliis nationibus et regionibus concessurum non dubium erit aut forte iam concessisse si quidem iis virtutibus excellere coeperint: morum enim vicissitudo et mutatio quotidie sit; sic ergo et imperiorum fiet, siquidem mores imperia insequi intellexerimus", *Vasquii Menachensis Controversiarum illustrium aliarumque usu frequentium libri tres*, liber primus, Venetiis, Apud Franciscum Rampazetum, 1564, c. 20, n. 32–32, 64v. However, it is likely that in the face of this reelaboration the reasons for Duck's objections not only remain but even increase.

90 "Concludunt aliqui imperium Deo nullum fuisse institutum", *Monarchia Petri de Monte veneti episcopi Brixiensis in qua generalium conciliorum materia de postestate prestantia & excellentia Romani pontificis & imperatoris plenissime discutitur ex proprio originali Felini Sandei transcripta*, Lugduni, editore sub signo Angeli [Vincent de Portonariis], 1512, 95. The *De summis pontificis, generalis concilii et imperialis maiestatis origine et potestate* (circa 1434), was given the new title *Monarchia* from the late 1400s onwards, due to its strongly anticonciliarist tone. On Pietro del Monte, who incidentally spent five years in England as the pontifical legate, see the entry by Diego Quaglioni in the *Dizionario Biografico dei Giuristi Italiani* I, 740–741, and David Rundle, "Carneades' Legacy: The Morality of Eloquence in the Humanist and Papalist Writings of Pietro del Monte", *The English Historical Review*, Vol. 117, No. 471 (Apr., 2002), 284–305. There is also a mention of Del Monte in England and his relationship with Henry Chichele, whose biography Duck wrote as a young man (*Vita Henrici Chichele Archiepiscopi Cantuariensis sub Regibus Henrici V et VI descripta ab Arthuro Duck*, Oxoniae, Excudebat Josephus Barnesius, 1617), in Anthony Black, *Monarchy and Community: Political Ideas in the Later Conciliar Controversy 1430–1450* (Cambridge: Cambridge University Press, 1970), 99–102.

of the preceding paragraph is relevant to the next controversial passage. The legitimacy of the Romans' command over the provinces is time limited: "dum tamen Resplublicae et populi eos tolerabant, eorum constitutiones et præcepta observare tenebantur". The providential dimension that sees the transfer of kingdoms and empires in virtue of the punishment of sins thus has a prosaic and secular impact.

Duck then addresses the other two lines of argument that claim the *iustitia* of the empire. Although presented separately, they are strongly interrelated and had already been anticipated in the attached references. The first concerns the *consent* of defeated princes and peoples, who, although initially unjustly forced to submit by violence, had ended up accepting Roman rule and thereby made it just. This would therefore be analogous to what canon law (*Decretum*, xv, 1.21–xv, 17.7) argues in relation to a marriage originally contracted *per vim et metum* that becomes legitimate only by subsequent consent. This is the *purgatio* thesis, which, as we have already seen, was supported by Albericus de Rosate and Paciani, and before that by Molina and Salas, to which Duck here adds Castaldi[91] again and the Bolognese Francesco Giovannetti,[92] thus

91 *Restauri Castaldi Perusini Iureconsulti, Amplissimus tractatus de imperatore* q. 69 n. 10, 125r, that relies heavily on *De regimine principum* on *c. omnes* to affirm the virtuous singularity of the Roman Empire over the three previous empires described in Daniel's prophecy. The whole of Castaldi's *quaestio* plays an important role for Duck because it offers a broad survey of the pro-imperial material that he needs for his references. It is worth nothing the use that Castaldi makes of the booklet that the Venetian humanist Girolamo Balbi writes on the occassion of the coronation of Carlo V in Bologna, *Hieronimi Balbi Episcopi Gurcensis, De Coronatione Liber Singularis ad Carolum V*, Argentorati, Typis Iosiae Rihelio, per Andream Rietschium, 1530, where the title *De potestate papali et imperiali* (but it was modelled on Albericiano) reappears for the text by Quidort, in connection with Dante, Aquinas and, "omnium postremus", Antonio Roselli. Balbi considered the coronation of the emperor by the pope not to be necessary, which resulted in his excommunication. On Balbi and his fate, see Marco Cavina, *Imperator romanorum triplici corona coronatur: Studi sull'incoronazione imperiale nella scienza giuridica italiana fra Tre e Cinquecento* (Milano: Giuffrè, 1991), 173-181. Balbi is linked with the earlier Roselli in the critique by Navarro; see *Relectio C. Novit de Iudiciis non minus sublimis quam celebris pronunciata ... per Martinum ab Azpilcueta*, Lugduni, apud Guilelmum Rovillum, 1576, III Notabile, n. 43, 104.

92 *Francisci Zoannetti De Romano Imperio ac eius Iurisdictione*, Ingolstadii, Per Vueyssenhornios fratres, 1563, 54r. The point in question is 231, but it is important to bear in mind that this adds fuel to a critique, also shared by Castaldi, but here expressed in extremely violent terms, against the famous *consilium* 69 (*Consuevit dubitari an omnes reges*) by Oldrado da Ponte from Lodi, which clearly, even two centuries later, continued to be a subject of controversy for those who supported the empire, as shown in Chapter VI ("L'*auctoritas* di Oldrado da Ponte e la sua influenza sul pensiero giuridico successivo") of Chiara Valsecchi's wide-ranging work, *Un'auctoritas del primo Trecento: Oldrado da Ponte e i suoi consilia* (Milano: Giuffrè, 2000) 673–715. Oldrado is an author who Duck knew well (vedi *infra*) and in *De Usu* his role goes beyond the specific moments in which he is referred to. For more on Oldrado, see all of Valsecchi's book and, specifically on *consilium* 69, see Gerald Montagu, "Roman Law and the Emperor: The Rationale of 'Written Reason' in some *Consilia* of Oldradus da Ponte", *History of Political Thought* 15, No. 1 (Spring 1994), 1–56, that reproduces the text of *consilium* 69 in its appendix. On Francesco Giovannetti or Zoanetti, a former student of Alciato and for a long

demonstrating the existence of a doctrinal path stretching right up to the sixteenth century.

Here, however, it is not the analogy that is at issue, but the consent, of which there is no clear testimony, even in cases in which we can assume it was expressed, and it certainly cannot be seen as a general condition. "Non constat omnes consentisse, dum pauci consenserint" (*DUA*, 8r). Duck rather obliquely attributes this opinion to the canonist Martín de Azpilcueta, from Navarra, the *doctor Navarrus*, in a contracted argumentative step, the thrust of which lies in the references.[93] Navarrus disputes that the universal uniqueness of the *imperium laicum*[94] can be deduced from Jerome's well-known passage in the *Decretum* (C.7 q.1 c.41) on the subject of bees and cranes having only one king. In fact, while it is true that a *civitas* governed by one is dictated by nature, it is equally true that there is a multiplicity of *civitates*, a thesis Navarrus had formulated in the preceding passage in words taken explicitly from Quidort's *De Potestate*. In short, every beehive has a monarch, but there are multiple beehives, and so the imperial claim is groundless "nulla naturali ratione". So Duck adds, explaining for those who might not have understood: "neque constat de consensu Principum, de quorum jure praesertim agitur". He then goes on to question the legitimacy of consent given in a state of enduring fear, which must be understood as forced and therefore not capable of creating an obligation, as is said in D.4.2.1 about the edict of the praetor, whose words to Baldo, which cite the Spanish canonist Raimundo de Peñafort,

time a teacher at Ingolstadt, then returning to Bologna, see: the work of Luigi Rossi, *Gli scrittori politici bolognesi* (Bologna: Società Tipografica già Compositori, 1888), 110–117; and the entry by Angela de Benedictis in the *Dizionario Biografico dei Giuristi Italiani* I, 1007–1008. David A. Lines, "Managing Academic Insubordination at the University of Bologna", in Jill Kraye, Marc Laureys, and David A. Lines (eds.), *Management and Resolution of Conflict and Rivalries in Renaissance Europe* (Göttingen: Bonn University Press, 2023) 139–159, also supplies biographical and contextual information on his Bolognese period. A detailed survey of all these authors is given by Vincenzo Piano Mortari in the first chapter ("L'impero all'inizio dell'età moderna") of his *Il potere sovrano nella dottrina giuridica del secolo XVI* (Napoli: Liguori, 1973), 7–33, which points out that "non può sfuggire, in ogni modo, un disinteresse sempre più diffuso nella letteratura giuridica europea del secolo XVI per i problemi cui si è fatto cenno", 16.

93 *Relectio C. Novit de Iudiciis non minus sublimis quam celebris pronunciata … per Martinum ab Azpilcueta*, Lugduni, apud Guilelmum Rovillum, 1576, 132. The point in question is III Notabile, n. 160. Duck had already mentioned De Azpilcueta in Chapter XVIII, naming him as one of those who accepted the argument that imperial justice was based on merit. On him see Vincenzo Lavenia, "Martin de Azpilcueta (1492–1586). Un profilo", Archivio italiano di storia della pietà, 16 (2003), 15–148.

94 An overview of the metaphor on bees and beehives can be found in Pietro Costa, "Le api e l'alveare: Immagini dell'ordine fra 'antico' e 'moderno'", AA.VV. *Ordo Iuris: Storia e forma dell'esperienza giuridica*, (Milano: Giuffrè, 2023), 373–409. The figure of the beehive returns repeatedly, used in reference both to the church and to the kingdom, as evidenced by the influential interventions of Calvin and Bellarmine. Useful on this subject is Jonathan Woolfson, "The Renaissance of Bees", *Renaissance Studies* 24:2 (2010), 281–300.

seem to be inspired by the Holy Spirit.[95] Rather than stressing the cliché of the *sanctissimae leges*, Duck is keen to counterpose them to the supporters of the Impero *iustum*, a position that he develops fully in the conclusion.

A Matter of Fact Rather Than of Law

The second line of argument claiming the *iustitia* of the empire revolves around the claim of the prescriptive force of duration, which for Duck is the other side of tacit consent. Those princes and peoples defeated by Roman armies had been dominated for so long that the Romans had established a prescriptive right to what they had acquired without title. Time cleansed violence and *vitium* and transformed the subjugation of the vanquished into acceptance of the victors. Although this argument had its supporters, it was in conflict with the "communis Jurisconsultorum sententia," which for every prescription requires title and good faith,[96] which, as taught by "Romanae leges et omnia iura", are necessarily lacking in a line of succession that has persisted in "vitio et culpa": "insistentes possessioni injustae vim continuo exercere dicantur." Without qualification, time only reproduces injustice and "praescrivere volentibus mala fides in aeternum obstetet," since "in re per vim possessa origo semper spectanda" (Q. 41.2.6). Duck insists on the figure of prescription, separating off its acquisitive variant, but his approach is essentially "negative": any reference to canonical tradition seems to be primarily aimed at tracing its limits.[97]

95 *Baldi Ubaldi Perusini in usus feudorum commentaria*, Venetiis, apud Iuncta, 1580, n. 8, 11v.

96 Here Duck gives as a reference, as well as the already cited work by Villalobos (ibidem, n. 4, 1v), the work, dedicated to Richelieu, of the theologist of Coimbra Francisco Macedo, *Ius succedendi in Lusitaniae regnum dominae Catharinae regis Emmanuelis ex Eduardo filio neptis, ...Nunc ab Lusitano Anonymo latinitate donatum*, Parisiis, apud Sebatianum Cramoisy, 1641, *Corollarium VI* of the Appendix, 24–27 in the second numeration. Macedo offers an example of a contemporary case in which there is no prescriptive material when he vehemently defends the arguments of Caterina of Braganza and her dynastic line against the king of Castiglia, stressing *mala fides* e *metus*. And even if we wanted to accept his opponents' position that it is possible to talk of prescription, he points out that in this case the period in question is less than the century that prescription requires.

97 On this point Duck puts together both civilist and canonist sources, presenting them as coherent with each other: C. 8.4.3; C. 11.67(66).2; X 2.26.17 e X 2.26.20; VI 5.13.2. Duck's use of the figure of prescription, even when it is not done in a particularly original way, deserves attention because it demonstrates an overcoming of the original distance between the *praescriptio romana* and the *praescriptio canonica* through rethinking the former in light of developments in the latter, allowing him to use Romanist terms outside of their usual terrain of private law. This is clearly a complex issue. The work of Francesco Ruffini is still useful: *La buona fede in materia di prescrizione: Storia della teoria canonistica* (Torino: Bocca, 1892), especially 130–177. More recent, but more distant from this problem, see Noel Vilain, "Prescription et droit canonique: du Décret de Gratien (1140) a Jean d'André (†1348)", *Traditio*, 14 (1958), 121–189, and Harry Dondorp, "Bona fides presumitur in classical Canon Law", *Zeitschrift der Savigny-Stiftung für Rechtsgeschichte. Kanonistische Abteilung* 102:1 (2016), 99–122.

The issue of the impossibility of prescription for the empire prevails over that of prescription vis-à-vis the empire and, although it does not render it void, it changes its scope. *De Usu* rarely gives a prominent position to those arguments that insist that kingdoms should gain independence by prescription in the face of an empire that had long ceased to fulfill its role. These arguments were quite frequent, and they seem to represent a widely held position among jurisconsults as a result of the undeniable fact of the empire losing its grip while maintaining its legal claims. For this reason, jurisconsults needed to come to terms with the emergence of territoriality as the exclusive sphere of legitimacy. It is unsurprising that, in a kind of compromise, these arguments are sometimes found in the works of jurists alongside the idea of an exemption given by the empire to certain peoples from the obligation to obey, exemplified by the case of the Venetians. When, at the beginning of the second book (II, 1, 4-5), Duck returns to the issue of whether the emperor is *Dominus in Orbe Terrarum*, he does not hesitate to call it, following Paciani, a question of fact rather than of law.[98] Indeed, the prescription against the empire seems to hold only a secondary argumentative role in *De Usu* as whole, with the exception perhaps of a mention of Britannia being "abandoned" by the Romans (II, 8, p. I, 9): "[S]ingularum Europae nationum Principes ex imbecillitate & declinatione Romani Imperii opportunum tempus afferendæ suæ libertatis nacti, Regna sua propria constituerunt, nullius Superioris (post Deum solum) Potestati obnoxi; eademque tot seculis ab Imperatorum Dominatione libera possederunt ut, si omnes alii tituli deessent, ex sola tanti temporis præscriptione se adversus Romanum Imperatorem tueri possent" (*DUA*, 57r). However, Duck's references – including those related to more recent cases, such as those in Iberian countries – all focus on the conditions that generally make it impossible to claim prescription, thus preventing it from becoming a source of legitimacy for continued imperial rule.

Reiterating the Divergence between leges *and* arma

Paragraph XX brings the long premise on *arma* and *leges* to a close. Duck concludes that, even after a thousand years, those who have been unjustly conquered can always recover their freedom and the dominion over them is always revocable, in the same way – and this comparison seems intentionally

98 "Hæc controversia est potius questio facti, quam iuris, ex eoque pendet, an Romani subiugaverint universum orbem, et an iuste, an iniuste, de qua re tamen satis clara sunt plures historiæ: sed quicquid sit, quando etiam vellemus fateri Romanum Imperium habuisse initium à violentia, et tyrannide, quam opinionem tenet Oldra[dus] in cons. 68. [sic] *consuevit dubitari, vers.per quam statuam*, col.2. ubi dicit, quod quatuor monarchiæ mundi, id est Assyriorum, Persarum, Græcorum, et Romanorum, omnes initium à violentia, & usurpatione ceperunt, ...", *Tractatus Fulvii Paciani Mutinensis, ... cui incumbat onus probandi*, nn. 52–53–54 cit 662. Straight afterwards Paciani draws conclusions that, as we have seen, are completely at odds with what we find in the above citation.

controversial – that the escape of the servant who has committed *furtum sui* is imprescriptible (C. 6.1.1). That which was lost by war can be recovered by war, particularly (*praesertim*) in those provinces that were acquired by violence and *non titulo oneroso*. Thus, those peoples who fight back have not disobeyed, as their obedience is only presumed (*postulata*), but have, in fact, regained their freedom. Duck's argument is a stronger version of that of Grotius, whom he refers to immediately afterwards.[99]

Again, Duck does not hesitate to reference authors whose general positions go against his own, but from whom he can retrieve arguments in support of his position. This is even the case when his position is the object of *reprobatio* by the cited author, as in the case of Antonio Roselli, or in which the arguments are not explicitly stated but have to be found within a more general treatment of the subject, as with Castaldi's *quaestio*. This allows the reader to identify the moments of agreement between these authors and Duck's position, such as in the reference to the discussion on the Hispanics who liberated themselves from the Moors with their own forces.[100] Immediately afterwards, however, a second series of references contains a more structured refutation of the *de jure* universality of imperial rule. The shift to the contemporary is clearer in the references to the aforementioned de Azpilcueta, Grotius, and *De Iure Maiestatis*, published in 1610 by the Lutheran Henning Arnisaeus. Arnisaeus's text is very significant (not only the attached paragraph, but the entire chapter, "Cui Maiestas competat, et an soli Imperatori"), tying together many of the threads of Duck's argument.[101] In fact, the opening chapter of *De Usu* seems to reflect Arnisaeus's refutation of imperial universalism. They largely touch on the same points – from the interpretation of Daniel's prophecy to the use of Zwingli in order to reconstruct the meanings assumed historically by the term *imperator* – and on the same authors, ranging from John Calvin's thesis (*Institution de la*

99 "Ne in omnia quidem quae olim fuere populi Romani, Imperator Romanus jus nunc habet, multa enim ut bello quaesita, ita bello amissa sunt, alia pactionibus, alia derelictione in aliarum gentium aut regum transierunt. Quaedam etiam civitates olim plane subdita, postea tantum ex parte subditae, aut tantum inaequaliter foederatae esse coeperunt. Nam omnes hi modi aut amittendi aut mutandi juris, non minus adversus Rom. Imperatorem, quam adversus alios valent", Grotius, *De Jure Belli ac Pacis* lib. II, cap. XII, n. 13, 387. This brief but dense paragraph by Grotius begins by contesting the position of Bartolus, "Iurisconsultorum diu princeps habitus", who dismissed as heretical those who denied the right of the emperor over all his peoples, including those in distant places who are unknown to him. Grotius also critiques Dante, saying his idea of a universal monarchy could never work and had no legal title.

100 On this point, in relation to Roselli, Duck refers again to the already cited *De conciliis ac synodis generalibus* (65v), clearly inspired by the expressive force of one of its formulations, even if it is later contested by Roselli himself. In relation to Castaldi, he makes reference to *Restauri Castaldi Perusini Iureconsulti, Amplissimus tractatus de imperatore* q. 53 n. 10, 99r and n. 16, 99v.

101 *Henningi Arnisaei Halbertstadiensis De Jure Maiestatis Libri Tres*, Francofurti, Sumptibus Johannis Thymii, 1610, I, 2, 15–38, the point is n. 3: "Ex quibus argumentis universale dominium colligatur, et eorum reprobatio, una cum assertione contraria", 19–24.

religion chrétienne, IV, 6, 8) on the plurality of beehives and flocks of cranes, all ruled by monarchies but *singulatim* – an image that Arnisaeus transposes from the Church to the empire, replacing bishops with kings – to the consideration that what the *lex regia* supposedly gave to the emperor could not be *pluris juris* of what was previously in the possession of the Roman people. Arnisaeus had a "constitutional" interest in bringing the imperial territories back under the general category of *maiestas*, adopting Bodin's formulation ("La souveraineté est la puissance absolue et perpetuelle d'une République, que les Latins appellent *maiestatem*", *Les Six Livres de la République* I, 8), but he rejects the latter's thesis on the aristocratic and non-monarchical character of the elective empire. Arnisaeus thus limits the emperor's superiority over European sovereigns to *dignitas* alone. Although different in terms of historical legacy, he holds that the empire, now irrevocably only German, shares a common condition with other territorial monarchies. He argues that its specificity can be found only within this condition, pointing out the variety of ways in which *maiestas* is articulated within it. He takes up the traditional Lutheran interpretation of the empire and redetermines it, also in relation to the challenge of Calvinist federalism. Arnisaeus's conceptual delimitation of the empire is of clear interest to Duck, who analyses it and uses it in support of his own position.

"Ideoque hallucinati sunt qui tradunt imperatores Germanicos Provincias a Romanorum Imperio olim avulsas posse Jure sibi restitui petere" (*DUA*, 8–9).[102] However, we should be careful not to misunderstand the vehement tone of Duck's writing here. This is a dispute between jurists, and it is in this context that Duck's argument must be read; he aims to do much more than make a politically outdated claim. At this point he calls on two figures. The first is Enea Silvio Piccolomini, who would become Pope Pius II, and who had been taught by Antonio Roselli, among others, in Siena. Duck makes reference to the epistle written to Emperor Frederick III on 1 March 1446 by Piccolomini when he was still working for the Imperial Chancellery. This text is widely known, being included in collections by both Schard and Goldast under the title *De ortu et auctoritate imperii Romani*.[103] It would become a classic reference of German nationalism and does not present many problems in terms of interpretation. The second is the admittedly less well known but more recent Georg Valentin von Winther,[104] Pomeranian of Treptow, who wrote *Parthenius Litigiosus seu Discursus Politicus-Iuridicus* under the

102 The Neapolitan edition of 1719 omits the phrase and then adjusts the text around it. The French version instead simply moderates the phrase ("ceux-là se sont lourdement trompez…", 23.

103 *De imperiali jurisdictione*, 314–328; *Monarchiae S. Romani Imperii, sive Tractatuum de Iurisdictione Imperiali seu Regia et Pontificia seu Sacerdotali*, Tomus Secundus, Francofordiae, typis Nicolai Hoffmanni, 1614, 1558–1566.

104 Duck cites him on various occassions as Minther, which is a clear typographical error (the inversion of a character, M for W), which remained in all of the editions and also in the

pseudonym Ventura de Valentiis, which would immediately be placed in the index of prohibited books. Whereas Piccolomini's text was celebratory and implicitly exhortatory.[105] functional to a complex personal strategy to connect papacy and empire, Winther's is recriminatory and nostalgic, with an eye to the contemporary jurisdictional issues of the imperial territories.[106] Apart from the fact that they lived at different times and had different biographies, the position Duck seems to attribute to them is fairly unproblematic, if not a little obvious. In addition to these names, Duck reintroduces Gentili because he was criticized on this point by Winther (see footnote 105). Although Gentili's position is very distant from that of Piccolomini and Winther, and although he is also explicitly rejected by the latter, his inclusion by Duck could be seen to suggest (although this inference is a little risky), if not that he is internal to the same doctrinal tradition, at least that he is contiguous with it.

It is more useful to consider the reference Duck makes to the sixth chapter ("De Ditione Romani Imperii, et subditis eius") of the first book of Konrad Braun's *De Seditionibus*,[107] placed in a somewhat confusing position immediately after that on Arnisaeus and just before that on the "hallucinati", who demanded the restoration of the original empire. It could be seen as playing an introductory role with respect to the latter. And in many ways Braun's text mirrors that of Arnisaeus, almost serving as its implicit critical object. Put together, the two texts include most of the themes and authors we have so far found in *De Usu*, and so help us to understand the latter's argumentative structure. Braun recognizes that the issue of obedience to the empire has always been a point of major disagreement (*magna altercatio*) between jurisconsults: there are those who affirm that the emperor is a universal lord, and that therefore no one is exempt from his jurisdiction, and those who argue that, on the contrary, many kings, princes, nations, and peoples are

French version. There is little literature on him, but see von Bülow, "Winther, Georg Valentin", *Allgemeine Deutsche Biographie*, 43 (1898), 501–502.

105 "Romana Regia potestas, quam sacrum Romanum Imperium appellamus, ab ipsa humanæ naturæ ratione, quæ optima vivendi dux est, cuique omnes parere oportet originem ducit": so begins the section of the text that Duck attaches, which can be found right at the beginning of the epistle. On Piccolomini and the empire, as well as returning to A.J. Carlyle, *A History of Medieval Political Theory in the West*, vol. 6, *Political Theory from 1300 to 1600* (Edinburgh: Blackwood, 1936), 188–191, this essay is useful: John B. Toews, "The Views of Empire in Aeneas Sylvius Piccolomini (Pope Pius II)", *Traditio*, 24 (1968), 471–487.

106 "Tot tantæque potentissimæ provinciæ, melioribus sine dubio nervis antiquo corpori adhuc cohæreret, aut aliquâ ex parte recuperari possent (quicquid statuat Alberic[us] lib. 1. de jur. bell. c. 23. Quod Imperator non agit ad ea quæ ante secula fuerunt imperij) si supremus omnium Monarcha Imperator Romano – Germanicus supremam imperij curam solummodo ageret, remotis privatorum litibus atque malitijs, ad Cameras Serenissimæ suae Maiestatis remittendis", *Parthenius Litigiosus seu Discursus Politicus-Iuridicus, in duos distributus libros. Auctore Ventura de Valentys, ICto Veronense, Comite S. Palati, Equite aurato, Cive Romano*, Veronae, Anno Instante Deo pIa ÇaVfa trIUMphat, apud Paulum Ledertz (but in fact published in Frankfurt a. M, 1628), Lib. I, cap. xvi, n. 33, 251.

107 *De Seditionibus*, 27–40.

exempt from it. This is why Braun, who had attended the Council of Trent in person as a representative of the archbishop of Mainz, intervenes directly in the matter, proposing seventeen *conclusiones* whose dominant tone is that of Tridentine theology. Duck accepts a number of Braun's arguments without much trouble, in particular on the origin of worldly empires and the distinction between *potestas a Deo iubente* (or *cooperante*) and *a Deo permittente* and between legitimate and tyrannical power. But then when the empire becomes Christian, Braun uses Constantine's conversion to redraw the providentialist picture. The "Imperium Romanum, etsi iustissimis legibus fundatum et latissime propagatum" remained tyrannical until, "Imperio in Ecclesiam per Christum translatum, simul etiam Romanae Monarchiae qualitas et conditio mutata est". From the Constantinian donation onwards the age of full imperial legitimacy began, resting on the recognition that Christ transferred the *pleno iure* the *imperium* to Peter and his successors, the Roman pontiffs. This completely shifts the argument, with the articulation between the spiritual and temporal dimension of the Church's *potestas* taking centre stage in the following *conclusiones*. Analysing the long debate on the doctrine of the two swords from this perspective, Braun redefines the empire in relation to the Church. The Church is the true guarantor of the empire's consistency and thus the latter must be understood on the basis of the Church. The outcome is clear: obedience to the empire is imprescriptible for its subjects, although there is nothing to prevent them from being exempt from the *iura* "vel privilegio Principis vel diuturnitate principis" to the extent of enjoying in their own kingdoms the same full power that the emperor possesses "in universo Imperio".[108] However, the empire's subjects are in no way exempt from obedience to the Roman Church, and this is how Braun, while recognizing that the empire has always been delimited in its spatial boundaries, recovers its universality on a pastoral level (clear reference is made to the flock), and thus also its universal legitimacy.

At the end of the chapter, in Paragraph XXI, Duck reiterates the divergence between *leges* ed *arma*, claiming that *per famam iustitiae* the laws of the Romans spread farther than their armies, so much so that those who had freed themselves from imperial domination or had never been subjected to it voluntarily upheld them as their own laws. Although Duck aimed to discuss this again later on, this passage is supported only by anecdotal and oratory

108 "Quo casu non oboedientia abiecta, sed libertas potius data vel praescripta esse censetur". Below Braun refers to the Venetians: "Atque ad hunc modum Venetorum dominio, a Iurisdictione Romani Imperii, privilegio Principis exemptum esse fertur. Quod privilegium Alber[icus] de Ros[ate] vidisse se testatur: ut alibi tradit Jason [Mainus]". However, Braun does admit that the Venetians argue that their exemption is "jure ipso romano", because their city is built on the sea (op. cit., 38). It is worth noting that Arnisaeus also refers to the Venetians in a way that inverts Braun's argument; see *Henningi Arnisaei Halbertstadiensis De Jure Maiestatis* n. 4 "Utrum Veneti de iure sint subiecti imperio", 24–26.

evidence and is therefore a little weak.[109] Much stronger is the main argument of the first chapter, which influences the rest of the work, and it is fully developed in the second and ninth chapter of Book I and the first chapter of Book II. For Duck the *leges* are not the correlate of the empire, which means that not only do they not coincide with the empire, but also that the stratifications of Roman-canon law can be accepted without requiring any relation to the empire. He holds that its normative dimension *as such* can be separated from it, in keeping with his conviction that there is a gap between empire and *leges* from the beginning. The insistence on the "miraculous" character and providence of *leges* creates a rhetoric that is able to account for this gap.

Universalism, Authorization, and the Issue of Apocalyptic

Three specific issues seem to govern Duck's analysis in *De Usu*. The first is that the semantic significance of the term "common" cannot be resolved in the sequence Roman law/imperial law/*ius commune*. This term refers only to specific contexts: in some of these contexts Roman law is common law, such as in the German territories and in many European countries; however, in others, such as England and Venice, a different law is common law. Duck reiterates this at various points in *De Usu*. For Duck, Roman law is Roman-canon law, the *utrumque jus* of the jurists, which, in its dual nature is under neither the Roman Empire nor the Roman Church, even though it can be traced back to them. The parallelism of the two laws is visible in the maintenance of the canonical tradition, or at least in its practical use. This is also the case in places where there is no longer a relationship with the papal authorities, such as the Protestant German territories where "post ejuratam Romani Pontificis Postestatem, Principes aliqui Germanici adhuc juris Canonici usum in Ditionibus suis conservent" (*DUA*, 68) or in England where canon law is transformed into the ecclesiastical law of the kingdom. This patrimony of thought and practice has its own rationality but cannot be reduced to that

109 Again, Duck puts an antique and modern thinker together. The first is **Valerius Maximus**, a moralist of the first century who had lasting success amongst jurists with humanist leanings (Luca da Penne made a compendium of his work around 1374), making reference to the sixth book of *Factorum et dictorum memorabilium*). The second is the French jurist Guillaume du Vair, magistrate and then bishop, a major exponent of *éloquence délibérative*, for whom Duck's reference is a speech he gave, as the first president of the parliament of Provence *A l'ouverture du Parlament de la Sainct Remy mil six cens quatre* (*Les Œuvres de messire Guillaume Du Vair, reveues par l'autheur avant sa mort et augmentées de plusieurs pièces non encore imprimées*, Paris, chez Sebastien Cramoisy, 1625, 858–863). On him see the entries by M-F. Renoux-Zagamé in P. Arabeyre, JL. Halperin, J. Krynen (eds.), *Dictionnaire historique des juristes francais xiie–xxe siècle* (Paris: PUF, 2015²), 394–395, and by Jacqueline Boucher in A. Jouanna, J. Boucher, D. Biloghi, G. Le Thiec (eds.), *Histoire et Dictionnaire des guerres de religion* (Paris: Laffont, 1998), 866–868, as well as that written by Marc Fumaroli, *L'âge de l'éloquence. Rhétorique et "res literaria" de la Renaissance au seuil de l'époque classique* (Paris : Albin Michel, 1994), 492–519 and *passim*.

rationality in any way. The consideration of Roman law as a *ratio scripta*, which Duck takes up enthusiastically, explicitly referencing French jurists, is clearly a central doctrinal element in *De Usu* that supports a universalist tendency covering both natural law and the law of nations. This gives legitimacy to the conviction of the jurisconsults that Roman law can be thought of as a universal *ius commune*, valid for all nations, for which some scholars would find evidence in the use of Roman law *in casibus non decisis* even in non-Christian contexts, such as among Jewish and Turkish people. However, regardless of the meaning given to the term *ratio*, it cannot be measured against an original authenticity, something that interpreters might hide behind or use as a filter. *Ratio* continues to indicate a form of knowledge, *scientia juris*, that, for Duck, it is worth repeating, is an open terrain and includes elements of controversy and conflict within it. This is precisely because it is always related to jurisdictional practices and institutions. For Duck, this is a matter for jurists and not for philosophers, a position in which he again displays extreme loyalty to his identity as a *civilian*.

This is strongly linked to the second issue. The autonomy of this normative inheritance coincides with the necessity for its authorization. This creates a complex and plural relationship between *usus* and *authoritas* that creates a tension between the different laws and the legal regimes in which they operate, or, to use two terms that were conceptually foreign to Duck and his time, between legal languages and legal systems.[110] The English *difference*, what Duck calls its position at the margins, here becomes a strategic resource that obviously must be considered in terms of its results, but not only. The traditional notion of *ius commune*, which assigns a globally subsidiary role to Roman law, is thus called into question, laying the groundwork, if not for its repudiation, at least for its careful reconsideration. Duck thus brings the relationships between law, politics, and history to the foreground, whilst always reading them from within the law.

The third issue is of a theological character, or perhaps a theological-political character, and regards the position of the empire on the eschatological level. For the entire first chapter Duck constantly returns to the prophecy of Daniel, fairly clearly implying that he accepts its contemporary relevance. His reflections on the prophecy emerge again and again throughout the book and in his dense web of sources, being taken up at various points only to be abandoned again. It is in the second paragraph of the second chapter that he makes his position most clear, precisely in the light of what he had previously said. The Roman Empire is the fourth monarchy of the prophecy, it is the last

110 We are a bit puzzled by the choice of Alain Wijffels, in his valuable contribution on Duck, mainly on the chapter of Book II of *De Usu* on France ("Arthur Duck et le *ius commune* europeen", *Revue d'histoire des Facultés de droit et de la science juridique*, 1990, n° 10–11, 193–221) to speak of the different laws as different legal systems. It seems to us that this choice makes a misleading comparative assumption.

earthly monarchy and after that there will be no other empire. This is a thesis on which there is almost universal consensus: "cum in eo fere omnes consentiant Monarchiam Romanam esse ultimam, neque aliam futuram Monarchiam usque ad secundum Domini nostri adventum, quae Leges orbi terrarum praescribere possit". Here Duck attaches a reference supporting the shared character of that affirmation, which we will now examine.

At this point, Duck refers to four authors, two belonging to the Lutheran world, Johannes Carion and Johannes Sleidanus, and two Italian jurists, the aforementioned Castaldi and the fourteenth-century Luca da Penne. But whereas for the latter two he does little more than again reiterate the identification of the final kingdom with the Roman Empire in contexts that bring us back to the confrontation between the papacy and the empire,[111] with the Germans he goes further. In the latter we find a complete narrative structure that supports the image of the four monarchies, beginning from the situation created by the Reformation, integrating the matter of the empire with that of the Church (the issue of the Antichrist), and elaborating on the idea of the maturity of the times already indicated in the early Lutheran phase. Their contemporaneity thus plays a major part in their construction of interpretative keys for reading history, and, in turn, these keys help them to understand the threatening present. Carion was a mathematician and astrologer with the Brandenburg court of the elector, becoming famous due to his precognitions, including of the onset of the Reformation, which he drew up in a *Chronica* at the beginning of the 1530s, a sort of calendar of world history in which the realization of Daniel's prophecy played a key part. His old classmate from Tubinga, Philipp Schwarzert, later known as Melanchthon, intervened in the *Chronica* at various points. In German Protestantism, Melanchthon was second in importance only to Luther and, as well as his theological vocation, had astrological and humanistic interests (as well as a legal education). In the version published in Wittenberg in 1632 as *Chronica durch Magistrum Johan Carion vleissig zusamen gezogen meniglich nützlich zu lesen*, Melanchthon's authorial imprint is clear. This edition included many alterations, some of which are fairly significant, including a large number by Melanchthon's

111 *Quaestio* 72 of the treatise of Castaldi, (*De imperatore*, 129–131), referred to by Duck on this point, addresses the question of the duration of the empire until the end of time and its possible final reintegration, in conversation with *De Potestate Papae* of the Dominican Agostino Trionfo (Augustinus de Ancona), one of the theorists who was most explicit on the issue of the supremacy of the Church, also in temporal terms. The attitude of Castaldi is rather prudent and seems to weaken the most markedly apocalytic aspects of the subject. "Notanter rationibus divine scripturae nam cum haec citra ordinem iuris nostri ac disciplinam sunt in messem non omnino meam falcem non immittam". More elusive is Duck's reference to *Commentaria in tres posteriores libros Codicis Iustiniani* by Luca da Penne on *De conductoribus et procuratoribus*, C. 11.72.1 (in the edition that we are using, Lugduni, apud Ioannam Iacobi Iuntae, 1542, n. 6, 638). This does not seem to add much new to the argument, but it is worth noting due to da Penne's authority.

son-in-law Caspar Peucher. These changes distance it from the apocalyptic aspect, which is relegated to an indeterminate time, and stabilizes the idea of the Sacred Roman Empire as the ultimate monarchy, which will last until the end of time and "de utroque adventu Cristi".

Sleidanus, born in the Habsburg Netherlands in 1506, moves along similar lines, although he has a different background: he was an annalist and diplomat and had studied law in Paris and Orléans. In 1555, Sleidanus published *De statu religionis & reipublicae, Carolo Quinto, Caesare commentariorum libri XXVI* and then, the following year, *De quatuor summis imperiis, libri très.* The first book detailed the events of the Reformation and for a long time was a primary historiographical resource, even by those who did not share its interpretation. The second book, as much as it differed from the *Chronica Carionis,* also insisted on understanding the story of Daniel as having documentary reliability, and, perhaps more than the *Chronica,* it included elements that went beyond the merely annalistic towards a more historical reading of events. Sleidanus's work immediately received widespread attention, with many reprints, translations, and compendiums, including in England where it had two different editions and was welcomed across confessional divides.[112] What the two authors share is their reelaboration – using somewhat different language and images – of the old Lutherian idea that the empire, although weakened, constituted an indestructible root at the eschatological level. And this establishes their position in Duck's text, not as a consensus but as a screen on which to project a specific dissent. Duck accepted the thesis of the *translatio imperii,* even if he understood it as weak and residual, unlike the strong readings of the Germans, of the pro-imperial Italian jurists or of Alberico Gentili, the latter of which was ultimately completely secular. The fact that the empire became *imbecillius,* as Jerome, who is cited again in the text, reminds us as early as the fourth century, is a constant in Christan reflection and is

112 For both authors Duck provides general indications as well as references to specific passages in the texts. The latter are roughly identifiable ("in finis" of book I and III for Sleidan, "in principio" for Charion), but they are difficult to link to specific editions. A reconstruction of the intellectual profiles of Carion and of Sleidanus can be found in the classic work by Claude-Gilbert Dubois, *La conception de l'histoire en France au XVIe siècle* (1977) (Genève: Slaktine, 2011), 424–443, that works with the contemporary French edition. It should be read alongside Mario Miegge's chapters on this subject in *Il sogno del re di Babilonia,* 41-66. Still interesting observations on Luther, Melanchthon and astrology can be found in Aby Warburg, *Heidnisch-antike Weissagungen in Wort und Bild zu Luthers Zeiten* (Heidelberg: Carl Winters Universitätsbuchhandlung,1920). More recently, Mark A. Lotito, has written an impressive book completely dedicated to *Chronica Carionis,* exploring its background and reception, also giving an overview of the various editions (*The Reformation of Historical Thought* (Leiden: Brill, 2019)). The literature on Sleidanus has, above all, concentrated on his book on the events of the Reformation; see Donald R. Kelley, "Johann Sleidan and the Origins of History as a Profession", *Journal of Modern History,* 52:4 (Dec., 1980), 573–598; and Alexandra H. Kess, *Johann Sleidan and the Protestant Vision of History* (Aldershot: Ashgate, 2008), which, in its wide-ranging analysis, also deals with *De quatuor summis imperiis.*

insufficient to support Duck's image of the destiny of the empire. He says that the empire, limited now to the German territories, is only *reliquae et umbra*, that is, something very different. There will thus not be a universalistic reintegration of empire, but neither will there be a redemption of the divergence between empire and *leges*. The *foelix* persistence of the latter does not depend on the former. The definition of *reliquae et umbra* acts as a sort of seal reminding us that after the Roman Empire only the return of Christ will give the world a new law. While we wait for that, the *leges* alone can give the world a scintilla of justice, as Zonaras says, and this, of course, remains the merit of the Romans. Although the terms that connect the final monarchy and the second coming in *De Usu et Authoritate* are the same as those found in the *Chronica* and Sleidanus, they differ radically in their emphasis. Thus Duck recovers the apocalyptic theme, although dealing with it in an unconventional manner. All this points to the need for a further investigation of the theological and intellectual background of Duck, beyond his uneasy position within the church of Archbishop Laud.[113] The paragraph closes with that which we might call the "etsi daremus" of the *civilian* Arthur Duck: "Et licet nihil aliud de magno illo Imperio superesset, habemus tamen eorum Leges, quas omnes deinceps nationes cum admiratione receperunt" (DUA, 9). For him this is a programmatic stance in relation to law, but it is also a tool for his investigation.

Cores within *De Usu et Authoritate* (2): The Use of Civil Law in the Dominions of the Italian Princes

In the second part of his "history of law on a European scale",[114] Duck explores the notion of empire and the idea of Roman civil law as imperial law, discussing both the dominion "imperatoris Romani in Orbem Terrarum" (*DUA*, 56r-66r) and the history of *ius civile* "in Dominiis Imperii Germanici" (*DUA*, 66v–69r). Then, in the third chapter, he examines the use of civil law in the dominions of the Italian princes. It is worth stressing that he does not refer to either the German or the Italian territories in a merely geographical sense but makes a clearly political reference to the "Dominii" of the emperor and the princes.

However, he uses this expression only for the German and Italian territories, identifying the monarchical states with the more precise expression "regnum", as he would do in later chapters when referring to southern Italy and

113 See Francisco J. Andrés Santos, "Ius commune vs Common Law", 73–78. However, there is still a lot left to explore on this topic.

114 Andrés Santos, "Ius Commune vs Common Law", 89, described Duck's work as "una obra histórico-jurídica", and Peter Stein as "the first history of law on a European scale" (Peter Stein, "Duck, Arthur," in *Oxford Dictionary of National Biography* (Oxford: Oxford University Press, 2004), accessed 20 March 2024, https://doi.org/10.1093/ref:odnb/8128.

the rest of Europe.[115] Following the same logic, instead of beginning his analysis from northern Italy and proceeding to the south, he begins from Rome and then moves out to the peripheries. As the "seat and source" of the Roman Empire and its laws, Rome is thus the starting point, although, like all Italian dominions, it is now liberated from the empire.

The thesis that Duck aimed to demonstrate, analysing all of the various dominions in turn, is clear from the very first lines of this chapter, in which he repeats three times that although the Italian princes had shaken off imperial power they continued to demonstrate a spontaneous "obedience" to its laws. Thus there seems to be a separation between the borders of the empire, now very limited in geographical terms, and the borders of *ius commune*, which still encompassed the whole of Italy and even all of Europe. The chapter's binary structure reflects this logic. The first part is dedicated to showing that the Italian princes – from the pope to the last of the local lords – do not recognize any superiors, and the second part is more specifically focused on the normative sources and the validity of Roman law in the Italian Peninsula. This validity is constantly reiterated by Duck, although not without pointing out all of the possible nuances arising as a result of the stratification and interweaving of local and regional norms and of the political-institutional vicissitudes of the different territories.

As we have already seen in relation to England, in both his description of political-institutional relations and in the way he structures his sources, Duck's argumentative style and the authorities on which he bases his assertions[116] place him fully within a European and what he calls "Italic" legal culture of jurists of late common law. Although he adopts some aspects of the new currents of legal humanism, he does not share all of their positions, above all their rejection of Justinian law.[117] He does not renounce the academy, but he is certainly more interested in jurisprudential *practice*.[118] Alongside a few treatises, such as Ristoro Castaldi's *De imperio*, and some fundamental commentaries,

115 This applies to all the later chapters, which were focused on the following countries: Naples and Sicily (chapter 4); France (for which he uses the antiquated name, the Kingdom of the Gauls, chapter 5); Spain (chapter 6); Lusitania, (chapter 7); obviously England (chapter 8); "Hibernia" (chapter 9); Scotland (chapter 10); Poland (chapter 11); Hungary (chapter 12); Denmark (chapter 13); Sweden (cap. 14); and Bohemia (chapter 15).

116 For an overview of these, beyond those already indicated, see Andrés Santos, "Ius Commune vs Common Law", 94 ff.

117 Also on this point, see Andrés Santos, "Ius Commune vs Common Law", 102–103.

118 On this, Andrés Santos describes the work of Duck as aimed particularly at "determinar la vigencia y el alcance del Derecho romano como ordenamiento aplicable por los tribunales en los diversos territorios europeos escogidos, lo que exige definir en cada caso las fronteras y delimitaciones del *ius commune* respecto a los distintos *iura propria*" and specifically to answer one question: "si el Derecho romano es o no ius commune en el territorio de que se trate (es decir, Derecho de aplicación supletoria para los casos de laguna normativa en el ordenamiento propio) y cómo viene aprendido y aplicado en él." (Andrés Santos, "Ius Commune vs Common Law", 90).

a central role is played by the *consilia* and *decisiones* in the organization of the references. These are cited individually and collected together, both by Duck and by those he references, to form the *communis opinio*, meaning the predominant thought of the time.[119]

Duck clearly knows Zasius, Cujas, and Andrea Alciato, the latter of whom he cites more than forty times, reproducing his critiques of Accursio (*DUA*, 21rv) and his doubts on the Latin text of the *novellae* (*DUA*, 21rv, 24v–25r). However, Duck gives a very simplistic and mistaken reading of the famous dispute between Alciato and Deciani. It seems more likely that he wanted to mould this debate to his purposes rather than that he simply misunderstood it. He presents the debate as entirely confined to the world of jurists, just one of the frequent differences of opinion (*dissensiones*) that emerge between jurists whenever situations arise that are not clearly determined by the law.

Duck devotes the entire eighth chapter of the first part of his book to the issue of interpretation.[120] He explains that when a complex situation arises that is not regulated by law, judges must refer to the doctrinal interpretation ("necesse est ut ad interpretes confugiant iudices"). Jurists can and indeed must be called upon: courts have to abide by the *communis opinio* where one exists. Indeed, it could be claimed that if a judge decides "contra communem opinionem" that would reveal their inexperience or, worse still, their bad faith.[121] The issue obviously becomes more complex if there are differing interpretations. In describing the points of contention and the criteria that should be adopted to identify the most reliable solution, Duck refers to the debate between Alciato and Deciani on whether the opinions expressed in commentaries and treatises or those found in the *consilia* are more reliable. According to Duck, Alciato was "pro commentariis et tractatibus", while Deciani was "pro Consiliis", arguing that most *consilia* were written with greater conviction and attention.[122] The two sixteenth-century masters are presented by Duck as the leaders of two distinct camps. Deciani's camp was that which was

119 Duck has no doubts about the binding nature of *communis opinio*. In the first part he presents this issue in general terms (*DUA*, 50rv), also providing the criteria that the world of jurists, of which he was a part ("regulae nobis traditae"), traditionally use to choose between majority and minority opinions (*DUA*, 50v ff.) and makes reference to this in his work on various occasions. As examples, see expressions such as "omnes Jurisconsulti affirmant" (*DUA*, 70r), "et generalites apud iurisconsultos receptum est" (*DUA*, 78r), or "sed frequentius recepta est contraria sententia" (*DUA*, 79v).

120 The expression "in infinita vero negotiorum humanorum varietate quandoque occurrunt Controversiae Legibus non determinatae, quae vix humani ingenii acumine possunt dissolvi" is found at the beginning of §. VII (*DUA*, 21r).

121 "in quo ab omnibus communiter receptum est: quotiens interpretes inter se consentiunt et communem opinionem constituunt, eam omnes iudices in sententiis suis sequi tenentur" (*DUA*, 50r).

122 "quod consilia magis deliberate plerumque scribantur" (*DUA*, 51rv).

prevalent in Italy and Germany,[123] although he saw that there were also many sound reasons to support Alciato's position, as others had already pointed out before him.

Confirmation that his reading of Alciato is a little strange can be found in the people he chooses to make reference to in support of the greater reliability of the commentaries. Duck's argument is that, unlike the *consilia*, the *commentari* are written with a mind free from greed, sympathy, or hatred, or any other personal sentiment ("cupiditas aeris, gratia, odium et omnis affectus"). In addition to citing the decisions of the *Supreme Chamber Imperii Germanici*,[124] he also cites Menochio in his treatise on legal presumptions (*De praesumptionibus*). Aimone Cravetta, Pier Paolo Parisio (in a *consilium*!), and Conrad Rittershus, in his observations in the margins of Fulgosius's "posthumous" collection of *consilia*. The name of Menochio is the first to stand out, as he is certainly not a well-known critic of the *consilia*. In fact, on closer inspection, he reports on the two positions without taking sides and indeed seems to lean towards the idea that, when in doubt, the judge has broad discretion to decide freely.[125] Aimone Cravetta, who, like Menochio, is also not a humanist, was a respected consultant, but despite this Duck cites his historical

123 He finds evidence of this both in the statutory provisions requiring municipal judges to make recourse to the *consilium sapientis* and in the regulations, which he understands as similar, of the German princes (ibidem).

124 Duck is familiar with the *Supreme Chamber Imperii Germanici* through reading the sixteenth-century German jurist Joachim Mysinger von Frundeck, which he repeats almost verbatim. Von Frundeck reports on it in his *Observationes* on the activity of the court. In Observation No. 60 of the sixth and last Centuria, in which he cites the *Sylva* of Giovanni Nevizzano d'Asti, he writes that, when confronted with the divergent opinions between doctors – some written in lectures or treatises, others in *consilia* – many jurists ask themselves whether they should put more faith in the theses expressed in the treatises or the *consilia* ("Saepenumero dubitari consuevit, quando reperiuntur opiniones Doctorum diversae, quas vel in eorum lecturis, vel tractatibus, vel etiam consiliis, sive responsis asseruerunt, quibus magis credendum sit, aut quae sint potiores habendae, aut praeferendae, maxime quando Doctores vel inter sese, vel etiam a seipsos discrepant"). Von Frundeck says he sides with those who claim that more faith should be placed in the lectures or treatises but admits that his thesis is not always approved by the Imperial High Court ("veluti veriorem in summo Imperii Tribunali meo tempore non semel adprobatam"), Joachim Mysinger von Frundeck, *Observationum imper. Camera Centuriae VI*, Lugduni, Apud Antonium Candidum, 1608. *Centuria* VI, *Observatio* 60, nn. 1–3, 335–336.

125 Menochio refers, with his usual excess of quotations, to the two positions, that favouring "in legendo" and that favouring "in consulendo", and adds that, in an analogous dispute between theologians and canonists, the latter are to be preferred in ecclesiastical courts. He concludes, however, that when opinions vary so much that it is impossible to identify which is correct, the judge can decide the dispute on the basis of equity ("quando opiniones sunt adeo dubiae, ut discerni nequeat veritas, iure suo poterit iudex rem controversam dividere aequaliter inter concedentes", Jacopo Menochio, *De praesumptionibus, coniecturis, signis et indiciis Commentaria, in sex distincta libros*, Tomus primus, Genevae, Sumptibus Samuelis Chouët, 1570, *praesumptio* 71, nn. 48–51, 244).

works.[126] Duck next adds a *consilium* by Pier Paolo Parisio,[127] and then makes the peculiar choice to cite Rittershus, the German publisher of a number of Fulgosius's *consilia*. In the work's dedication, which, strangely, is addressed to the Venetian doge Leonardo Donà, Rittershus defends his decision to seek out and publish new *consilia* by Fulgosius, arguing that the latter's capacity for synthesis is particularly evident in his *consilia*, when he does not digress from the subject at hand, or use complicated language and linguistic tricks, but instead completely focuses on the search for equity and justice, expressing himself in clear and precise terms.[128]

Thus, there is no escape even here from the *mos italicus*, and even Alciato seems to be "enlisted" by him to support the role of jurisprudence in the development and functioning of the legal system.

It is worth confirming this by briefly running through the long list of the most frequently mentioned names in Duck's work.[129] There is an array of well-known and even famous authors within the long list of people he cites. These include the most important civilists and canonists of the fourteenth and fifteenth centuries, such as Bartolus and Baldo, Oldrado da Ponte, Giovanni d'Andrea, Nicolò dei Tedeschi, Paolo di Castro, Fulgosio, Tartagni, the two Socini (senior and junior); the great jurists of the sixteenth and early seventeenth century, such as Rolando della Valle, Jacopo Menochio, Tiberio Deciani, Marcantonio Pellegrini, and Francesco Mantica[130]; and many others whom Duck read and is clearly very familiar with. In his search for "direct" witnesses of local practices, especially those who were connoisseurs of statutory legislation or collectors of *decisiones*, Duck even cites provincial jurists, whom had inevitably been

126 Aimone Cravetta, *Tractatus de antiquitate temporis*, Lugduni, Apud haeredes Iacobi Giuntae, 1550, p. 1 §. *Propositis* (rectius *Propositum*), n. 48, f. 19r: I find that doctors get closer to the truth in teaching than in consilia, because greed for money does not interfere in lectures; a dangerous sentiment that often leads mortal souls to hell ("reperio quod doctores in legendo magis mituntur veritati, quam in consulendo: quia in lectura cessat effectio et cupiditas aeris cuius libido, ehei! quot mortalium animas inferos trahit?"). It is also worth noting the choice of the historian of law, Alberto Lupano, who wrote Cravetta's academic biography, to describe Cravetta as a "jurist of common law": Alberto Lupano, *Aimone Cravetta (1504–1569): giurista del diritto comune* (Torino: Deputazione subalpina di storia patria, 2008).

127 Pier Paolo Parisio, *Tertia pars consiliorum*, Venetiis, Apud Nicolaum Bevilaquam et socios, 1570, cons. 91 n. 48, f. 156r.

128 "de accurata brevitate, qua in respondendo omissis ambagibus et ampullis et truffis usus est auctor noster, vel de studio aequitatis et iusticiae ubique elucente, vel de latinitate, quam adhibet, puriorem certe quam pro illo aevo": Raffaele Fulgosio, *Consilia posthuma ... quae et ipsa antehac numquam impressa fuerunt. Cunradus Rittershusius JC recensuit*, Ambergae, sumptibus a typis Johannis Schönfeldi, 1607, in principio.

129 See above, in this chapter, Andrés Santos, "Ius Commune vs Common Law", 94 ff.

130 The last four of these are explicitly identified as professors called upon by the Republic of Venice to give prestige to the University of Padova, in which Duck sees an indirect confirmation of the authorities of the Serenissima's admiration for Roman civil law, despite everything (*DUA*, 75v–76r cfr. Claudia Passarella, *"Negari tamen non potest Venetos ius civile romanorum colere et venerari": Venetian Law and* Ius Commune *between the 17th and 18th Centuries*, in this book).

relegated to the margins in history and historiography.[131] Perceiving himself as 'external', he seems to seek confirmation and endorsement from the 'locals' for his historical-institutional and, more importantly, normative and practical reconstruction of the legal system. This explains his repeated references to 'Italic' jurisconsults, either choosing the most authoritative among them or implying they are unanimous or in broad agreement on various matters. For example, he states that the pontifical power not to extradite those who had committed crimes in foreign countries was a teaching of "Roman" jurisconsults.[132] He also cites Italians when discussing the freedom of the Genoese (*DUA*, 73v) and the power of the various minor duchies (*DUA*, 74rv), citing the "Lucenses"[133] on Lucca and the "Mediolanenses" on Milan.[134] He does

131 There is some doubt surrounding Duck's precise knowledge of these authors, whom he might have found only in "chains" of citations traditionally repeated in various works, since many of their surnames are misspelt in the transcription. In these cases, as elsewhere for even well-known jurists, the z is written as r in all Latin editions of the work: Giovanni Battista Fenzoni, author of *Annotationes* on the Statute of Rome, becomes "Fenron"; the author of *consilia* Bartolomeo Bertazzoli is abbreviated to "Bertarrol"; Barnaba Cornazzano becomes "Cornarron."; and Giovanni Nevizzano, whose *Summarium decretorum Sabaudie ordinem iudiciarium concernentium* is cited, that introduces and comments on *Decreta seu Statuta vetera serenissimorum ac praepotentum Sabaudiae ducum*, Augustae Taurinorum, apud haeredem Nicolai Beuilaquae, 1586, becomes "Neviran", and in one case (see later nt. 142) even Azzone becomes "Aronem", despite the fact that elsewhere he is cited correctly (see for example the Portuguese Ordinances, *DUA*, 121r). There are also many other small errors, such as the Sarzanese Alderano Mascardi, repeatedly abbreviated as "Muscard", Laerte Cherubini, author of a *Bollario* of Pope Pius V, who becomes Lorenzo ("Lauren"), and the Neapolitan jurist Gaspare de Leo written as "Gosp. De Leo." (*DUA*, 86v).

132 *DUA*, 71r. Called on to confirm this are a famous *consilium* by Oldrado da Ponte concerning the lack of extradition to England of the banker Pepo Frescobaldi in 1312 (Oldrado da Ponte, *Consilia seu Responsa et quaestiones aureae*, Venetiis, ex officina Damiani Zenari, 1585, cons. 124, f. 58v), a commentary on the Digest of Pedro Barbosa that extensively elaborates on the theme of jurisdiction (Pedro Barbosa, *Commentarii ad interpretationem tituli ff. De iudicis*, Lugduni, Suptibus Ludovici Prost haeredis Rouille, 1622, ad l. 2 §. *Legatis*, 111 ff.), and a passage from the criminal *praxis* of Farinacci (Prospero Farinacci, *Praxis et theoricae criminalis pars prima*, Duaci, ex officina Marci Wyon, typographi Iurati sub signo Phoenicis, 1618, quaestio VII, n. 12, 56), the only one of these jurists who is properly "Roman".

133 *DUA*, 76rv. The attestation of the observance of *ius civile* in the Duchy of Lucca is taken from Magonio's *decisiones* (Gerolamo Magonio, *Decisiones causarum tam Rotae Florentinae quam Rotae Lucensis*, Venetiis, Apud Sessas, 1605, *decisio Rotae Lucensis* XCI n. 10, 21, and *decisio Rotae Lucensis* VI n. 5, 17). He also mentions the *decisiones* collected by Barnaba Cornazzano, whose name has been misspelt as "Cornarron." Decisio 236 does not exist in the two most well-known editions of the work. It cannot be found in Barnaba Cornazzani (Bernabò Cornazzani), *Novissimae decisiones Rotae Lucensis*, Venetiis, apud Damianum Zenarium, 1598, which contains only 215 decisiones. And neither can it be found in Bernabò Cornazzani, *Decisiones novissimarum Rotae Lucensis centuriae duae*, Francofurti, cura et studio Collegii Musarum Novenarum Paltheniani, 1600, that contains only 216. Decisio 236 could be a misprint (present in all editions) for Decisio 136, which deals with the relationship between statute and common law. However, the doubt remains as to whether Duck had direct access to the work.

134 *DUA*, 78v-79r. Duck has more detailed knowledge of the latter. In the text he specifically mentions Filippo Sacco, president of the Senato, the senators Francesco Lampugnano and Egidio Bossi, the 'reviewer' of the Milanese constitutions, Francesco Crasso (Grassi), whose

the same for the different case of the Kingdom of Naples, here referring to the opinions of the "iurisconsulti Neapolitani et Siculi" (*DUA*, 86rv).

However, in many other cases, the community of jurisconsults is shown to cross all geographical boundaries, being presented as united and unique. Duck demonstrates that he feels fully part of this community; thus, in these cases he assumes a gaze "from within", even going so far as to use expressions such as "Interpretes nostri", as we pointed out at the beginning of this chapter.[135] He shares this cultural context with other well-known seventeenth century European jurists, such as the Italian De Luca, who a few decades later would collect all of his theoretical-practical knowledge together in his *Theatrum veritatis et iustitiae*.[136] In the most doubtful cases, where differences of opinion can be seen between the vast range of interpreters, Duck prioritizes the positions of the most recent and up-to-date jurists on the developments of a system that he still clearly considers to be jurisprudential.

With regard to Constantine's donation, for example, Duck could not be seen to be unaware of the controversies initiated by Lorenzo Valla, recalling the heated debates between jurists, canonists and civilians. He finds a more secure position ("tutius") among more recent jurists, including his contemporaries, who built their theories on papal power starting from the mechanism of acquisitive prescription (*DUA*, 69v–70r) so as to be able to arrive at what mattered most in practice, namely that all jurists affirm that the pontiff is the absolute master of his dominions and can perform all of the acts that are the

De origine iuris Mediolanensis libellus is referenced, and the commentators Catellano Cotta and Antonio Rossi, whom he definitely read and the 1594 Bergamasque edition of the Milanese statutes, precisely cited recalling the place and year (indeed, the complete title of the work is *Mediolanensium statuta olim a iureconsulto Catelano Cotta scholijs illustrata, et ab Antonio Rubeo annotationibus locupletata: in hac vero postrema editione ipsius Antonij Rubei annotationes, quae in calce ipsorum statutorum reperiebantur, suis locis collocatae*, Bergomi, typis Comini Venturae sumptibus Antonij de Antonijs bibliopolae Mediolanensis, 1594). He points out that these Milanese jurists, in their comments on the constitutions, adapt them to Roman civil law as common law and refer to them to decide cases in court when there are no statutes or "constitutions" ("quas etiam ad ius Civile Romanorum ut ad ius commune in iudiciis accomodant et ab eo Decisiones Causarum in Statutis et Costitutionibus omissarum petunt" *DUA*, 79r).

135 He uses it, for example, in relation to the position of the Veneti, referring in the text to Bartolus and in a footnote to Antonio da Budrio, Alberico da Rosciate, Paolo di Castro and others, all of whom are Italian (*DUA*, 74v–75r), and repeats it in relation to the interpretation of the statutes "in Dominiis Italiae", with regard to which "iurisconsulti nostri tradiderunt": they state that the interpretation should be restrictive whenever the statute deviates from or "corrects" common law (*DUA*, 78v–79r).

136 The words used by Alessandro Dani to describe the "vast and composite" legal culture underpinning De Luca's Theatrum seem to apply perfectly to Duck (A. Dani, "De Luca, Giovanni Battista", in *Il contributo italiano alla storia del pensiero. Diritto* (Roma: Istituto dell'Enciclopedia italiana, 2012), 177–180.

responsibility of kings in their kingdoms and emperors in their empires.[137] Similarly, with regard to the position of the Duke of Savoy, he dismisses the idea that, being an imperial fiefdom, the ducal powers of that territory were limited by the feudal hierarchy.[138]

His position is therefore in clear opposition to the decision taken from the fifteenth century onwards by some European princes, such as those in Castille, to promulgate the "laws of citations", which Duck also somehow knew about and referenced. Either consciously or unconsciously, Duck seems to some extent to misunderstand the meaning of those measures, particularly those promulgated in the Iberian Peninsula. According to the established view of legal historians today, these were, in fact, an initial reaction by sovereigns to a law that was not only chaotic and uncertain, but which also had for too long been the monopoly of the legal class. Simplifying a little, this reaction could be categorized as evidence of a rising anti-jurisprudential ideology.[139]

However, Duck appears to find in them a confirmation of the importance of the legal class.[140] Talking about Spain, for example, he writes that kings had long allowed imperial and canon law to be taught in the academies in their kingdoms, and they understood it as "iura communia", with the force of law across their territories in cases not covered by local laws. Finally, they allowed it to be used and cited ("allegari concesserunt") in all trials and all courts. Furthermore, according to Spanish law, this force of law was attributed not only to the text of civil and canon law, but also to the interpretations of the *doctors*.[141] He also makes similar comments in relation to the Portuguese Ordinances (*DUA*, 121rv).

Strangely, he seems to have a clearer sense of the only Italian case of his time, of which he probably had only indirect and vague knowledge.[142] Duck

137 "omnes jurisconsulti affirmant Pontificem Romanum esse Dominum Supremum in suis Dominiis Temporalibus, omnia posse facere quae Reges in Regnis suis et Imperator in Imperio possunt" (*DUA*, 70rv). A similar unanimity is specified for the *potestas* of the Fiorentini (*DUA*, 72r). For the Duke of Milan it is said that "constans est iurisconsultorum sententia" (*DUA*, 72v).

138 *DUA*, 73r: "iurisconsulti tamen recentiores omnes affirmant eundem per investituram accepisse Supremam et Imperatoriam Potestatem".

139 On their "typically antijurisprudential" character, see, for an overview of the subject, Adriano Cavanna, *Storia del diritto moderno in Europa: Le fonti e il pensiero giuridico*, I, (Milano: Giuffrè, 1982), 247.

140 In a way Duck is right here: as Cavanna points out, "the jurists who were in that way granted 'exclusive' authority were thuse literally 'canonised', constituting a kind of supreme court of the dead" (Cavanna, *Storia del diritto*, 248).

141 "reges enim Hispaniae in Regnis suis, diu permiserunt ius Caesareum et Canonicum in Academiis suis publice doceri ... eademque iura in Legibus suis post iura Municipalia, uniuscuisque Regni iura Communia appellant eaque in omnibus iudiciis et Curiis suis per iudices et causarum patronos allegari concesserunt ... et Lege Hispania tribuitur vis Legis, non solum ius Caesareo et Canonico, sed et Doctorum Interpretationibus" (*DUA*, 116rv).

142 For an overview and bibliographical references on the Italian citation laws, see Maria Morello, "Il problema delle citazioni nella crisi del diritto comune: Interventi a carattere

sees the law promulgated by Francesco Maria della Rovere for his small Duchy of Urbino as an attempt to restrict reference to jurists, and perhaps for this reason describes it as "singulare" (peculiar) (*DUA*, 77v–78r), which he does not do for the Spanish and Portuguese laws. Cleverly adapting his own language, in describing the relationship between Justinian law and Italian princely or statutory and "municipal" legislation, he constantly uses the expression "*ius commune*". After having clarified its meaning in the first part, the term is particularly prevalent in the second part, where it is used in the *technical* sense, as the doctrine had been taught from the Middle Ages onwards, to indicate a law that applies in a subsidiary manner to the *iura propria*. In Part I, following Du Moulin ("Carolus Molineus"), he had already very explicitly stated that Roman law was so fair and reasonable that it was applied and practiced by almost all peoples[143] and that all the "iuris interpretes" referred to Roman law as "*ius commune*", so much so that every time they use the expression "*ius commune*" they meant Roman law.[144] He adopts this line of reasoning throughout his analysis of the various European systems.

Ius commune can be found wherever there are local laws with which it can be related, but it is more influential where there are "educated" interpreters and judges capable of constructing and theorizing the relationship between common law and local law and, above all, of rendering it effective in practice.[145] In line with this view, the two peculiar and "eccentric" cases of the Church State and the Republic of Venice are at the centre of his analysis in

antigiurisprudenziale in alcuni ordinamenti italiani tra XV e XVIII secolo", *Studi Urbinati*, new series A - 68, 1–2 (2017), 159–222. For Francesco Maria della Rovere's measure of 1613, Morello recalls Duck's citation, pointing out, in keeping with Marongiu (Alessando Marongiu, "L'ultimo Duca d'Urbino e la sua 'legge delle citazioni'", in *Studi Urbinati*, vol. XI, n. 3–4, 1937, 1–3), that this was an indirect citation and perhaps for this reason partial and inaccurate, also in indicating the names of jurists involved in the measure (see particularly the transcription error in which z and r were swapped, transforming Azzone into "Aronem" and the omission of other names, Morello, 184-185). It is reasonable to assume that Duck gets his information from P. D'Avity, *Description générale de l'Europe avec tous ses empires, royaumes, estats et républiques*, t. II, Paris, chez Claude Sonnius et Denys Bechet 1637, 907, annexed by him.

143 "ut omnium fere Christianarum gentium usu et approbatione commune sit effectum". See Charles Du Moulin, *Prima pars commentariorum in consuetudines parisienses*, Parisiis, Excudebat Ioannes le Preux, 1572, *Titulus primus*, *De matiere foedal*, f. 7v, quoted verbatim in DUA, Lib. I, chapt. II, §. VI, 11v. He similarly claims that the kings of Spain also "appellant leges Romanas ius commune" (*DUA*, 12r).

144 "omnes iuris interpretes appellant Ius Romanum Ius Commune, et quotiescumque de Iure Communi loquuntur intelliguntur de Romano" (*ibidem*). The references here go from Luca da Penne to Zasio and Deciani, up to Toschi and the German Matthias Stephani from Greifswald (Matthias Stephani, *Tractatus De officio iudicis*, Francofurti ad Moenum, Impensis Petri Kopfhi, 1625, lib. I, chapt. 1, 1–4).

145 This is why, for example, reporting on the legal-historical events of Sweden, Duck notes how as a result of the lack of "properly" trained jurists, there is little evidence of the presence of Roman law in this area ("apud Suecos pauca habemus Legum Romanorum indicia", *DUA*, 178rv) and similarly in the brief conclusions of his work, where it seems clear that, more so

the part of his book dedicated to the legal system in force in the Italian territories.[146] In Rome and the cities under papal rule, civil law naturally had to contend not only with municipal laws, but also with canon law. Although he emphasizes some factors that seem to him to be irrefutable evidence of the practical application and *auctoritas* of Roman law in all territories under papal rule, such as its teaching in universities, the required presence of *doctores* in the adjudicating colleges, and its priority over canon law in civil cases, he does not use the term "*ius commune*" in the parts focusing on Rome. This is probably because the subsidiary function is here ultimately performed not by civil law but by canon law,[147] even though in Bologna, as in Ancona of course, the statute – which preceded the inclusion of the city in the dominions of the Church – indicates that "ubi ius municipale eius loci deficit, ius civile debet observari" (*DUA*, 75r).

Of course, the anomaly par excellence is Venice.[148] The "veneration"[149] that even the proud Venetians had for Roman laws was demonstrated for Duck above all by the existence of the University of Padua and the respect for it shown by the Venetian government, as well as by the *assessores* and *consultors in iure*, despite the fact that there was no direct application of Roman laws except in the mainland cities.

Duck's argument in relation to the other Italian dominions is very different, for which "minor est dubitatio": *ius civile* is "*ius commune*" for Florence, as well as for Lucca.[150] Similarly, the Milanese jurists study the constitutions promulgated for the Duchy by Charles V, adapting them, in their court cases,

---

than the academics, Duck sees the practitioners as the true builders and custodians of the *ius commune*, as we argued earlier in this chapter.

146 *DUA*, 69v–80r, for the centre-north of Italy and *DUA*, 80v–87r, dedicated to the Kingdom of Naples.

147 Duck says that in Rome and its territory, the same statute prescribes that judgements must be made according to civil law, with canon law being used only when there is no civil law on the matter ("ex iure civili sit iudicandum, et non recurratur ad canones, nisi ubi ius civile deficit", *DUA*, 74v–75r), that in some cases canon law "corrects" civil law and finally that in all other cases, when there is no civil law, canon law must be applied ("de caetero ubi ius civile deficit, vel in casibus superius expressis, ius Canonicum in Dominiis Ecclesiae Romanae servandum est").

148 Even in the mid-eighteenth century, the Venetian Marco Foscarini, who was to become Doge in 1662, attributed in his *Della letteratura veneziana* (In Padova, nella Stamperia del Seminario, 1652, 10) to Duck the merit of having most effectively indicated the difference ("il divario") of Venetian law compared to the *ius commune* in force in other Italian territories. See, in this volume, Silvia Gasparini, "Lawyers in Venice"; Alfredo Viggiano, "Venetian Law and *ius commune*"; and, above all, Claudia Passarella, "*Negari tamen non potest,*" which sets out Duck's thought on Venice in its opening pages.

149 "venerari" is the exact verb that Duck uses, *DUA*, 75v.

150 *DUA*, 76r: civil law is common law in Florence and also in Lucca ("ius civile apud Florentinos est ius commune", "idemque esse ius commune apud Lucenses").

to Roman civil law considered as common law.[151] It is used in Genoa in cases that are not covered by the local laws and in the interpretation of statutes[152], and it is definitely common law for the judges of the Senate of Mantua. Although aware of various critiques of Tiberio Deciani,[153] Duck follows the latter's staunch position, finding him particularly authoritative on the case of Ferrara. Here too, therefore, civil law has the status of common law.[154] Duck also claims that *ius civile* in the Savoy territories is not only considered to be common law, but also continues to develop through the rulings of the Senate of Turin, published by the president Cacherano d'Ozascho and others,[155] while in Parma and Urbino civil law was applied in trials.[156] In relation to the duchy of Urbino, Duck says he is aware that it is not really a question of *ius commune*, but rather only of the "leges Iustinianeas" and a small number of jurists.[157]

Conclusion: Looking from the Margins

The conclusion that Duck draws from this overview, in order to then more closely examine the relationship of statutes and "leges Municipales" with Roman law, is that, in general, according to the most widespread opinions of jurists, Roman civil law is common law in the whole of Italy.[158] Traversing

151 "quas etiam ad ius Civile Romanorum ut ad ius Commune in iudiciis accomodant" (*DUA*, 78v–79r).

152 "in casibus omissis et pro statutorum interpretatione" (*DUA*, 79rv).

153 Duck recalls a position expressed by Cefali in one of his *consilia* (Giovanni Cefali, *Consiliorum sive Responsorum iuris liber quartus*, Francofurti, Sumptibus Gotefridi Tampachii Bibliopolae, 1624, cons. 586 n. 6, 359). The same position is expressed, also in a *consilium*, by Cardinal Zabarella (Francesco Zabarella, *Consilia*, Venetiis, Apud Ioannem Baptistam a Porta, 1581, cons. 2, 1v) and then taken up again by Cardinal Toschi in his *conclusio* 95, entitled *Ferrariae Civitas* (Domenico Toschi, *Practicarum conclusionum iuris tomus tertius*, Romae, ex Typographia Stephani Paulini, 1605, *conclusio* 95, 606–610).

154 "ius civile habet vim iuris communis" (*DUA*, 79v).

155 "non esse tantum ius Commune sed et florescere praeter doctissimas Senatus Pedemontani Decisiones". In particular, besides Cacherano, Duck cites the "acutissimus superioris saeculi Iurisconsultus" Antoine Fabre (*DUA*, 77v).

156 Also in relation to Parma, as already pointed out by Morello for the duchy of Urbino (see supra, nt. 142), there is only a reference to D'Avity's text and not to local sources or authors (*DUA*, 78r).

157 "et Urbini pariter et Parmae ius civile in iudiciis observatur, nullique praeter iuris civilis Professores ad ius dicendum admittuntur, et in Dominiis Ducis Urbini illud singulare est, quod Advocati possint coram senatum tantum allegare Leges *Iustinianeas* et ex Doctoribus solos *Accursium*, *Bartolum*, *Baldum*, *Aronem* (sic), *Alexandrum*, *Castrensem* et *Iasonem*, in criminalibus solum Angelum de Maleficiis, iuris Canonici vero interpretum omnium possunt authoritate uti" (*DUA*, 78r).

158 "generaliter apud iurisconsultorum receptum est, ius Civile Romanorum esse ius Commune in Italiam" (*DUA*, 78r). The list of *auctoritates* cited here becomes longer and more varied and is bundled together without too much attention being paid to context and period: it begins with commentaries on the *Decretales* (X.5.33.28) by Antonio da Budrio and Gio-

political and cultural boundaries that had already become *topoi* in his own time, Duck presents himself not only as an English "civilian" – with particular expertise in canonical and ecclesiastical matters, who is called upon in this capacity to consult the courts,[159] a role he is always ready to defend as central to the English system[160] – but also, to all intents and purposes, as an "Italic" jurist,[161] or, in other words, a jurist of late European common law, as we have argued from the beginning of this chapter.

To further test this hypothesis, we should analyse the reasoning of, and, above all, what "common law" would mean to, the theoretical and practical jurists of "late common law" whom Duck cites in his *De usu et auctoritate iuris civilis romanorum*. Perhaps Duck understood and made this particular subject his own when reading the numerous collections of *consilia* and *decisiones* that he had at his disposal and to which he chooses to refer.[162] As one might expect,

vanni d'Andrea (Antonio da Budrio, *Super quinto libro decretalium*, *De privilegiis*, c. *Super specula*, Venetiis, per Ioannem Gregorium de Gregoriis fratres, 1503, 102v e Giovanni d'Andrea, *Novella super V Decretalium*, *De privilegiis*, c. *Super specula*, Venetiis, Per Ioannem de Furlivio et Gregorium fratres, 1489, f. without numbers). This is followed by the piacentino Pietro Antonio de Petra (Pietro Antonio de Petra, *Tractatus De potestate principis et inferioribus ab eo*, Francofurti ad Moenum, 1600, c. 3, quaestio 4, n. 48, 48), then the Sarzanese Alderano Mascardi (also here referred to as "Muscard", see Alderano Mascardi *Communes I. U. conclusiones ad generalem quorumcumque statutorum interpretationem accomodatae*, Ferrariae, Apud Victorium Baldinum Typographum Cameralem, 1608, *conclusio* 2, n. 89, 104), which is followed by other consilia, such as that of Pellegrini (Marco Antonio Pellegrini, *Consiliorum sive Responsorum volumen primum*, cons. 63 n. 5, 170r) and that of Charles Du Moulin (Charles Du Moulin, *Consilia at Responsa iuris analytica*, Lugduni, Apud Bartholomaeum Vincentium, 1582, cons. 15 n. 14, 69); he then goes back to Rolandino's *Summa notarile* (p. 3 §. *De iure civili*) and returns to more recent authors such as Guy Coquille and to the preface of his commentary on the customs of the Nivernois (here erroneously abbreviated to "Ninern"), who, in order to emphasize the difference between the French and the Italian situation, writes: "Car en Italie le Droict commun c' est le mesme droict ciuil des Romains. Et les Loix particulieres que chacune ville avéc son contat a voulu avoir contraires, ou diuerses ou outre le droict commun et Romain, sont les Statuts: lesquels pource qu'ils sont exorbitans du dit droict Romain et commun, ont esté tenus et reputez de droict estroit. Qui a donné occasion audits Docteurs d'exercer leurs entendemens à faire regles de diuerses sortes pour l'interpretation et intelligence desdits Statuts, et autres tant que pour le Droict Romain et Commun."(Guy Coquille, *La coustume de Nivernois*, in *Les Oevvres*, Paris, chez Henry Le Gras, 1646, 1. On the author, a strong defender of the value of *coutumes*, see Paolo Slongo, *La forza della consuetudine: Costumi, costituzione, governo in Montaigne e Montesquieu* (Milano: FrancoAngeli, 2020).

159 See the article by Richard H. Helmholz, "Common Lawyers and Civil Lawyers In England: Barriers and Connections between Them", in this book.

160 Andrés Santos, "Ius Commune vs Common Law", 71 ff.

161 Santos, particularly in relation to the second part of the work, defines Duck as an "avezado jurista práctico, probablemente imbuido de las construcciones escolásticas de los grandes autores italianos de la Baja Edad Media (el llamado mos Italicus), con cuyas obras se muestra muy familiarizado" (Andrés Santos, "Ius Commune vs Common Law", 83).

162 As previously mentioned, there are still some doubts as to whether the author had direct access to some of these collections, which were very local in nature (see above).

citations of the *consilia*, although not completely absent,[163] are sporadic only in those chapters in the second part of the work devoted to Europe. However, it is clear that, together with judicial case law, advisory case law is Duck's main guide not only to understanding the Italian situation in which it dominates,[164] but also in trying to pose the question he wants to answer. The *consilia* are thus a broad and constant reference in the first part.[165]

It might therefore be interesting to explore the way practical and specific issues were dealt with in cases of disputes for which *consilia* were requested from leading jurists, which in the second half of the sixteenth and the early seventeenth century still involved the emperor and were linked to the feudal relations between the Italian princes and the emperor's jurisdictional powers. The positions taken by jurisprudence in these cases is revealing of the meaning and boundaries of *ius commune* in Italy and Europe at the height of the modern age. It is no surprise that Duck chooses a number of *consilia* by Jacopo Menochio to outline the position of the Italian principalities and other issues, as they are particularly good examples of this mentality and culture. The *consilia* that Duck most frequently quotes in *De Usu*, even referring to diverse editions,[166] is the advice requested by the Republic of Genoa in its case against

163 For Naples, only those of Gaspare de Leo and Fabio de Anna are mentioned as *consilia*; for France, as well as Paolo di Castro, the Frenchmen François Clapier and Charles Du Moulin are mentioned, and even for England there are two references to Filippo Decio and Jacopo Menochio, and Tiberio Deciani is mentioned in chapter 10 on Scotland. It is not surprising that a more prominent role is assigned to Oldrado da Ponte, whose *consilium* 69, for centuries almost a *sedes materiae* for discussing the king's and emperor's powers, is cited in note for France (*DUA*, Lib. II, chapt V, §. IX, 90v) and many times in the text on Spain (*DUA*, 108r; 112v; 115v).

164 In these pages as many as twenty-five authors are cited, sometimes repeatedly and with different *consilia*: Pietro D'Ancarano, Angelo degli Ubaldi, Baldus degli Ubaldi (10 *consilia*), Bartolomeo Bertazzoli (3 *consilia*), Francesco Borsati (3 *consilia*), Benedetto Capra, Giovanni Cefali, Francesco Corti iunior, Tiberio Deciani (3 *consilia*), Filippo Decio, Charles Du Moulin, Raffaele Fulgosio, Jacopo Menochio, (3 *consilia*), Niccolò dei Tedeschi (2 *consilia*), Oldrado da Ponte, Fulvio Paciani, Paolo di Castro (4 *consilia*), Marco Antonio Pellegrini, Rolando della Valle, Ludovico Romano, Carlo Ruini, Mariano Socini, Alessandro Tartagni (3 *consilia*), and Francesco Zabarella.

165 There are fourteen authors of *consilia* cited in the first part and in the first chapter of the second part, which is on imperial rule "in Orbem Terrarum" and can thus be considered part of the general reflection. With the exception of only Charles du Moulin and Étienne Bertrand, the authors cited are all Italian: Angelo degli Ubaldi, Bartolomeo Bertazzoli, Giovanni Cefali, Filippo Decio, Prospero Farinacci, Girolamo Gabrielli, Jacopo Menochio, Niccolò dei Tedeschi, Oldrado da Ponte, Pier Paolo Parisio, Ludovico Romano, and Mariano Socini. Menochio is cited three times, with three different *consilia*, (2, 21, and 75). In particular, as we shall see below, *consilium* 2 is for Duck an essential source of information and legal arguments in relation to various Italian states.

166 Menochio's opinion, which is "fearlessly" opposed to that presented to the emperor by the College of Jurists in Pavia, is then immediately published by him together with those of the Bolognese and Paduan colleges, as an appendix to his treatise on possession, where they were reproduced in various different versions and updates, and it was also published on its own

the Marquis of Finale Ligure (the so-called *causa finariensis*) and in which, like the other famous feudal dispute in which Menochio had intervened,[167] the emperor played the role of superior and judge.

After centuries of wars with Genoa, in the mid-fifteenth century the Marquisate of Finale became independent again under the Del Carretto family, but thanks in part to the misrule of Marquis Alfonso II it was invaded by the Republic in 1558. Menochio's *consilium* dates from 1567, when an attempt was made to shift the matter from the battlefield to the legal sphere. Not long afterwards, the dispute was resolved politically: after Alfonso II's brief return to power in 1571, the Spanish, eager to gain control of a port, fomented a new revolt and then sent their troops "to garrison" the Ligurian city. From that moment on the Spanish retained their hold over the marquisate, tightening their power when the last marquis, Andrea Sforza, gave up his feudal rights to Spain in 1598. Their rule eventually became definitive at the latter's death in 1602. However, the arguments that the legal world of the mid-sixteenth century had used to tackle this delicate question were still useful a century later for understanding the "status" of the Italian princes in relation to the empire and for shedding light on the legal system in force in their territories.

In response to the various *dubitationes* submitted to him, Menochio courageously promoted the limitation of imperial powers, which his own college in Pavia did not dare do, but which Duck was strongly in agreement with. Menochio first dealt with the emperor's jurisdication, which was called into question on the basis of the Republic of Genoa's political position: the competent judge in a dispute is clearly he who has jurisdiction and has the power to impose his will on the *subditi*.[168] It was therefore the Republic that had the power and obligation to "ius dicere" on the case concerning the fief of Finale. Despite the many learned arguments that could be used to validate the

(see, for example, *Responsa causae finariensis*, Coloniae Agrippinae, Apud Ioannem Gymnicum, 1587). Menochio then included it as the second *consilium* after that of Monferrato in the first volume of the collection of *consilia*, which over the years would become very extensive. He was clearly conscious that it was precisely thanks to these prestigious commissions that he started to become very successful in his career as a consultant (see Chiara Valsecchi, "Menochio, Giacomo", in *Dizionario Biografico degli Italiani*, vol. 73 (Roma: Istituto della Enciclopedia italiana, 2009), 521–524, and Chiara Valsecchi, "Menochio, Jacopo" in *Dizionario Biografico dei Giuristi Italiani (XII–XX secolo)* II, 1328–1330).

167 This is the famous case of the possession of Monferrato. See Chiara Valsecchi, "Prìncipi e giuristi nell'Europa moderna: Il contributo della giurisprudenza consulente nelle crisi dinastiche", in *Rivista internazionale di diritto comune*, 28 (2017), 75–139; and Chiara Valsecchi, "Consilia and Dynastic Successions in Modern Europe", in *Succession Law, Practice and Society in Europe across the Centuries*, ed. by M.G. di Renzo Villata, (Cham: Springer, 2018), 417–472.

168 "in suos iurisdictionem exercet, sibique subditos coercere potest" (Jacopo Menochio, *Consiliorum sive Responsorum, Liber primus*, Francofurti ad Moenum, Typis et sumptibus Wechelianorum, apud Danielem et Davidem Aubrios et Clementem Schleichium, 1575, cons. 2, n. 1, 43).

competence and role of the empire, Menochio declared that he was convinced that the opposite position was stronger primarily because the Genoese were "liberi et exempti" from imperial jurisdiction.[169] The *auctoritates* cited in support of the idea that Genoa had always been free dated back to none other than Dionysius of Halicarnassus, who described the Ligurians as a free people. According to Menochio, there was also no evidence in the works of ancient historians such as Livy or Plutarch[170] that the Ligurians were subject to Rome. Leaping skilfully over an argument that must have appeared to him as a bit of a stretch, in just a few lines Menochio jumps from ancient Rome to the year 1162, the date in which Frederick I Barbarossa granted full autonomy to the republic, later confirmed by his successor Henry VI in 1191, a freedom which it had enjoyed ever since. Menochio could take it as an established fact, confirmed by the chronicles[171] and by major legal minds of the Middle Ages,[172] that from then on the Republic of Genoa did not recognize any authority higher than its own.[173] Many years later, Charles V, during a stay in the Ligurian city in 1529, reconfirmed the well-established Genoese freedoms.

To corroborate his thesis on Genoa, Menochio clearly found it helpful to make a sort of comparative analysis with other Italian cities and republics that also enjoyed freedom "absoluta".[174] Duck, who cited this *consilium* with regard to Genoa, clearly also found it useful for its statements and doctrinal references on the rest of the Italian Peninsula and beyond, so much so that he used it again in support of the more general statement that all of these lords, having received perpetual investiture for themselves and their heirs, had supreme power over their subjects, over whom they exercised all imperial rights.[175] In Menochio's round up of examples supporting the principle that free republics have all the rights of the empire, he above all and inevitably cites

169 Menochio, *Consiliorum sive Responsorum, Liber primus*, cons. 2, nn. 41 ff., 45.

170 Menochio, *Consiliorum sive Responsorum, Liber primus*, cons. 2, nn. 47-48, 45.

171 Menochio, *Consiliorum sive Responsorum, Liber primus*, cons. 2, n. 49, 45: reference is made to the Genoese scholar Agostino Giustiniani, bishop of the diocese of Nebbio in Corsica ("nebiensis episcopus"), which was published posthumously in 1537 as *Castigatissimi annali ... della eccelsa e illustrissima Repubblica di Genova* (see Aurelio Cevolotto, *Agostino Giustiniani. Un umanista tra bibbia e cabala* (Genova: EGIG, 1992) and Aurelio Cevolotto, "Giustiniani, Agostino", in *Dizionario biografico degli Italiani*, 57 (Roma: Istituto dell'enciclopedia italiana, 2001), 303–306.

172 Menochio points out that "many of us" claim that, ("ex nostris multi affirmarunt"), citing the *consilium* by Baldus (Baldo degli Ubaldi, *Consiliorum sive Responsorum Volumen Quintum*, Venetiis, Apud Haeredes Alexandri Paganini 1608, cons. 182, 47v–48v; cfr. Menochio, *Consiliorum sive Responsorum, Liber primus*, cons. 2, n. 49, 45).

173 "nullum vel imperatorem vel regem aliumve in superiorem ac dominum recognoscere" (Menochio, *Consiliorum sive Responsorum, Liber primus*, cons. 2, n. 53, 45. n. 53).

174 Menochio, *Consiliorum sive Responsorum, Liber primus*, cons. 2, nn. 63 ff., 46.

175 "omnes vero post investituram perpetuam, sibi et haeredibus suis supremam potestatem habent in subditos suos, in quos exercent omnia imperialia et maiestatis iura" (*DUA*, 74rv).

Venice, whose independence from the empire was documented by Bartolus and Ristoro Castaldi, and then by Parisio, Socini, and Fulgosio.[176]

The situation in Florence was similar, at least until the advent of "Dux prudentissimus simul ac liberalissimus" Cosimo de' Medici.[177] Again, numerous jurists and other authors attest to this.[178] In Menochio's list of examples, like in Duck's exposition – which seems to closely mirror the former – Lucca follows Florence.[179] Via a complex web of arguments on the relations between "civitas" and "iura imperii", the system of appeals,[180] and the concept of "iurisdictio fundativa",[181] Menochio ends up concluding that the emperor is not (can no longer be, but perhaps never really was) "dominus totius mundi".[182] He seeks confirmation of this by referring not only to the "Catholic king" of Spain and to the situation in France,[183] but, perhaps wanting to complete the picture of the Italic context, also to the case of Savoy and the Duchy of Milan,[184] none of which "recognoscet" the emperor as superior.

This remained, almost to the letter, Duck's position in the mid-seventeenth century: although his training and experience differed from that of Menochio and of Duck's near-contemporary De Luca, from his position at the "margins" Duck seemed to perfectly grasp the features of *ius commune* in what would end up being the last century of its history.

176 "respublicae liberae iura habent fisci et imperii" (Menochio, *Consiliorum sive Responsorum, Liber primus*, cons. 2, nn. 63–64, 46).

177 Menochio, *Consiliorum sive Responsorum, Liber primus*, cons. 2, n. 65, 46.

178 Menochio cites Mariano Socino senior, Giasone del Maino, Felino Sandei, the decisions collected by Porporato, and again Ristoro Castaldi, and the life of Onorio III del Platina (Menochio, *Consiliorum sive Responsorum, Liber primus*, cons. 2, n. 66, 46).

179 Menochio, *Consiliorum sive Responsorum, Liber primus*, cons. 2, n. 68, 46.

180 Menochio, *Consiliorum sive Responsorum, Liber primus*, cons. 2, nn. 72–73, 46.

181 Menochio, *Consiliorum sive Responsorum, Liber primus*, cons. 2, n. 92, 47.

182 Menochio, *Consiliorum sive Responsorum, Liber primus*, cons. 2, n. 98, 48. On this point Menochio unsurprisingly recalls the authoritative position expressed at the beginning of the fourteenth century by Oldrado da Ponte, who, as mentioned above, Duck also refers to.

183 Menochio, *Consiliorum sive Responsorum, Liber primus*, cons. 2, nn. 102–103, 48.

184 Menochio, *Consiliorum sive Responsorum, Liber primus*, cons. 2, nn. 104–105, 48.

Index

FSC
www.fsc.org
MIX
Papier | Fördert
gute Waldnutzung
FSC® C083411

Kolibri 360 GmbH
Ferdinand-Jühlke-Straße 7
99095 Erfurt, Deutschland
produktsicherheit@kolibri360.de